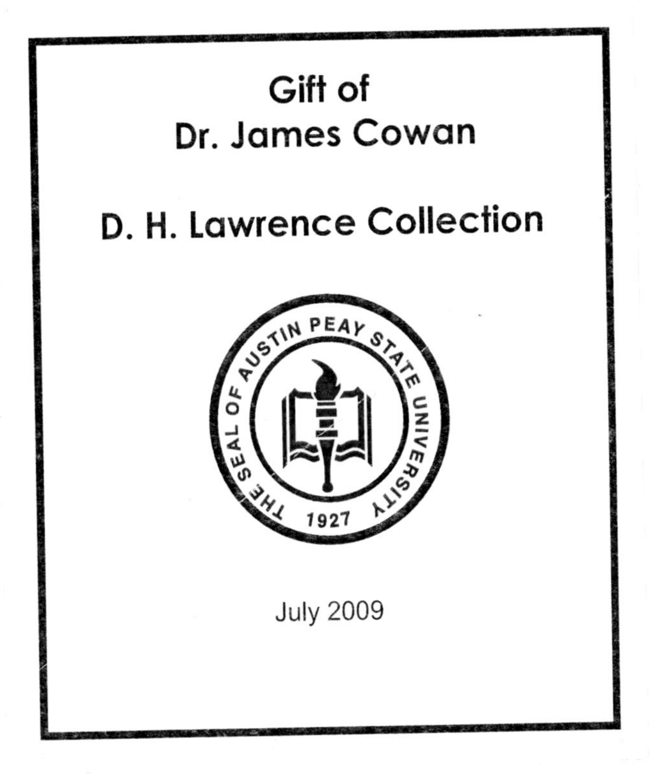

D. H. LAWRENCE:

The Cosmic Adventure

D. H. LAWRENCE:
The Cosmic Adventure

Studies of his Ideas, Works, and Literary Relationships

Essays Based on Selected Papers from the Fifth International D.H. Lawrence Conference held at the University of Ottawa, Canada, June 24-28, 1993

Lawrence Gamache, Editor

Phyllis Sternberg Perrakis, Associate Editor

bp

Borealis Press
9 Ashburn Drive
Nepean, Ontario, Canada K2E 6N4

The Publisher gratefully acknowledges the financial assistance of the Ontario Arts Council, and the D.H. Lawrence Society of North America

CANADIAN CATALOGUING IN PUBLICATION DATA

Main entry until title:

D.H. Lawrence : the cosmic adventure

1st ed.
Sixteen essays selected from the 140 presentations at the 5th International D.H. Lawrence Conference, held June, 1993, at the University of Ottawa.
Includes biographical references.
ISBN 0-88887-152-X (bound) -
ISBN 0-88887-154-6 (pbk.)

1. Lawrence, D.H. (David Herbert), 1885-1930—Criticism and interpretation. I. Gamache, Lawrence II. International D.H. Lawrence Conference (5th : 1993 : University of Ottawa).

PR6023.A93Z62 1993 823'.912 C95-900020-8

Cover design by Pierre LaFlamme, Ottawa

Contents

Introduction

The title of this collection suggests the breadth and spirit of D. H. Lawrence's concerns as a man living in a confusing and challenging twentieth-century milieu. It is also intended to reflect the depth of questioning he brought, both intellectually and emotionally, to confronting such a universe so newly described and newly experienced after the modernists reshaped human perceptions of the individual, the community, and the cosmos. He rejected as dangerous many contemporary religious, moral, and ideological approaches to life that he thought misdirected, even distorted, individual and social realities; he was convinced that people as individuals and as members of communities, both small, like families, and large, like nations, were dissociated from any felt cosmic source for human vitality, from any sense of wonder or adventure in the face of the cosmic mystery. It was his quest within himself and in the world he wandered for much of his life, to renew a sense of place in this world and in the cosmos that would justify living passionately and fully as beings composed of flesh and blood, mind and spirit. It is our hope that these essays will express something of Lawrence's breadth and depth of awareness through their study of his works, his life, and his relationships to others in his time and after who were of like mind or who were driven by equally profound values. He searched as a man and as a writer to find the means and the perceptions of human life that would clarify and display values expressive of positive yet modernist cultural imperatives.

These essays are based on papers presented at the Fifth International D. H. Lawrence Conference held in Ottawa, Canada, June 24–28, 1993, which was sponsored by the various D. H.Lawrence societies of Europe, Asia, and North America and by the University of Ottawa and Cornell University. This conference was one in a series begun at the University of Southern Illinois, Carbondale, promoted by Harry T. Moore and supported by the D. H.Lawrence Society of North America. In 1981, during the Houston MLA meetings, Moore and others at the Lawrence sessions began to discuss holding a Centenary Conference, which eventually occurred at Tufts University in 1985. This major gathering of Lawrence scholars from around the world, organized by Dennis Jackson and Keith Cushman, became the Second International D. H.Lawrence Conference and inspired the notion of having such meetings periodically in different sites around the world. The third such conference was planned for Shanghai, China, when it became known that Liu Xiang Xi wanted to hold a Lawrence conference in conjunction with the founding of the D. H. Lawrence Society of China. This led to the Third International D. H. Lawrence Conference that met in Shanghai in 1988. At that time, another conference was projected, to take place in France in 1990 or 1991. In Montpelier, The Fourth International D. H. Lawrence Conference, organized by Peter Preston, met in the summer of 1991. During this conference the proposal for the next meeting, in 1993 in Ottawa, Canada, chaired by L. Gamache and Ian MacNiven, was approved and a recommendation that an international governing body be organized to oversee the arrangements for international Lawrence conferences was also recommended. In Ottawa, the Committee for Organizing International D. H. Lawrence Conferences was established, its by–laws were approved, and it took over the responsibility for developing the Sixth International D. H. Lawrence Conference, to be Chaired by John Worthen and planned for Nottingham, England, in 1996. This brief recapitulation of the history of international Lawrence conferences, now supported by all the D. H. Lawrence societies and journals across five continents, is intended to explain the stimulus for the papers included in this collection, and to explain the genesis of the series of texts that have emanated from these conferences since 1985.

As indicated above, these essays attempt to clarify Lawrence's contribution to English literature by elucidating his ideas, his work, or his life as part of the modernist tradition. Their selection is intended to represent the current state of Lawrence studies, as exemplified by such established Lawrence scholars as James C. Cowan, H. M. Daleski, Paul Delany, Holly Laird, Ginette Katz-Roy, Mark Spilka, Michael Squires, and George Zytaruk. Essays by a number of younger writers who participated in the discussions at the conference reflect the continuing vitality and range of interests in contemporary Lawrence studies. Some essays explore the relationship between Lawrence and such other writers as Hardy (H.M. Daleski), Anaïs Nin (Jane Eblen Keller), Margaret Laurence (Nora Foster Stovel), Lawrence Durrell (Carol Peirce), and

Tennessee Williams (M. Elizabeth Sargent). Other contributions consider his personal life and its relationship to his works, as does Wayne Templeton, who examines Lawrence's illness and its influence on his works. His ideological vision is considered by Kaien Kitazaki who compares Lawrence's ideas about the nature of man and his cosmic relationships to analogous conceptions in the Buddhist tradition. Some essays analyze his works—either textually, as does John Henry Raleigh, who considers the new edition of *Sons and Lovers*, or critically, as does Joan Douglas Peters, who studies "dialogues of form" in *The Rainbow*.

From the evidence of the list of studies included in this volume, it is clear that scholars today are less preoccupied with either Lawrence's idiosyncratic behavior and personality or with his views of sexuality as sensationally revolutionary; they tend to consider Lawrence's exploration of human realities, his "cosmic adventure" as a writer and as a person and his modernist approach to novelistic and poetic techniques. It has become clear also that he developed his texts through a dynamic process, discovering by the act of writing itself what he needed to comprehend as a man and as an artist. He did not work from a preconceived design or from a strict set of prescriptions about novelistic techniques or poetic form and style. The variety and complexity of current approaches to Lawrence is represented by the following examples in these essays: H. M. Daleski freshly reconsiders the relationship between Lawrence and Hardy, based in large measure on an examination of Lawrence's "Study of Thomas Hardy"; Ginette Katz-Roy compares Lawrence's "psychology of crowds" and "a science founded by [Gustave Le Bon and Gabriel Tarde] two Frenchmen who were near contemporaries of Lawrence"; James Cowan applies two recent psychoanalytic models to Lawrence; Paul Delany views the "tension between universalist and particularist feminism" in *The Rainbow*; Michael Squires, whose article first appeared in *Criticism* 37 (1995): 469-92, studies the "philosophical and narratological connections between narrators, knowledge, and coherence" in Lawrence; and Mark Spilka examines domestic violence in "The White Stocking." What concerns today's readers is clearly reflected in the range of concerns in these and the other articles included in this volume. However, the scholarly interest in Lawrence is also reflective of the on-going development of literary studies as such, clear evidence of their relevance to current intellectual endeavors that seek to understand Lawrence's struggle to survive in the modern world—a struggle that can reveal much to the rest of us who similarly confront a complex universe.

The editors wish to thank all those who have contributed to the production of this volume. Our special appreciation must be stated for the help and encouragement provided by Ian MacNiven and his wife Susan. The valuable work of the editorial assistants of Borealis Press, Julie Sévigny-Roy, Joanne Kloeble, and Marie Tremblay-Chénier, is gratefully acknowledged. The D. H. Lawrence Society of North America provided both financial and moral support througout the time spent on preparing the conference and this volume of essays it has generated. Christine Zerbinis deserves special recognition for the generous help she has given us in her editorial suggestions and in proofreading. Finally, Glenn Clever and Borealis Press must receive our deepest appreciation for helping us publish these papers.

We wish also to thank Penguin Books, U.S.A. Inc., Lawrence Pollinger Ltd., the Harry Ransom Research Centre—The University of Texas at Austin, and the University of Nottingham Library for permission to quote from Lawrence's poetry in Holly Laird's essay.

Lawrence Gamache
University of Ottawa

Phyllis Sternberg Perrakis
University of Ottawa

1

Lawrence and Hardy: The Music of Figures

H.M. DALESKI

Some years ago in an essay entitled "Lawrence and George Eliot: The Genesis of *The White Peacock*," I argued that George Eliot was the main initial influence on Lawrence, to a degree that *The White Peacock* may be read as a rewriting of *The Mill on the Floss*; and I furthermore suggested that, in pushing beyond Eliot in his first novel, Lawrence may be said to have found himself through her.[1] I stand by this view today, but wish now to qualify it by joining those who have long viewed Thomas Hardy as Lawrence's most significant precursor. I believe, however, that it is only in the writings of Lawrence's major phase, in *The Rainbow* and *Women in Love*, that Eliot gives way to Hardy; and that the marks of Lawrence's imaginative engagement with Hardy are stamped in particular on these two novels. Though Lawrence had read Hardy before, his intense response to him at this point in his career was accidental. In July 1914 Lawrence was unexpectedly invited by James Nisbet and Co. to do a short book on Hardy, and was then presented with a complete set of Hardy's works by Edward Marsh. In September 1914 he began the "Study of Thomas Hardy," and he completed a revised version of it by early December. At the same time—that is, in November 1914—Lawrence began to rewrite the novel that became *The Rainbow*.[2] The rewriting of *The Rainbow* thus went hand in hand with the rereading of Hardy and the composition of the "Study"; and the writing of *Women in Love* followed in 1916–17.

At first sight it might seem wilful to assert a connection between Lawrence in his new modernist phase and Hardy since the latter, in his critical pronouncements and many of his practices, is so typically Victorian. For Hardy the novel had above all to tell a story. In "The

Profitable Reading of Fiction," the most substantial of his few critical essays, he held that the novel should be viewed as "an exemplification of the art of storytelling," and consequently that "the story naturally takes the first place."[3] But story—what E.M. Forster called "this low atavistic form"[4]—was precisely what Lawrence, in *The Rainbow* as compared, say, with *Sons and Lovers*, tried to do without, reducing this element to the barest possible minimum since, as Forster saw, it was impossible to eliminate it altogether.

In the same essay Hardy insisted that the "telling" of the story had to be "artistically carried on" and that the story had to be "an organism," by which he meant its parts should be organically related, held together in "well-knit interdependence" (121). He accepted as fundamental, that is, the need for plot, the organization of the story in a tight mechanism of cause and effect, in what (in another essay) he called "a selected chain of action,"[5] from which anything not relevant to the ongoing drama of incident would be rigorously excluded. By the time of *The Rainbow* the confinement of the narrative within a plot seemed artificial to Lawrence, and he sought to find a place in it for all that novels with plots seemed constrained to leave out. For Hardy, however, a plot had its own aesthetic justification. "To a masterpiece in story," he said (in "The Profitable Reading of Fiction"), "there appertains a beauty of shape, no less than to a masterpiece in pictorial or plastic art" (120); a finely wrought plot, therefore, could be regarded as possessing "the quality which makes the Apollo and the Aphrodite a charm in marble" (122). Hardy's image is startlingly similar to one used by Lawrence in February 1914: "I know it [i.e., *The Wedding Ring*] is quite a lovely novel really—you know that the perfect statue is in the marble, the kernel of it. But the thing is the getting it out clean."[6] The correspondence of image, however, actually provides a measure of Lawrence's difference from Hardy by the time of *The Rainbow*. Marble statues may certainly have both beauty and charm, but they are rigid and fixed—like novels with taut, chain-like plots. In *The Rainbow* Lawrence experimented with a new way of unifying a narrative, substituting for plot as an organizing principle rhythmic repetitions and variations in the lives of his three generations of characters. Statues, that is, give way to music.

If there are thus some fundamental divergences between the two novelists, they nonetheless have in common striking affinities of outlook.

It is not merely that in the metaphysical sections of the "Study" Lawrence formulated what was to become the ideological substructure of his mature art, a formulation that was clearly triggered by his reading of Hardy; a key phrase in the "Study," one that may be said to sum up Lawrence's thought (in so far as this is possible) directly links him to Hardy. At the end of the "Study" Lawrence implicitly announces his intention to aim at a "supreme art," an art which would be defined by its reconciliation of the law of the man and the law of the woman, an art in which both would be "equal, two-in-one, complete."[7] The idea of two-in-one is so central in Lawrence because it relates not only to art but to the coming together of man and woman in marriage and to the consummation of a self comprising two major opposed forces. The phrase itself is straight out of *Jude the Obscure*: after the death of their children, Sue says to Jude, "O my comrade, our perfect union—our two-in-oneness—is now stained with blood."[8]

In the "Study" Lawrence frames his direct analysis of Hardy's novels with a general statement of their motivating impulse:

> none of [Hardy's] heroes and heroines care very much for money, or immediate self-preservation, and all of them are struggling hard to come into being. . . . The via media to being, for man or woman, is love, and love alone. . . . The tale is about becoming complete, or about the failure to become complete. (20)

The statement is not only illuminating in regard to Hardy but also clearly reflects Lawrence's own interests, and it could well serve as an epigraph to *The Rainbow* and *Women in Love*, which he at one time regarded as a single two-volume work.[9] The sense we get here of kindred spirits is enhanced by their common view of the importance of the novel: "Our true object," says Hardy, "is a lesson in life";[10] "the novel," says Lawrence, "can help us to live, as nothing else can . . ."[11] Indeed Lawrence memorably called the novel "the one bright book of life,"[12] always steadfastly putting life before art and thus aligning himself with a writer such as Hardy rather than with a fellow modernist such as James Joyce, for whom the novel became primarily a text, a play of words. Lawrence is furthermore aligned with Hardy in their mutual attempt to give due weight in the novel to the significance of sexual relations and to pursue a new candour in their portrayal, a candour that led both writers into conflict with a restrictive censorship.

These, then, are some of the large affinities that link Lawrence and Hardy. But I am more concerned in this paper to trace certain indirect connections between them, connections that manifest themselves in recurrences of image and scene. It is as if the work of Hardy foreshadows certain episodes or descriptions or themes in *The Rainbow* and *Women in Love*. These large intertextual units in the novel are the equivalent of the more limited verbal echoes in poetry that John Hollander has studied in *The Figure of Echo*. Hollander stresses that such echoes may be deliberate but do not "depend on conscious intention" and may also "be unconscious or inadvertent."[13] Much the same may be said of Lawrence's echoing of Hardy.

Perhaps the best way of approaching such correspondences in the novel is by way of Roland Barthes' suggestive metaphor of "a music of figures": "The intertext," says Barthes, "is not necessarily a field of influences; rather it is a music of figures, metaphors, thought-words; it is the signifier as siren."[14] It is indeed as if a Hardy music plays in the Lawrence passages I will refer to. But Odysseus, we recall, while the music of the sirens was ringing in his ears, was bound to his own craft, which kept straight ahead; and he continued to hold firmly to his own course as the sound of the sirens became no more than an indistinct reverberation in his inner ear.

II

The opening of *The Rainbow* is justly famous, and one never tires of hearing the well-known lines:

> But heaven and earth was teeming around them, and how should this cease? They felt the rush of the sap in the spring, they knew the wave which cannot halt, but every year throws forward the seed to begetting, and falling back, leaves the young-born on the earth. They knew the intercourse between heaven and earth, sunshine drawn into the breast and bowels, the rain sucked up in the daytime, nakedness that comes under the wind in autumn, showing the birds' nests no longer worth hiding. Their life and inter-relations were such; feeling the pulse and body of the soil, that opened to their furrow for the grain, and became smooth and supple after their ploughing, and clung to their feet with a weight that pulled like desire, lying hard and unresponsive when the crops were to be shorn away.[15]

This passage may well be regarded as prototypically Lawrencean, but it is instructive to put beside it the following description from *Far from the Madding Crowd*:

> It was the first day of June, and the sheep-shearing season culminated, the landscape, even to the leanest pasture, being all health and colour. Every green was young, every pore was open, and every stalk was swollen with racing currents of juice. . . . Flossy catkins of the later kinds, fern-sprouts like bishops' croziers, the square-headed moschatel, the old cuckoo-pint,—like an apoplectic saint in a niche of malachite,—snow-white ladies'-smocks, the toothwort, approximating to human flesh, the enchanter's night-shade, and the black-petaled doleful-bells, were among the quainter objects of the vegetable world in and about Weatherbury at this teeming time . . .[16]

Both passages are devoted to evoking a sense of the "teeming" natural world, the adjective being pivotal in each. And both are thoroughly anthropomorphic in the way they do this, the earth and its bounty being made, like Hardy's toothwort, to "approximate to human flesh." Hence, in Hardy, the flowers and plants that are like man and his appurtenances, and the "leanest pasture" that is "all health and colour"; hence, in Lawrence, the breast and bowels and nakedness of the earth, and "the pulse and body of the soil." But it is of course the repeated employment of sexual imagery that most suggestively links the two passages. Hardy's imagery in this respect is circumspectly embedded in bishops' croziers and apoplectic saints where Lawrence is explicit with his "intercourse between heaven and earth" and the earth that opens to the farmers' ploughing, but Hardy is no less evocative with his pores that are open and his phallic stalks that, like "the rush of the sap" in Lawrence, are "swollen with racing currents of juice." The sense of universal fecundity is so strong in both writers that it is a moot point whether human beings are reflected in nature or nature in them.

Will Brangwen and Jude Fawley might at first sight seem an unlikely pair of characters, but in their spiritual ecstasies they are fellow souls. Will is roused to ecstasy at the mere thought of visiting Lincoln Cathedral, his "beloved" cathedral. When he sees the cathedral in the distance, "his soul [runs] ahead," his "heart [leaps]," and his face is "glowing, ecstatic," while his mouth opens "with a strange, ecstatic grin" (186). The strange grin gives an illicit tinge to his ecstasy, and he almost at once reveals that his passion for the church is compounded of more mundane elements than he would care to admit—or that he is aware of: "There she is," he says, as Anna and he approach the cathedral. His use of the feminine pronoun "irritates" Anna, and it soon becomes apparent why. As they come near the precincts, his veins seem "to break into fiery blossom," and he is "transported":

> In a little ecstasy he found himself in the porch, on the brink of the unrevealed. He looked up to the lovely unfolding of the stone. He was to pass within to the perfect womb.
>
> Then he pushed open the door, and the great, pillared gloom was before him, in which his soul shuddered and rose from her nest. His soul leapt, soared up into the great church. His body stood still, absorbed by the height. His soul leapt up into the gloom, into possession, it reeled, it swooned with a great escape, it quivered in the womb, in the hush and the gloom of fecundity, like seed of procreation in ecstasy. (186–87)

It is Will's soul that leaps up into the church while his body stands still, but the experience is rendered, substantially, in terms of physical entry and possession. Possession, however, is the condition of "a great escape." Will, that is, seeks to lose himself in the church in much the same way that he does sexually with Anna. Spiritual and sexual ecstasy become indistinguishable in the "consummation" Will comes to in the cathedral (187).

Jude's ecstasy is evoked by a city, the university city of Christminster, rather than by a cathedral, but the city has a cathedral-like name and his ecstasy has related overtones. When in an epiphanic moment Jude first sees Christminster from afar, this constitutes "his first ecstasy" as well as his "vision" of the city (71). In his imagination thereafter, though before he actually goes to Christminster, he is "always beholding a gorgeous city—the fancied place he had likened to the new Jerusalem," and he calls it "a city of light" (62, 66). At this period he thus lives in spiritual altitudes, becoming "entirely lost to his bodily situation" as he hears in the wind "the voice of the city" conveying to him a "message" from "some soul residing there" (63). Concurrently, however, the new Jerusalem, like Will's cathedral, begins to take on a female allure: "He was getting so romantically attached to Christminster," says the narrator, "that, like a young lover alluding to his mistress, he felt bashful at mentioning its name . . ." (64). For Jude Christminster is its colleges, and when one night he finally gets to his beloved city, his encounter with "the first ancient mediaeval pile" he comes across recalls Will and the cathedral, for it is portrayed in terms of entry and penetration and sensual satisfaction:

> It was a college, as he could see by the gateway. He entered it, walked around, and penetrated to dark corners which no lamplight reached. Close to this college was another; and a little further on another; and then he began to be encircled as it were with the breath and sentiment of the venerable city. . . .
>
> When the gates were shut, and he could no longer get into the quadrangles, he rambled under the walls and doorways, feeling with his fingers the contours of their mouldings and carving. (125)

The shutting of the gates is ominous, indicative of the response Jude will experience not only in respect of Christminster but of his other beloved, Sue Bridehead, for Jude, unlike Will, never attains to full possession. Ruefully he is forced to conclude that he is "outside the gates of everything, colleges included: perhaps some day he would be inside" (133). He also registers the hollowness of his youthful dream of becoming "imbued with the *genius loci*" (165), as if, in contradistinction to Will's consummation in the cathedral, he had wished to impregnate himself.[17]

The scene in which Ursula Brangwen dances with Skrebensky under the moon bears so strong a resemblance to that in which Clym Yeobright's wife, Eustacia, dances with Wildeve on the village green in *The Return of the Native* that the Lawrence seems to be a rewriting of the Hardy.[18] The feelings of the women prior to the dancing are similar and provide it with a common frame. Each is disillusioned in her man. Eustacia finds it "dreadful" that her husband is a furze–cutter, has "a forlorn look" about her, feels "depressed," and worries that her sense of their "wasted lives" may drive her "out of [her] mind."[19] Ursula is repelled by Skrebensky's view of his life as a soldier, tells him that he seems "like nothing" to her, is filled with "a sense of potent unrealities," and feels he has "created a deadness round her, a sterility, as if the world were ashes" (287–89, 294). Her encounter with the bargeman, however, makes her "feel the richness of her own life" (293), just as Eustacia, watching the dancers, senses that to them "the pride of life was all in all," and begins "to hunger" for a similar "hope and happiness" (321). When Wildeve unexpectedly appears and asks her to dance with him, "the enchantment of the dance" surprises her; and, despite their previous differences, she is conscious of a physical and emotional closeness to him as they "[tread] one measure" (323). Ursula does not turn to another man, and it is she who invites Skrebensky to dance, but initially she too has a sense of oneness with her partner, two-in-oneness, one might say: they become "one movement, one dual movement, dancing on the slippery grass"; they are "locked in one motion, yet never fusing, never yielding one to the other" (295).

Then in both texts the moon exerts an overwhelming influence on the dancers—with ultimately fateful consequences. When Eustacia reaches the green, "a round yellow moon" is rising, and it is in "increasing moonlight" that she meets Wildeve (320–21). When they begin to dance and the light of the moon is "added" to the movement of the dance, "it drives the emotions to rankness" (322). A "new vitality" enters Eustacia (322), and she experiences "tropical sensations" in comparison with the "arctic frigidity" in which she has been steeped (323); but for the dancing couple the dance becomes "a riding upon the whirlwind" and "an irresistible attack upon whatever sense of social order there was in their minds" (324). The dance leads to the re-establishment of the relationship between Eustacia and Wildeve, and so in the end to the tragic conclusion in which both of them lose their lives. In the metaphorical terms of *The Rainbow*, terms which force us to relate to words in new contexts and so to give them new, Lawrencean meanings, the rising of the moon while Ursula and Skrebensky are dancing also leads to a death, to his "annihilation" by her. Ursula becomes "aware of some influence looking-in upon her," feels "some powerful, glowing sight" is looking "right into her," and when the music stops, she stands "filled with the full moon, offering herself" (296). She offers herself to the moon, not Skrebensky, and it drives her to a frenzied self-assertion. She is filled with "a rage to tear things asunder," and their renewed dancing is for her "only a kind of waiting, of using up the time that intervened between her and her pure being" (297). After the dance, when he kisses her, it is "like putting his face into some awful death" (298), and he is "annihilated" in the kiss (299).

Ursula is involved in another unusual episode that has suggestive connections to Hardy. If Lawrence was daring in depicting Ursula's love relationship with Winifred Inger, Hardy was there before him in his account in *Desperate Remedies* (his first published novel) of an encounter between Miss Aldclyffe and Cytherea Graye that has strong Lesbian overtones. Cytherea is serving as Miss Aldclyffe's maid, and late at night the older woman comes to her room and gets into bed with her:

> The instant they were in bed Miss Aldclyffe freed herself from the last remnant of restraint. She flung her arms round the young girl, and pressed her gently to her heart.
> "Now kiss me," she said.[20]

Lawrence was more graphic than Hardy in his physical descriptions, as restored passages in the Cambridge edition now reveal:

> [Ursula] swam blinded with passion. Ah, the beauty of the firm, white, cool flesh! Ah, the wonderful firm limbs. If she could but hold them, hug them, press them between her own small breasts! . . .
> [Miss Inger] caught Ursula round the waist, in the water, and held her for a moment against herself. The bodies of the two women touched, heaved against each other for a moment, then were separate. (313–14)

In Hardy the two women have "cooled from their fires" by the morning (123), but, unlike developments in *The Rainbow*, it is the older woman who breaks away: Miss Aldclyffe, when she discovers Cytherea is in love with a man, is repelled by the thought that she has been "sipping at [Cytherea's] mouth as if it were honey" because she "fancied no wasting lover knew the spot" (116).

The language Ursula uses when she breaks away from Winifred composes a music of figures at its most subtle and indirect. Ursula withdraws from "the perverted life of the elder woman," and her revulsion is concretized in her sense of Winifred as "clayey," "big and earthy," as suggesting the "heavy cleaving of moist clay" (319). The clay image subsequently expands into that of a marsh. Ursula disengages from Winifred by throwing her together with her uncle Tom, feeling that they share a "marshy, bitter-sweet corruption" (326): "He too had something marshy about him—the succulent moistness and turgidity, and the same brackish, nauseating effect of a marsh, where life and decaying are one" (325). In a note on this passage, the editor of the Cambridge edition directs us to one of Lawrence's letters to Bertrand Russell, in which he writes: "It is true Cambridge made me very black and down. I cannot bear its smell of rottenness, marsh-stagnancy."[21] The coincidence of image in *The Rainbow* and the 1915 letter suggests that what had depressed Lawrence about Cambridge was the homosexuality of numbers of those he had encountered there, but it does not throw light on the provenance of the image. I suggest that, in the mysterious manner of imaginative reverberation, the image harks back to Hardy.

When Ursula first sees Winifred in her bathing dress, she reflects "how lovely she [looks]": "Her knees were so white and strong and proud, she was firm-bodied as Diana" (313). Diana, says the Cambridge editor in a note, is "the virgin hunter-goddess, rejecter of men, associated with the moon." The image, then, gestures in two directions: in one, it points to the sort of self-assertion Ursula exhibits in the moon-scene previously discussed; in another, it suggests the idea of enclosed self-sufficiency, for Winifred is said to be "a fearless-seeming, clean type of modern girl whose very independence betrays her sorrow" (311). The image thus also points to the first of a number of Diana-characters in Hardy, to Bathsheba Everdene in *Far from the Madding Crowd*:

> Although she scarcely knew the divinity's name, Diana was the goddess whom Bathsheba instinctively adored. That she had never, by look, word, or sign, encouraged a man to approach her—that she had felt herself sufficient to herself, and had in the independence of her girlish heart fancied there was a certain degradation in renouncing the simplicity of a maiden existence to become the humbler half of an indifferent whole—were facts now bitterly remembered. (334)

When Troy denounces Bathsheba in the famous coffin-scene in this novel, he in effect accuses her of having wanted to remain sufficient unto herself even in marriage. Bathsheba flees from him and runs outdoors, where she spends the night. In the morning she first sees where she has been.

> From her feet . . . the ground sloped downwards to a hollow, in which was a species of swamp, dotted with fungi. . . . The general aspect of the swamp was malignant. From its moist and poisonous coat seemed to be exhaled the essences of evil things in the earth, and in the waters under the earth. . . .

> The hollow seemed a nursery of pestilences small and great, in the immediate neighbourhood of comfort and health . . . (363)

III

The swamp imagery carries over into *Women in Love*. At the Water-Party Birkin says to Ursula as he sniffs the air, "Do you smell this little marsh?" and then adds that he finds it "alarming" because "it seethes and seethes, a river of darkness." He goes on to talk of two rivers that are "rolling" in them both, "the silver river of life" and "the other river, the black river," which he defines as "the dark river of dissolution" and "the black river of corruption."[22] Given the dimension of "marsh-stagnancy" already referred to, it seems permissible to relate the image, in at least one sense, to Birkin's own latent homosexuality. Such a tendency in Birkin is by no means merely latent in the unused "Prologue" to the novel (included as an appendix in the Cambridge edition), and the recurrence there of the idea of dissolution throws light on one aspect of the dark black river. In the "Prologue" it is said that, even if Birkin's "fundamental desire" is to love a woman "completely," "both body and soul at once," it is with him "always a case of one or the other," though he knows that each "alone" is "deadly." Since he cannot love, he becomes "more hollow and deathly," and he knows that he is "not very far from dissolution":

> All the time, he recognised that, although he was always drawn to women, feeling more at home with a woman than a man, yet it was for men that he felt the hot, flushing, roused attraction which a man is supposed to feel for the other sex. (501)

The connection between this sort of feeling and the two rivers referred to above is implicit in the "Prologue": "He could never grant . . . that it was well for him to feel this keen desire to have and to possess" the bodies of men, a desire that is said to be "the passion to *bathe* in the very substance of such men, the substance of living, eternal light, like eternal snow, and the flux of heavy, rank-smelling darkness" (504; my emphasis).

In the published novel Birkin's desire for an "eternal union with a man too: another kind of love" (481) is described more cautiously in the depiction of his relationship with Gerald Crich. Nevertheless, he does propose that they "swear a Blutbrüderschaft," that is, that they "swear to love each other" and to be "given to each other, organically" (206–7). The word takes on flesh, as it were, in the well-known wrestling encounter between the two men, in which they strip naked and seem "to drive their white flesh deeper and deeper against each other, as if they would break into a oneness" (270). There is nothing quite like this in Hardy, but there are some striking parallels between the relationship of Birkin and Gerald and that of Michael Henchard and Donald Farfrae in *The Mayor of Casterbridge*, the only close man to man relationship in Hardy.

The relationship is inaugurated when Farfrae restores Henchard's grown wheat and the latter offers him a position as manager of the corn branch of his business. Henchard says to him:

> "Your forehead, Farfrae, is something like my poor brother's—now dead and gone; and the nose, too, isn't unlike his. You must be, what—five foot nine, I reckon? I am six foot one and a half out of my shoes. But what of that? In my business, 'tis true that strength and bustle build up a firm. But judgement and knowledge are what keep it established. Unluckily, I am bad at science, Farfrae; bad at figures—a rule o' thumb sort of man. You are just the reverse—I can see that . . ."[23]

Henchard does not propose a bloodbrotherhood, but he is clearly drawn to Farfrae as a displacement of his dead brother. Emotionally isolated as he is, he feels the need for a close friend even more than a manager: "[H]ow that fellow does draw me," he says to himself. "I suppose 'tis because I'm so lonely" (125). It is significant that Henchard moves so abruptly and seemingly inconsequently from the supposed resemblance of Farfrae to his brother to a reckoning of the differences, physical and temperamental, between himself and Farfrae. He is also drawn to Farfrae, that is, as his complement, for all the world as if he were relating to a woman. That Henchard does perhaps unconsciously wish to possess Farfrae, to take him into himself, so to speak, is suggested to us by Elizabeth-Jane, whose discerning eye detects the mayor's devouring feeling for him: though he puts his arm on the manager's shoulder, "as if Farfrae were a younger brother," she recognizes "Henchard's tigerish affection for the younger man" (161).

Farfrae correlates with Gerald Crich in a different connection too. Just as Gerald is responsible for the mechanization of his mines, so Farfrae recommends the introduction of a "new-fashioned agricultural implement called a horse-drill" not previously known in that part of the country (238). Where Elizabeth-Jane laments that "the romance of the sower is gone for good," Farfrae declares that the drill "will revolutionize sowing heerabout": "Each grain," he says, "will go straight to its intended place, and nowhere else whatever!" (240). Farfrae furthermore plays a similar role to that of Gerald when Henchard arranges the wrestling match with him. The wrestle is forced on him, and Henchard intends it to be a fight to the death, but the struggle knits the men together, as it does Birkin and Gerald: they "[rock] and [writhe] like trees in a gale"; Farfrae "[locks] himself to his adversary" (347). Henchard comes close to killing Farfrae, but what the wrestling does finally is to elicit a declaration of his love for him:

> "Now," said Henchard between his gasps, "this is the end of what you began this morning. Your life is in my hands."
>
> "Then take it, take it!" said Farfrae. "Ye've wished to long enough!"
>
> Henchard looked down upon him in silence, and their eyes met. "O Farfrae!—that's not true!" he said bitterly. "God is my witness that no man ever loved another as I did thee at one time . . . And now—though I came here to kill 'ee, I cannot hurt thee! . . ." (347–48)

The homoerotic dimension of this relationship is much more muted than in the corresponding relationship in *Women in Love*. But when we read back from Lawrence to Hardy, the relationship in *The Mayor of Casterbridge* is placed in a context that brings out its undertones.[24] This kind of correspondence, indeed, is what Hollander calls "a true ghost": "like all phenomena of this sort," he says, "we must always wonder what our own contribution [is]" (99).

Though there are other aspects of *Women in Love* that have parallels in Hardy, I turn finally to two scenes that have an astonishing resemblance to each other—yet are quintessentially Lawrence and Hardy, respectively.

In *Women in Love* Lawrence perfected a special kind of symbolic action, whereby a dramatic scene, rendered in vivid immediacy, is made to project a significance far beyond its apparent meaning; and he imparted a distinctive twist to the technique when he yoked it to animals and sex, showing how the attitudes of men and women to animals may reveal their own sexual proclivities. The most striking of these scenes is that in which Gerald forces the frightened red Arab mare he is riding to stand at the railway crossing while a colliery train slowly passes. The scene radiates in a number of directions, but sexual overtones are an insistent feature of it: Gerald is "pleased with the delicate quivering of the creature between his knees," and he sits "soft and close on the slender red mare" (110). The mare bucks and rears in its terror, but Gerald "[bites] himself down" on her "like a keen edge biting home, and [*forces*] her round." It is his mastery that Gerald asserts, as he remains "calm as a ray of cold sunshine"; and as he digs his spurs into the mare's sides and makes them bleed, he is watched by Gudrun, who is horrified but drawn to him, "looking at him with black-dilated, spell-bound eyes" (111). The destructive battle for dominance between Gerald and Gudrun is joined in effect at the crossing.

The scene is pure Lawrence, no doubt, but it echoes a scene in *Tess of the d'Urbervilles*. When Alec drives Tess in his gig, he urges the horse, which is also a mare, into a reckless plunge downhill. With "the figure of the horse rising and falling in undulations before them,"[25] this scene too has strong sexual overtones. What is figured for Tess is the sort of abandon Alec wishes to drive her to. And here too the issue is one of mastery. The mare is no ordinary horse, but "has killed one chap" and "nearly killed" Alec himself on another occasion (95). In the wild gallop, Alec pits himself against the mare, and—like Gerald—he tests his power over it and demonstrates his mastery. "If any living man," he tells Tess, "can manage this horse I can:—I won't say any living man can do it—but if such has the power, I am he" (94). And as in the case of Gerald, the condition of Alec's mastery is his own coolness, urging the horse to madness but never losing control of it. Issues of abandon, submission, and mastery, which will dominate the relationship of Tess and Alec, are sharply if indirectly adumbrated.

With the sirens singing lustily, the music of figures reaches a crescendo in these scenes. When it ends, the rest is silence—or rather we return to the rich but different sounds of *The Rainbow* and *Women in Love* in their own unique mode.

Notes

1. See Jeffrey Meyers, ed., *D. H. Lawrence and Tradition* (London: The Athlone Press, 1985), 51–68.
2. See Bruce Steele, Introduction to *Study of Thomas Hardy and Other Essays*, ed. Bruce Steele (Cambridge: Cambridge University Press, 1985), xix–xxiv.
3. *Thomas Hardy's Personal Writings*, ed. Harold Orel (Lawrence: University Press of Kansas, 1966), 120.
4. *Aspects of the Novel* (London: Edward Arnold, 1949; first published 1927), 27.
5. "Candour in English Fiction," *Personal Writings*, 126.
6. Letter to Arthur McLeod, 9 February 1914. *The Letters of D.H. Lawrence*, Vol. 2 June 1913-October 1916, ed. George J. Zytaruk and James T. Boulton (Cambridge: Cambridge University Press, 1981), 146. The image provides the title of a fine essay by Mark Kinkead–Weekes on the evolution of *The Rainbow* and *Women in Love* and the relation between the "Study" and *The Rainbow*. See "The Marble and the Statue: The Exploratory Imagination of D.H. Lawrence," *Imagined Worlds: Essays on Some English Novels and Novelists in Honour of John Butt*, ed. Maynard Mack and Ian Gregor (London: Methuen, 1968), 371–418.
7. "Study of Thomas Hardy," 128.
8. *Jude the Obscure*, ed. C.H. Sisson (Harmondsworth: Penguin English Library, 1978), 412.
9. The last page of the manuscript of *The Rainbow* is marked "End of Volume I." See Lawrence Clark Powell, *The Manuscripts of D.H. Lawrence: A Descriptive Catalogue* (Los Angeles, 1937), 5.
10. "The Profitable Reading of Fiction," 114.
11. "Morality and the Novel," *Study of Thomas Hardy and Other Essays*, 175.
12. "Why the Novel Matters," *ibid.*, 195.
13. *The Figure of Echo: A Mode of Allusion in Milton and After* (Berkeley: University of California Press, 1981), 64.
14. *Remarks* (1). This quotation is used as the epigraph to Kevin Z. Moore's *The Descent of the Imagination: Postromantic Culture in the Later Novels of Thomas Hardy* (New York & London: New York University Press, 1990). Moore traces connections between Hardy and writers who preceded him.
15. *The Rainbow*, ed. Mark Kinkead–Weekes (Cambridge: Cambridge University Press, 1989), 9–10.
16. *Far from the Madding Crowd*, ed. Ronald Blythe (Harmondsworth: Penguin English Library, 1978), 194.
17. Richard Swigg says that Will shares with Jude a "mystic devotionalism," a "self–absorbed inarticulate fervour without conscious, fitting ethic." *Lawrence, Hardy, and American Literature* (London: Oxford University Press, 1972), 110. Marjorie Garson refers only to Jude, but she too notes the force of the gates being shut against him, and says that Christminster is "a metaphorically female

body." *Hardy's Fables of Integrity: Woman, Body, Text* (Oxford: Clarendon Press, 1991), 169–70.

18. Robert Langbaum says that the scene in *The Rainbow* "echoes" the scene in *The Return of the Native*, but he merely states that both scenes depict the "erotic release" of the couples. "Lawrence and Hardy," *D.H. Lawrence and Tradition*, 78.
19. *The Return of the Native*, ed. George Woodcock (Harmondsworth: Penguin English Library, 1978), 317, 318.
20. *Desperate Remedies*, The New Wessex (paperback) Edition (London: Macmillan, 1975), 112.
21. Letter to Bertrand Russell, 19? March 1915. *Letters*, 2: 309.
22. *Women in Love*, ed. David Farmer, Lindeth Vasey and John Worthen (Cambridge: Cambridge University Press, 1987), 172.
23. *The Mayor of Casterbridge*, ed. Martin Seymour-Smith (Harmondsworth: Penguin English Library, 1978), 117.
24. Marjorie Garson insists that the nature of Henchard's feeling for Farfrae remains "undefined and unexaminable"; by contrast it is Lawrence in *Women in Love* who "[rewrites] the wrestling match to release its erotic potential." *Hardy's Fables of Integrity*, 110. Robert Langbaum also refers to *Women in Love* but for similar purposes of negative contrast: "Henchard's sudden passion for Farfrae, which is striking after his coolness toward women, suggests homosexuality on his side (Farfrae's response never exceeds cool affection). But their relationship does not develop in a way that bears out this hypothesis; for it quickly turns into male power rivalry once Farfrae breaks out of Henchard's proprietorship. Another sign is that the wrestling between them is not, like the match between Gerald and Birkin in *Women in Love*, given a homosexually erotic colour." "The Minimisation of Sexuality in *The Mayor of Casterbridge*," *The Thomas Hardy Journal*, 8 (February 1992), 22.
25. *Tess of the d'Urbervilles*, ed. David Skilton (Harmondsworth: Penguin English Library, 1978), 95.

2

Living by Lawrence: Anaïs Nin's Revelations of Passional Experience

JANE EBLEN KELLER

> It is the way our sympathy flows and recoils that really determines our lives. And here lies the vast importance of the novel, properly handled. It can inform and lead into new places the flow of our sympathetic consciousness, and it can lead our sympathy away in recoil from things gone dead. Therefore, the novel, properly handled, can reveal the most secret places of life: for it is in the *passional* secret places of life, above all, that the tide of sensitive awareness needs to ebb and flow, cleansing and freshening.
>
> D.H. Lawrence, *Lady Chatterley's Lover* (94)

In the fall and early winter of 1929, at the beginning of a new cycle of cataclysm and ruin in Europe, Anaïs Nin—just before she discovered D. H. Lawrence—was nearly 27, married, respectable, relatively affluent, and living in a comfortable apartment in Paris. But she was tormented by restlessness and boredom. "Something in me curses away all peace," she wrote in the diary she had kept since childhood (*Early Diary* 4: 244). The empty conversations at polite tea parties maddened her. "'And is your sister's sore throat better? Is your new cook satisfactory? Yes, things do cost ten percent more out here. Oh, dear, is that so? Children *are* troublesome. I'm sorry you hate long dresses. . . .' Mon Dieu, these people are going to make me egotistical and neurasthenic" (363–64). Her stylish social life, the dinners and receptions depressed her: "the hollow speeches, the political flatteries, the tactful diplomatic moves, the bromides of so-called great men. . . ." (249). Her friends were "irritatingly 'insuffisant'" (262). Her husband, a handsome American banker, was tender but reserved and preoccupied with business, always to Nin the hateful, cold, heartless business of money and power. Worse, he was so exasperatingly *good*. "I live with a saint," she wrote despairingly (266). He worshipped her with too much reverence and not enough passion. A long, never-consummated fascination with another man (the novelist John Erskine) had left her frustrated and full of longing for—something. "[T]his insatiable hunger of the mind, of which I am ashamed, drives me mad," she wrote (256). "I am being slowly starved" (264).

The similarities to Constance Chatterley's state of mind at the same age—just before she found Mellors—are obvious. Connie, at 27, was restless and bored. She too was married to a man who was preoccupied with his work and who revered but could never satisfy her sexually or emotionally. She, too, felt empty after a failed love affair, and she feared a confrontation with the knowledge that "the only reality was nothingness, and over it the hypocrisy of words" (*Lady Chatterley* 47).

Yet, if Anaïs Nin's season of discontent was an astonishingly close imitation of D.H. Lawrence's artful portrayal of Connie's, the striking parallels between the two were, at this point, accidental. Nin only discovered Lawrence some time in late December, 1929. On Christmas Eve, amidst bleak, windy weather—one imagines dark clouds now and then opening to reveal a full moon—she wrote that she had read "a strange and wonderful book (*Women in Love* by D.H. Lawrence), concerned . . . with the physical only as a transcription of spirit. . . . [Lawrence] has an occult power over human life and sees deeper than almost anyone I know. . . ." And, she concluded prophetically, "Lawrence is dangerous to the mind, because he flounders. He knows and he doesn't know. At least, he doesn't know what to do with what he knows" (*Early Diary* 4: 266–67).

By the following spring, she had read much more of Lawrence and had experienced a kind of liberation of her own spirit. It wouldn't be long before Nin did know what to do with what Lawrence knew. Soon his ideas would loosen her loins as she embarked on a remarkable series of amorous adventures. But first, Lawrence loosened her tongue.

In April 1930, Nin writes, "Lawrence has loosened my tongue so much, broken down my reticence. . . . In his treatment of language, in the poetic intensity of his prose, I find courage for my own writing" (294). And at last she had something substantial to write *about*. She temporarily set aside the stories and plays no one had yet accepted and wrote an essay about Lawrence. It was to be her first published piece. "D.H. Lawrence Mystic of Sex"—"a short, undistinguished essay" according to the critics—appeared in *The Canadian Forum* in October 1930 (Franklin and Schneider

269). With the encouragement of Edward Titus, who had a bookstore and small press in Paris, Nin, in a white-hot blaze of energy, spent two weeks expanding the essay, which became her first published book and one of the early defenses of Lawrence's work. Titus brought it out as *D.H. Lawrence: An Unprofessional Study* in 1932.

Harry T. Moore, in his introduction to the American edition of the book, published in 1964 by the Swallow Press, pays tribute to Nin's precocious understanding of Lawrence. But her 110-page volume of sometimes embarrassingly breathless prose and praise sheds at least as much light on Anaïs Nin as on Lawrence. It does represent a small milestone in Lawrence criticism but is perhaps less a belletristic event than a personal *cri de coeur*, a manifesto, a working out of a philosophy of living to which she would remain faithful all her life. It is interesting that Nin's working title for the first essay was "When D.H. Lawrence Found Himself" (*Early Diary* 4: 291). The little book that grew out of the essay could easily be called "How I, Anaïs Nin, Found Myself through D.H. Lawrence."

* * *

Anaïs Nin, the writer and the person, presents numerous problems. Her fiction is virtually unreadable, and if latter-day critics such as Anna Balakian defend it, the novels often drew critical scorn, if any attention at all, when they first came out. On the other hand, her *Diary*, as originally published (seven volumes appearing between 1966 and 1980), earned her a kind of cult following, invitations to speak on college campuses, a place on the soft side of the counter-culture of the era, and some serious consideration from critics such as Karl Shapiro. What attention the originally published *Diary* did get is sometimes strange to read in the wake of the whole new series of unexpurgated versions that began to appear in 1986 and that reveal what was left out the first time around.

The first volume of the unexpurgated volumes, *Henry and June*, purports to give us the real story—with lots of sex—of Nin's affair with Henry Miller. The second volume, *Incest*, which came out in 1992, reveals new twists and turns of the Miller saga as well as the details of her concurrent and steamy affairs with her first therapist, René Allendy, with the eminent analyst Otto Rank, and most sensational of all, with her father, the musician Joaquin Nin. Thus Oliver Evans's disclaimers in his critical study of 1968, *Anaïs Nin*, seem odd indeed. "Now that portions of the work [the originally published *Diary*] have been published," Evans writes, "the public which imagined that Miss Nin was writing another *Life and Loves à la* Frank Harris has had occasion to learn how false was their impression" (4). Instead, of course, the public is now learning that Nin's journals *do* have something in common with Frank Harris's memoirs, much more, many would think, than with the confessions of St. Augustine, Petronius, Abélard, Rousseau, or Proust to which works Henry Miller compared the *Diary* in an often-quoted article in *Criterion* in 1937 (33).

With the gradual appearance of Nin's "true" true confessions, everyone who has written about her has words and thoughts to eat. This is annoying and sometimes embarrassing. Perhaps to some extent as a consequence, many critics are focusing more on her life and less on her work, more on the material she wrote about, i.e. herself, her adventures, her confusions, and emotions, and less on her literary achievement. All those wrestling with how to evaluate Nin get tangled up in the strange mixture of fact, fiction, truth, untruth, and half-truth resulting from the new layers of information—a tangle all the more dispiriting because all the various versions of the *Diary* pretend to be the unvarnished, no-holds-barred inner truth about a woman and thus to reveal what Nin always claimed were certain universal truths about Woman. Meanwhile, the problem of Anaïs Nin is further complicated by the shape of mainstream feminism which can only decry and pity much of what she thought, did, and wrote.

Critics are having a field day of disdain over the corpse of "the atrocious Anaïs Nin," as Elizabeth Pochoda, writing in a recent edition of the *Nation* (417), calls her. Katha Pollitt, reviewing *Incest* in the *New York Times Book Review*, admits Nin's flair for pornography but doesn't fail to dwell on the "tremulous and vaporous prose, staggering self-absorption and endless analysis of this or that tiny flutter of emotion" (3). Michiko Kakutani, writing in the *New York Times*, condemns the "hothouse prose . . . [that] hardly supports Nin's claims to greatness as [an] artist" (4 Dec. 1992). And Claudia Roth Pierpont, in the *New Yorker*, paints a devastating portrait of a woman of limited vision and intelligence whose subject "is not sex, or the flowering of womanhood, but deceit" (76), whose celebrated erotica are, "in disconcerting proportion, tales of harrowing female frustration" (88), and whose "career of trivial wickedness and familiar vice" is raised to a level of even mild importance only for its sad revelation of what can happen to a woman who "made herself into a character rather than an author . . . —a Madame Bovary sitting down with a pen and the notion 'Flaubert, *c'est moi*'" (90).

This sort of thing is fun to write, and one senses that Nin's critics are having a wonderful time picking her apart—and not overlooking the Lawrence factor. Pierpont leaps on it. "Lawrence's ideal of sex as transcendent rite," she writes, "offered a defense and high justification" for many of Nin's excesses. Added to the incendiary mix, Pierpont emphasizes, was Nin's reading of Freud "who gave the imprimatur of science to the same quest for physical fulfillment that Lawrence cast in terms of religion" (75). Dangerous stuff indeed in Pierpont's view, to be both pitied *and* censured.

* * *

Yet to dismiss Nin's experiment in living by Lawrence as merely ridiculous, pitiable, or evil is to miss the exploration of a 20th-century phenomenon notable if only for its uniqueness. That Lawrence was a powerful force in the evolution of British and American ideas about sex is by now axiomatic. As V.S. Pritchett writes, he was a "great influence, like Wells . . . on ordinary conduct; a whole generation dropped the puritan tradition and made love after the fashion of Lawrence's new puritanism" (*Complete Essays* 252). Much of the study of his influence, literary and otherwise, focuses on the male of our species. Many women were surely influenced as well, but Nin is the only female to record in such detail what it was like to live—or try to—by Lawrence.

Her story, if occasionally lurid, is not ultimately sordid. Lawrence may well have given her, secondarily, a "defense and high justification" for her adventures. But one can also argue that Nin was acting primarily on a kind of high Lawrencean principle, one which she considered to be blazingly truthful, courageous, liberating, and, it must be said, sometimes exhilarating. Lawrence gave her a reason, not merely an excuse, for much of what she did. Pritchett says that "no one could possibly believe what Lawrence believed, and Lawrence hated people if they tried" (252). But Nin, I think, did believe, and a number of people in high places are hating *her* for trying. If her *Diary* is a kind of addendum to 20th-century letters, it is at least, now, an uninhibited one with elements of daring, even courage, few women have risked—or admitted to.

The really interesting issues are: how Nin, this most ardent disciple, reads, and perhaps misreads, Lawrence's ideas as liberating for women; if our assessment of her basic ideas needs to be revised as a result of the new series of the *Diary*; and whether or not her decision to live by Lawrence was satisfying to her, if not to her critics. These are topics that cannot be treated fully here, and there is still much to learn about what happened to Anaïs Nin after 1934. But I can suggest that her interpretation of and belief in Lawrence are more complex than a story of mere promiscuity or, as Elizabeth Pochoda writes (*Nation* 417), "Olympian dishonesty," both so eagerly condemned—and with a sense of shock and moral outrage (one is tempted to announce the arrival of a "new" new puritanism) that isn't all that different from that which initially accompanied much of Lawrence's work. Nin's behavior and philosophy were nonconformist and strangely naïve by contemporary standards. But they were shaped, I would argue, around a distinctly "modern" romantic idealism she learned from Lawrence.

In literature and in life, Nin tried hard to break through the traditions and rituals of classically romantic love with all its conventions and what she would call game-playing and illusion-making. "The classics were content to describe the romantic (neurotic) illusion which separated the lover from his love, but in our time it was illusion which had to be conquered to win love," she writes in *The Novel of the Future* (69). This model, established in her mind as she read and interpreted Lawrence, replaced the old one and was based on a breaking down of ritual, a submission to naked reality, and a male/female fusion of love, art, and sex she believed Lawrence posited and promised. Nin may have been silly and misguided at times. Yet she was also serious about her ideas, ideals, and goals and was thoroughly modern in her search for personal identity and authenticity.[1] Before condemning, dismissing, or even approving, we should suspend moralistic judgment and look carefully at what she set out to do.

* * *

The whole process must begin, Nin writes of Lawrence's philosophy, with "a *transcending of ordinary values* [the italics are hers]" (*Study* 13) and the overthrow of evasion and reticence, both of which haunted Nin's own life. Life fully lived, a theme she returns to over and over again in the *Diary*, was certainly not a matter of intellect—indeed the intellect was always to be suspect if not positively spurned—but a deep jump into "instincts and intuitions" (13). She quotes Lawrence's dictum, without giving the source, that real life must be "'obedience to the urge that arises in the soul, the urge that is life itself, urging us to new gestures, new embraces, new emotions, new combinations, new creations'" (14).

The sex part of all this holds great interest, of course, for nearly everyone, Nin included. But she tries hard to separate Lawrence from mere prurience or pornography and to explain, rather convolutedly, that sex, itself, for him, is neither animalistic, pleasure-seeking self-indulgence nor some quirky, quasi-religious experience. The mysticism of sex for Lawrence, she insists, is almost an anti-mysticism for being counter to outmoded idealism. Sex is a breaking through to reality, an openness to "life itself," a creative act of faith in a basic life force that is in opposition to the old ideas of bogus glorification. Thus, Nin writes that the "violent union of Anton and Ursula" in *the Rainbow* is "devastating" because the lovers use sex for the wrong reasons and invest in it too many hopes and ambitions. They "seek violently in each other a satisfaction they do not find." At the same time, sex is a paradigm for a greater struggle, [again Nin's italics] "*the creator's craving for a climax far bigger than the climaxes life has to offer*" (26). Nin's own longing for so comprehensive a climax was evident before she read Lawrence. It must have been thrilling to discover a soul-mate who understood the power of that longing as well as its insatiability. It must also have been thrilling to think that sex could be at once powerfully symbolic as well as earthily primitive, important enough to have meaning but unimportant enough to be invested with miscast sacredness—terrific, in short, for the few who could see both sides of it.

She must have felt tapped as one of the elect because Lawrence, Nin writes, believes the celebration of sensation should be limited to a few initiates who understand its limitations and its possibilities. She writes: he "did not mean to incite everyone to action in sex; only those who should act must." Lawrence was doing little more than giving those already capable of "real life" the freedom to let go and live it; but, Nin emphasizes, "no feeling can be awakened in us unless we have the roots of it in ourselves; no ideas can be put into our heads. They can only be developed when the seed of them is already growing in us" (109).

Nin believed she had the seed. Lawrence merely watered it. In 1931, when she met Henry Miller, it looked as if the Lawrencean promise of fusion and absolute love—the trinity of love, sex, and art—was about to be fulfilled. Up to a point, their affair followed with remarkable faithfulness that of Constance Chatterley and Oliver Mellors. The beautiful, repressed, aristocratic lady is fascinated and liberated by the raw but savagely noble manliness of Miller. "I am a peasant, Anaïs," Miller writes to her at one point (*Henry and June* 56), playing the part of Mellors beautifully. Soon they embark on an odyssey of ecstatic lovemaking that "transpires, it blazes . . . ," Nin writes, all the more so because Miller, she believed, sought her core just as Lawrence, she writes approvingly, "sought the *core* of the woman" and found that the [again, the italics are Nin's] "*core of a woman is her relation to man*" (*Study* 49).

Such a statement elicits tongue-clicking pity at best in the late 20th century among feminists. But to give Nin her due—and she *was* writing in 1931—she credited Lawrence with a deeper understanding of "the problems of the modern woman!" (50) and went on to develop a credo of femininity/feminism rooted in her early description of what she believed to be Lawrence's.

This credo rests on three key points. The first grows out of the overall objective to break out of the straight-jacket of ordinary values. Both men and women must smash the man-made patterns of, among other things, male-female relations. Lawrence, Nin writes, "understands the problem of woman, who has effaced her real self in order to satisfy man-made images" (49), and he admits "that most men's patterns [her italics] *had not been much good*" (50). Starting with this clean slate, the second step for women is a matter of creating their own identities, independent of men, neither imitative nor submissive. An element of this independent identity is timing. Women should learn when to be demure and when to be dauntless. "The woman," she interprets Lawrence's views, "does not want to live in dim sureness, with purely domestic, material proofs of her activity: eggs—but neither is the man's life a satisfaction to her." In certain activities, a woman must be dauntless, but if she is also feminine, demure, at the right times, the man will behave well and everyone will be happy; "he will . . . be magnificent with her. And she will have both the vote and the hatchable egg" (52).

The third part of all this is the establishment of male/female balance, finally and most compellingly articulated in *Lady Chatterley's Lover*, Lawrence's best novel in Nin's view. Here, she claims, he resolves the issue he has been wrestling with throughout his life and work. In *The Rainbow*, Nin writes, Lawrence explores the disastrous consequences of imbalance in love. The union between Anton and Ursula is a waste for several reasons but ultimately because the two are not balanced forces. Lawrence "realizes the tragedy of inequality in love as no one else ever realizes it" (27). In *Kangaroo*, Nin writes, Lawrence explores the idea of balance further by suggesting that it requires a certain resistance and independence on the part of both partners. But Lawrence doesn't conclude anything; "he compromises," Nin writes, when he says that "'each human being is a ship that must sail its own course, even if it go in the company with another ship'" (56). In *Women in Love*, Lawrence still hasn't made up his mind about the true relationship between the sexes. He is still "writing the two sides of the case, himself really seeking and wondering who is right" (*Study* 80)—whether Birkin's or Ursula's idea is the real one, whether it is possible to have "two kinds of loves" and thus a divided love.

Only with *Lady Chatterley* does Lawrence come to the end of his "*progression in perfection*." The novel is, Nin writes, "a more perfect expression of his mystical attitude towards the flesh than any other book he wrote" (37). That mystical attitude, she explains in a chapter devoted to the novel, is rooted as much in the earth as in the stars, as much in seasonal rhythms as in celestial connections, in a kind of comprehensive embrace of the carnal and the sublime. But everything depends on faithfulness to that "inner vital connection which is the mystery of marriage . . . [And again her italics] *The most immediate union is woman, the wife*'" (37). The implication, for Nin, is that if the core of a woman is in her relation to man, the reverse is also true. The core of man is marriage to woman. Once accepted on each side, Nin suggests, both men and women can go on about their work as Nin says Mellors and Lady Chatterley are at last free to do. Yes, she quotes without the slightest wink or embarrassment Lawrence's famous passage that "'marriage is no marriage that is not basically and permanently phallic'" (108). Yes, at the end of what Nin seems to take not as a fairy tale but as a promise of happiness, Constance chooses motherhood as her work while Mellors "can go on . . . to the building of their world" (110). But both, Nin implies, are choices, not impositions, free choices possible only because of the transfiguration that comes from living intensely and sincerely, not by intellectual counterfeit. It is always necessary to "dethrone mentally directed love," she writes (108). Latter-day views of her unenlightened opinion notwithstanding, we can see Nin's opinion of Lawrence's phallic emphasis as symbolic of his "defiant justification of a life of free physical sensation" (108).

For Nin, *Lady Chatterley* is a resolution, a ringing affirmation, in part because it is a final "revolt from the white idealistic love of the past" (108). The lovers achieve earth-bound balance in and through each other. They represent a new beginning, "an instinctive beginning" (109). This was the happy ending Lawrence promised Nin, the reward of a steady progression for those who are willing to engage fully in experience and who believe in "real" love.

So, Nin, who believed, would first throw off ordinary values and seek to obey the urgings of her soul and the promptings of her instinct in order to create an independent female identity, not modeled on man's, and to find what Mellors and Lady Chatterley found, what she called the "only complete modern love story" (107).

Until the end of her life, Nin reiterated this tripartite credo and suggested that the promise, at least in her case, had been fulfilled. Her insistence on the development of the female/feminine identity may seem somehow quaint. But again to give her due, she stuck with her beliefs, and some of them are being echoed unexpectedly in the ideologies of the "new" feminism and the exploration of the nature and theory of feminist literature and criticism.[2]

"I would like to see women creating their own language," Nin said in 1972. "Not fighting like men, but trying really to find a language for her feelings, a language for these things which come from the unconscious, which are instinctive" (Hinz 80). In 1973, she said that the "crucial issue, which some of the women's liberationists don't recognize, is for women to discover and appreciate the true nature of *femininity* and to strengthen that. They don't have to become men and they don't have to create the world in the same way" (94). As late as 1972, she was still crediting Lawrence with putting her on this path. "He was the one who said that women would have to make their own patterns, they were being created by men. . . . [You] have to take Lawrence as a whole and see his contribution. He put me on the track that there was a language for emotions and instincts and sensation" (99).

Moreover, Nin suggests that the process of self-creation actually leads to fulfillment in love, "that the perfectly balanced couple will conquer all and be together" as Mellors writes to Constance at the end of *Lady Chatterley's Lover* (282). In 1972, five years before she died, at an Esalen Seminar (appropriately enough!), Nin said that "you *can* find a person who answers to all the multiple needs. I think you find it when these conflicting elements in yourself stop conflicting, and when you're willing to make certain balances in yourself" (Hinz 62). Citing Lawrence's metaphor of the five-pointed star, "with the ideal relationship being one in which two individuals balance each other at all points," she declared her belief that such was possible: " . . . only rarely do you find a match for all five [points]. But it can happen. . . . And then it can become monogamous, in the sense that it is self-fulfilling" (63).

* * *

In a further example of life imitating art, Nin's own search for fulfillment—so shocking to her critics for being so experiential and so labyrinthine with lies—recapitulates with a curious faithfulness her description of Lawrence's novelistic explorations and progress. Throughout *Incest*, as she juggles multiple lovers and a husband, it is as if Nin is arguing—and living out—several sides of the case for love, just as, she claims, Lawrence writes out his own bafflements and conflicts in his novels.

Henry Miller, who perhaps should have been the alpha and omega of her love life (I kept rooting for him even though I know how things turn out), disappoints in the end. He breaks too many Lawrencean rules. "I stood before Henry with the submissiveness of a Latin woman, ready to be overwhelmed," she writes. But Miller "has let me overwhelm *him*" (*Henry and June* 183). Worse, he allows his intelligence to dominate and get in the way. "Lawrence had divined that the intelligence is a juggler," Nin writes in her *Study*, who distorts and denies the greater force of instinct, "that flow of blood-life" (18). Miller falls into that trap, to his peril. "He has let thinking interfere with our happiness" (*Henry and June* 183). The phallocenter does not hold. Besides, other temptations and experiences present themselves. If Miller could have his whores, his intellect, and other weaknesses, Nin could find her own side alleys to explore.

Lawrence, Nin writes in her *Study*, teaches that the "more you know of decadence, the more virile the reaction back to livingness" (34). René Allendy, her first analyst, gives her a chance to test this when he brings out a whip during one of their assignations. She sees the comic side of this, "the dime-novel quality of it all" (*Incest* 147), which is relatively rare for the very earnest Nin. She also sees the decadence and brutality, the empty imbalance, and seems nearly as frightened by her cold indifference as by the seediness of the episode. Throughout, she remains cool, the detached observer, not the participant. "I wonder if Allendy knows how uncapturable I have been" (148).

The story of her incest with her father, almost a parody of *Sons and Lovers*, is a merger of symbolism and sensuality true to Nin's view of Lawrence's ideas. The exploration of her dual self is the obvious symbolism. The explicit descriptions of the sex are satisfactorily earthy. As interesting is the eerily Lawrencean dialogue she records. At one point, for example, Nin *père* says: "'We burned away all the prejudices. We flamed up with a new passion'" (210). Later he wonders at "Such a tenuous balance. . . . Our balance hangs on the most tenuous thread" (213). Meanwhile, she has a different kind of balance to maintain because she is telling different lies to her father, to Miller, and to her husband so she can find time to be with all of them, to sustain "that divine feeling of liberation from the one love . . . the feeling of *security in multiplicity*" (227)—at least for the moment, because at the same time, the Lawrencean ideal shimmers in the background, tempting, appealing, unreal. "Both of us [she and her father] are always wishing for an end to our amorous careers—an ideal end—a dream of fidelity! But it's only smoke" (264).

Otto Rank offers a renewed brush with the "ecstasy . . . of a new love" (334) and an intensified psychoanalytic slant. Again, some of the dialogue she records is strangely Lawrencean. "'When the neurotic woman gets cured,'" Rank says to her, "'she becomes a woman. When the neurotic man gets cured, he becomes an artist. . . . For the moment, you need to become a woman'" (301)—in order to knit up the pieces of her being, she interprets, and realize the true artist in her.

Her own prescription for healing, for knitting up the devil and angel in her, is her art. "I have been living out an angel pattern—but only externally. Internally diabolical. . . . Art. Slowly, by art, I will fuse the two women" (343). For Nin, as for Lawrence, writing is a kind of catharsis. She may have read Lawrence's letter to Arthur McLeod, published in 1933 in *Lawrence and Brett* (Meyers 403), in which he writes that "one sheds ones [sic] sicknesses in books—repeats and presents again ones [sic] emotions, to be master of them" (*Letters* 90). She comes to the same conclusion.

As the shedding process continues, I gather we'll get a political slant to love, à la *Kangaroo*, when the next volume of the so-called *Journal of Love* gives us the details of Nin's affair with Gonzalo, a Peruvian revolutionary. Who knows what else may come, further to besmirch or to elevate or finally to redeem Nin's image.

* * *

Anaïs Nin could defend herself through it all by referring to what she calls Lawrence's system of mobility in which "stability is merely an obstacle to creative livingness" (*Study* 14) and living "is a process of *becoming*, a combination of states we have to go through. Where people fail is that they wish to elect a state and remain in it. This is a kind of death" (20).

No one will ever accuse Anaïs Nin of stultifying stability, though the current fashion tends toward damnation for stultifying self-absorption and silliness, at best, and obscenity at worst. Claudia Roth Pierpont is particularly horrified by the abortion Nin had in 1934. Nin presented the episode as a still-birth in Volume I of the originally published *Diary*, reworked it as a short story that won the praise of Edmund Wilson and Lawrence Durrell, and tells "the truth" about it in *Incest*. (Nin claims the child was Henry Miller's. As soon as she discovered she was pregnant, she decided to abort, although for reasons that are not entirely clear, the procedure did not take place until her sixth month.) Pierpont is scathing in her outrage over "so brutal and frivolously self-serving an account . . . [E]ven in an age of hard-won and vulnerable freedoms, the truth we are offered now is recognizably obscene" (*New Yorker* 90).

Pierpont's final appraisal of Nin's work and life is one of "shuddering pity" (90). Her powerfully written portrait is so far the most widely distributed portrayal of Nin as a pathetically misguided, deceitful little minx who shamelessly and surreptitiously uses her husband's money to support her lovers, enjoys wearing romantic clothes and playing the *artiste*, is swept away by a destructive Lawrencean/Freudian fantasy of redemptory promiscuity and self-deluding fraudulence, and who writes badly into the bargain. Pierpont stops short only of citing Nin as a prime example of the evil effects of Lawrence's work, a case history of what Aldous Huxley predicted would happen when "Lawrence's doctrine is . . . invoked by people, of whom Lawrence himself would passionately have disapproved, in defence of a behavior, which he would have found deplorable or even revolting" (Meyers 362).

What would Lawrence have thought of Anaïs Nin, her headlong leap into a life of instinct, and the *Diary* that explored and revealed "the most secret places of [her] life," indeed, with the new volumes, the "*passional* secret places"? One can argue that Nin betrayed Lawrence, her hero, by her excesses as she regularly betrayed her husband and her lovers. One can apply popular psychological diagnoses to explain her. She lacked self-esteem. She was dependent on male admiration and caught in a neurotic cycle requiring love invariably followed by masochistic disappointment. One can condemn her on various moral grounds—for her adulteries, her deceitfulness, for having had an abortion at all, for not admitting to it sooner, or for admitting it at all. One can criticize her notions of feminism. One can poke fun at her quaint English. Anatole Broyard, reviewing Volume IV of the *Diary* in 1971 in the *New York Times*, tweaks her for a "vocabulary . . . out of some Victorian antique shop of literature: Like feather boas, faded satins, ambiguous furs, words such as illusion, dream, beauty, soul, spontaneity, infinite, inspire and create are her stock in trade. Some of her passages are gnomic to the point of camp." Claudia Roth Pierpont, much less gently, ridicules her fondness for the word *ensorcelled* and cites numerous passages she describes as "free-floating nebulae" (*New Yorker* 88).

Finding fault with Anaïs Nin is easy, and it is not my intention to be an apologist for her. I do feel obliged to say, however, that it took a measure of courage for her to make arrangements for the new series of the *Diary* to be published, to set the record, with all its flaws, straight and to risk a hostile reaction. That she did so inclines me to accord her the benefit of the doubt that her motives were rather purer—cleansing and freshening—than not. The truth is that I, along with Katha Pollitt, like her better in *Henry and June* and *Incest* than in the original *Diary*. A muscular candor and defiance, in counterpoint to the fluffy dreaminess, characterize the unexpurgated confessions. If nothing else, I can't help being glad that a woman finally goes one better than Frank Harris. A kind of balance has been restored here. Surely a good number of Nin's readers smile vicariously rather than sniff with supercilious or pious scorn when they read how a woman got away with exploits so long associated with men, even if, and perhaps because, most of Nin's encounters were in the name of love, not in order to collect sexual scalps. To find her feminine center, Nin wasn't afraid to step into the territory long held by men.

I do think there is something touching and brave about Nin's steadfast belief in Lawrence's ideas, as she read them. She was, perhaps, more faithful to her ideas about him than she was to most of the other men in her life. At the beginning of her career, she defended him from those who charged him with salaciousness. Near the end of her life, she took his side against those who attacked his phallocentricity and sexism. "I paid my tribute to Lawrence by defending him against the narrow-mindedness of the militant women," she writes in the last *Diary* in the original series (7: 301).

Perhaps the best way to respond to Anaïs Nin is to say that the early volumes, at least, of the *Diary* deserve a respected place in the literary heritage of the 20th century as metaliterary[3] documents with an immediacy comparable to the gossip, the Tevershall talk, that disturbed and fascinated Constance Chatterley. We might say, with her, of Nin: "After all, one may hear the most private affairs of other people, but only in a spirit of respect for the struggling, battered thing which any human soul is" (*Lady Chatterley* 94).

Notes

1. The philosopher Charles Taylor cites the search for self and personal authenticity as one of the least understood and most important emblems of the modern world. "What we need to understand here is the moral force behind notions like self-fulfillment. . . . Talk of 'permissiveness' misses this point. Moral laxity there is, and our age is not alone in this. What we need to explain is what is

peculiar to our time" (*The Ethics of Authenticity* 16–17). Anaïs Nin's work can be seen as a herald in the elevation of self-fulfillment as a moral imperative—a phenomenon Taylor worries about and considers dangerous. But even from this point of view, the serious study of Nin's work is all the more valid because it is an individual expression of a cultural phenomenon.

2. That Nin and many feminists arrive at different conclusions (Nin sought union with men; many feminists do not) shouldn't undermine a shared interest in the importance of developing a feminine center. This is far too broad a topic for exploration here. But Elaine Showalter, among others, summarizes the academic literary situation well when she writes in the introduction to *The New Feminist Criticism* that the field "has established gender as a fundamental category of literary analysis" (3)—almost, or so she suggests in an essay in the same volume, without wanting to. Here she confesses that she and many of her colleagues once thought they were working toward a "promised land in which gender would lose its power, in which all texts would be sexless and equal, like angels." Instead, she discovered that femaleness in literature was "a fundamental and continually determining reality" and that "the land promised to us is not the serenely undifferentiated universality of texts but the tumultuous and intriguing wilderness of difference itself" ("Feminist Criticism in the Wilderness," 266–67). In another essay in this collection, "Toward a Feminist Poetics," she writes that "the program of gynocritics is to construct a female framework for the analysis of women's literature, to develop new models based on the study of female experience, rather than to adapt male models and theories" (131).

   Meanwhile, the outrageously exuberant and provocative Camille Paglia explores her own new-found "femininity as difference." She writes further, in "*Sexual Personae*: The Cancelled Preface," that "[a]t midlife, I now accept that there are fundamental sex differences. . . . Sexual geography, our body image, alters our perception of the world. Man is contoured for invasion, while woman remains *the hidden*. . . . No legislation or grievance committee can change these eternal facts. . . . Equality of opportunity, a crucial political ideal that all must support, should not be confused with sexual similitude, which remains a wishful fiction" (*Sex, Art, and American Culture* 107–9). She accepts and celebrates.

   As a final example, this time from the popular-but-respectable-self-help-sector, Clarissa Pinkola Estés's best selling *Women Who Run with the Wolves* is all about recovering femaleness, creating an authentic female identity, and rescuing it from predatory world/male-imposed restrictions. Freeing the Wild Woman, she writes, is tapping into "the female soul. . . . She is all that is of instinct, of the worlds both seen and hidden. . . . She is ideas, feelings, urges, and memory. She has been lost and half forgotten for a long, long time" (13).

3. This is a word borrowed from Peter Dronke, the medievalist, who uses it, in *Women Writers of the Middle Ages*, to describe the work of a number of women

whose writings "show excellingly a quality (literary, but also 'metaliterary') of immediacy. . . . This immediacy can lend women's writing qualities beside which all technical flawlessness is pallid" (x). The early volumes of Nin's *Diary*, it seems to me, have a parallel immediacy and certain other characteristics described quite well as "metaliterary."

Works cited

Broyard, Anatole. "Of Art, Ecstasy and Water." Rev. of *The Diary of Anaïs Nin: Volume 4, 1944–1947*, by Anaïs Nin. *New York Times* 26 Oct. 1971.

Dronke, Peter. *Women Writers of the Middle Ages: A Critical Study of Texts from Perpetua (203) to Marguerite Porete* (1310). Cambridge: Cambridge UP, 1984.

Estés, Clarissa Pinkola. *Women Who Run with the Wolves: Myths and Stories of the Wild Woman Archetype*. New York: Ballantine, 1992.

Evans, Oliver. *Anaïs Nin*. Carbondale: Southern Illinois UP, 1968.

Franklin, Benjamin V, and Duane Schneider. *Anaïs Nin: An Introduction*. 1979. Athens: Ohio UP, 1982.

Hinz, Evelyn J., ed. *A Women Speaks: The Lectures, Seminars, and Interviews of Anaïs Nin*. Chicago: Swallow, 1975.

Kakutani, Michiko. "The Diary as an End Rather Than the Means." Rev. of *Incest* by Anaïs Nin. *New York Times* 4 Dec. 1992.

Lawrence, D.H. *Lady Chatterley's Lover*. 1928. New York: Signet Books–The New American Library, 1959.

———. "To Arthur McLeod." 26 Oct. 1913. Letter 667 in *The Letters of D.H. Lawrence*. Ed. George J. Zytaruk and James T. Boulton. Vol. 2. Cambridge: Cambridge UP, 1981. 7 vols.

Meyers, Jeffrey. *D.H. Lawrence, A Biography*. New York: Knopf, 1990.

Miller, Henry. "Un Etre Etoilique." *Criterion* 17.66 Oct. 1937: 33–52.

Nin, Anaïs. *The Diary of Anaïs Nin, 1966–1974*. Vol. 7. San Diego: A Harvest/HBJ Book–Harcourt, Brace, Jovanovich, 1980. 7 vols. 1966–80.

———. *D.H. Lawrence: An Unprofessional Study*. 1932. Chicago: Swallow, 1964.

———. *The Early Diary of Anaïs Nin, 1927-1931*. Vol. 4. San Diego: A Harvest/HBJ Book–Harcourt, Brace, Jovanovich, 1986. 4 vols. 1978–86.

———. *Henry and June: From the Unexpurgated Diary of Anaïs Nin*. 1986. San Diego: A Harvest/HBJ Book–Harcourt, Brace, Jovanovich, 1989.

———. *Incest: From "A Journal of Love," The Unexpurgated Diary of Anaïs Nin, 1932–1934*. San Diego: A Harvest/HBJ Book–Harcourt, Brace, Jovanovich, 1992.

———. *The Novel of the Future*. New York: Macmillan, 1968.

Paglia, Camille. "*Sexual Personae*: The Cancelled Preface." *Sex, Art, and American Culture: Essays*. New York: Vintage Books, 1992. 101–24.

Pierpont, Claudia Roth. "Sex, Lies, and Thirty–Five Thousand Pages." *New Yorker* 1 Mar. 1993: 74-90.

Pochoda, Elizabeth. "Reading Around." *Nation* 29 Mar. 1993: 417.

Pollitt, Katha. "Sins of the Nins." Rev. of *Incest*, by Anaïs Nin. *New York Times Book Review* 22 Nov. 1992: 3.
Pritchett, V.S. "Sons and Lovers." *Complete Collected Essays*. New York: Random House, 1991. 252–57.
Showalter, Elaine. "Feminist Criticism in the Wilderness." *Critical Inquiry* 8 (Winter 1981). Rpt. in *The New Feminist Criticism, Essays on Women, Literature, and Theory*. Ed. Elaine Showalter. New York: Pantheon, 1985. 243–70.
———. Introduction. *The New Feminist Criticism*. 3–17.
———. "Toward a Feminist Poetics." *Women's Writing and Writing About Women*. Ed., Mary Jacobus. London: Croom Helm, 1979. Rpt. in *The New Feminist Criticism*. 125–43.
Taylor, Charles. *The Ethics of Authenticity*. Cambridge: Harvard UP, 1992.

3

The Long Shadow of D.H. Lawrence on Lawrence Durrell's *Alexandria Quartet*

CAROL PEIRCE

Lawrence Durrell wrote to Richard Aldington in 1959, as he was well into the composition of *The Alexandria Quartet*: "I don't know who your literary influences were and how you thought of them but when I was young just names like Roy Campbell, Aldington, Lawrence were like clouds in the sky. Like I suppose the Olympians, Zeus, Hera and Co" (*Literary Lifelines* 73). Like "clouds in the sky" they certainly were, D. H. Lawrence being to him always a master.

Durrell mentions Lawrence by name several times in the *Quartet*, but the "Olympian" casts an even longer shadow over it than that. Durrell refers in letters, interviews, and various writings to Lawrence's central importance to him. And the ways Lawrence is important essentially affect the *Quartet*. In such areas as theme, plotting and scene description, character development, sense of place, and use of symbolism and myth, Lawrence's thought and writings inform Durrell's work. In spite of some real creative and intellectual differences—and even disagreements—with Lawrence, Durrell acknowledges the profound relationship. In his Preface to *Lady Chatterley's Lover* he puts it, "Writers of this size impose their vision upon us even if it does not always conform to what we believe to be our own" (xi). And in the *Quartet* he gives to his cynical, philosophical novelist, Pursewarden, whose ideas preside over the four volumes—*Justine*, *Balthazar*, *Mountolive*, and *Clea*—of the novel, the greater, loving praise, "Dear D.H.L. so wrong, so right, so great, may his ghost breathe on us all!" (*Clea* 127).

Both writers' themes seem ultimately to center on love, friendship, and death. Lawrence called himself "a priest of love" (*Letters I* 493), and Durrell characterized the *Quartet* as centrally "an investigation of modern love" (*Balthazar*, Note). When asked in an interview whether this was a serious claim, Durrell responded:

> Yes, it is a serious claim I suppose—love as the *point faible* of the psyche; human and divine love. . . . There is such a thing as "modern love." But I hope to suggest that it itself is only a way of growing, a nourishment which prepares one for other problems, perhaps deeper ones. ("Lawrence Durrell Answers a Few Questions" 157)

Again, in his Preface to *Lady Chatterley's Lover*, he says that Lawrence was deeply concerned with "tracing the springs of psychic awareness, psychic growth" (viii). Durrell does suggest elsewhere that Lawrence is overly concerned with blood knowledge to the detriment of mental: "I feel that to cut off the head and exclude the reason in order to locate the affective nature of man in the abdomen, as he did, is to make the river flow backwards" (Young 62). But George Steiner writes about the two: "Both men see in the act of love the crucial affirmation of human identity and the only true bridge for the soul" (17).

Of course every modern and postmodern writer owes a tremendous debt to Lawrence, along with Joyce, for spearheading the movement toward sexual freedom within the novel. Durrell, with Henry Miller and Anaïs Nin, especially admired Lawrence's breaking barriers toward sexual freedom in his works—even as he lamented his own inability to write with the absolute freedom that he wanted and still get his novels published in England. Richard Aldington notes this breakthrough in a letter to Durrell in 1959, "You owe a lot to DHL's valiant fight—if your things had come out between 1912 and 1928, as his did, you'd have been in all sorts of woes" (*Literary Lifelines* 109).

Lawrence wanted to break the rules of the old novel not only in relation to sexual knowledge but in regard to form:

> Tell Arnold Bennett that all rules of construction hold good only for novels which are copies of other novels. A book which is not a copy of other books has its own construction, and what he calls faults, he being an old imitator, I call characteristics." (*Letters II* 479)

He wanted to give a sense of life itself by moving, not according to a set pattern of plot, but according to rhythms of natural life, of breathing and feeling.

Durrell's works, in fact, challenge the old novel's pattern even more vitally than do Lawrence's. While Lawrence's apparently random movement (though actually studied) challenges the tight-knit concept of the "Big" Victorian novel with its "beginning," "middle," and "end," Durrell tears it apart so thoroughly that he feels constrained to apologize when he recreates the form in *Mountolive*. He goes even further to attempt to show life in all its variations through multiple views—"a sort of prism-sightedness" (*Justine* 27). Talking about Proust, Lawrence, and the early modernists, Durrell explains in the *Paris Review* interview:

> what we as artists are trying to do is to sum up in a sort of metaphor the cosmology of a particular moment in which we are living. When an artist does that completely and satisfactorily he creates a crisis in the form. The artists immediately following him become dissatisfied with the existing forms and try to invent or grope around for new forms. ("Lawrence Durrell" 277)

But here again he parts company from Lawrence, for he tells the reader who is watchful that he has, beneath the randomness and leaps of presentation, a careful plan. Although he gives to Arnauti, his older writer, the desire to create "drama freed from the burden of form" (*Justine* 75), he voices the young narrator Darley's creed early and clearly near the opening of *Justine*: "Our common actions in reality are simply the sackcloth covering which hides the cloth-of-gold—the meaning of the pattern" (17).

Both Lawrence and Durrell create memorable scenes—pictures in the web—that continue in memory long after the reading. Some affective relation between them can be seen here too. One of the most memorable scenes in *Women in Love* is that of the water-party:

> As the golden swim of light overhead died out, the moon gained brightness, and seemed to begin to smile forth her ascendancy. The dark woods on the opposite shore melted into universal shadow. And amid this universal under-shadow, there was a scattered intrusion of lights. . . . Here and there, close against the faint water, and at the far end of the lake, where the water lay milky in the last whiteness of the sky, and there was no shadow, solitary, frail flames of lanterns floated from the unseen boats. There was a sound of oars, and a boat passed from the pallor into the darkness under the wood, where her lanterns seemed to kindle into fire, hanging in ruddy lovely globes. (165-66)

Durrell draws toward the end of *Justine* with a description of the great duck shoot:

> With a lithe swing of the pole Faraj drives us out into the channel and suddenly we are scoring across the heart of a black diamond. The water is full of stars, Orion down, Capella tossing out its brilliant sparks. For a long while now we crawl upon this diamond-pointed star-floor in silence save for the suck and lisp of the pole in the mud. (213)

The common elements in each include, to begin with, similar treatments of light, reflection, sound, movement, and even personification. The mood of each has a luminous quality to it.

Also, within each work, the beautiful scene ends in a drowning or apparent drowning so underplayed that it seems almost not to have happened at all. Yet each occurrence is of signal importance to the plot. Lawrence's scene, however, is presented almost as part of the accidental circumstance of life, while Durrell's set piece strikingly climaxes the development of *Justine* and adumbrates the plotted conspiracy that is revealed later.

Another similar use of scene is that of the horse-taming by Gerald in *Women in Love* and by Narouz in the *Quartet*. Both are men of extraordinary will, and each scene is remarkable both for its descriptive power and for its revelation of the character of the man involved. Both characters, also, seem charged with a drive toward the "flux of death," as Lawrence characterizes it. Narouz is one of the few characters in the *Quartet*, however, whom Durrell endows with that desire for dominance that is evident in so many Lawrence characters. This is one important aspect in which the two authors differ. To Lawrence the tug of will often defines a character. To Durrell, will is not, on the whole, a major issue—though it is important to an understanding of Narouz and becomes vital to an understanding of the love between Nessim Hosnani, Narouz's brother, and his magnificent wife, Justine.

A chief concern of Lawrence in regard to his characters is to progress from creating the same clearly-defined, predictable personalities that he saw in the novels preceding him. He writes:

> You mustn't look in my novel for the old stable ego of the character. There is another ego, according to whose action the individual is unrecognisable,

> and passes through, as it were, allotropic states which it needs a deeper sense than any we've been used to exercise, to discover are states of the same single radically-unchanged element. (Like as diamond and coal are the same pure single element of carbon. The ordinary novel would trace the history of the diamond—But I say, 'diamond, what! This is carbon.' And my diamond might be coal or soot, and my theme is carbon.) (*Letters II* 183)

Durrell was fascinated by this quotation and the idea behind it. He used part of it as an epigraph to a chapter in his *Key to Modern British Poetry* (49), and he quoted it many times, as late even as his critical address, "From the Elephant's Back," given in 1981, where he reiterates, "The stable ego of fiction has disintegrated—Lawrence says so in his letters" (4). He uses the concept both in discussion of what he is doing—and in the actual doing. In one interview he says,

> Human character? A sort of rainbow I should say, which includes the whole range of the spectrum. I imagine that what we call personality may be an illusion, and in thinking of it as a stable thing we are trying to put a lid on a box with no sides. (*Kneller Tape* 163).

In *Clea* Darley muses on the woman he loves,

> And if human personality is an illusion? And if, as biology tells us, every single cell in our bodies is replaced every seven years by another? At the most I hold in my arms something like a fountain of flesh, continuously playing, and in my mind a rainbow of dust. (98)

In terms of character development, too, there are striking interior analogues or lines of connection running between *The Alexandria Quartet* and *Women in Love* that, when explored, become almost sliding panels opening to reveal like patterns and affinities of mind and spirit. Both the *Quartet* and *Women in Love* deal with the relationship among a foursome of lovers. An epigraph to *Justine* quotes Freud: "I am accustoming myself to the idea of regarding every sexual act as a process in which four persons are involved. We shall have a lot to discuss about that." The progress of love itself in the heart of each major protagonist seems to follow and ultimately define "love" in the same way. And both writers see love as a search, not just for physical fulfillment, but for creative and intellectual partnership as well. Each author reaches toward defining the truly modern woman as well as man.

Indeed, both *Women in Love* and *The Alexandria Quartet* posit a quest toward the ultimate relationship of men and women and ask what that relationship is. In *Women in Love* the two couples, Rupert Birkin and Ursula Brangwen and Gerald Crich and Ursula's sister Gudrun, move in opposite directions, the first upward toward the light, toward wholeness and understanding; the second inexorably downward toward division, hatred, and extinction.

Ursula is often framed in a golden light: "Her face was now one dazzle of released, golden light. . . . She was beautiful as a new marvellous flower opened at his knees, a paradisal flower she was, beyond womanhood, such a flower of luminousness" (305). Birkin hopes for "a strange conjunction with you . . . an equilibrium, a pure balance of two single beings:—as the stars balance each other" (139). Lawrence explains further:

> He believed in sex marriage. But beyond this, he wanted a further conjunction, where man had being and woman had being, two pure beings, each constituting the freedom of the other, balancing each other like two poles of one force, like two angels, or two demons. (191)

Birkin also loved Gerald and longed for "blood-brotherhood" with him. In the end the closeness of the four is destroyed forever through the battling wills of Gudrun and Gerald; his death leaves an aching void for Birkin. But the union of Ursula and Birkin is a quest achieved.

Durrell's "four persons" actually include five, for the frail Melissa, Darley's first love, is dead except in memory before the *Quartet* begins, and her place is taken finally by his last love Clea, "honey-gold" and "poured, while still warm, into the body of a young grace" (*Justine* 128). This quartet is somewhat more complicated than Lawrence's as Darley loves Justine, who seems to love him but is eventually revealed to love only her husband Nessim, who loves Darley as a friend, but has in sadness a brief affair with Melissa; "The four of us were unrecognized complementaries of one another, inextricably bound together" (203), Darley says. Clea loves all intimately as a friend of Nessim, as the lesbian lover of Justine, and as an artist who is trying to find with Darley the same kind of equilibrium that Birkin achieves with Ursula. Darley's quest takes him through love as pity and love as passion to love as understanding and equality. He is able to save Clea's life when she is nearly drowned and "by an act of will force her to live," to attain "rebirth" (*Clea* 251–52). As Darley and Clea's love is achieved, Justine and Nessim's disintegrates into bitterness but returns stronger than ever in the end. Interestingly, some of the same comparisons are introduced for Ursula and Justine. Ursula "too was the awful, arrogant queen of life, as if she were a queen bee on whom all the rest depended" (192). Clea "spoke of her [Justine] with a wonder and tenderness such as people might use in talking of a beloved yet infuriating queen" (*Justine* 228).

But there is one other major theme Durrell develops in the *Quartet* that is not touched on in *Women in Love*, that of the quest and growth of the artist. And that is the theme of Lawrence's *Sons and Lovers*. Darley, like Paul Morel, sets out to achieve himself and his artisthood and by the end of the novel has found his way. Each protagonist has also progressed through young love and love as passion toward a resolution. We imagine intuitively today that artisthood and a life with someone like Frieda loom ahead for Paul (who is autobiographically Lawrence) in Italy and through the world, even as he walks "towards the faintly humming, glowing town, quickly" (420). And Clea, who also is coming of age as an artist, predicts that Darley will join her in France where "the bitter-sweet herb of their self-discovery" will grow (*Clea* 279). Darley concludes:

> Yes, one day I found myself writing down with trembling fingers the four words (four letters! four faces!) with which every story-teller since the world began has staked his slender claim to the attention of his fellow-men. Words which presage simply the old story of an artist coming of age. I wrote "Once upon a time. . . ." (282)

Durrell is an heir to Lawrence in many ways!

One of the most striking characters of the *Quartet* is Pursewarden, the great novelist and Darley's mentor. When Durrell daringly gives him a personal relationship with Lawrence, not unlike the one that he is trying to draw between Darley and Pursewarden himself, Durrell is suggesting his own debt to and admiration for Lawrence. More than that, he impishly quotes their correspondence, allowing Pursewarden to retort to Lawrence and, thus, gently accentuating his own differences with Lawrence as well. Darley writes:

> He showed me once a letter . . . in which Lawrence had written: "*In you I feel a sort of profanity—almost a hate for the tender growing quick in things, the dark Gods. . . .*" He chuckled. He deeply loved Lawrence but had no hesitation in replying on a postcard: "*My dear DHL. This side idolatry—I am simply trying not to copy your habit of building a Taj Mahal around anything as simple as a good f--k.*" (*Balthazar* 113–14)

Just as Lawrence recreates himself in Birkin, Durrell is partially Pursewarden (Durrell mocks himself, also, in some of the characterization of Darley), though he has attributes too of other writers as varied as Henry Miller, Wyndham Lewis, Blake, and Byron. But, most important here, he is like Lawrence in many ways. And, yes, he does care for the "tender growing quick in things." In almost the ultimate word of the novel on Pursewarden's personality, Clea writes: "Underneath all his preoccupations with sex, society, religion, etc. (all the staple abstractions which allow the forebrain to chatter) there is, quite simply, a man *tortured beyond endurance by the lack of tenderness in the world*" (*Justine* 244). It could be an epitaph for Lawrence.

Along with his cynicism, irony, and soft underbelly, Pursewarden is, like Birkin and Lawrence, a preacher and a prophet. In fact, while Durrell laments Lawrence's tendency to "prophecy" and philosophical speculation, he too has become a prophet.

At one point in *Women in Love* Birkin and Gerald are talking about the future and about social equality: "There had been some discussion, on the whole quite intellectual and artificial, about a new state, a new world of man. Supposing this old social state *were* broken and destroyed, then, out of the chaos, what then?" (95). Later Birkin comes back to the topic talking to Ursula:

> Do you think that creation depends on *man*! It merely doesn't. There are the trees and the grass and birds. I much prefer to think of the lark rising up in the morning upon a humanless world. Man is a mistake, he must go. There is the grass, and hares and adders, and the unseen hosts, actual angels that go about freely when a dirty humanity doesn't interrupt them—and good pure-tissued demons: very nice. . . . But humanity never gets beyond the caterpillar stage—it rots in the chrysalis, it never will have wings. It is anti-creation, like monkeys and baboons. (120)

Pursewarden, in a passage that is clearly in dialogue with Birkin and

Lawrence—Durrell moves on to refer to Lawrence himself during the discussion—responds:

> But when it comes, this great blinding second of illumination—only then shall we be able to dispense with hierarchy as a social form. The new society—so different from anything we can imagine now—will be born around the small strict white temple of the infant Joy! . . . Nothing stands in the way of this Ideal Commonwealth, save that in every generation the vanity and laziness of the artist has always matched the self-indulgent blindness of the people. But prepare, prepare! It is on the way. It is here, there, nowhere!
>
> The great schools of love will arise, and sensual and intellectual knowledge will draw their impetus from each other. The human animal will be uncaged, all his dirty cultural straw and coprolitic refuse of belief cleaned out. And the human spirit, radiating light and laughter, will softly tread the green grass like a dancer; will emerge to cohabit with the time-forms and give children to the world of the elementaries—undines and salamanders, sylphs and sylvestres, Gnomi and Vulcani, angels and gnomes.[1] (*Clea* 140)

One can almost hear Pursewarden's wicked chuckle, as he touches almost every chord of Lawrence's serious philosophy, not to mention nuances of suggestion. Rananim is here!

One of Pursewarden's most insistent emphases, as he seeks to guide Darley toward the light artistically, is symbolism. "Symbolism!" he exclaims. "The abbreviation of language into poem. The heraldic aspect of reality! Symbolism is the great repair-outfit of the psyche, Brother Ass" (as he called Darley), "the *fond de pouvoir* of the soul" (*Clea* 137–38). More follows. But he clearly agrees with Lawrence, who maintains in his "Introduction to *The Dragon of the Apocalypse*":

> Symbols are organic units of consciousness with a life of their own, and you can never explain them away, because their value is dynamic, emotional, belonging to the sense-consciousness of the body and soul, and not simply mental. . . . And the power of the symbol is to arouse the deep emotional self, and the dynamic self, beyond comprehension. (*Selected Literary Criticism* 157–58)

Of course others, such as Yeats, were insisting on the power of the symbol at this time too, but it is a signal aspect of both men's prose styles. It runs through Lawrence in the meaning of flowers and of nature, both sexually and mystically. One thinks of Mrs. Morel swooning among the white lilies, their yellow pollen shining in the moonlight (*Sons and Lovers* 24) or of Ursula watching the daisies drifting down the "dark, lustrous water": "Why did they move her so strongly and mystically?" (*Women in Love* 123). But perhaps the greatest of Lawrence's natural symbols are the rainbow (in *The Rainbow*) and the moon (in the "Moony" chapter of *Women in Love*). The rainbow carries the Christian symbolism of hope and redemption; it "strengthened itself till it arched indomitable . . . its arch the top of heaven" (495). The moon, on the other hand, reflected in the water, gathers into itself all the mystery of Diana and Cybele, of the powers of the White Goddess. In one of Lawrence's most wonderful symbols, Birkin throws stone after stone into its heart; it shatters but returns, "reasserted, renewed." "Why should you hate the moon?" Ursula asks. Obliquely he answers in another context: "There is a golden light in you, which I wish you would give me" (240–41).

Durrell's symbols are no less meaningful though often more deeply woven into the pattern of the whole—the mirrors of *Justine*, the masks of *Balthazar*, for instance. One close parallel, however, to Lawrence's use is that of the pool of phosphorescent water and underground grotto in which Clea nearly dies but is reborn: "Its beauty was spell-binding. It was like diving into the nave of a cathedral whose stained-glass windows filtered the sunlight through a dozen rainbows" (*Clea* 226).

This love of symbols with their elusive connotations is related in both Lawrence and Durrell to their use of myth, for, as Lawrence says, symbols are "the images of myth"; and "Myth is an attempt to narrate a whole human experience, of which the purpose is too deep, going too deep in the blood and soul, for mental explanation or description" (*Selected Literary Criticism* 158). In both Lawrence and Durrell, as well, myth is closely related to their concepts of the "spirit of place" so closely connected to each and another bond between them. They saw place differently, it is true, Lawrence loving to wander and Durrell forever striving to put down roots (*Durrell-Miller Letters* 283). Lawrence, though, might well have agreed with Durrell's definition of landscape "as a field dominated by the human wish. . . . scribbled with the signatures of men and epochs" (*Justine* 112) and would have understood his poem to the god of place, "Deus Loci," enshrining as it does a little spot of his beloved Italy:

> All our religion founder, you
> remain, small sunburnt *deus loci*
> safe in your natal shrine,
> landscape of the precocious southern heart.
> (*Collected Poems* 214)

Myth is important to the modernists. Joyce uses the *Odyssey* as the running analogue beneath *Ulysses*. It is in commentary on *Ulysses* that T.S. Eliot makes his important pronouncement that myth "is simply a way of controlling, of ordering, of giving a shape and a significance to the immense panorama of futility and anarchy which is contemporary history. . . . Instead of narrative method, we may now use the mythical method" (Eliot 177–78).

Durrell, however, uses myth more symbolically as the underlying layer of "some medieval palimpsest where different sorts of truth are thrown down one upon the other, the one obliterating or perhaps supplementing another" (*Balthazar* 183). Thus ancient Alexandria lies beneath the modern city, and the story of Antony and Cleopatra lies beneath that of Nessim and Justine. On the second page of the *Quartet* the connection is made: "A drunken whore walks in a dark street at night, shedding snatches of song like petals. Was it in this that Anthony heard the heart-numbing strains of the great music which persuaded him to surrender for ever to the city he loved?" (*Justine* 14). From this point on, the historic myth glimmers symbolically beneath the tale.

Closer to Durrell's method than to Joyce's careful correlation, the myth of the Northland is counter-poised with intimations of the warm south in *Women in Love*. Gerald is early characterized as "Like a Nibelung" by Ursula (40). The name, Gudrun, is that of Sigurd's wife. And throughout Gerald is described in terms of that myth:

> Birkin thought of Gerald. He was one of these strange white wonderful demons from the north, fulfilled in the destructive frost mystery. And was he fated to pass away in this knowledge, this one process of frost-knowledge, death by perfect cold? Was he a messenger, an omen of the universal dissolution into whiteness and snow? (246–47)

In the end he dies through Gudrun's betrayal with Loerke who, like Loki, enjoys the mischief of the gods. Lawrence writes of his lover, "Not a word, not a tear—ha! Gudrun was cold, a cold woman" (466). One thinks of the *Volsunga Saga*: "Yet for her grief Gudrun could not weep./ So hard was her heart by the hero's body" (Hamilton 306).

There is a moment toward the end of the *Quartet* that movingly confirms Durrell's relationship to Lawrence. When Durrell writes through the voice of Pursewarden a deep tribute to Lawrence's power, he reveals both his own "burden of influence" and his deep love: "How wonderful the death–struggle of Lawrence: to realise his sexual nature fully, to break free from the manacles of the Old Testament; flashing down through the firmament like a great white struggling man–fish, the last Christian martyr. His struggle is ours. . . ." (141) One thinks of Zeus and Co. streaking from among the clouds.

In another letter to Aldington, Durrell writes of Lawrence, "Currents run through him" (*Literary Lifelines* 98). Yes, and from him, blazing down from the sky—currents that found their way into Durrell's mind and heart—and merged there with currents coursing through Durrell's own blood to unite the two of them deeply in spirit. Across the pages of *The Alexandria Quartet* flashes the long shadow of that great "man–fish."

Notes

1. This description of the Ideal Commonwealth by Pursewarden refers not only to Lawrence but also to the Sun card (XIX) of the Tarot, one of the major symbol systems in *The Alexandria Quartet*. The two different references simply reveal two different layers of meaning in Durrell's many–layered palimpsest.

Works Cited

Aldington, Richard, and Lawrence Durrell. *Literary Lifelines: The Richard Aldington–Lawrence Durrell Correspondence*. Ed. Ian S. MacNiven, and Harry T. Moore. New York: Viking, 1981.

Durrell, Lawrence. *Balthazar*. New York: Dutton, 1958.

———. *Clea*. New York: Dutton, 1960.

———. *Collected Poems: 1931–1974*. New York: Viking, 1980.

———. "From the Elephant's Back." *Poetry London/Apple Magazine* 2 (1982): 1–9.

———. *Justine*. New York: E.P. Dutton, 1957.

———. A Key to Modern British Poetry. Norman: U of Oklahoma P, 1952.

———. "The Kneller Tape (Hamburg)." *The World of Lawrence Durrell*. Moore 161–68.

———. "Lawrence Durrell." *Writers at Work: The Paris Review Interviews*. Ed. George Plimpton. 2nd Series. 1962. New York: Penguin, 1977.
———. "Lawrence Durrell Answers a Few Questions." *The World of Lawrence Durrell*. Moore 156–60.
———. *Mountolive*. New York: Dutton, 1959.
———. Preface. *Lady Chatterley's Lover*. By D.H. Lawrence. Ed. Ronald Friedland. New York: Bantam, 1968.
Durrell, Lawrence, and Henry Miller. *The Durrell-Miller Letters, 1935–80*. Ed. Ian S. MacNiven. New York: New Directions, 1988.
Eliot, T.S. *Selected Prose*. Ed. Frank Kermode. New York: Harcourt Brace Jovanovich, 1975.
Hamilton, Edith. *Mythology*. New York: New American Library, 1940.
Lawrence, D.H. "Introduction to *The Dragon of the Apocalypse*." *Selected Literary Criticism*. Ed. Anthony Beal. New York: Viking, 1966.
———. *The Letters of D.H. Lawrence: Volume I: September 1901–May 1913*. Ed. James T. Boulton. Cambridge: Cambridge UP, 1979.
———. *The Letters of D.H. Lawrence: Volume II: June 1913–October 1916*. Ed. George J. Zytaruk, and James T. Boulton. Cambridge: Cambridge UP, 1981.
———. *The Rainbow*. 1915. New York: Penguin, 1978.
———. *Sons and Lovers*. 1913. New York: Penguin, 1979.
———. *Women in Love*. 1920. New York: Penguin, 1979.
MacNiven, Ian S. "Lawrence and Durrell; on the Same Tram." *D.H. Lawrence's Literary Inheritors*. Ed. Keith Cushman and Dennis Jackson. New York: St. Martin's Press, 1991.
Moore, Harry T., ed. *The World of Lawrence Durrell*. 1962. New York: Dutton, 1964.
Steiner, George. "Lawrence Durrell: The Baroque Novel." *The World of Lawrence Durrell*. Moore 13–23.
Young, Kenneth. "A Dialogue with Durrell." *Encounter* 8 (December 1959): 61–68.

4

Lawrencean Legacy: *Sons and Lovers* and *The Stone Angel*

NORA FOSTER STOVEL

D. H. Lawrence's indelible influence on subsequent writers, including novelists, dramatists and poets, from Tennessee Williams to William Carlos Williams, was convincingly demonstrated in *D. H. Lawrence's Literary Inheritors* (1991). However, since Kate Millett's influential *Sexual Politics* (1970), where she argues Lawrence transformed "masculine ascendancy into a mystical religion" (238), feminist critical attitudes to Lawrence have been largely negative, right through to Cornelia Nixon's study of *Lawrence's Leadership Politics and the Turn Against Women* (1986). Recently, some critics, both male and female, have begun to appreciate Lawrence's influence on women writers, both British and American—including eminent authors such as Margaret Drabble, Doris Lessing and Joyce Carol Oates—who reflect Lawrence's legacy.[1]

Margaret Laurence, called "Canada's most successful novelist" in *The Oxford Companion to Canadian Literature*, is another major woman novelist who reflects Lawrence's influence. Indeed, the two Lau/wrences, David Herbert and Margaret, are surprisingly similar in some ways. I say *surprisingly* because the differences are obvious: one author is eminently English, the other quintessentially Canadian; one is male, one female; and one is modern, the other contemporary. And yet they *are* similar. Indeed, one wonders how any writer in this century named Lau/wrence, albeit by marriage, could fail to be aware of his or her famous (or infamous) namesake or fail to be influenced by him—even though Margaret, curiously, never mentions David Herbert in essays such as "Books That Mattered to Me."[2] Nor have critics compared these two authors, perhaps because Margaret Laurence is viewed in a Canadian context, rather than in the great tradition of English literature in which she was educated.[3] Similarities between Lawrence and Laurence may be demonstrated by comparing their novels *Sons and Lovers* (1913) and *The Stone Angel* (1964).

In spite of the fact that one novel is laid in England and the other in Canada, the settings are remarkably parallel, because both texts are set in a small town that serves as a microcosm of society. D. H. Lawrence's home, Eastwood, becomes the stifling Bestwood of *Sons and Lovers*, and Margaret Laurence's Neepawa, Manitoba becomes her mythical Manawaka, a "town of the mind" (*HS* 3). Laurence completed *The Stone Angel* in Elm Cottage in Penn, a Buckinghamshire village not unlike her own birthplace. Perhaps this English village aided her perception of her small prairie home town and its parallels with D.H. Lawrence's birthplace. Certainly Laurence is the primary novelist of the Canadian prairies, just as D.H. Lawrence is the preeminent novelist of Nottinghamshire, in the tradition of regional novelists such as Walter Scott and Thomas Hardy. Both novelists highlight this town setting in opening sentences that suggest a moralized, almost allegorical, landscape: *Sons and Lovers* begins, "'The Bottoms' succeeded to 'Hell Row'" (7), and *The Stone Angel* begins, "Above the town, on the hill brow, the stone angel used to stand" (3).[4] So both openings suggest a Manichaean cosmology that frames the dynamics of the characters, providing each microcosm with mythic proportions and each protagonist with heroic stature.

Although D. H. Lawrence's novel was published in 1913 and Margaret Laurence's over half a century later in 1964, even the eras in which the two novels begin are parallel. Lawrence's autobiographical fiction begins essentially with the birth of Paul Morel, modelled on Lawrence himself, who was born in 1885. Margaret Laurence's first Canadian novel is set at the same time: indeed, the first date mentioned, on the second page, in the childhood of Laurence's nonagenarian heroine, Hagar Shipley, is 1886, precisely one year after David Herbert Lawrence's birth date. Margaret Laurence explains that, when she first set novels in Canada, "I had to begin approaching my background and my past through my grandparents' generation, the generation of pioneers of Scots Presbyterian origin, who had been among the first to people the town I called Manawaka. . . . Hagar, in *The Stone Angel*, was not drawn from life, but she incorporates many of the qualities of my grandparents' generation. Her speech is their speech, and her gods their gods" (*HS* 3–4).

Comparing *Sons and Lovers* with *The Stone Angel*—a *bildungsroman* about a boy facing life and a *vollendungsroman*[5] about a ninety-year-old woman facing death—may appear peculiar, but the parallels between Paul Morel's mother Gertrude Coppard (based on Lawrence's mother Lydia Lawrence) and Hagar Currie, the Stone Angel made flesh, are manifold. Despite differences in narrative method and viewpoint—Hagar's tale told in her voice through a series of flashbacks and Paul Morel's story narrated from an omniscient viewpoint centred in his perspective—these two central female characters are remarkably similar. The primary parallellism between the novels centres on Part One of *Sons and Lovers*, especially the initial chapters: "The Early Married Life of the Morels," "The Birth of Paul, and Another Battle," "The Casting Off of Morel—The Taking on of William," and "The Young Life of Paul," through to "Death in the Family."

Both matriarchs, Gertrude Coppard and Hagar Currie, spring from the bourgeoisie, daughters of proud citizens and denizens of the Victorian culture. In *Sons and Lovers*, Lawrence writes:

> Mrs Morel came of a good old burgher family, famous independents who had fought with Colonel Hutchinson, and who remained stout Congregationalists. Her grandfather had gone bankrupt in the lace-market at a time when so many lace-manufacturers were ruined in Nottingham. Her father, George Coppard, was an engineer—a large, handsome, haughty man, proud of his fair skin and blue eyes, but more proud still of his integrity. (14-15)

Hagar, heroine of *The Stone Angel*, is the daughter of "Jason Currie, businessman" (16), the first merchant of Manawaka. As the owner of Manawaka's first General Store, Jason Currie is a "fledgling pharaoh in an uncouth land" (3). His daughter Hagar thinks he is equal to God himself: "Auntie Doll was always telling us that Father was a God-fearing man. I never for a moment believed it, of course. I couldn't imagine Father fearing anyone, God included, especially when he didn't even owe his existence to the Almighty. God might have created heaven and earth and the majority of people, but Father was a self-made man, as he himself had told us often enough" (17). This Scots-Presbyterian pioneer of commerce is proud of his British mercantile heritage, inviting his daughter to admire the portrait of his father, Sir Daniel Currie, who served with distinction in India and imported silks to Scotland (14). Jason instructs Hagar in her proud heritage: the Curries are Highlanders, sept of the Clanranald MacDonalds. Jason gives Hagar his grandfather's plaid pin bearing the Currie crest—"three-towered castle and an arm holding a sword"—and the motto *Gainsay Who Dare* (124). Hagar recalls proudly "strutting the board sidewalk like a pint-sized peacock, resplendent, haughty, hoity-toity, Jason Currie's black-haired daughter" (6).

Each woman is indeed her father's daughter: in *Sons and Lovers*, D. H. Lawrence observes, "Gertrude resembled her mother in her small build. But her temper, proud and unyielding, she had from the Coppards" (15). In *The Stone Angel*, Currie declares, "You take after me. . . . You've got backbone," and Hagar acknowledges, "I did take after him" (10). She explains, "My brothers took after our mother [who gave up the ghost at Hagar's birth], graceful unspirited boys who tried to please him but rarely could. Only I, who didn't want to resemble him in the least, was sturdy like him and bore his hawkish nose and stare that could meet anyone's without blinking an eyelash" (7–8). Both women pride themselves on their puritanical nature: D. H. Lawrence writes, "[Gertrude Coppard] was a puritan, like her father, high-minded, and really stern" (18). Hagar recalls, "How anxious I was to be neat and orderly, imagining life had been created only to celebrate tidiness, like prissy Pippa as she passed" (5). Hagar and her friends resemble "dainty-nosed czarinas" (27).

Both women are unusually highly educated for their eras, and both intend to be teachers. Gertrude Coppard assists the mistress at the private school in Sheerness, where she was a student (15). Hagar Currie, unlike her elder brothers Matt and Dan, is sent away to college in Toronto, to learn how to "behave like a lady" (42). When she returns home to Manawaka, she intends to be a teacher in a one-room schoolhouse in South Wachakwa, but her father has other plans for her. He wants his ladylike daughter to be his chatelaine, hosting his dinner parties and decorating his table: "I was Pharaoh's daughter reluctantly returning to his roof, the square brick palace so oddly antimacassared in the wilderness" (43), Hagar recalls resentfully.

Each woman is attracted to a man who is her opposite in every way—lower class and less educated, but vivacious and virile—Dionysian to her Apollonian. D. H. Lawrence writes:

> [Walter Morel] was well set-up, erect, and very smart. He had wavy black hair that shone again, and a vigorous black beard that had never been shaved. His cheeks were ruddy, and his red, moist mouth was noticeable because he laughed so often and so heartily. He had that rare thing, a rich, ringing laugh. Gertrude Coppard had watched him, fascinated. He was so full of colour and animation, his voice ran so easily into comic grotesque, he was so ready and so pleasant with everybody. Her own father had a rich fund of humour, but it was satiric. This man's was different: soft, non-intellectual, warm, a kind of gambolling. (16-17)

Brampton Shipley is built in the same mould as Walter Morel, an archetypal Lawrencean male—"Strong as a horse [with] a beard black as the ace of spades. He was a handsome man" (272), Hagar recalls: "I reveled in his fingernails with crescents of ingrown earth that never met a file. I fancied I heard in his laughter the bravery of battalions. I thought he looked a bearded Indian, so brown and beaked a face. The black hair thrusting from his chin was rough as thistles" (45-46).

The men are connected to the land—Morel as a miner and Bram as a farmer: even Brampton's name suggests *bran*, full of fibre. Gertrude and Hagar, town-bred and school-educated, initially revel in their lover's link with the land. When Walter tells Gertrude that he is a miner (modelled on Lawrence's own collier father, Arthur Lawrence), "She looked at him, startled. This was a new tract of life suddenly opened before her. She realized the life of the miners, hundreds of them toiling below earth and coming up at evening. He seemed to her noble. He risked his life daily, and with gaiety" (19). Similarly, in *The Stone Angel*, Hagar delights, initially, that her husband Bram comes home at supper time "smelling of sweat and sun" (113). But Bram is "so hey-day, go-day, God-send-Sunday" (168), Hagar declares, that his "land . . . was never lucky" (29).

Both men embody natural forces in opposition to the world of commerce represented by the women's families. Both novels are constructed around this basic opposition introduced in the opening moralized landscapes. On the first page of *Sons and Lovers*, Lawrence suggests the rape of the fair country by the collieries: "The brook ran under the alder-trees, scarcely soiled by these small mines" (7). Similarly, in *The Stone Angel*, Laurence describes the Manawaka cemetery thus:

> sometimes through the hot rush of disrespectful wind that shook the scrub oak and the coarse couchgrass encroaching upon the dutifully cared-for habitations of the dead, the scent of the cowslips would rise momentarily. They were tough-rooted, these wild and gaudy flowers, and although they were held back at the cemetery's edge, torn out by loving relatives determined to keep the plots clear and clearly civilized, for a second or two a person walking there could catch the faint, musky, dust-tinged smell of things that grew untended and had grown always, before the portly peonies and the angels with rigid wings, when the prairie bluffs were walked through only by Cree with enigmatic faces and greasy hair. (5)

Brampton Shipley embodies the wind that blows off the prairies, disturbing the cultivated blooms.

The men are attracted to the women as their diametrical antithesis in class and education. D.H. Lawrence writes of Gertrude: "She herself was opposite. She had a curious, receptive mind, which found much pleasure and amusement in listening to other folk. She was clever in leading folk on to talk. She loved ideas, and was considered very intellectual. What she liked most of all was an argument on religion or philosophy or politics with some educated man. This she did not often enjoy. So she always had people tell her about themselves, finding her pleasure so" (17). Walter Morel, like Arthur Lawrence, is semi-literate, reading aloud from the newspaper with the deliberation of "a man pitching quoits" (62–63). Brampton Shipley reads only Eaton's catalogue "to improve his mind" (113), and his handwriting looks like "sparrow tracks on snow" (166).

D. H. Lawrence clarifies the attraction: "[Gertrude] was still perfectly intact, deeply religious, and full of beautiful candour [and] Walter Morel seemed melted away before her. She was to the miner that thing of mystery and fascination, a *lady*" (my italics 17). After all, "His grandfather was a French refugee who had married an English barmaid—if it had been a marriage" (17), Lawrence explains. Brampton Shipley, like Walter Morel, is no gentleman: he acknowledges Hagar's social superiority, albeit grudgingly: "by Christ, you're respectable—I'll give you that" (116).

Lawrence explains in his "Autobiographical Sketch" that this unlikely union of the puritanical bourgoise and the elemental miner is based on his own parents: "My father was a collier, and only a collier, nothing praiseworthy about him. He wasn't even respectable, in so far as he got drunk rather frequently, never went near a chapel, and was usually rather rude to his little immediate bosses at the pit. . . . My mother was, I suppose, superior. She came from town and belonged really to the lower bourgoisie" (592). As Margaret Laurence explains in *Heart of a Stranger*, *The Stone Angel* is based on her grandparents' deities and idioms.

The contrast in background in this attraction of opposites is best exemplified in their speech: D.H. Lawrence writes, "When [Gertrude] spoke to [Walter], it was with a southern pronunciation and a purity of English which thrilled him to hear" (17). On the other hand, he notes, "She had never been 'thee'd' and 'thou'd' before" (19). Initially, she finds his local dialect charming, when he addresses her as "tha mucky little 'ussy" (28). This class distinction in speech reflects Lawrence's own parents: in his "Autobiographical Sketch," he recounts, "My mother spoke King's English, without an accent, and never in her life could imitate a sentence of the dialect which my father spoke, and which we children spoke out of doors" (592). In *The Stone Angel*, Hagar recalls, "[Bram] was a big-built man, and he carried himself so well. I could have been proud, going to town or church with him, if only he'd never opened his mouth" (69–70), for "He couldn't string two words together without some crudity" (79). Bram swears: "Judas priest, woman. . . . I talk the way I talk, and I ain't likely to change now. If it's not good enough, that's too damn bad" (71). Hagar acknowledges, "And yet—here's the joker in the pack—we'd each married for those qualities we later found we couldn't bear, he for my manners and speech, I for his flouting of them" (79).

Both men, gifted dancers, win the woman by dancing with her, overwhelming her with their vitality. Walter Morel, "a famous one for dancing" (22), "danced well, as if it were natural and joyous in him to dance" (17): "Gertrude Coppard watched the young miner as he danced, a certain subtle exultation like glamour in his movement, and his face the flower of his body, ruddy, with tumbled black hair, and laughing alike whatever partner he bowed above" (17–18). Gertrude was "contemptuous of dancing" (18) in general, but when Walter bowed above her, inviting her to dance, Lawrence writes, "A warmth radiated through her as if she had drunk wine" (18). Hagar Currie, surrounded by eligible suitors, recalls meeting the unsuitable Brampton Shipley at a dance:

> As we went spinning like tumbleweed in a Viennese waltz, disguised and hidden by the whirling crowd, quite suddenly he pulled me to him and pressed his outheld groin against my thigh. Not by accident. There was no mistaking it. No one had ever dared in this way before. Outraged, I pushed at his shoulders, and he grinned. I, mortified beyond words, couldn't look at him except dartingly. But when he asked me for another dance, I danced with him. (47)

The men, curiously, are compared to pigs: Walter Morel observes to Gertrude, "I'm like a pig's tail, I curl because I canna help it." However, he also remarks, "Tha'rt not long in taking the curl out of me" (18). Hagar tries equally hard to uncurl Bram, who is called "Common as dirt" (47). Bram is termed "Lazy as a pet pig" (46) by Jason Currie who calls Hagar "pig- headed" (49). Thus, both authors suggest the males' natural animal spirits so antithetical to the starchy women.

Indeed, both women marry a man who is not only antithetical to themselves but also opposite to their upright fathers, for the men are sheerly sensual, while the wives are proudly puritanical. D. H. Lawrence writes of Walter and Gertrude, "She thought him rather wonderful, never having met anyone like him. Her father was to her the type of all men. And George Coppard, proud in his bearing, handsome and rather bitter; who preferred theology in reading, and who drew near in sympathy only to one man, the Apostle Paul; who was harsh in government, and in familiarity ironic; who ignored all sensuous pleasure;—he was very different from the miner" (18). Therefore, "the dusky, golden softness of this man's sensuous flame of life, that flowed off his flesh like the flame from a candle, not baffled and gripped into incandescence by thought and spirit as her life was, seemed to her something wonderful, beyond her" (18). In the case of *The Stone Angel*, there is even the suggestion of an incestuous attachment of the widowed Jason Currie to his chatelaine daughter Hagar. Certainly she rejects the nambypamby suitors he parades before her and selects the most unsuitable spouse to spite her father, who disinherits her in revenge. Hagar exults in her heroic defiance, "drunk with exhilaration at my daring" (49). She flings her father's family motto in his face—*Gainsay who dare*! (15). Hagar's exhilaration, as "I rode in the black-topped buggy beside the man who was now my mate" (50), resembles Alvina Houghton's riding with her Italian actor-lover, Ciccio Marasca, atop a Woodhouse tram in Lawrence's *The Lost Girl* (215).

Marital bliss is short-lived, however. Lawrence writes of the Morels, "The next Christmas they were married, and for three months she was perfectly happy: for six months she was very happy" (19). Hagar's happiness is even briefer: since *the birds and the bees* are news to Hagar, her *deflowering* comes as a shock: "I had not known, and when he'd bent, enormous and giant, I could not believe there could be within me a room to house such magnitude. When I found there was, I felt as one might feel discovering a second head, an unsuspected area. Pleasure or pain were one to me, meaningless. I only thought—well, thank the Lord now I know, and at least it's possible, without the massacre it looked like being. I was a very practical girl in many ways" (52). Elbow-grease provides the antidote to sex for Hagar: convinced, like most Victorian housewives, that cleanliness is next to Godliness, she "worked like a dray horse" (112), and the morning after, she scrubbed the Shipley place, to make it ship-shape, "as though I'd been driven by a whip" (52).

Both women marry for love but live in hate, exhibiting frigidity in the marriage bed, never giving their husbands the satisfaction of acknowledging their attraction. Hagar recalls:

> It was not so very long after we wed, when first I felt my blood and vitals rise to meet his. He never knew. I never let him know. I never spoke aloud, and I made certain that the trembling was all inner. He had an innocence about him, I guess, or he'd have known. How could he not have known? Didn't I betray myself in rising sap, like a heedless and compelled maple after a winter? But no. He never expected any such a thing, and so he never perceived it. I prided myself upon keeping my pride intact, like some maidenhead. (81)

She confesses, "I'd sucked my secret pleasure from his skin" (100), but Bram, unconscious of her secret, always said he was "*sorry* to bother me" (116 italics mine).[6] As an old woman, condemned to a bed as "cold as winter," where she imagines lying on the snow to make an image of "an angel with spread wings" (81), Hagar finally acknowledges to herself half a century later: "*His banner over me was love*. . . . I never thought it love, though, after we wed. Love, I fancied, must consist of words and deeds delicate as lavender sachets, not like the things he did sprawled on the high white bedstead that rattled like a train. . . . His banner over me was only his own skin, and now I no longer know why it should have shamed me" (80-81).

The narrative perspective of *Sons and Lovers* allows us less insight into Gertrude Morel's intimate feelings, but Lawrence suggests that the sexual relation of the married couple outlasts their love, causing the birth of Paul and a concommitent guilt on Gertrude's part for "having brought it into the world unloved" (51). Lawrence writes, "After this she scarcely desired him" (62). Although infant Arthur is the "fruit of this little peace and tenderness between the separating parents," during Walter's convalescence, Lawrence insists, "she did not love her husband" (63).

Both husbands seek solace for their wives' frigidity in the bottle: Walter Morel squanders his pay carousing at the Moon and Stars or swilling beer at the Miner's Arms (26); Bram drinks red biddy with his buddy Charlie Bean in a shack on the wrong side of the tracks (115). Equally important, both men find affection in animals. Walter is fond of the pit pony Taffy and delights in regaling the children with tales of this "little 'oss" who is such "a fawce un!" (83). Bram seeks solace in his stallion Soldier. Hagar hates horses, even though she enjoys tossing her *black mane* at men (46). She keeps a picture of Rosa Bonheur's *The Horse Fair* on her wall: "and still in my room the great-flanked horses strut eternally. Bram never cared for that picture," she recalls.

> "You never gave a damn for living horses, Hagar," he said once. But when you seen them put onto paper where they couldn't drop manure, then it's dandy, eh? Well, keep your bloody paper horses. I'd as soon have nothing on my walls."
>
> He was quite right that I never cared for horses. I was frightened of them, so high and heavy they seemed, so muscular, so much their own masters--I never felt I could handle them. I didn't let Bram see I was afraid, preferring to let him think I merely objected to them because they were smelly. Bram was crazy about horses. (83)

Hagar's fear of horses recalls Ursula Brangwen's trauma at the conclusion of *The Rainbow* (489). Her characterization of equine virility is essentially Lawrencean, recalling *St Mawr* or Miss Limb's beloved stallion in *Sons and Lovers* (288). Hagar is uneasy with animals: although she is the *egg woman* (132), who admits "the damnable chickens were a godsend" (173), she is just as repelled to touch the chickens as that "mardy-kid" Miriam Leivers in *Sons and Lovers* (158).

One of the most poignant episodes in *The Stone Angel* occurs one winter night when Bram goes in quest of Soldier—after the stallion followed the *black mare with the wandering streak* into a snowstorm and got lost in the blizzard—only to discover the horse the next spring with its leg caught in a barbed wire fence in a scene that is richly reminiscent of D.H. Lawrence (85–88). Bram erects a rock to mark Soldier's grave, recalling the stone angel that Jason Currie erected to memorialize "the brood mare [who'd] proved no match for his stud" (43). Ironically, Bram's loss of Soldier inspires Hagar's sympathy so that she thinks, "I might have opened to him openly" (88), but Bram considers that "the greatest favour he could do me" (88) is to leave his wife alone. And so, with their customary bad timing, they miss their moment of intimacy. Hagar recalls that in the "moment when we might have touched our hands together, Bram and I, and wished each other well [at the birth of their son] the thought uppermost in my mind was—*the nerve of him*" (101).

Both women, teachers by training, try to *educate* their men, to transform their husbands into their fathers. Lawrence writes, "[Gertrude] still continued to strive with [Walter]. She still had her high moral sense, inherited from generations of Puritans. It was now a religious instinct, and she was almost a fanatic with him, because she loved him, or had loved him. If he sinned, she tortured him. If he drank, and lied, was often a poltroon, sometimes a knave, she wielded the lash unmercifully" (25). In *The Stone Angel*, Hagar is certain that "Father would soften and yield, when he saw how Brampton Shipley prospered, gentled, learned cravats and grammar" (50).

But there is no communication between the puritanical bourgeoise and the elemental miner or farmer who make such strange bedfellows. Lawrence writes, "Sometimes, when she herself wearied of love-talk, she tried to open her heart seriously to him. She saw him listen deferentially, but without understanding. This killed her efforts at a finer intimacy, and she had flashes of fear" (20). Likewise, "his soul would reach out in its blind way to her and find her gone" (63). Similarly, Hagar records, "I couldn't speak, nor reach out to [Bram] in any way at all" (100).

Thus, the battle of the sexes is exacerbated by the class war, and both works portray a marital state that degenerates into a martial state.

Lawrence writes, "There began a battle between the husband and wife—a fearful, bloody battle that ended only with the death of one. She fought to make him undertake his own responsibilities, to make him fulfil his obligations. But he was too different from her. His nature was purely sensuous, and she strove to make him moral, religious. She tried to force him to face things. He could not endure it—it drove him out of his mind" (23). When Gertrude discovers that Walter does not even own their own home, "She was her father now" (21), Lawrence writes, for "Something in her proud, honourable soul had crystallized out hard as rock" (22)—recalling the stone angel that symbolizes Hagar.

The Morel marriage becomes a dance of death: "They were now at battle-pitch. Each forgot everything save the hatred of the other and the battle between them" (33). Lawrence concludes, "And so he broke himself. So she merely left him alone. There was this deadlock of passion between them, and she was stronger" (56). Hagar summarizes a quarter-century succinctly: "Twenty-four years, in all, were scoured away like sandbanks under the spate of our wrangle and bicker" (116). She acknowledges, "I'd be the last one to maintain that marriages are made in heaven, unless, as I've sometimes thought, the idea is to see what will happen, put this or that unlikely pair together, observe how they spar" (167)—suggesting God, the "brutal joker" (*JG* 42).

The initial attraction of opposites degenerates into a war of attrition, as the "vulgar gusto" (*SL* 57) of the husband, originally so appealing to the bride, becomes detestable to the wife. Both women end by loathing the very qualities they initially loved, eventually subduing their mates to the degenerate, drunken derelicts they believe them to be. In an unpublished autobiographical commentary, D. H. Lawrence clarifies this destructive dynamic: "My mother fought with deadly hostility against my father, all her life. He was not hostile, till provoked, then he too was a devil. But my mother began it. She seemed to begrudge his very existence. She begrudged him and hated her own love for him, she fought against his natural charm, vindictively" (Ford, 43).

The breakdown of the marriage causes each man to degenerate into drunkenness and, in the case of Bram Shipley, death. The woman's heart hardens to stone, against which the man batters helplessly, shattering his substance, until he is a mere shell. Each husband becomes a hollow man. Initially of virile physique, the man shrinks physically under the weight of wifely disapprobation, diminishing from hearty exuberance into peevish meanness. In *Sons and Lovers*, Lawrence writes, "Morel fell into a slow ruin" (142): "there was a slight shrinking, a diminishing in his assurance. Physically even, he shrank, and his fine full presence waned. He never grew in the least stout, so that, as he sank from his erect, assertive bearing, his physique seemed to contract along with his pride and moral strength" (38). Finally, "his manhood broke" (54), for "He had denied the God in him" (82). Still, "the real tragedy went on in Morel in spite of himself" (488), Lawrence insists.

Hagar recalls that Bram too, "changed, put away the laughter he once wore and replaced it with a shabbier garment" (113). The nadir of Bram's Dionysian descent is the night he is thrown in jail for relieving himself on the steps of *Currie's General Store*. After that, the children call him "Bramble Shitley" (131). When Hagar, appalled by her own transformation reflected in the mirror of a public convenience, goes to Currie's Store to get herself some decent clothes and encounters a drunken Bram buying day-old doughnuts and lemon extract to sell to his buddy Charlie Bean, she walks out of the store side by side with Bram, with all the pride she can muster: "and that was the last time we ever walked anywhere together, Brampton Shipley and myself" (135), she recalls. Ultimately, Hagar is shocked that the big bearlike Bram is shrunken to "an ancient child" (183).

Each family home reflects this marital discord. When the Morels move up in the world—"from the Bottoms to a house on the brow of the hill, commanding a view of the valley, which spread out like a convex cockle-shell, or a clamp-shell, before it" (77)—the children love the new Scargill Street house, but they fear the old ash-tree in front of the house that shrieks in the wind, striking terror into the hearts of the children: "This terror came in from the shrieking of the tree and the anguish of the home discord" (78). The Morels may have moved from "Hell's Row" (7) up to the hill brow, but the misery of the marital malaise poisons their pleasure. Similarly, the Shipley house seems like an empty shell to Hagar, symbolizing the breakdown of their marriage. When Hagar returns to Manawaka as Bram lies dying, she is struck by the farm's dereliction: "At the Shipley place the rusty machinery stood like aged bodies gradually expiring from exposure, ribs turned to the sun . . . [and] the front porch . . . had been given a final pliers twist by frost and wore a caved-in look, like toothless jaws" (169)—prefiguring the shrunken man she finds within. Hagar "worked like a dray horse" (112) to get the Shipley place ship-shape, but when she abandoned it the house, like the husband, decayed. This "grey shell of a house" (208) is like a cadaver from which the life or soul has departed. In *Sons and Lovers* Lawrence calls Miriam Leivers *anthropomorphic* (184), but this term could apply to both novelists, for both present the home in human terms.

Both married couples develop a vicious cycle: in *Sons and Lovers* D. H. Lawrence writes, "The estrangement between them caused him, knowingly or unknowingly, grossly to offend her where he would not have done" (23-24), and "Having hurt her, he hated her" (57). Both husbands become derelict drunkards, humiliating their proud mates. Lawrence summarizes this insidious syndrome succinctly: "The pity was, she was too much his opposite. She could not be content with the little he might be; she would have him the much that he ought to be. So in seeking to make him nobler than he could be, she destroyed him. She injured and hurt and scarred herself, but she lost none of her worth. She also had the children" (25-26). The Morel children side with their mother against their father: "All the children, but particularly Paul, were peculiarly *against* their father, along with their mother" (76). Morel realizes that "His wife was casting him off, half regretfully, but relentlessly; casting him off and turning now for love and life to the children" (62).

Each father's treatment of the cherished child causes each mother to despise her spouse more energetically and cleave even more passionately to her son. In *Sons and Lovers*, Lawrence writes, "the hard hands of the collier hit the baby. Then Mrs. Morel loathed her husband, loathed him for days; and he went out and drank; and she cared very little what he did. Only, on his return, she scathed him with her satire" (23). Both turning-points are conveyed through vivid vignettes. When Gertrude finds her child standing between his father's legs, "cropped like a sheep" and surrounded by "a myriad of crescent-shaped curls, like the petals of a marigold scattered in the reddening firelight" (24), Lawrence writes, "This act of masculine clumsiness was the spear through the side of her love for Morel" (25). The father's act of drunken violence—causing a drop of the mother's blood to fall onto the head of her newborn baby Paul, like a ritual blood bond—renders Gertrude "as cold and impassive as stone" (54)—recalling Hagar, the stone angel, again.

Hagar witnesses a similarly epiphanic scene in a very Lawrencean vignette. Bram Shipley was a bee-keeper who could thrust his arm into the hive without receiving a sting. Hagar recalls:

> Once I followed John out to the boxed bee village, and saw Bram, taking out the full combs, cut a slab of waxen honey and hold it out, and the child opened his mouth, afraid to do otherwise, and stand stock-still and white, while the honeyed butcher knife rammed in, his father's generosity, offering sweetness on a steel that in another season slit the pigs' carcasses. I stood unmoving, afraid to speak, as though they had been sleepwalkers, and startled, might fall. The blade drew away with such slowness it seemed to be drawn out of my very flesh, and when I screamed at Bram, he turned, holding in his hands the knife still drizzling honey like blood, and his beard and mouth drew up into a jester's grin. (125)

The war between the sexes is never so fierce as when children provide the battleground. The attachment of each mother to her son in despite of her spouse creates a familial love triangle, making the son the lover. Indeed, the title *Sons and Lovers* could apply equally to either novel. While D. H. Lawrence is most famous, or infamous, for depicting romantic relationships, his greatest genius is arguably for portraying family relations, which are just as passionate in their way. For Lawrence, the *family romance* inspires the most intense rivalry. Nativity, for Lawrence, provides not completion but conflict, as the love triangle of mother, father, and child creates a deadlock that can only be dissolved by death. Margaret Laurence's novel pivots on the same axis.

Both matrons assuage their pain by turning to their sons for the understanding and tenderness they fail to find from their husbands, trying unconsciously to turn their sons into their lovers. Lawrence writes of William, Gertrude's firstborn, modelled on Lawrence's deceased elder brother Ernest: "His mother loved him passionately. He came just when her own bitterness of disillusion was hardest to bear; when her faith in life was shaken, and her soul felt dreary and lonely. She made much of the child, and the father was jealous. At last Mrs. Morel despised her husband. She turned to the child; she turned from the father" (23). The transference of affections is complete.

Gertrude has great expectations for William: "She saw him a man, young, full of vigour, making the world glow again for her" (63). "She loved him so much! More than that, she hoped in him so much. Almost she lived by him" (72-73). The mother is very ambitious for her first-born, and he absorbs her ambition, socializing with "the bourgeois of Bestwood" (69) and taking a job as a clerk in London. She lives vicariously through him, and all his triumphs are for her: when, at age twelve, William wins first prize in a race, he gives his mother his award, a glass inkstand shaped like an anvil, as his "first real tribute to herself. She took it like a queen" (69). As William launches out on life, "he was like her knight who wore *her* favour in the battle" (101).

After William's departure, Gertrude transfers her affections to Paul, inspiring sibling rivalry: "when William went to Nottingham, and was not so much at home, the mother made a companion of Paul.The latter was unconsciously jealous of his brother, and William was jealous of him. At the same time, they were good friends" (89). But this maternal-filial bond is different, for "Mrs. Morel's intimacy with her second son was more subtle and fine, perhaps not so passionate as with her eldest" (89). Mother and son have been bound together since Paul's birth: "She felt as if the navel string that had connected its frail little body with hers had not been broken. A wave of hot love went over her to the infant" (50–51). As a child, Paul is his mother's *shadow* (64): "His soul seemed always attentive to her" (75). As an adolescent, he is her *secret sharer*: "she felt he was coming to share her burden" (108). Ultimately, "she shared almost everything with him without knowing" (111)—including her hatred of her husband: "Paul hated his father. As a boy he had a fervent private religion. . . . 'Lord let my father die,' he prayed very often" (79). Paul wishes to replace his father: his ambition in life is to make up to his mother for loss of "her life's fulfilment," and he suffers from "a sense of impotence" (85). When his father is in hospital, he tells his mother joyfully, "'I'm the man in the house now'" (112). His life's ambition is to "live happy ever after" (113) with his mother after his father's death. When mother and son journey to Nottingham for Paul's interview at Jordan's Surgical Appliances, Gertrude is "gay, like a sweetheart" (116), and the pair are like "lovers having an adventure together" (117). While Walter complains, "What dost ter ma'e a stool-harsed Jack on 'im for?" (68), Gertrude is glad when Paul gains employment in the grisly factory, for she feels "she had two sons in the world" who would do "what *she* wanted; they were derived from her, they were of her, and their works also would be hers" (127–28). Clearly, she lives vicariously through her sons: "[Paul's] life-story, like an Arabian Nights, was told night after night to his mother. It was almost as if it were her own life" (142). Thus, she bleeds him of his right to live and love freely.

The "mother of men" (SL 44) like Gertrude, Hagar has two sons, Marvin and John. She finds similar solace in her younger son John. "I took to him at once" (122), she says, unlike his brother Marvin: "I almost felt as though Marvin weren't my son" (62), she confesses. Like Gertrude with Paul, Hagar perceives John as frail and in need of protection (123). The two boys even resemble each other physically, with their slight builds, searching eyes and sensitive physiognomies. Hagar plays favourites, manifestly preferring her younger son, John, to her elder, Marvin, whom she sees as "a Shipley through and through" (64). His father's son, who "speaks as Bram did" (30), Marvin shares in his mother's contempt for the shiftless Shipleys: his very name, a "Shipley family name," is detestable, for their "squat brown names [are] common as bottled beer" (32). Unlike John, a fanciful boy like Paul Morel, forever "spinning his spiderwebs" (157), Marvin is "a stolid soul" who "lives in a dreamless sleep" (58). A "serious and plodding little boy" (112), he does his chores doggedly. No messiah, Marvin is a disciple: "High day or holiday or Judgment Day—no difference to Marvin. He would have put his elbow on the table if he'd been an apostle at the Last Supper" (34). When Marvin, Hagar's "unknown soldier" (182), goes off to war as a boy of seventeen, she waits "for him to make himself known to me." But, tragically, "he was never a quick thinker. . . . Words would not come to his bidding, and so the moment eluded us both" (130). When Hagar tells an old woman that she has "two sons. . . . I mean, I had two. One was killed—in the last war" (104), she seems to suggest that she wishes Marvin, not John, had died.

Hagar believes that John takes after the Curries, the strong son her father Jason never had: she laments, "Jason Currie never saw my second son or knew at all that the sort of boy he'd wanted had waited a generation to appear" (64); "A great pity your grandfather never saw you, for you're a boy after his own heart" (123). Hagar gives John her precious plaid-pin, emblem of her heritage, polishing the blackened sterling (124), but John confesses he traded his mother's prized talisman to Lazarus Tonnerre for a hunting knife (177), signifying his contempt for her proud Scottish lineage. His horse, named *Pibroch*, after a Gaelic dirge, foreshadows his doom. Even when John, as an adolescent, grows "wild as mustard seed" (127), Hagar refuses to see him for what he really is—Bram's son and a Shipley. Hagar views John as a natural aristocrat, taking after her titled grandfather Sir Daniel Currie, and Marvin as a peasant, like his father. She insists, "I always thought John took after the Curries" (202), but John corrects her: "'You always bet on the wrong horse. . . . Marv was your boy, but you never saw that, did you?'" (237). Hagar imposes Paul Morel's personality and filial devotion on her own son John, although it is clearly a mismatch.

While Gertrude and Paul are like "lovers having an adventure" and Paul dreams of living alone with his mother after the death of his father, Hagar really does abandon Bram her husband, taking her younger son John with her, leaving Manawaka to travel to the west coast of Canada, where she serves as paid housekeeper in a *stone house* (156) like her aunt Dolly Stonehouse (17). She tells John, "I'll have a man in the house" (141)—parallel to Paul Morel, who boasts, "I'm the man in the house now" (112). In *Sons and Lovers*, the son makes this claim, however, whereas in *The Stone Angel*, the mother asserts it. No momma's boy, John is his father's son, *taking after* Brampton Shipley and *taking care* of him. John abandons his mother in Mr. Oatley's house on the coast to return home to Manawaka to look after his father while Bram dies of sclerosis of the liver. John feeds his father his *medicine*—homebrew—treating himself to a generous allowance.

Hagar feels uncomfortable with her son's sexuality. When she eavesdrops on John tumbling a girl in the garden or overhears "the stifled storming of his breath in the night," she acknowledges, "I didn't care to dwell on the thought of his manhood. I suppose it reminded me of the things I'd sealed away in daytime, the unacknowledged nights I'd lie sleepless even now, until I'd finally accept the necessity of the sedative to blot away the image of Bram's heavy manhood" (159–60). Hagar wishes to deny her son's sexuality, just as she did her husband's, with fatal consequences.

Neither mother can accept her son's mortality. For D.H. Lawrence, nativity represents not completion but conflict, for his most passionate love triangle is composed of the family trinity of mother, father, and son.

The Christian terminology is apt, for the nativity of both baby boys is presented in epiphanic terms: Gertrude Morel imagines the shocks of corn bowing to her infant son and wonders if he will be a Joseph (49); she thrusts him "forward to the crimson, throbbing sun," declaring, "I will call him 'Paul'" (51). Gertrude's scene with the lilies in the moonlight (35) suggests a feminist immaculate conception with Diana, virgin goddess of the moon, as progenitor, making Paul, the Lawrence figure, messianic. Hagar, named for the biblical Abraham's handmaid, calls herself "a stout Madonna" (122), suggesting her baby is messianic or prophetic, a John the Baptist figure. When John would "hold his tantrum breath," Hagar "prayed to him as though he were some infant and relentless Jesus" (54), while pragmatic Bram would just slap him to make him draw breath, like a midwife bringing to life a newborn. Where Bram's favourite profanity is *Judas priest*, John swears by *jumping Jesus* (128). Bram tells John that he was born in a barn—"Me and Jesus" (125)—and he believes his barns will rise "miraculous as Jesus from the tomb" (114), but when Charlotte Tappen mischievously asks Bram his opinion of the Manawaka Glee Club's plan to perform *The Messiah*, he responds cavalierly, "I don't give a good goddamn" (70).

Hagar views John as Jacob wrestling with the angel, just as Gertrude sees Paul as Joseph (49). And Hagar makes John wrestle with the angel literally when mother and son encounter the stone angel overturned and desecrated. Although John does right the angel after a struggle, the reader suspects the culprit who first toppled the old lady was John. Hagar recalls, "I wish he could have looked like Jacob then, wrestling with the angel and besting it, wringing a blessing from it with his might. But no. He sweated and grunted angrily. His feet slipped and he hit his forehead on a marble ear, and swore" (179). John's feet of clay are apparent to the reader, if not to the mother.

Both sons, stifled by their mother's affections, turn to surrogate families for relief—Paul to the Leivers of Willey Farm and John to the Tonnerre family of Métis blood—exacerbating the conflict. John even trades Hagar's proud plaid pin to Lazarus Tonnerre for a hunting knife like the knife Bram fed him honey on, choosing his father's cutting instrument over his mother's connecting one. This familial disaffection is a prelude to the romantic transference of affections in both novels.

Gertrude, her name recalling Hamlet's Oedipal attachment to his mother, blocks both sons' loves, driving them to distraction. Lawrence believed "*Oedipus* is the finest drama of *all* time" (*CL* 276), and his greatest fictional and dramatic works pivot on this maternal–filial devotion. This Oedipal stalemate is complicated with time, when the inital family romance of mother, father, and son interlocks with the subsequent romantic love triangle of mother, son, and sweetheart. *The Stone Angel* parallels *Sons and Lovers*, for the dramatic tension of both narratives is generated by the conflict of these twisted triangles, and the resolution of their rigidity forms the climax of both works, for the two interlocking triangles create a deadlock that can only be dissolved by death.

By trying to possess their sons as men and by trying to force them to give up the young women upon whom they have become emotionally and sexually dependent, both mothers destroy their sons. Gertrude's firstborn attends dances where he meets "flower-like ladies [who] lived like cut blooms in William's heart for a brief fortnight" (70). When some "flame" pursues her "errant swain" (70), Gertrude repels the girl rudely. Symbolically, William "burned his love-letters" (73), giving his younger brother, Paul, his *Postle*, "the birds and flowers" (73)—perhaps inspiring Paul to "the sacrifice of Missis Arabella" (76), his sister Annie's doll that Paul burns in a sacrificial rite.

Later, in London, William *falls* for the fascinating Louisa Lily Denys Western, "supposed to be a lady" (126), bringing her home for Christmas to present to his family: "Miss Western was the princess" (147) in the Morel home, queening it amid the Morels with "her *blessed* airs" (148). Gertrude is jealous of her son's attachment to Lily, because "She loved him passionately" (105). Torn by the conflict between his mother and his mistress, William ultimately dies of brain fever, an appropriate extroversion of his intolerable tension, leaving his *Gypsy* to flirt with other men.

Similarly, Hagar is appalled to discover, when she follows John home to Manawaka after the death of Bram, that he has *fallen* for Arlene Simmons, "No-Name Lottie Dreiser's daughter" (204). Just as contemptuous of the Dreiser dynasty as her father Jason was half a century before, Hagar assumes that "Arlene was taking pleasure from flaunting him like a ragged flag" (199)—just as she, Hagar, flaunted Bram Shipley before Jason Currie like a red flag before a bull. Overhearing the couple "playing at house" (192)—making love while she lies on her "Afghan cocoon like an old brown caterpillar" (208)—she "burned [and] fumed in silence" (208). Mistaking her jealousy for indignation, she plots with Arlene's mother to send the girl east to prevent the lovers' marriage. Warning him, "you have to avoid not only evil but the appearance of evil" (238), Hagar forbids John to bring Arlene home, driving the lovers to ditches: "They never played at house again in the Shipley place" (237). Drunk, John accepts the challenge of Lazarus Tonnerre and dies, along with Arlene, after a collision of his truck with a train on the trestle bridge in Manawaka—a convergence of the twain that forms a graphic symbol of conflicting impulses (240). Hagar recalls, "The night my son died I was transformed to stone and never wept at all" (243)—the stone angel made flesh.

After the death of William in *Sons and Lovers*, Paul contracts pneumonia. Realizing, "I should have watched the living, not the dead" (175), the mother transfers her devotion to her second son: "The two knitted together in perfect intimacy. Mrs Morel's life now rooted itself in Paul" (175–76). The pattern repeats itself with Paul. Driven out of his home by the marital misery, he relies on the Leivers for relief: "Paul fell under Mrs Leivers' spell" (184), finding a surrogate family at Willey Farm. His mother rejects his growing intimacy with Miriam: "it is disgusting—bits of lads and girls courting" (200), Gertrude declares. Her possessive love for her son is thwarted by Miriam's spiritual intensity: "She could feel Paul being drawn away by this girl. And she did not care for Miriam. 'She is one of those who will want to suck a man's soul out till he had none of his own left'" (199); "'She exults—she exults as she carries him off from me,' Mrs Morel cried in her heart when Paul had gone. 'She's not like an ordinary woman, who can leave me my share in him. She wants to absorb him. She wants to draw him out and absorb him till there is nothing left of him, even for himself. He will never be a man on his own feet—she will suck him up'" (237).

So Paul is torn by the conflict between his love for his mother and his need for his lover: "It caused a violent conflict in him. . . . His consciousness seemed to split" (214). Because Gertrude hates Miriam, Paul loathes her: "If Miriam caused his mother suffering, then he hated her" (238). "Strife in Love" climaxes with Paul's capitulation: when his mother confesses, "I've never had a husband—not really," Paul succumbs, "I don't love her, Mother" (262); "Instinctively he realized that he was life to her. And, after all, she was the chief thing to him, the only supreme thing" (261). Following a fight with his father, Paul, echoing Hamlet, begs Gertrude, "Don't sleep with him, Mother" (264): "He pressed his face upon the pillow in a fury of misery. And yet, somewhere in his soul, he was at peace because he loved his mother best. It was the bitter peace of resignation" (264). "Defeat of Miriam" follows logically, for "The deepest of his love belonged to his mother" (264). Jessie Chambers, Lawrence's first betrothed, the model for Miriam, declares in her memoir, "In *Sons and Lovers*, Lawrence handed his mother the laurels of victory" (201).[7]

Both novels climax with the death of the female figure, for not until these possessive mothers relinquish their grip on life can their remaining sons, Paul Morel and Marvin Shipley, live and love freely. Both women incubate death, as cancers consume them. Hagar can "feel the pain beating its wings against my rib cage" (256), for her heart is imaged as a bird desperate to be freed from the (rib)cage of the body: "My heart is pulsing too fast, beating like a berserk bird . . . against the cage of bones. . . . in a frenzy to get out" (95). The epigraph by Dylan Thomas that Margaret Laurence employs for *The Stone Angel*—"*Do not go gentle into that good night. Rage, rage against the dying of the light*"—could apply to either novel, for both mothers fight death to the last.

In *Sons and Lovers*, Paul tells Gertrude, "I never shall meet the right woman while you live" (427). In her memoir *Not I But the Wind*, Frieda Lawrence reports that D. H. Lawrence insisted, "If my mother had lived I could never have loved you, she wouldn't have let me go" (57). In *The Stone Angel*, it is Hagar who realizes, of her son Marvin, "[I] can only release myself by releasing him" (304). The difference is that, while Hagar frees her son, Gertrude clings to Paul to the last. Consequently, Paul speeds his mother's departure, feeding her an overdose of morphine in her nighttime cup of milk, while Marvin does everything he can to please and preserve his mother. Only in death can Paul see his mother purged of the sensual flesh and returned to maidenhood: "She lay like a maiden asleep. . . .dreaming of her love" (485)—images of purity echoed in "The Bride" and "The Virgin Mother," poems on the death of Lydia Lawrence in December, 1910.

The difference is that Gertrude Morel goes to her grave unconscious and unrepentant of her crimes of the heart,[8] whereas Hagar achieves salvation by lying for love. Hagar's sheer longevity and Laurence's narrative method of flashbacks allow Hagar, who is "rampant with memory" (5), to relive her life, revising her actions as a novelist might revise a story. Initially, she lamented, "Oh, my lost men" (6), but it is only through realizing her responsibility and asking forgiveness for her failures of love that she can atone and attain salvation. Reliving her rejection of John's love for Arlene with her father-confessor figure, insurance salesman Murray Ferney Lees, Hagar reaches out to Lees, thinking he is her son John and apologizes: "I didn't really mean it, about not bringing her here. . . .You could come here in the evenings. I wouldn't say a word. . . .I'd not get in your way" (247). Lees, impersonating John, gives her absolution: "I knew all the time you never meant it. Everything is all right" (248). Together they consume crackers and wine in a mock eucharist.

Mr. Troy, the minister, triggers Hagar's *anagnorisis* by singing at her request her favourite hymn, "*All people that on earth do dwell*," making her feel like "a sleepwalker wakened" (285):

> This knowing comes upon me so forcefully, so shatteringly, and with such a bitterness as I have never felt before. I must always, always have wanted that—simply to rejoice. How is it I never could? I know. I know. How long have I known? Or have I always known, in some far crevice of my heart, some cave too deeply buried, too concealed? Every good joy I might have held, in my man or any child of mine or even the plain light of morning, of walking the earth, all were forced to a standstill by some brake of proper appearances—oh, proper to whom? When did I ever speak the heart's truth?
>
> Pride was my wilderness, and the demon that led me there was fear. I was alone, never anything else, and never free, for I carried my chains within me, and they spread out from me and shackled all I touched. Oh, my two, my dead. Dead by your own hands or by mine? Nothing can take away those years. (292)

Realizing on her deathbed that it is her elder, unloved son Marvin, not John, who "is truly Jacob, gripping with all his strength, and bargaining. *I will not let thee go, except thou bless me*," Hagar reassures Marvin, "You've been good to me, always. A better son than John." She considers: "The dead don't bear a grudge nor seek a blessing. The dead don't rest uneasy. Only the living. Marvin, looking at me from anxious elderly eyes, believes me. It doesn't occur to him that a person in my place would ever lie" (304). When she overhears Marvin declare to a nurse, "She's a holy terror" (304), Hagar feels blessed: "I feel like it is more than I could now reasonably have expected out of life, for he has spoken with such anger and such tenderness" (305). Maybe you *can* get blood from a stone: by melting her marble heart, dissolving the *stone*, Hagar frees the *angel*, her soul.

Thus, Hagar liberates herself for death and her son for life: "I lie here and try to recall something truly free that I've done in ninety years. I can think of only two acts that might be so, both recent. One was a joke—yet a joke only as all victories are, the paraphernalia being unequal to the event's reach [that is, Hagar's gargantuan effort when she fetched the bedpan—"gained the shiny steel grail" (301)—for her suffering young roommate Sandra Wong]. The other was a lie—yet not a lie, for it was spoken at least and at last with what may perhaps be a kind of love" (307). Hagar is granted her own grail, as she holds her cup of water in her own hands,[9] redeeming in this baptismal metaphor the perverted picture of the mother's milk in the poisoned cup that Paul feeds Gertrude in *Sons and Lovers*. *The Stone Angel* concludes with embarkation, as Hagar's last words are those of breathless anticipation: "And then—" (308).

Sons and Lovers concludes with a different kind of embarkation, as Paul Morel, following the death of his mother, determines—despite "the gap in life, the tear in the veil, through which his life seemed to drift slowly, as if he were drawn towards death . . . the lapse toward death following in the wake of his beloved" (495)—that "He would not take that direction, to the darkness, to follow her. He walked towards the faintly humming, glowing town, quickly" (511).

A comparison between *Sons and Lovers* and *The Stone Angel* demonstrates manifold parallels that suggest how much the Canadian novelist resembles her English predecessor in portraying this archetypal family romance. The differences between the deaths of the mothers and the lives of the surviving sons, however, suggest that the woman writer has responded to the male author by redeeming the maternal–filial relation, for, while *Sons and Lovers* ends in a tragic tone, *The Stone Angel* concludes on a note of divine comedy.

Notes

1. *D. H. Lawrence's Literary Inheritors* includes Carol Siegel's "Floods of Female Desire in Lawrence and Eudora Welty," Diane Bonds's "Joyce Carol Oates: Testing the Lawrentian Hypothesis," and Nora Foster Stovel's "'A Great Kick at Misery': Lawrence's and Drabble's Rebellion Against the Fatalism of Bennett." *The Legacy of D. H. Lawrence*, ed. Jeffrey Meyers, includes James Gindin's discussion of Lawrence's influence on Doris Lessing in "Lawrence and the Contemporary English Novel" (30–53).
2. Margaret Laurence was born Jean Margaret Wemyss; she married a civil engineer named Jack Laurence and adopted his surname as her pen–name.
3. In *Dance on the Earth*, Margaret Laurence recalls reading the great English writers with Miss Mildred Musgrove in high school in Neepawa (77), as well as studying English literature with such instructors as Malcolm Ross in the Honours English program at United College in Winnipeg (95). Canadian poet Al Purdy recognized the affinity between the two Lau/wrences and urged Margaret to read D. H. Lawrence's 1923 collection of poems, *Birds, Beasts and Flowers* (Lennox 167). Purdy linked both Lau/wrences in "Lawrence to Laurence" in *The Woman on the Shore* (71).
4. Margaret Laurence inserted this famous first sentence by hand into the typescript of *The Stone Angel*, which is held at the Mills Memorial Library at McMaster University in Hamilton, Canada. D. H. Lawrence's manuscript of *Sons and Lovers*, showing few revisions besides some excisions requested by Duckworth editor Edward Garnett, is in the Bancroft Library of the University of California at Berkeley.
5. *Vollendungsroman* is a term, meaning a novel of winding down, used by Constance Rooke to refer to a group of novels, including *The Stone Angel*, that portray a protagonist facing death.
6. In "A Bird in the House," Vanessa says that in the MacLeod family the "magic word. . . . was sorry" (77). Indeed *sorry* seems to be the magic word in Manawaka.
7. This conflict is discussed in more detail in "D. H. Lawrence, Playwright to Novelist: 'Strife in Love' in *A Collier's Friday Night* and *Sons and Lovers*."
8. Lawrence dramatizes this realization in *The Widowing of Mrs Holroyd*, as I demonstrate in "D.H. Lawrence and 'The Dignity of Death': Tragic Recognition in 'Odour of Chrysanthemums', *The Widowing of Mrs Holroyd*, and *Sons and Lovers*."
9. This image recalls a striking scene in *The Prophet's Camel Bell* where Margaret and Jack Laurence offer a cup of water to a mother and child in the Somali desert during the drought (77). George Woodcock parallels these two passages, observing, "Here was a Hagar in real life" (32).

Works Cited

Chambers, Jessie. *D. H. Lawrence: A Personal Record.* London: Frank Cass, 1935. p. 201.

Coldwell, Joan. "Margaret Laurence." *The Oxford Companion to English Literature.* Gen. Ed. William Toy. Toronto: Oxford UP, 1983. pp. 434–36.

Cushman, Keith and Jackson, Dennis, Eds. *D.H. Lawrence's Literary Inheritors.* New York: St. Martins, 1991.

Ford, George H. "The 'S' Curve: Persephone to Pluto." *Double Measure.* New York: Holt, Reinhart and Winston, 1965.

Gindin, James. "Lawrence and the Contemporary English Novel." *The Legacy of D.H. Lawrence.* Ed. Jeffrey Meyers. New York: St. Martin's Press, 1987. pp. 30–53.

Laurence, Margaret. *A Bird in the House.* Toronto: McClelland and Stewart, 1970.

———. "Books That Mattered to Me." *Margaret Laurence: An Appreciation. Journal of Canadian Studies.* Ed. Christl Verduyn. Peterborough: Broadview Press, 1988. 239–49.

———. *Dance on the Earth: A Memoir.* Toronto: McClelland and Stewart, 1989.

———. *The Diviners.* Toronto: McClelland and Stewart, 1974.

———. *Heart of a Stranger.* Toronto: McClelland and Stewart, 1976.

———. *A Jest of God.* Toronto: McClelland and Stewart, 1966.

———. *The Stone Angel.* Toronto: McCLelland and Stewart, 1964.

Lawrence, D. H. "Autobiographical Sketch." *Phoenix II: Uncollected, Unpublished, and Other Prose Works by D.H. Lawrence.* Ed. Warren Roberts and Harry T. Moore. New York: Viking, 1959. pp. 592–96.

———. *The Letters of D.H. Lawrence: Volume I: September 1901–May 1913.* Ed. James T. Boulton and Andrew Robertson. Cambridge: Cambridge UP, 1985.

———. *The Lost Girl.* Ed. John Worthen. Cambridge: Cambridge UP, 1981.

———. *The Complete Plays of D.H. Lawrence.* London: Heinemann, 1965.

———. *The Complete Poems of D.H. Lawrence.* Ed. Vivian de Sola Pinto and Warren Roberts. New York: Viking, 1964.

———. *The Rainbow.* Harmondsworth: Penguin, 1915.

———. *Sons and Lovers.* Harmondsworth: Penguin, 1948.

———. *St. Mawr and The Man Who Died.* New York: Vintage, 1925.

Lawrence, Frieda. *Not I But the Wind.* New York: Viking, 1934.

Lennox, John, Ed. *Margaret Laurence-Al Purdy: A Friendship in Letters.* Toronto: McClelland and Stewart, 1993.

Millett, Kate. *Sexual Politics.* New York: Doubleday, 1970.

Moore, Harry T. *The Priest of Love: The Life of D.H. Lawrence.* New York: Farrar, Straus, and Giroux, 1974.

Nixon, Cornelia. *Lawrence's Leadership Politics and the Turn Against Women.* Berkeley: U of California P, 1986.

Purdy, Al. *The Woman on the Shore*. Toronto: McClelland and Stewart, 1990.

Rooke, Constance. "Hagar's Old Age: *The Stone Angel* as *Vollendungsroman*." *Crossing the River: Essays in Honour of Margaret Laurence*. Ed. Kristjana Gunnars. Winnipeg: Turnstone Press, 1988, pp. 25–42.

Stoval, Nora Foster. "'A Great Kick at Misery': Lawrence's and Drabble's Rebellion Against the Fatalism of Bennett: Bennett's *Anna of the Five Towns*, Lawrence's *Lost Girl*, and Drabble's *Jerusalem the Golden*." *D. H. Lawrence's Literary Influences*. Ed. Keith Cushman and Dennis Jackson. London: Macmillan; New York: St. Martin's, 1992, 131.

———. "D.H. Lawrence and 'The Dignity of Death': Tragic Recognition in 'Odour of Chrysanthemums,' *The Widowing of Mrs. Holroyd*, and *Sons and Lovers*." *The D.H. Lawrence Review*, 16 (1983): 59–82.

———. "D.H. Lawrence, Playwright to Novelist: 'Strife in Love' in *A Collier's Friday Night* and *Sons and Lovers*," *English Studies in Canada*, 13 (1987): 451–56. Reprinted in *D.H. Lawrence*. Ed. Ornella De Zordo. Bromley: C. Helm, 1994.

Woodcock, George. *Margaret Laurence's THE STONE ANGEL*. Toronto: ECW Press, 1989.

5

Rereading D.H. Lawrence in Tennessee Williams's *Glass Menagerie*

M. ELIZABETH SARGENT

"While All the World Was Waiting for Bombardments,"
January 15, 1991

I heard we were bombing Baghdad at 4 pm Oregon time on a gray January afternoon after classes were over for the day. A few hours later, on the half-hour commute home, my car kept slowing down and drifting off to the shoulder of the highway. I didn't have the strength to steer or even keep my foot down on the gas pedal. When I got home, all I seemed able to do was stare at the TV news and then reread parts of my favorite essay, D.H. Lawrence's *Study of Thomas Hardy*—which, as Lawrence's reaction to England's entry into World War I ("what colossal idiocy this war—in sheer rage I've begun my book about Thomas Hardy"), suddenly moved me more deeply than ever before as a statement on why creativity is necessary in the midst of wholesale destruction. Here I was barely able to muster the energy to drive home, and Lawrence—poor and sick and jobless in the autumn of 1914—was finding a way to believe that rewriting *The Rainbow* and continuing to write for an often hostile and unreceptive public was still important even with all creation crashing down around him.

The next day I found myself telling the students in my Introduction to Drama class that creation is slow and hard, destruction fast and easy—that I wouldn't ignore what was going on and the fear we all felt, but that the reason I was going to continue teaching my classes—and hoped that they would keep coming—was my belief in the slow, hard, creative work we did there. If there was anything in our way of life worth protecting and preserving, that thoughtful work was it, and it would be my personal protest against destruction to keep it going.

Then we went on to the assigned subject for the day, Tennessee William's *Glass Menagerie*. What all of us began to see in the play—and what I had paid little attention to in previous readings over the years— was its strong anti-war feeling and its sense of impending chaos. We suddenly focussed on the fact that *The Glass Menagerie* was first produced during World War II, the most popular war of this century. Williams's courage in declaring his anti-war sentiments struck all of us, both those who supported Bush's move against Iraq and those who did not. These are stated most fully in Tom's long speech to Jim before dinner in Scene 6:

> People go to the movies instead of moving! Hollywood characters are supposed to have all the adventures for everybody in America, while everybody in America sits in a dark room and watches them have them! Yes, until there's a war. That's when adventure becomes available to the masses! Everyone's dish, not only Gable's! Then the people in the dark room come out of the dark room to have some adventures themselves—goody, goody! It's our turn now, to go to the South Sea Island—to make a safari—to be exotic, far-off!

Earlier, in Scene 5, Tom—playing his narrator role—had broken into the middle of the play to make sure we didn't forget the larger setting of this softly-lighted domestic drama. Describing the Paradise Dance Hall across the alley with its large, turning glass sphere giving off "delicate rainbow colors," he underscored the sense of threat and the attempt at escape:

> Couples would come outside, to the relative privacy of the alley. You could see them kissing behind ash pits and telephone poles. This was the compensation for lives that passed like mine, without any change or adventure. Adventure and change were imminent in this year. They were waiting around the corner for all these kids. Suspended in the mist over Berchtesgaden, caught in the folds of Chamberlain's umbrella. In Spain there was Guernica! But here there was only hot swing music and liquor, dance halls, bars, and movies, and sex that hung in the gloom like a chandelier and flooded the world with brief, deceptive rainbows. . . . All the world was waiting for bombardments!

Narrating at the end, looking back from the present, Tom makes sure we realize that the threat has now become reality. In his memory, Laura has to blow her candles out because "nowadays the world is lit by lightning!" World War II has arrived.

While my class was focussing on William's reaction to World War II and their own fear of a potential World War III (and of possibly being drafted into it), I was being struck by a third thing—Lawrence's reaction to World War I and a growing certainty that Williams had read Lawrence's *Study of Thomas Hardy* and that *The Glass Menagerie* was filled with echoes from what Lawrence had called his "confessio fidei," his confession of faith.

William's debt to Lawrence, obvious in plays up to and including *The Glass Menagerie* (Blanchard 17), is well-known, but has always been assumed to rest on Lawrence's poetry, letters and fiction. Norman Fedder, in his study of Lawrence's influence on Williams, found that Williams had read much of Lawrence's poetry, letters, and short fiction, and—among the novels—at least *Sons and Lovers*, *The Virgin and the Gipsy*, and *Lady Chatterley's Lover* (11–12). However, no links have been made to Lawrence's non-fiction. Yet as I read and re-read *The Glass Menagerie* under these new conditions, I became convinced that the strong anti-war message and wartime context of the *Study of Thomas Hardy* were a major influence on *The Glass Menagerie*, and that as much as Williams may have misread and distorted Lawrence on matters of sex (Blanchard is convincing on this subject), he read Lawrence supremely well on the underlying causes of war.

References to Guernica and a newspaper headline, "Franco triumphs," make clear that the Wingfield's story is set in the late 30's—that time, Tom says, when "the huge middle class of America was matriculating in a school for the blind. Their eyes had failed them, or they had failed their eyes . . ." (23). Everyone is trying to avoid the oncoming reality of World War II by escaping into one sort of illusion or another. The Wingfields are experts at this: Tom has his movies, Amanda has the past, and Laura has her Victrola and her little glass animals. Even Jim O'Connor, the gentleman caller, has his public speaking and his naive belief in progress.

The first, full published version of *Study of Thomas Hardy*, which Lawrence originally titled *Le Gai Savaire*, was contained in *Phoenix: The Posthumous Papers of D.H. Lawrence*; it came out in New York with Viking in October 1936 (in London with Heinemann simultaneously) and was reviewed widely that fall and winter.[1] Also in 1936, Williams enrolled at Washington University, St. Louis, and undertook a thorough study of Chekhov, D.H. Lawrence, and Hart Crane. It's hard to imagine Williams not being drawn to *Phoenix* when it came out, especially considering his use of the phoenix image in his play about Lawrence's death, *I Rise in Flame, Cried the Phoenix*, written about the same time as *The Glass Menagerie* although not published until 1951. It's even tempting to think of *Phoenix* as the book referred to in *The Glass Menagerie* (Scene 3) as "that hideous book by that insane Mr. Lawrence," the book Amanda returned to the library —but she also calls it "that horrible novel," so viewers have always assumed it to be *Lady Chatterley* or possibly *Sons and Lovers*, the novel with the clearest connections to Tom and Amanda. However, *Menagerie* echoes the long *Study of Thomas Hardy,* described by an early reviewer as "the most central and synthesizing of the major expository pieces" in *Phoenix* ("Flame": 956), much more frequently and exactly than it echoes any of Lawrence's novels.

The strangest and one of the earliest echoes is visual—William's puzzling first three screens, those insulting audio-visual aids that have, thankfully, never been used in any major production of *The Glass Menagerie*. The first screen, just before Amanda calls Tom to supper as the play begins, is in French: "Òu sont les neiges" [Where are the snows?]. Then, as Amanda begins her story of the seventeen gentlemen callers, the second screen—a picture of her as a girl on a porch—appears. Finally, as she lists the callers by name, the third screen repeats, but with an addition: "Òu sont les neiges d'antan?" [Where are the snows of yesteryear?].

Now, certainly Williams could be quoting directly from François Villon's medieval poem, "Balade des dames du temps jadis." Or, if that seems unlikely, Williams could be translating back into the French from Dante Gabriel Rossetti's 1870 translation of the poem, which Rossetti entitled, "The Ballad of the Dead Ladies." But Williams could with much more reason assume his audience to be familiar with a recent and widely reviewed publication of Lawrence's than with either Villon or Rossetti; and the context of Lawrence's quoting of Villon suggests that William's use of it in *Menagerie* is a gentle appreciation, almost a tribute to Amanda in her moment of glory. The connection to Villon and Lawrence helps students make sense of these two French scenes, which otherwise distract them. For Lawrence, the Villon passage is linked to the development of the phoenix and the poppy images that become central to the Hardy study. In the following passage from the *Study of Thomas Hardy*, notice that the grandfather speaks of a *female* phoenix:

> "I have seen the eternal phoenix escape away into flame, leaving life behind in her ashes. Suddenly she went up into red flame, and was gone, leaving life to rise from her ashes."
> "And did it?"
> "Oh yes, it rose up."
> "What did it do then?"
> "It grew up, and burst into flame again."
> And the flame was all the story and all triumph. The old man knew this. It was this he praised, the red outburst at the top of the poppy, in his innermost heart that had no fear of winter. . . .
>
> The phoenix grows up to maturity and fulness of wisdom, it attains to fatness and wealth and all things desirable, only to burst into flame and expire in ash. And the flame and the ash are the be-all and the end-all, and the fatness and wisdom and wealth are but the fuel spent. It is a wasteful ordering of things, indeed, to be sure. . . . But I will chase that flamy phoenix that gadded off into nothingness. Whoop and halloo and away we go into nothingness, in hot pursuit. Say, where are the flowers of yesteryear? Où sont les neiges d'antan? Where's Hippolita, where's Thais, each one loveliest among women? Who knows? Where are the snows of yesteryear? (399–401)[2]

After this recalling of Hippolita and Thais from the Villon poem, Lawrence goes on in the *Study* to write about Dido, a legendary beauty who burst into flame, a "dead lady" (Rossetti's term, not Lawrence's) who burned like a phoenix. Lawrence develops her connection with the phoenix and then moves back into the flame-red flower / poppy image of bright being and fulfillment. Lawrence mocks the reductionist idea that blossoms are just the excess that accompanies reproduction, a necessary lure for pollination and no more:

> What then of this excess that accompanies reproduction? The excess is the thing itself at its maximum of being. If it had stopped short of this excess, it would not have been at all. If this excess were missing, darkness would cover the face of the earth. In this excess, the plant is transfigured into flower, it achieves at last itself. The aim, the culmination of all is the red of the poppy,

> this flame of the phoenix, this extravagant being of Dido, even her so-called waste.
>
> But no, we dare not. We dare not fulfil the past part of our programme. We linger into inactivity at the vegetable, self-preserving stage. As if we preserved ourselves merely for the sake of remaining as we are. (*Study* 402–3)

The echoes of the Hardy *Study* in William's first three screens suggest that Amanda is not fabricating the story about her gentleman callers, even if she is using her past to escape from the hard reality of her present. Her rhapsodic speech to Laura in Scene 6 reveals that Amanda did have her flowering, her moment of maximum or extravagant being. Her memory of it keeps her alive. And Williams underscores the Lawrentian connection by the emphasis on flowers, Amanda's "craze for jonquils" that spring:

> "Finally there were no more vases to hold them, every available space was filled with jonquils. No vases to hold them? All right, I'll hold them myself! And then I—met your father! Malaria fever and jonquils and then—this—boy."

Not only does Amanda live most fully in the memory of that spring she fell in love, but she also wants Laura to have a moment like that—perhaps even more than she wants her to have security and a home. Williams uses not only the screens, but, more effectively, flower imagery to suggest that, short-lived and painful as it is, Laura has such a moment: she blossoms as Blue Roses on her evening with Jim and under his kiss. (Laura is connected with fragile and unreal flowers like the blue roses, unlike Amanda's abundant natural jonquils—instead of attending business college, she tells her mother, "Lately I've been spending most of my afternoons in the Jewel Box, that big glass house where they raise the tropical flowers," Scene 2). Amanda has worked for Laura to have this moment—"the climax of her secret life," Williams calls it—even though she and Laura and Tom—and Jim—are all aware that no further growth or fulfillment can come from it, that in fact Laura may retreat even further into herself and be permanently damaged ("a wasteful ordering of things, to be sure," as Lawrence says). Amanda seems almost to know ahead of time what will happen, if we consider her prophetic but otherwise strange and hurtful comment to Laura moments before Jim arrives in Scene 6—"This is the prettiest you will ever be."

The Lawrence echoes here in *The Glass Menagerie* also jarred me into noticing the echoes of Virginia Woolf for the first time in Jim's repeated reference to Laura as "Shakespeare's sister" (see Chapter 3 of Woolf's *A Room of One's Own*, 1929)—the talented sister of the poet who, as Woolf imagines her, dies as a result of love. "Who shall measure the heat and violence of the poet's heart when caught and tangled in a woman's body?" (Woolf 50). Tom Wingfield, like Judith Shakespeare's brother, escapes and manages to find some form and outlet for his poetic nature; his sister is not so lucky.

An inexplicable stage direction near the end of the play (inexplicable because there's no way an audience could ever see the detail Williams is insisting on) reinforces the *Study of Thomas Hardy* connection: just after Jim has kissed Laura, Amanda arrives with a pitcher of lemonade and a plate of macaroons and we are told, "The plate has a gold border and poppies painted on it."

Lawrence's anger at World War I and his beliefs about the causes of the war become clear as he explores Villon, Dido, the phoenix, and especially the poppy:

> Instead of producing our flower, instead of continuing our activity, satisfying our true desire, climbing and clambering till, like the poppy, we lean on the sill of all the unknown, and run our flag out there in the colour and shine of being, having surpassed that which has been before, we hang back, we dare not even peep forth, but, safely shut up in bud, safely and darkly and snugly enclosed, like the regulation cabbage, we remain secure till our hearts go rotten, saying all the while how safe we are.
>
> No wonder there is a war. No wonder there is a great waste and squandering of life. Anything, anything to prove that we are not altogether sealed in our own self-preservation as dying chrysalides. Better the light be blown out, wilfully, recklessly, in the wildest wind, than remain secure under the bushel, saved from every draught.
>
> So we go to war to show that we can throw our lives away. . . . Does not the war show us how little, under all our carefulness, we count human life and human suffering, how little we value ourselves at bottom, how we hate our own security? . . . Tell me no more we care about human life and suffering. We are, every one of us, revelling at this moment in the squandering of human life as if it were something we needed. And it is shameful. And all because that, to live, we are afraid to risk ourselves. We can only die . . . this is the only good that can result . . . that we realize once

> more that self-preservation is not the final goal of life; that we realize that we can still squander life and property and inflict suffering wholesale. (*Study* 406–7)

I quote this passage at some length because the echoes from it throughout *The Glass Menagerie* are so strong and also because, as it builds, I am reminded of how uncomfortable it was to read out loud in my class the day after we started bombing Iraq. It angered and upset and moved my students—and me. And it strengthened on our ears the noise of passages in *The Glass Menagerie* that are too easily overlooked and in fact often cut from film and live productions of the play. For instance, the televised version starring Katherine Hepburn and Sam Waterston, which we had watched in class, cut almost every passage where Tom referred to the civil war in Spain or the imminence of a world war, thus focusing the audience's attention entirely on the personal encounter between Jim and Laura.

The debate between Tom and Amanda over self-preservation versus "all that [Tom] dreams of doing and being, ever" continues throughout the play, and Amanda's complexity is revealed in her understanding that Tom plans to leave and *must* leave eventually—he must have his moment too. But not until Laura is "provided" for. That a lifetime of work in the warehouse, that security and safety, can kill as surely as physical want, is a knowledge Tom has to set against his guilt about abandoning Laura. Williams wisely doesn't try to resolve this opposition, any more than Lawrence does in this passage from the *Study of Thomas Hardy*:

> Man has made such a mighty struggle to feel at home on the face of the earth. . . . Even his religion has for the systole of its heart-beat, propitiation of the Unknown God who controls death and the sources of nourishment. But for the diastole of the heart-beat, there is something more, something else, thank heaven, than this unappeased rage of self-preservation. . . . Working in contradiction to the will of self-preservation, from the very first man wasted himself begetting children, colouring himself and dancing and howling and sticking feathers in his hair, in scratching pictures on the walls of his cave, and making graven images of his unutterable feelings. So he went on wildly and with gorgeousness taking no thought for the morrow. . . . (*Study* 398)

This necessary systole / diastole rhythm is as central to Lawrence's essay as it is to Williams's play. Both Tom and Amanda seem rounder, richer in character, when they're set against this inevitable systole / diastole Lawrence insists on. It's often too easy to stereotype Amanda because of exchanges like the following where Tom is clearly on the side of supposedly "Lawrentian" man:

> TOM: Man is by instinct a lover, a hunter, a fighter, and none of those instincts are given much play at the warehouse!
> AMANDA: Man is by instinct! Don't quote instinct to me! Instinct is something that people have got away from! It belongs to animals! Christian adults don't want it! (Scene 4)

But clearly Tom understands the need for self-preservation—and Amanda from her own experience understands and sympathizes with the need for "going on wildly and with gorgeousness."

I haven't the space here to discuss yet another fruitful link with the *Study of Thomas Hardy*—the emphasis on light (both in Williams's text and in the handling of light in stage directions) and the emphasis on images of the madonna—so I will, instead, move on to a final, even more important link. In Williams's treatment of Amanda and Laura—indeed, in his repeated portrayal in many of his plays of the genteel but vital woman of the old South lost in the callous present—I also see strong debts to Lawrence's essay. After Lawrence's long discussion of Hardy's novel *Jude the Obscure* and of Sue Bridehead's refusal to sleep with Jude or marry him, Lawrence unsettles our expectations by rising to a lengthy and passionate defense of Sue. He castigates Jude for forcing Sue to marry and mate with him:

> Sue had a being, special and beautiful. Why must not Jude recognize it in all its speciality?. . . . Why must it be assumed that Sue is an "ordinary" woman—as if such a thing existed? (*Study* 510)

If *The Glass Menagerie* is anything, it is an unforgettable portrait of two women who were *not* ordinary, two women who live on in Tom's reverent but accurate and funny and painful memories. Tom insists on Amanda's "dignity and tragic beauty" at the end of the play, just as Williams insists on "the tenderness in her slight person" in her character description at its beginning: "her characterization must be carefully created, not copied from type. . . . There is much to admire in Amanda, and as much to love and pity as there is to laugh at." Although Williams, in the prefatory notes to *I Rise in Flame*, criticizes Lawrence's supposed insistence upon woman's subservience to the male (while in the play itself, as Blanchard notes, distorting the facts of Lawrence's death to emphasize female subservience), Williams's more accurate reading of Lawrence and greater tribute to him is the portrayal of Amanda in all her complexity in *The Glass Menagerie*.

Finally, however, how are we to relate the strong anti-war feeling in *Menagerie* to the private story of the Wingfields? The internal evidence of Williams's reading of Lawrence's *Study of Thomas Hardy* led me back to Lawrence for clues, where the final passage defending Hardy's Sue Bridehead provided the link to Lawrence's earlier tirade against the war.

> Why are we so foul that we have no reverence for that which we are and for that which is amongst us? If we had reverence for our life, our life would take at once religious form. But as it is, in our filthy irreverence, it remains a disgusting slough, where each one of us goes so thoroughly disguised in dirt that we are all alike and indistinguishable. If we had reverence for what we are, our life would take real form, and Sue would have a place . . . she would have a place which does not yet exist, because we are all so vulgar, we have nothing. (*Study* 510)

Our inability to honor the difference, the unique being of the other, is inextricably bound up with our inability to honor, recognize, and satisfy our own unique being. We go to war out of shame that we lack "some new courage to let go the securities, and to be, to risk ourselves in a forward venture of life, as we are willing to risk ourselves in a rush of death" (*Study* 408).

In a world headed for war, Tom Wingfield made his own protest—not only by claiming the value of his own life, his own "maximum of being," his need to go to sea (compare Tom's chosen life with the full final paragraph of Chapter 2 of the *Study*: "and the rest of his life he will be a stirring at the unknown, cast out upon the waters" 409), but by remembering Laura and his mother in exact detail. Williams made his protest against destruction—against both his sister Rose's lobotomy and the insanity of war—by creating an inviolable place for Laura and Amanda in a world that would otherwise crush them, a world of lightning instead of candlelight. Williams's debt to Lawrence is often characterized as the simple lifting of "Lawrence primitives uncorrupted" (Falk 37), but a deeper, truer lifelong debt is to Lawrence's passionate devotion to the patient, hard, risky individual work of creation in a world in love with the illusion, escapism, and mass destruction of war.

Notes

1. In October, November, and December, 1936, reviews appeared in—to name a few—*The Chicago Daily Tribune*, *The Spectator*, *The Christian Science Monitor*, *The Times Literary Supplement*, *New Statesman*, *London Mercury*, *The Boston Transcript*, *The New Republic*, *The New York Times Book Review*, *Booklist*, *The Nation*, *The New York Herald Tribune*, and *The Saturday Review of Literature*.
2. Page numbers throughout refer to the edition of *Phoenix* Williams would have used, Viking, 1936, instead of the recent Cambridge edition edited by Bruce Steele, 1985.

Works Cited

Blanchard, Lydia. "The Fox and the Phoenix: Tennessee Williams's Strong Misreading of Lawrence." In *D.H. Lawrence's Literary Inheritors*. Eds. Keith Cushman and Dennis Jackson. MacMillan, 1991.

Falk, Signi. *Tennessee Williams*. 2nd edition. Boston: Twayne, 1978.

Fedder, Norman. *The Influence of D.H. Lawrence on Tennessee Williams*. The Hague: Mouton, 1966.

"The Flame of Another Phoenix: D.H. Lawrence as Expositor and Artist." *Times Literary Supplement*. 21 Nov. 1936: 956 (unsigned review).

Lawrence, D.H. *Study of Thomas Hardy*. In *Phoenix: The Posthumous Papers of D.H. Lawrence*. Ed. Edward D. McDonald. London: Heinemann and New York: Viking, 1936. 398-516.

Steele, Bruce, ed. *Study of Thomas Hardy and Other Essays*. Cambridge: Cambridge UP, 1985.

Williams, Tennessee. *The Glass Menagerie*. 1945. New York: New Directions, 1949.

Woolf, Virginia. *A Room of One's Own*. London: Harcourt Brace, 1929.

6

Domestic Violence in "The White Stocking:" A Lawrencean Case Study

MARK SPILKA

I

No reading of D.H. Lawrence's "The White Stocking" can proceed very far without acknowledging Keith Cushman's useful precedent. In Chapter VI of *D.H. Lawrence at Work* (148–66) Cushman traces the story's development from its conception in 1907 through its magazine publication in *The Smart Set* in October 1914 to its final appearance in *The Prussian Officer and Other Stories* in December of that year. His most startling discovery, moreover, is one on which my own speculations depend: for it was not until that final version that Lawrence would include the episode of domestic violence which gives the story its remarkably modern resonance. As Cushman demonstrates, the original story was merely an amusing anecdote, and the more serious *Smart Set* revision had avoided violence through the heroine's timely change of heart and mind in the final paragraphs. Thus, when Elsie Whiston sees how upset her husband Ted has become over Valentine gifts and messages from her former employer, she embraces Ted, stops her defiant flirtation, and quietly sends the gifts back the next day. In the final version, however, Whiston bloodies her mouth with a backslap of his hand, advances as if to destroy her, then backs off "in shame and nausea," before returning the offending gifts himself. His closing embrace of his wife combines his own guilty penitence, moreover, with her equally anguished repentance (Cushman 149–50, 162–65).

Cushman calls the first ending "sentimental" and considers the second ending a great improvement. "[T]he addition of the blow makes the story more psychologically persuasive," he writes, "and greatly increases its effectiveness. The blow provides a needed catharsis." Later he embellishes these points by arguing that "violence is a transgression of the mores of modern life" and that husband and wife "are shocked back to social reality" by it (164,165).

Such aesthetic considerations are not uncommon among critical discussions of domestic violence in our time. They suggest a certain edginess about dealing directly with moral implications. Cushman himself exhibits such edginess when he notes, in preceding remarks, that "Too much has been written about the dishes Lawrence and Frieda sometimes threw at each other, but we do know that Lawrence believed that a strong passional impulse should not be resisted." As if to reinforce this odd authorial sanction for violence, Cushman then quotes George Orwell's flip deduction of the story's moral: namely, "that women behave better if they get a sock on the jaw occasionally"—"an interpretation," says Cushman, "that might not have upset Lawrence" (164). Nor Hemingway, one might add, nor Steinbeck, nor many a male writer of hardboiled film and fiction in our time. The incorporation of domestic violence into modern literary fare is legion; it often proceeds without moral comment, or with the implicit sanction of harsh domestic realism or naturalism, a sort of tonic male version of how things really are.

My own comments are going to be less tonic, but no less realistic. They are also going to be much more insistent on the moral and social hazards of aesthetic treatments of this theme. I have called this paper a "Lawrencean Case Study" in my subtitle, for instance, for two good reasons: first, because the story seems to me an almost classic narration of the terms and stages of domestic violence as defined today by professionals in that social service field; and second, because it not only prefigures the directions Lawrence himself would take in his later treatments of domestic violence, it also contains an implicit critique of those directions. I will combine these reasons in my remarks, as the occasion requires; but I want to point out now that the story itself anticipates the professional critique of domestic violence of the 1990s even as it makes its own prescient case against some of Lawrence's most cherished future convictions. As Lawrence himself wisely noted in his *Study of Thomas Hardy* (1914), "every work of art . . . must contain the essential criticism on the morality to which it adheres" ("Study" 185). The early story at hand not only contains that essential moral criticism: it helps us to understand how and where Lawrence himself lost sight of it in later fictions, and how and where he restored it.

I want to stress, in this light, the early appearance in this tale of the dominance–submission problem in Lawrence's later fictions. In his edginess about domestic violence, Cushman overlooks this theme almost entirely; but it is crucial to the story's dramatic tensions and unspoken assumptions and needs to be spelled out. From the opening sentence—"I'm getting up, Teddilinks," said Mrs. Whiston, and she sprang out of bed briskly"—the story is about sex and power, or more precisely, about the liberating freedom Mrs. Whiston finds by leaving herself "utterly in [her husband's] power" ("The White Stocking" 148,153). On this Valentine's Day she exercises this liberation, paradoxically enough, in the interest of the coming postman's delivery of expected Valentines from her former employer. She springs out of bed with a "careless abandon" that makes her husband's spirit glow; she seems a thoughtless "pretty little thing," an "untidy minx" "quick and handy" in her careless ways, intent on her secret rendezvous with the postman and with those confirming letters and packages which indicate that her former employer, Sam Adams, is following up for a second year a flirtation that began before her marriage to Teddilinks. And as her lighthearted name–play on tiddly winks suggests, her liberation allows now for thoughtless romantic games with another power player, the bald bachelor roue who runs the local lace factory where she and her husband and their bachelor boss once tiddled winks with each other at the Christmas ball.

This thoughtless but loving wife carries the heavy burden, then, of Lawrence's future concern with sexual politics. She is about to test the limits of her freedom in consequential ways that the early Lawrence wants to explore and understand. The problem he poses will recur in different ways in his mature fiction; but from the very beginning—"The White Stocking" was among the first three stories that he and Jessie Chambers entered in a story contest in 1907—the problem surfaces; and by 1914—in sequence with the composition of *The Rainbow*—it receives its lasting imprint of domestic violence. Thus Elsie Whiston's paradoxical dependence on her husband's reassuring masculine power is carefully spelled out. In Part I the spelling comes through the kind of washing scene that Lawrence would employ early and late to indicate male vitality:

> Presently he rose, and went to wash himself, rolling back his sleeves and pulling open his shirt at the breast. It was as if his fine, clear–cut temples and

> steady eyes were degraded by the lower, rather brutal part of his face. But she loved it. As she whisked about, clearing the table, she loved the way in which he stood washing himself. He was such a man. She liked to see his neck glistening with water as he swilled it. It amused her and pleased her and thrilled her. He was so sure, so permanent, he had her so utterly in his power. It gave her a delightful mischievous sense of liberty. Within his grasp, she could dart about excitingly. (153)

The physical description of Whiston's face recalls that of Lawrence himself, and the emphasis on the brutal lower jaw will have its fictional relevance to the author's marriage; but the frivolousness of this wife within her husband's power hardly recalls Frieda. These are ordinary Nottingham characters from whom Lawrence is able to gain some distance from his own marital troubles while speaking to the terms of every marriage. And the terms are those of male responsibility for female conduct. Thus in Part III of the tale the dominant responsibility theme is even more carefully articulated:

> Inside of marriage she found her liberty. She was rid of the responsibility of herself. Her husband must look after that. She was free to get what she could out of her time. (165)

This is the rather biblical tenet to which Lawrence would return in *The Fox* and the American and Mexican stories and novels of his middle period, after striving so bravely for "star–equilibrium" in *Women in Love* and for balanced roles freely chosen in *The Captain's Doll*. It is also the tenet he would abandon by stressing mutual submission, in *Lady Chatterley's Lover*, to the spontaneities and responsibilities of tender passional love. Meanwhile he is able to see with startling clarity some limits of the tenet in this striking early tale.

II

Among those limits are the husband's secret dependency upon his wife. Though Lawrence insists that Whiston has found himself in this marriage, that his wife's passionate abandon has given him "a permanent surety and sense of realness in himself," he is also a man who "would be miserable all day without" his goodbye kiss from Elsie, and who feels "as if all his life and warmth were taken away" when she leaves the room. Cushman makes the nice point that Lawrence was equally dependent on Frieda in these early years of marital discovery, that he too had found himself in marriage, yet felt it was hopeless for him to do anything without a woman at his back, upon whom he could draw for strength (Cushman 150–51). In this early story, then, he tests the limits of his own paradoxical dependency and self-discovery: in Elsie's defiant liberation tactics on this Valentine morning, and in Whiston's violent reactions, he tests his own half-formed convictions about male responsibility and sheltering power, about female liberation and submission—and finds them sorely wanting!

Whiston's jealousy about Sam Adams's Valentine attentions offers another biographical clue to these paradoxes. One thinks of Lawrence's rather platonic surface reactions to Frieda's defiant flirtations and infidelities, during their early relations, and of the comic alpine travel narrative that Lawrence would devote to that period in *Mr. Noon* (1920-21), with its oddly calm acceptance of cuckoldry. Perhaps Lawrence's frequent fights with Frieda, his own angry violence about apparently unrelated matters, speak more tellingly to those early triangulations than we have hitherto supposed. Certainly his recognition that Whiston, in his violence with Elsie, is paying back old scores, has the ring of authorial self- knowledge behind it.

It rings also with the power side of sexual politics. Cushman's observation, that "Whiston's 'lust to see [Elsie] bleed, to break her and destroy her' and his desire for 'satisfaction' are obviously and violently sexual," is certainly well-taken; and his tracing of the sensual emendations of the dance imagery in the middle section, as they prefigure similar rhythmic scenes of sexual import in *The Rainbow* (1915), is the triumphant heart of his valuable chapter on this story. But Cushman wrote before the development of an insightful discourse about domestic violence in the 1980s and 1990s. The more recent stress is on male power and control, on mastery and possession and the denial of female equality, and Lawrence's tale rings truer to that emphasis than Cushman is able to show us. The instructive difference between sexual and social potency in males, with its different basis in physical and sensual powers, is what matters here; and Elsie's confused attribution of Ted's sensual powers in that washing scene—his male vitality—to his physical ability to hold her in his power ("He was such a man"), helps to explain why it matters. One has only to recall Lady Chatterley's similar reaction to the gamekeeper's male vitality as she comes upon him washing his upper body in that later novel—her shock of recognition at the beauty of male sensual potency in a rather frail male physique—to grasp the crucial difference (*Lady Chatterley's Lover* 75–76).

The early game, then, is power and control, as our current professionals tell us. Men batter women, even as they rape them, for that very different and decidedly more deadly kind of satisfaction. And the story's structure and texture speak steadily to that deadly end.

Lawrence's use of the flashback in Part II is a functional case in point. In Part I he introduces the Valentine's Day flirtation between Elsie and Sam Adams that has been going on for the past two years. When Whiston surprises Elsie in the front hall, where she has been winking at herself in the mirror, admiring her new earrings, she begins a sequence of delayed confessions by which she ultimately reveals that Sam Adams is the sender of white handkerchiefs, white stockings, earrings, an amethyst brooch, and romantic verses. The confession is staggered over Parts I and III, and by the end of Part I, when Whiston has learned only that she has lied about the white stocking by calling it a sample rather than a gift, and that she has in fact met with Adams once for a drink of coffee and benedictine at a local pub, Whiston has lost that "permanent surety and sense of realness in himself" that came with marriage. In fact, he leaves the house deeply hurt, burned by her flirtation, dangerously roused by her partial confession, and spends his day at work "yearning for surety, and kept tense by not getting it."

Part II, the flashback to the Christmas party for employees at Adams's house two years before, after which the Whistons quickly married, is accordingly our explanatory source for those old scores with Elsie which Whiston settles so violently in Part III. As Cushman shows, Lawrence has added two dance scenes to the original one and has emphasized in all three the seductive sensual power by which bachelor Sam Adams appeals to Elsie, dazes her into unconscious connection, until she swims away "out of contact with the room," passing "into him" sensually, so that the "delicious" movements of his strong supporting body are her own (Cushman 159–60). In Part I we have watched her swinging from her husband's neck, like a child who delights in the sheer physicality of masculine power. Now, in her passive submission to Adam's seductive movements, we see the blend of sexual and physical power which appeals to her. That Whiston also sees it, and is disturbed by her touch while she is roused by the other man, is the dynamic tension of Part II. Unable to dance himself, he is forced to play cards while his partner enjoys herself so thoroughly in the arms of their common boss that she resists going home, late in the party, to his intense chagrin; and when he warns her against being "too free" with the rakish Adams, she even admits to liking him. Then the tension breaks into the open when Adams comes to her for another dance, and she accidentally drops what she takes to be her pocket handkerchief, but which turns out to be a white stocking as it falls to the floor. Adams picks it up with a triumphant laugh:

> "That'll do for me," he whispered—seeming to take possession of her. And he stuffed the stocking in his trousers pocket, and quickly offered her his handkerchief.
>
> The dance began. She felt weak and faint, as if her will were turned to water. A heavy sense of loss came over her. She could not help herself any more. But it was peace. (163)

Plainly Elsie has become the unlucky pawn in an intimate power play. Throughout this scene her self-division between the attractions of these two men has been evident. Now she belongs to Adams. But Whiston intervenes and soon reclaims her. Incensed by the boss's appropriation of her stocking, and by her acquiescence in that seizure, he demands to know what it means, refuses to stay any longer, and explodes with rage outside when he faces her attachment to "That great hog, an' all." As the sequence ends he holds her safe in his arms while she pleads with him to be good to her, not to be cruel to her, and is restored at last by his "white-hot love and belief in her." As Part III begins we learn that they get married within a few weeks and that the white stocking episode, though touched upon once or twice, has never been resolved.

III

The white stocking story had begun with an episode in the early life of Lawrence's mother. She had worked at a lace factory, had gone to the Christmas party for employees, and had been so embarrassed when the white handkerchief she pulled from her pocket turned out to be a white stocking that she never forgot the incident (Cushman 149–50). She told her children about it, and one of them at least understood the embarrassing sexual subtext so well that he made an artful story about it during his own early manhood. The sensual dancing and the problem of divided sexual attraction came from his own early experiences with fickle girlfriends at such parties and from his own troubled reactions to his older wife Frieda's infidelities and flirtations: but the marvellous grasp of these matters comes from his characteristic identification with the woman's point of view. He was close to his mother, and (as we have seen) strongly dependent on his wife for the strength to create his new fictions: the revision of the story to include the new sensualized dancing scenes and the closing violence—this artful realization of the meaning of his early materials—comes from that strong identification with how the women in his life might think and feel. Troubled by his father's brutalities with his mother, and by his own repetition of those brutalities in his fights with Frieda, he created this rare exposition of domestic violence and its causes in characters close to his own sense of himself, his own male and female aspects. There is nothing quite this intimate, quite this close to home, wife and mother, and to his own battering propensities, in his later fiction.[1] The story functions accordingly as a useful case study of the nature of domestic violence and of his early apprehension of the deadly struggle he would later place at the heart of modern marriage.

In Part III Lawrence turns to the culmination of that deadly struggle in the Whiston household. As Cushman shows, he had worked in an intimation of impending violence in Part I (154). Thus, when Elsie tells Ted of her drink with Sam Adams at a local pub:

> The blood came up into his neck and face[;] he stood motionless, dangerous.
>
> "It was cold, and it was such fun to go into the Royal," she said.
>
> "You'd go off with a nigger for a packet of chocolate," he said, in anger and contempt, and some bitterness. Queer how he drew away from her, cut her off from him.
>
> "Ted—how beastly!" she cried. "You know quite well. . . ." She caught her lip, flushed, and the tears came to her eyes. (154)

That women and blacks share a subordinate status in our culture comes as no surprise in these days of raised consciousness about ethnic and gender differences. But it is worth citing Toni Morrison's recent observation of the disruptive presence of African darkness in white fictions as a sign of things "beastly" and black that threaten our white heterosexual partners (*Playing* 76,91). Elsie has just fallen measurably in human and social status as the angry Ted draws back in bitter contempt from his erstwhile prize possession. It is in this "dangerous" and demeaning manner that Ted claims his dependent goodbye kiss and goes off to work as the sequence closes. Meanwhile Elsie is further trivialized as thoughtless by her return to the frivolous morning mood of delight in her new earrings, which Whiston has not noticed, but which she wears all day, hoping the tradesmen will notice them; as indeed they do:

> All the tradesmen left her door with a glow in them, feeling elated, and unconsciously favoring the delightful little creature, though there had been nothing to notice in her behaviour.
>
> She was stimulated all the day. She did not think about her husband. He was the permanent basis from which she took these giddy little flights into nowhere. At night, like chickens and curses, she would come home to him, to roost. (154–55)

That ominous reference to curses indicates Lawrence's participation in Elsie's indictment in this story as a provocative, thoughtless minx, while she is at the same time being cherished as a woman who rests confident in her husband's power, his willingness to take responsibility for her behavior and her willingness to allow it. These contradictory meanings—or perhaps more accurately, these ambivalent leanings—are now exposed as Lawrence further develops Elsie's sportive play with Valentine fantasies of the past two years and her plans for future innocent deceptions of her now discouraged husband. Thus, when he returns home tired and depressed from his male insecurities, she is still caught up in imagined "liberations" and begins to mock and jeer and cut him off. Though these additional provocations make her uneasy, she can't help goading him on, as if testing the limits of her sportive freedom like a child asking for clarifying punishment.

Or perhaps like a woman who no longer wants to be treated like a child. That construction is my own, but it seems to me implicit in the story's ultimate exposure of its own ambivalences. "Elsie's Rebellion, or The White Stocking Revisited," might be a fair way of retitling this essay, in keeping with my reading of her supposedly thoughtless conduct and its contradictory meanings. If she is to learn to take her sportive ways, her harmless and supposedly innocent flirtations more seriously, she must herself be taken more seriously by her husband, her creator, and her self; and in all fairness to Lawrence and his awareness of more serious infidelities, I think he does arrive at a similar weighting of the inadequacy of his own assumptions here. He is true to the psychodynamics of this situation—to where the tale is taking him—and so creates a tale we can trust while at the same time questioning the artist's mixed intentions.[2]

Meanwhile he provides us with a nice version of the standard complaint of male batterers: that "she drove me to it." Thus Elsie does all she can to madden and infuriate her already jealous husband. When he asks why she doesn't put the stockings on the fire-back where they belong, she goes upstairs, pulls them onto her legs, and comes down to dance around her husband tauntingly, in defiant resentment of his commanding ways. His anger mounts dangerously.

> It was a war now. She bent forward, in a ballet-dancer's fashion, and put her tongue between her teeth.
>
> "I shan't back-fire them stockings," she sang, repeating his words, "I shan't, I shan't, I shan't."
>
> And she danced round the room doing a high kick to the tune of her words. There was a real biting indifference in her behaviour.
>
> "We'll see whether you will or not . . . trollops! You'd like Sam Adams to know you was wearing 'em, wouldn't you? . . ."
>
> "Yes, I'd like him to see how nicely they fit me, he might give me some more then."
>
> And she looked down at her pretty legs. . . . It made his anger go deep, almost to hatred.
>
> "Yer nasty trolley," he cried. "Put your petticoats down, and stop being so foul-minded."
>
> "I'm not foul-minded," she said. "My legs are my own. And why shouldn't Sam Adams think they're nice? . . ."
>
> "Them who has anything to do wi' him is too bad for me, I tell you."
>
> "Why, what are you frightened of him for?" she mocked.
>
> She was rousing all his uncontrollable anger. . . . Every one of her sentences stirred him up like a red-hot iron. Soon it would be too much. . . . A curious little grin of hate came on his face. He had a long score against her.
>
> "What am I frightened of him for? he repeated automatically. . . . "Why for you, you stray-running little bitch."
>
> She flushed. The insult went deep into her, right home. (167–68)

Bad, nasty, trollops, trolley, foul-minded, stray-running little bitch—the abusive litany of sexually degrading terms betrays Ted's fear of dispossession by another man. His long score against Elsie has its roots in those seductive dancing scenes two years back, in Adams's possession of her pawn-like body upon seizing the white stocking and making it his own. That unresolved incident still rankles Ted, rouses what Lawrence calls his "uncontrollable anger"—which, as domestic violence professionals know, is the rage at the bottom of the iceberg anger chart, where old scores are stored below our half-conscious feelings of resentment, loss, jealousy, inadequacy, insecurity, contempt, bitter hostility: old scores, that is, against the women in our lives, our sweethearts, wives, and mothers before them, as in those pre-oedipal infant rages that Margaret Storch explores through Melanie Klein,[3] or in those oedipal resentments that Lawrence and Freud explore between rivalrous sons and fathers. Long scores indeed; but scarcely uncontrollable. We work them up as we need them, we exploit them in our need for power and control, and then blame anger itself for our violent conduct, or blame our provocative partners, as the story now demonstrates.

Thus, when Elsie jeeringly suggests that she won't tell her husband about any future meetings with Adams, a strange thing happens:

> Her jeering scorn made him go white-hot, molten. He knew he was incoherent, scarcely responsible for what he might do. Slowly, unseeing, he rose and went out of doors, stifled, moved to kill her.
>
> He stood leaning against the garden fence, unable either to see or hear. Below him, far off, fumed lights of the town. He stood still, unconscious with a black storm of rage, his face lifted to the light. (169)

Here Whiston does instinctively what domestic violence counsellors advise their clients to do: butt out, cool off when rage rises, find time and space to talk yourself down, to regain full control of your hostile feelings. But "instinctively" is perhaps misleading since Whiston here *chooses* to go outside, exhibits the very control and responsibility he claims not to possess, and seeks to reinforce it. Actually he merely allows his rage to simmer: there is no talking down, and when he returns to the house, Lawrence emphasizes that he is "still unconscious of what he is doing."

It is at this point in the magazine version of the story that his wife Elsie had gone outside to look for him, had called his name and returned inside when he did not answer. He had then felt sorry for her and had come inside to confront her. "Taking courage," she had moved into his embrace, and they had reached each other's deepest feelings by holding fast, overcoming fear and hostility, until she had finally drawn his head down to kiss him, murmuring "My love, my love." Next day she had sent back both stockings and earrings, never telling her husband about the latter (Cushman 162–63).

This "sentimental ending," as Cushman calls it, is oddly true to Elsie's integrity as a responsible person, able to judge and act for herself, and not the biblical wife, the fallen Eve whose punishment is to look to her husband for spiritual and moral guidance. The revised ending in *The Prussian Officer* version is indeed an "improvement" on this easy moral gain, not as an aesthetic catharsis as Cushman argues, but in its recognition of the realities of sexual politics in our time. The story is true, that is to say, to the actualities of domestic violence, to its repetitive and recurrent nature, and to those devastatingly false assumptions about biblical responsibilities, about male power and control and female submission and childish "liberation," that go with the territory. Thus, when Whiston returns inside, Elsie confronts him stubbornly with his commanding ways: "*You're* not going to tell me everything I shall do, and everything I shan't," she declares; and then for the first time, when he threatens to break her neck, she tells him defiantly about the jewels that Adams has sent her over the past two years without his knowledge:

> "He what?" said Whiston, in a suddenly normal voice. His eyes were fixed on her.
>
> "Sent me a pair of pearl ear-rings and an amethyst brooch," she repeated, mechanically, pale to the lips.
>
> And her big, black, childish eyes watched him, fascinated, held in [his] spell.
>
> He seemed to thrust his face and eyes forward at her, as he rose slowly and came to her. She watched transfixed in terror. Her throat made a small sound, as she tried to scream.
>
> Then, quick as lightning, the back of his hand struck her with a crash across the mouth, and she was flung back blinded against the wall. The shock shook a queer sound out of her. And then she saw him still coming on, his fist drawn back, advancing slowly. . . . (169–70)

As Whiston's "suddenly normal voice" attests, he is able now to focus his full attention on the apparent meaning of his wife's defiant confession. In that sense he is in full control of his long-simmering rage when he slaps her; it is a deliberate slap, a choice of punishments, an interpretive response to those surprise romantic properties, those telltale jewels, and their apparent confirmation of lost power and control over his own romantic "property." His slow advance with fist drawn back indicates another deliberate action; but this time he is "slowly arrested" by the sight of his terrified wife:

> He hung before her, looking at her fixedly, as she stood crouched against the wall with open bleeding mouth, and wide-staring eyes, and two hands clawing over her temples. And his lust to see her bleed, to break her and destroy her, rose from an old source against her. It carried him. He wanted satisfaction.
>
> But he had seen her standing there, a piteous, horrified thing, and he turned his face aside in shame and nausea. He went and sat heavily in his chair, and a curious ease, almost like sleep, came over his brain. (170)

Again Lawrence refers to the "old source against [Elsie]," the old scores to be settled, as the origin of violence and of the rage that carries Ted toward it: but what Ted demonstrates is a controlled use of that rage, a series of choices, and a decision now to desist out of "shame and nausea" over the observed consequences of his own chosen conduct. Indeed, a moment later, after discovering that his wife has merely kept the jewelry for its own sake, and has had no carnal dealings with Adams, a weariness comes over him; he feels dreary and sick, and the sight of his wife's bloody handkerchief makes him "only more tired and sick of the responsibility of it, the violence, the shame."

The doubling here of the meaning of responsibility, the reference now to his own guilt and shame at striking her, along with the old biblical concern with responsibility for her conduct, is the story's striking reversal, its critique of its own moral system, here sharply undercut by Whiston's recognition of the double folly of his own assumptions. Still, those grimly doubled responsibilities continue as he now goes slowly about his unfinished biblical business: when his wife refuses to fetch the jewels, he goes upstairs to find them, wraps them up, and walks out in his slippers to post them back to Sam Adams. The Valentine's Day Massacre, such as it has been, is over. When he returns to his wife and sees "her tear-stained, swollen face," a flash of anguish goes over his body: *he* embraces *her* now, in this revised version of the ending, and it is he who says "My love, my little love" as the story ends.

As Cushman wisely observes, "Lawrence's art here is more convincing than the couple's reconciliation" (165). The event has been much too traumatic for easy resolution. A terrifying breach in the marriage has just occurred. Indeed, we have just witnessed what professionals call "the honeymoon phase" of the cycle of violence: the remorseful pleasures of kissing and making up after the dramatic flareup of ugly violence, with its damaging wounds and bruises, its anguished tears and hostile recriminations, its demeaning and bloody consequences for the wife, its exhilarating high for the power-hungry husband, his reactive guilt and shame as he reassures himself and his wife it won't happen again, and her own mistaken concurrence in that guilt. It is the honeymoon phase, with its mutually anguished repentance, that Lawrence records as the story closes. For in a way nothing has really changed: the wife's littleness, her childishness, and the husband's controlling role, remain intact. The cycle of violence will continue; it will repeat itself again and again, as in Lawrence's marriage to Frieda and in his own artistic reworkings of the theme. As with those battle-scarred antagonists, Walter and Gertrude Morel, in *Sons and Lovers*, there will be many, many stages in the ebbing of the Whistons' love, but it will always be ebbing.[4]

What are we to make, then, of Lawrence's undercutting of his own assumptions in this tale? What did he learn from revising and strengthening this story? Well, for one thing, he seems to have reached that mature understanding of the powerful psychodynamics of marital conflict, with its death or life options, that marks the next phase of his development; and for another, he seems to have revised upward his estimate of women's strength and worth and the seriousness of their own search for responsible freedom. In *The Rainbow* and *Women in Love*, where the new ethic of star-equilibrium emerges, his creation of strong questing women, his choice of creative life for questing characters of either sex, the personal resistance of such characters to the death-pulls of northern ice-destruction, is a decided cultural and moral advance over the merely personal predicament of the anguished and imbalanced Whistons. As late as *The Captain's Doll* (1921), moreover, he would balance the chauvinist premise that every woman wants to make a doll of the man she loves with the more strikingly accountable view that every man makes "a ghastly fool of *himself* with a woman at some time or other" (emphasis mine).[5]

Meanwhile the deadly weight of World War I, the police persecution in Cornwall, the estrangement of old friends, the suppression of *The Rainbow* and the delay of *Women in Love* (1920), took their cultural and personal toll. By the time Lawrence began his own postwar quest for political power and purpose, he had given himself permission to revive the dominance-submission ethos, with its essentially abusive posture toward women and its reduction of their common claim to life-responsibility, its biblical insistence that women should freely yield that claim in marriage to their supposedly protective partners;[6] and, in such disastrous cosmic fantasies as

The Plumed Serpent and "The Woman Who Rode Away," he would even try to reshape the world and its wives to conform to that ethos. At this point, however, two related personal changes of great moment occurred: he became impotent himself from the inroads of tuberculosis, and his own good wife Frieda rode away from him to England and the arms of John Middleton Murry. Of necessity, then, and with no little wisdom and courage, the phoenix-like Lawrence veered sharply away from the deadly willfulness of "the militant ideal," as he then called it, toward the mutual creaturely tenderness and sensual renewals and responsibilities of *Lady Chatterley's Lover* and *The Man Who Died*, and toward the final haunting humanity of his great poem, *The Ship of Death*. In these last years, at least, his own deadly propensities, his own cycle of violence, had finally been broken.

Notes

1. See my extensive account of Lawrence's treatment of the domestic violence theme in *Renewing the Normative D.H. Lawrence: A Personal Progress*, 211-31. As I observe on 219-20, though Lawrence gave a powerful account of his father's domestic violence in *Sons and Lovers*, he avoided direct autobiographical treatment of his own abusive behavior in all his fictions.
2. I allude here to Lawrence's famous dictum in his introduction to *Studies in Classic American Literature*: "Never trust the artist. Trust the tale. The proper function of the critic is to save the tale from the artist who created it."
3. See Margaret Storch's book, *Sons and Adversaries*, an in-depth Kleinian analysis of Blake and Lawrence as pre-oedipal cases.
4. This is what Lawrence says of Gertrude's love for Walter Morel in *Sons and Lovers*, 46: "There were many, many stages of her love for him, but it was always ebbing."
5. For a full discussion of this balanced opposition and the striking sense of male accountability it implies, see my chapter on *The Captain's Doll* on pp. 254-75 of *Renewing the Normative D.H. Lawrence*.
6. As early as *The White Peacock* (1911) Lawrence had granted the principle of "life-responsibility" (i.e. personal responsiblity for the quality and direction of one's life) to women as well as men. The intrusions of the dominance theme led to doctrinal conflicts in his own thinking and to the dubious resolution of having his women characters freely choose to yield that dominant role to their male partners—as in "The White Stocking" and in later derivative situations in *The Fox, The Plumed Serpent*, and "The Woman Who Rode Away." In *The Captain's Doll* he even tried the expedient of freely chosen *roles*, dominant and submissive,

as defined by the marriage service, as distinct from unpossessable modes of *being* for both partners. In *Lady Chatterley*, however, he returned to vital modes of being for equal partners and showed in several ways how the dominance drive can work against that freely chosen goal. Indeed, the dominance drive here dwindles, in my view, into the "sexual refinements" and expungings of shame through anal intercourse during the last of many conflictual stages—a stage which some critics aggrandize into the novel's true climax.

Works Cited

Cushman, Keith. *D.H. Lawrence at Work: The Emergence of The Prussian Officer Stories*. Charlottesville: UP of Virginia, 1978.

Lawrence, D.H. *The Captain's Doll. Four Short Novels of D.H. Lawrence*. New York: Viking Compass, 1965.

———. *Lady Chatterley's Lover*. New York: Grove, 1959.

———. *Sons and Lovers*. New York: Viking, 1958.

———. *Studies in Classic American Literature*. New York: Viking, 1964.

———. "Study of Thomas Hardy." *Selected Literary Criticism*. Ed. Anthony Beal. New York: Viking, 1956.

———. *The White Peacock*. Ed. Andrew Robinson. Cambridge, England: Cambridge UP, 1983.

———. "The White Stocking." *A Modern Lover and Other Stories*. Ed. Julian Moynahan. New York: Ballantine, 1969.

Morrison, Toni. *Playing in the Dark: Whiteness and the Literary Imagination*. Cambridge, MA: Harvard UP, 1992.

Spilka, Mark. *Renewing the Normative D.H. Lawrence: A Personal Progress*. Columbia: U of Missouri P, 1992.

Storch, Margaret. *Sons and Adversaries: Women in William Blake and D.H. Lawrence*. Knoxville: U of Tennessee P, 1990.

7

"A Secret Riches": Universal and Particular Feminism in *The Rainbow*

PAUL DELANY

It is the spring of 1900 and Ursula Brangwen, sixteen years old, is pondering her future:

> An all-containing will in her for complete independence, complete social independence, complete independence from any personal authority, kept her dullishly at her studies. For she knew that she had always her price of ransom—her femaleness. She was always a woman, and what she could not get because she was a human being, fellow to the rest of mankind, she would get because she was a female, other than the man. In her femaleness she felt a secret riches, a reserve, she had always the price of freedom.
> However, she was sufficiently reserved about this last resource. The other things should be tried first.[1]

Ursula's wavering between two kinds of adult identity raises the most complex and persistent question within the feminist tradition: the status of woman's difference (Ebert, Guillaumin). Her desire for a career and economic independence aligns her with the universalist feminism that would make her the formal equal of the male; but the idea of "secret riches" links Ursula to "female feminism"—the affirmation of woman's particularity (Braidotti 210). One kind of feminism seeks to erase gender difference, the other privileges it. In looking at Ursula's evolution in *The Rainbow* I want to suggest three perspectives on the tension between universalist and particularist feminism. One is historical, connecting Ursula's uncertainty about her gender identity with debates inside and around the suffragist movement. The second arises from a reading of the novel as a narrative of identity formation and displacement. Finally, that narrative includes a compromised and contradictory subtext: Lawrence's appropriation of the novel for his own project of "becoming-woman."

I

Any woman who entered the teaching profession around 1900 would have been obliged to situate herself in relation to contemporary feminist and suffragist movements. Ursula's three women friends in *The Rainbow* —Winifred Inger, Maggie Schofield, and Dorothy Russell—are all suffragists. In representing suffragist women, Lawrence drew on his experience of Eastwood feminists like his mother, Sallie Hopkin, and Alice Dax. As a young teacher he argued in favor of votes for women, and shared the suffragist enthusiasm of his fiancée Louie Burrows.[2] All these women who influenced him in youth were universalist feminists, who wanted to remove women's traditional disabilities and encourage them to be active in the public sphere on an equal basis with men. Yet in December 1912 Lawrence told Sallie Hopkin that he planned to write a novel about "Love Triumphant," by which "I shall do my work for women, better than the suffrage."[3] From 1912 on, he believed that women's liberation should not be limited by what Ursula calls, in *The Rainbow,* "the automatic system that contained the vote" (377). He remained sympathetic to the grievances and aspirations of the feminists he had known in Eastwood, but he was now urging them to move on from suffragism to a more radical rejection of the existing order of things.

The shift in Lawrence's views about female emancipation coincided with the transformation of his personal life. In 1912 he broke off his engagement to Louie Burrows, a fellow teacher, and eloped with Frieda Weekley. In doing so, Lawrence was rejecting a suffragist in favor of an intensely erotic individualist; one could say that he was "converted" from one kind of modern femininity to another. When he composed *The Rainbow* (between March 1913 and August 1915), he conflated the histories of the two women he had loved in succession—Louie and Frieda—into the single character of Ursula. In real life, both women remained consistent in their beliefs. Louie did not become disillusioned with teaching, like Ursula, but remained in the profession and fought for the equality of women teachers with men. Frieda never took part in the organized feminism of her time, though she was always a rebel against woman's conventional role. Ursula, however, changes from being like Louie to being like Frieda. Lawrence decided, in reality, that he wanted to love a different kind of woman; in the novel, Ursula decides that she wants to *be* a different kind of woman.

But *The Rainbow* is more than a justification of Lawrence's own erotic development. The change in Ursula's personal views corresponds to a crucial shift in feminist ideology around the time of World War I. Universalist and particularist feminisms were in dialogue with each other then, as they are now. "Equality feminism" took as its aim the erasure of differences in privilege and gender roles. As Winifred Holtby explained in 1924, its paradoxical aim was to succeed, and then to disappear:

> Personally, I am a feminist, and an Old Feminist, because I dislike everything that feminism implies. I desire an end of the whole business, the demands for equality, the suggestions of sex warfare, the very name of feminist. I want to be about the work in which my real interests lie, the study of inter-race relationships, the writing of novels, and so forth. But while the inequality exists, while injustice is done and opportunity denied to the great majority of women, I shall have to be a feminist, and an Old Feminist, with the motto Equality First. (Quoted in Riley 61)

Holtby was responding to the particularist "new feminism" of Eleanor Rathbone and her followers. "At last we can stop looking at all our problems through men's eyes and discussing them in men's phraseology," Rathbone said in 1925. "We can demand what we want for women, not because it is what men have got but because it is what women need to fulfil the potentialities of their own natures and to adjust themselves to the circumstances of their own lives."[4]

This "change of gear" within feminism (after the achievement of the suffrage in 1918) finds a modern parallel in Julia Kristeva's schema for feminism before and after 1968. Until 1968, Kristeva argues, the dynamic of the feminist movement centered on:

> The political demands of women; the struggles for equal pay for equal work; for taking power in social institutions on an equal footing . . . all are part of the *logic of identification* . . . with the logical and ontological values of a rationality dominant in the nation-state. (474)

In this phase, therefore, feminists invoked the abstract universalism of the Enlightenment to claim formal equality with men, to discredit all the modes of patriarchal discrimination, and "to gain a place in linear time as the time of project and history" (474). But after 1968, following a characteristic postmodern shift from universalism to particularism, many women rejected the aim of incorporating themselves into the male–constituted public sphere. It seemed that the logic of identification only worked in one direction: men expected to remain the same while women were invited to become like them. "Essentially interested in the specificity of female psychology and its symbolic realizations," Kristeva says, "these women [sought] to give a language to the intrasubjective and corporeal experiences left mute by culture in the past" (474–75). It seemed to them that universalism neutralized that which they wanted to affirm: their femaleness, which was now seen as irreducibly different from both male physique and consciousness. Because patriarchy (a form of *male* particularism) had defined woman as different in order to subdue her, universalist feminism claimed that woman, in her abstract human identity, was "no different." Postmodern feminism restores female difference; but now as *antagonistic* to the patriarchal order rather than *supplementary* to it (Ebert). Kristeva finds in postmodern feminism "an exacerbated distrust of the entire political dimension. . . . by demanding recognition of an irreducible identity, without equal in the opposite sex and, as such, exploded, plural, fluid, in a certain way nonidentical, this feminism situates itself outside the linear time of identities which communicate through projection and revindication" (474–75). Finally, postmodern feminist difference bases itself on that which seems most irreducibly to distinguish a woman from a man: her body (Braidotti 218–19). All these contemporary themes are anticipated in Ursula's search for an identity based on the "secret riches" of her femaleness.

II

Even before Ursula makes the transition to "female feminism," she has an instinctive sense that identity is constructed from difference, and her trajectory in the novel is driven by a succession of inner and outer negations. At school, "she was never herself, since she *had* no self"; all she could know was her paranoid relation to other people, who "walked as an upright menace to her" (311). In her wavering isolation, Ursula fastens on the apparently fearless and independent Miss Inger. But as soon as Miss Inger becomes dependent on *her,* Ursula turns away (319).

She does not want a symmetrical exchange of love, because she knows instinctively that the identity she seeks and pursues can only be generated from opposition; and a lesbian relationship does not, in her eyes, have sufficient difference between the partners. So she turns back to her mother—yet only, as Lawrence says, to fight:

> [Anna Brangwen] went about, big with child, slovenly, easy, having a certain lax dignity, taking her own time, pleasing herself, always, always doing things for the children, and feeling that thereby she fulfilled the whole of womanhood. (328)

This "dominance of physical maternity" (329) soon propels Ursula out into "The Man's World," where she can hope to win economic independence and contribute to "the great task which humanity is trying to fulfil" (332). This task appears to be ungendered, or at least a co-operation between men and women, and thus an escape from Anna Brangwen's fate as a complacent female "breeding animal" (329). But Ursula soon finds that teaching effaces sexual difference one-sidedly, by requiring women to conform to the male imperative of impersonal dominance over their pupils. For a while Ursula does conform, inserting herself into a symmetrical conflict of wills with her male students below and Mr. Harby above. Yet she persists because she fears the consequences of failure—an ignominious return to her mother—rather than because of any spontaneous relish for the struggle.

College is another link in the chain of reactions. At first, Ursula rejoices to have escaped the blinkered practicality of the school, and to be able to pursue knowledge for its own sake. But she soon realizes that the college is just as mundane and materialistic as the school, despite its professions of idealism. So beyond college there would be only "the next move into the world again," when the pendulum would return her to the masculine realm of impersonality and strife. Ursula now feels that she has been "always negative in her action," rejecting one ready-made social role only to be ensnared by another (405). In deciding to become a teacher, she thought that she was asserting her individuality. But the first thing she learnt at school was that she must leave "her feelings and her generosity" at home: "It was queer to feel that one ought to alter one's personality. She was nobody, there was no reality in herself, the reality was all outside of her, and she must apply herself to it" (347).

When Ursula left her family, society took over in writing the self, using schools and professions as its instruments. To continue her development she turned to the realm of personal relations, which she expected to be less coercive than either the family or society. However, personal relations are also marked for the female sphere, and devalued accordingly—so that an identity that would command respect in the "man's world" cannot easily be built on them.

This is the weakness of the solution chosen by Ursula's fellow teacher, Maggie Schofield, in spite of her having achieved "the freedom of the great world of responsible work":

> Maggie had taken her place there, she had even stood level with Mr Harby, and got free of him; and her soul was always wandering in far-off alleys and glades of poetry. Maggie was free. Yet there was something like subjection in Maggie's very freedom. Mr Harby, the man, disliked the reserved woman, Maggie. Mr Harby, the school-master, respected his teacher, Miss Schofield. (363)

The crucial phrase here is "the reserved woman," which echoes the earlier description of Ursula's "secret riches" (310). Maggie's reserve of femininity—shown in the "touch of pictures and flowers" in her classroom—complements her working life in the man's world (351). She balances between the professional and the personal, the masculine and feminine spheres. By separating her public and private lives, she avoids making a clear choice between universalist and particularist feminism. Yet the narrator perceives in her a "fundamental sadness of enclosure": she is not truly integrated or fulfilled, because in her professional activities her femininity must be suppressed (382).

In any case, Ursula has no talent for such compromises; she puts all of herself into each phase of life, and starts afresh if she does not find satisfaction. Once she launches into her search for "That which she was, positively" (405)—at the end of her college years—she finds that she must transgress the boundaries of the established social and economic order. Her recognition of identity as conventional pushes her towards some alternate realm where the self might elude the constitutive powers of society. That realm, defined as the personal, the natural, or the unconventional, awaits her in the darkness that lies beyond rules or borders:

> The inner circle of light in which she lived and moved, wherein the trains rushed and the factories ground out their machine-produce and the plants and the animals worked by the light of science and knowledge, suddenly it seemed like an area under an arc-lamp, wherein the moths and children played in the security of blinding light, not even knowing there was any darkness, because they stayed in the light. (405)

The darkness is a space of metaphysical adventure. Her suitor Skrebensky returns from his service in the Boer War professing to have shaken off all commitments to civilization; Ursula therefore expects him to enter the darkness with her. At the beginning of their affair, then, her gender ideal is of equal comradeship with Skrebensky, and the opponent she sees in front of her is not maleness, but social conformity. But the realms where she will act are marked for the female metonymic chain that links darkness and the sea to the moon, nature, emotion, and that opposes the male series of light, land, sun, culture, reason.[5] Once Ursula and Skrebensky become lovers there is a steady increase of conflict in their relation, corresponding to Ursula's progressive alignment with the female metonymic chain, and Skrebensky's with the male. At first Ursula mistakenly sees Skrebensky as an emissary from the realm of darkness: "She was caught up, entangled in the powerful vibration of the night. The man, what was he?—a dark, powerful vibration that encompassed her" (418). But the darkness is a projection of her own desire, rather than a true wildness in Skrebensky. Ursula wants to burn her bridges to the man's world of universalism, whereas Skrebensky is only on leave from it. When he returns to duty after his period of anarchism, he will support "civilizing" values in their most aggressive form, as colonial rule over the dark natives.

The sexual relation between Ursula and Skrebensky therefore becomes a confrontation between radical differences. In principle, Lawrence welcomes such confrontations, because they strengthen the individual self by a sharper definition of its boundaries:

> when she knows the fearful *other flesh,* ah, darkness unfathomable and fearful,
> contiguous and concrete,
> when she is slain against me, and lies in a heap like one outside the house,
> when she passes away as I have passed away,
> being pressed up against the *other,*
> then I shall be glad, I shall not be confused with her,[6]

But the encounters between Ursula and Skrebensky are destructive rather than creative. Skrebensky's ultimate wish is to possess Ursula as a conventional appendage to his social role—to reinforce his existing identity, not to renew it. For Ursula, self-discovery has always involved the identification of an object against which she can exercise her will. In her teaching career she aims at equal authority with the male, and achieves it by her violent subduing of the boy Williams. Standing erect and brandishing the cane, while the boy writhes on the floor at her feet, she has turned herself into a triumphant virago (370). But when she later renounces the "man's world" there is no diminution in the power of her will. She mobilizes against Skrebensky the specifically female energies of her body, and undermines the male power of his: "She owned his body and enjoyed it with all the delight and carelessness of a possessor. But he had become gradually afraid of her body" (426). For Ursula, nakedness and exposure signify her rejection of repressive culture: "She would not love [Skrebensky] in a house any more. She said she hated houses, and particularly she hated beds."[7] She makes Skrebensky run naked with her over the hills, and stay out all night. Nakedness becomes so much a display of Ursula's will that her body becomes, in Skrebensky's eyes, an implicit weapon.

Ursula thus recapitulates her mother's defeat of her husband Will by dancing naked and pregnant in front of him (170). For both mother and daughter, their nakedness asserts female self-sufficiency: woman's enjoyment of an unmediated relation with nature leaves the sexual male feeling diminished and dispensable. Lawrence's identification with the female, evident from early childhood, proposes that a fractured male identity can be healed through a woman sharing with him her closer access to Being; but what woman gives she can also take away, by denying the man's need. Even in his identification with Ursula, Lawrence is haunted by the idea of her dangerousness towards the male. Skrebensky's raw fear of Ursula's body (426) invokes such archetypes as the Medusa, Oedipus, and Candaules—myths proposing that the sight of the naked female body would strike down the man exposed to her. Ursula destroys Skrebensky by allying herself with elemental forces—the ocean, darkness, the moon —that overwhelm the merely social existence of her lover:

> The salt, bitter passion of the sea, its indifference to the earth, its swinging, definite motion, its strength, its attack, and its salt burning, seemed to provoke her to a pitch of madness, tantalizing her with vast suggestions of fulfilment. And then, for personification, would come Skrebensky, Skrebensky, whom she knew, whom she was fond of, who was attractive, but whose soul could not contain her in its waves of strength, nor his breast compel her in burning, salty passion. (443)

The sexual consummation that follows is a counterpart to Ursula's beating and subduing the boy Williams. In the earlier instance she was erect, dressed, and armed with the cane; now she is the naked succubus, who pulls Skrebensky down on her in order to have the life out of him, and also to punish him for not providing the "vast fulfilment" that her body demands. Yet authorial judgement of this episode remains ambiguous. It can be read as the triumphant consummation of the identity Ursula has been seeking; or, conversely, as the (literally) naked assertion of female sexual power over the vulnerable male.

There is no doubt about Skrebensky's response to the encounter. He flees from Ursula—"the darkness, the challenge, the horror"—back to daylight and a conventional marriage with the Colonel's daughter (447). If Ursula had become Mrs. Skrebensky, she too would have been left with an objectified female identity. Sexual adventurism was her escape from the universalist professionalism of the lady-teacher; but at the end of that path lies the destiny of being a wife. Ursula realizes that domesticity is just as conventional as professional independence—and just as restrictive of the radical femaleness that she still wants to assert, in spite of her disappointment in Skrebensky. This is why the novel must end with images of transfiguration and apocalypse, because all previous strategies of self-discovery have ended in contradiction. Ursula's state of sick unconsciousness, after rejecting Skrebensky, indicates her repudiation of the choices given her by society—between professional independence or wifely dependence, both equally inauthentic for her. His retreat from self-creation is obvious enough; but what remains for Ursula, apart from her sickness and her negative desire to "disengage herself from feeling, from her body, from all the vast encumbrance of the world that was in contact with her"? (456).

In the conclusion of *The Rainbow*, Lawrence tries to sum up the novel's concern with issues of women, politics, history, and time, in order to achieve a sense of completeness for his narrative. Defeated in his elemental maleness in the sexual encounter on the moonlit beach (443–45), Skrebensky returns to established society, where his masculinity will be protected by structural privilege. Ursula faces one more test, in her struggle to escape from the horses. This can best be understood as a final, though this time non-sexual encounter with "otherness."[8] When Ursula gets away over the hedge she "[falls] in a heap"—the same phrase used in "Manifesto"—and is left "unconscious, unchanging, unchangeable . . . in her final isolation" (454–4). Sick and alone though she may be, the self that she had struggled to construct is now complete. Yet the first act of Ursula's achieved self is to repudiate the conflict that made it:

> It was good that he was as he was. Who was she to have a man according to her own desire? It was not for her to create, but to recognise a man created by God. . . . She was glad she had nothing to do with his creation. She was glad that this lay within the scope of that vaster power in which she rested at last. The man would come out of Eternity to which she herself belonged. (457)

One recognizes here the accents of Lawrence's future "leadership phase," with its transcendental gender roles and ideology of male supremacy (Nixon).

The final vision of the rainbow proposes a dissolution of everything in the social order that was labelled earlier "The Man's World." Critical tradition has tended to take this as a direct authorial manifesto, an attempt to transcend the terrible public events of the year it was written, 1915. But why, then, is the vision tied so relentlessly to Ursula's subjective knowledge and response: "she saw" (repeated eleven times), "she was sick," "she knew." Yet if we locate that vision within Ursula, what relevance does it have to her previous preoccupations: with the construction of a specifically female identity for herself? The vision is indeed gendered, but now it assigns woman a merely instrumental role in social change, through such imagery as "the swelling and the heaving contour of the new germination" (458). If Ursula has been converted to a wise passivity, and if woman is made into a kind of surrogate womb that incubates the new order, it is not clear what kind of personal destiny Ursula might have under the rainbow's dispensation.

Ursula had two reasons for leaving behind her phase of male-identification. First, success in the "man's world"—which for Lawrence is really a neutered world of convention, reason, hierarchy, and the machine—required her to suppress all her specifically female desires. Second, the suffrage movement was using radical means in pursuit of conservative ends: at the end of the day, women would join in the institutional work of holding the existing social order in place. Ursula comes to believe that true radicalism requires her to move into the realm of the asocial—a realm which is also revealed to be gendered at a primal level. She believes, for a while, that Skrebensky has accompanied her; but he is too easily subdued, whether by the force of convention or by Ursula herself. At the end of the affair with Skrebensky, Ursula has passed through and exhausted three phases of female identity. The first is *complementarity,* the division of labour in marriage that her mother came to accept. Then, *identification,* the desire for an equal place in the masculine public sphere. And finally *difference,* her immersion in a female realm of water, darkness, and the moon. This last phase still has a potential for renewal, and a new dialectic of difference will emerge in *Women in Love*. There, Birkin's idea of "star–equilibrium" or "free proud singleness" envisions a mode of sexual difference that is non–antagonistic and not driven by the will (319, 254). In contrast, Gerald and Gudrun recapitulate the Skrebensky/Ursula relation—of destructive difference—to an even more deadly resolution.

III

What kind of feminism does Ursula arrive at, then; and where in the novel is the "work for women" that Lawrence boasted he would achieve? At the end of the novel Ursula is completely isolated: from other women, from the political feminism of her time, and even from history itself. Lawrence's work seems to be for a woman, rather than for women; and is "private feminism" not as problematic a concept as a private religion or a private language? Ursula's experiences within the novel become steadily more esoteric, analogous in this regard to practices like the ritual of blood–brotherhood that Lawrence proposed to J.M. Murry. Her first steps towards an adult identity are motivated by opposition to established forms of femininity: woman as mother, as lesbian, or as independent suffragette. She resists Skrebensky's conformist masculinism, but also uses it as a means of nourishing her own heterosexual erotic self–assertion.

Even after the relation with Skrebensky breaks down, Ursula orients herself towards some more adequate male replacement (who appears in due course as Rupert Birkin).[9]

Two fundamental Lawrentian beliefs condition his treatment of Ursula's *bildungsroman*. One is his faith in heterosexual love as the highest possible destiny—a faith reinforced by Frieda's transmission to him of the erotic ideology of Otto Gross (Green). The other is his conception of love as a radical confrontation of the "not-self" and of the unknown. From this arises Lawrence's mistrust of homosexual relations (seen as insufficiently differentiated and therefore sterile); and also his emphasis on primal encounters between male and female bodies. Carol Siegel has noted the uneasy attitudes within feminism to such agonistic heterosexual eroticism: "tension is evident between the desire to imagine female sexual experience as, at least potentially, rebelliously deconstructive and the desire to reject it as inevitably constructed by and contributive to patriarchy" (112). But she commends Lawrence for his participation in the "essentially feminist endeavor" of establishing "the intrinsic importance of female desire and the value of giving it free flow" (184). Against this endorsement, we may set Judith Butler's argument:

> Strategies of exclusion and hierarchy . . . persist in the formulation of the sex/gender distinction and its recourse to "sex" as the prediscursive as well as the priority of sexuality to culture and, in particular, the cultural construction of sexuality as the prediscursive. (148)

Lawrence is a limit case of the privileging of "prediscursive" sexuality, and of restricting woman's identity position to that realm. It could be argued, then, that prescriptive identities (such as the "compulsory heterosexuality" that Butler denounces) are left standing at the end of *The Rainbow*, and may even be reinforced. The aggressive masculinism of Lawrence's leadership phase would then appear as already implicit in Ursula's embrace of an essentialist solution to the contemporary "woman question."

In the early years of their relationship Lawrence displayed an almost masochistic identification with Frieda's eagerness to exhibit herself in the nude and bluntly offer herself to men she desired.[10] She seems to have been delighted by Otto Gross's salute to her as "the *woman of the future*," liberated from the great repressive forces of chastity, Christianity, and democracy (Turner 165). In a society that denied female sexuality, or at least tried to keep it invisible, Frieda could be revolutionary just by following her impulses. In *The Rainbow,* similarly, the hostile responses of Will Brangwen to Anna, and of Skrebensky to Ursula, show how woman's nakedness threatens the repressive Victorian sexual order. However, Lawrence's identification with female sexual assertiveness seems to have inspired a corresponding disillusionment with the suffragists, and a conviction that the idealism of suffragist women (such as Jessie Chambers, Alice Dax, Helen Corke, and Louie Burrows) was a symptom of sexual repression.[11] It was easy to see the suffragists as conspiring with the old order to suppress female eroticism: partly because they wanted to show themselves the equal of men in rationality, partly because they rejected "the methods of the harem."[12] Frieda's indifference to politics and her uninhibited sexual adventurousness would then release in Lawrence a potential that suffragism had denied.

One way of judging Frieda, and the "erotic feminism" that Lawrence absorbed from her example, would be to place her in a Continental rather than Anglo-Saxon tradition, extending from George Sand to Anais Nin and elements of recent French feminism. Naomi Schor provides a useful summary of this tradition, commenting on a quotation from Kristina Wingard Vareille:

> Far from confirming and consolidating an unjust system by aspiring to be a part of it, women must then preciously cling to their marginality, which thus becomes the visible sign of an inevitable change, the index of the necessity of creating a society founded on new principles. It's as though by refusing to endorse the most apparently radical claims of contemporary feminists, Sand was intent, on the level of mythical imagination if not that of rational reflection, on ensuring for female marginality a function of radical interrogation of existing society.
>
> Vareille's analysis of Sand's feminism would apply just as well to that of her contemporary heirs, Cixous and Irigaray, who (just like Sand) reject the egalitarian/reformist model of feminism, indeed feminism itself, in the name of a mythical feminine that might constitute a sort of reserve of alternate and superior moral values. This comparison is meant less to demonstrate the persistent utopian temptation of French feminists—with which I have great sympathy—than to emphasize the logic which necessarily links the theory of the separation of spheres to utopian feminism. The theory of the separation of spheres reinforces utopian feminism, to the extent that it enables one to imagine a protected locus where the Ideal prevails. (Schor 50–51).

Even if we accept the utopian potential of "female marginality," we still face the question of a *male* author's desire to occupy that position.[13] Like Ursula, Lawrence abandoned his career as a teacher to answer the call of erotic individualism. But Ursula's renunciation was a conventional and even a socially expected choice for a woman, whereas Lawrence was flouting gender expectations and giving up the power he might expect to wield in the public sphere.[14] Lawrence thus participated in the feminization of modernist male artists, and in their characteristic interest in creating female characters. Andreas Huyssen has argued that "such masculine identification with women, such imaginary femininity in the male writer, is itself historically determined . . . the phenomenon has a lot to do with the increasingly marginal position of literature and the arts in a society in which masculinity is identified with action, enterprise and progress—with the realms of business, industry, science, and law" (189). In *The Rainbow,* the realms of masculine action, such as schoolteaching or soldiering, are consistently devalued, as the author participates in Ursula's contempt for them; while true potency lies on the side of the female. Yet the male artist's "becoming woman" is always unstable, because it evokes the dangers of hysteria, effeminacy, and castration. From Flaubert through to Eliot, Joyce, and Lawrence himself in his leadership phase, empathy for female characters co–exists with ritualistic misogyny. Even Lawrence's identification with Ursula, which at the level of narrative voice seems quite undiluted, still contains misogynist elements at deeper symbolic levels, where female difference is equated with female danger.

We are left with an inevitable confusion in the way male authors articulate their female characters, through a mixture of ventriloquism, projection and representation. The ability to create a credible and sympathetic woman in fiction does not preclude her use as a vehicle for male doctrines of gender. This problematic is in fact co–extensive with the history of the English novel, from Moll Flanders and Clarissa through to Becky Sharp, Bathsheba Everdene, and Molly Bloom. Such heroines allow their authors to satisfy a grudge against the patriarchal order, often through identification with the heroine's anarchic or amoral individualism. At the same time, their construction of female character typically remains in complicity with the most archaic patterns of reified female identity: the author exploits female difference for his own ends, rather than interrogating it. Ursula's rejection of patriarchy, whether in institutions or in sexual arrangements, is not enough; we must consider how her successive identities are still implicated in existing structures; how radical is the sexual difference imputed to her; how far her strength is simply a projection of her author's will. It is in the light of these questions that we can finally judge how well Lawrence has "done his work," and for whom.

Notes

1. D.H. Lawrence, *The Rainbow* 310.
2. *Letters I,* 2, 122–24, 277. For Lawrence's early contact with feminism see Simpson 19–22. In *Sons and Lovers* we are told that "Paul had more or less got into connection with the socialist, suffragette, unitarian people in Nottingham, owing to his acquaintance with Clara" (301). The Eastwood branch of the Women's Co-operative Guild, the main field of Lydia Lawrence's political activity, does not seem to have been a hotbed of suffragism; but it was sufficiently feminist to be an irritation and threat to male miners (Worthen 21–22).
3. *Letters I* 490. Lawrence began "The Sisters," the precursor of *The Rainbow,* three months later; whether it was the novel of "Love Triumphant" he had in mind earlier is uncertain.
4. Presidential address to the National Union of Societies for Equal Citizenship, quoted in Land, 115. For a critique of "new feminism" in the context of World War I and its aftermath, see Kent.
5. On the female and male metonymic chains see, for example, Jardine 72.
6. Lawrence, "Manifesto" (*Complete Poems* I 267). The poem was composed in 1916, as part of the *Look! We Have Come Through* sequence.
7. The Rainbow 430. For Lawrence's own mistrust of houses and domesticity see Delany 162–64.
8. It seems significant that Lawrence nowhere identifies the "horse-group" as either male or female (451–54). For other readings of the encounter with the horses see Kalnins.
9. *Women in Love* is beyond the scope of this essay; but from early in the process of composition, Lawrence had envisioned for Ursula an eventual union with someone like Birkin: *Letters II* 142.
10. When married to Ernest Weekley Frieda liked to dance naked (except for a shawl)—not coincidentally, on Sunday mornings, when her respectable acquaintances were entertaining themselves in more inhibited fashion. She also is said to have demoralized Ernest Weekley by perching nude on top of a wardrobe on their wedding night.
11. A frequent theme in suffragism, of course, was woman's calling to control the natural brutality of the male, or else to dissociate herself from it. Christabel

Pankhurst's *The Great Scourge and How to End It* (1913) "advised women to remain celibate, as most men not only suffered from venereal disease but were in any case so perverted that intercourse with virtuous women did not satisfy them" (Simpson 47). See also the principles espoused by the suffragist Rhoda Nunn (significant name!) in Gissing's *The Odd Women.* When a suitor asks one of Rhoda's friends if she is "capable of falling in love?" the friend replies "She thinks it so much nobler to disregard such feelings" (Gissing 223).

12. E.M. Forster applies this phrase to Margaret Schlegel, when she wheedles a concession from Henry Wilcox: *Howards End* 228.
13. The subject positions and allegiances of gay male writers such as E.M. Forster would have an obvious relevance here, though I do not have space to pursue this issue.
14. In 1911, Lawrence had recommended to Louie Burrows the critique by Olive Schreiner of "parasitism"—that women were demeaned when they let themselves be supported by men, instead of seeking paid work. *Letters I*, 288.

Works Cited

Braidotti, Rosi. *Patterns of Dissonance: A Study of Women in Contemporary Philosophy*. Cambridge: Polity Press, 1991.

Butler, Judith. *Gender Trouble: Feminism and the Subversion of Identity*. New York: Routledge, 1990.

Delany, Paul. "*Sons and Lovers*: The Morel Marriage as a War of Position." *The D.H. Lawrence Review*. 21.2 (Summer 1989): 153–65.

Ebert, Teresa L. "The 'Difference' of Postmodern Feminism." *College English*. 53.8 (Dec. 1991): 886–904.

Forster, E.M. *Howards End*. Ed. Oliver Stallybrass. Harmondsworth: Penguin, 1975.

Gissing, George. *The Odd Women*. New York: New American Library, 1983.

Green, Martin. *The Von Richthofen Sisters: The Triumphant and the Tragic Modes of Love*. New York: Basic Books, 1974.

Guillaumin, Colette. "The Question of Difference." *French Connections: Voices from the Women's Movement in France*. Ed. and Trans. Claire Duchen. Amherst: U of Massachusetts P. 1987. 64–77.

Huyssen, Andreas. "Mass Culture as Woman: Modernism's Other." *Studies in Entertainment: Critical Approaches to Mass Culture*. Ed. Tania Modleski. Bloomington: Indiana UP, 1986.

Jardine, Alice. *Gynesis*. Ithaca: Cornell UP, 1985.

Kalnins, Mara. "Lawrence's Men and Women: Complements and Opposites." *Problems for Feminist Criticism*. Ed. Sally Minogue. London: Routledge, 1990. 145–78.

Kent, Susan Kingsley. "The Politics of Sexual Difference: World War I and the Demise of British Feminism." *Journal of British Studies* 27 (1988): 232–53.

Kristeva. Julia. "Women's Time." *Critical Theory Since 1965*. Ed. Hazard Adams and Leroy Searle. Tallahassee: UP of Florida, 1986. 471–84.

Land, Hilary. "Eleanor Rathbone and the Economy of the Family." Smith, *British Feminism*. 104–23.

Lawrence, D.H. *The Complete Poems of D.H. Lawrence. Volume One*. Ed. Vivian de Sola Pinto and Warren Roberts. New York: Viking, 1964.

———. *Sons and Lovers. The Unexpurgated Text*. Ed. Helen Baron and Carl Baron. Cambridge: Cambridge UP, 1992.

———. *The Letters of D.H. Lawrence: Volume I. 1901–1913*. Ed. James T. Boulton. Cambridge: Cambridge UP, 1979.

———. *The Rainbow*. Ed. Mark Kinkead-Weekes. Cambridge: Cambridge UP, 1989.

———. *Women in Love*. Ed. David Farmer, Lilndeth Vasey, and John Worthen. Cambridge: Cambridge UP, 1987.

Nixon, Cornelia. *Lawrence's Leadership Politics and the Turn against Women*. Berkeley: U of California P, 1986.

Riley, Denise. *"Am I That Name?" Feminism and the Category of "Women" in History*. Minneapolis: U of Minnesota P, 1988.

Schor, Naomi. "Feminism and George Sand: *Lettres à Marcie." Feminists Theorize the Political*. Ed. Judith Buter and Joan W. Scott. New York: Routledge, 1992. 41–53.

Schreiner, Olive. *Woman and Labour*. London: T. Fisher Unwin, 1911.

Siegel, Carol. *Lawrence among the Women: Wavering Boundaries in Women's Literary Traditions*. Charlottesville: UP of Virginia, 1991.

Simpson, Hilary. *D.H. Lawrence and Feminism*. London: Croom Helm, 1982.

Smith, Harold L. "British Feminism in the 1920s." *British Feminism in the Twentieth Century*. Ed. Harold L. Smith. Aldershot: Edward Elgar, 1990.

Turner, John, editor. "The Otto Gross–Freida Weekley Correspondence: Transcribed, Translated, and Annotated." *The D.H. Lawrence Review*. 22.2 (1990): 137–227.

Worthen, John. *D.H. Lawrence: The Early Years 1885–1912*. Cambridge: Cambridge UP, 1991.

8

Lawrence's Beginnings: Sexuality, Literary Success, and Gender in the Production of *Love Poems and Others*

HOLLY LAIRD

It was to Jessie Chambers that Lawrence said, "It will be *poetry*," and she responded, "Well, isn't that the very greatest thing?" But he worriedly countered, "Ah, *you* say that . . . But what will the others say? That I'm a fool. A collier's son a poet!" (57). In Chambers' anecdote, writing emerges for Lawrence as trespass, not only of the one boundary he names here—class—but also of the boundaries of sex and family this dialogue implies. His intensifying interchange with Chambers would produce a second sphere in his life—a locus for sexual as well as textual development—which tore at the strong ties binding him to his family. But if this effort to grow away from "others" failed, he would be seen as a fool. To play the fool was to become, instead of his own agent or productive maker of images, the passive recipient of others' constructions of him, their social ridicule or paternalistic shaming. The "fool" is a eunuch of intellect and sanity as well as body, exposed as a nought. Here in Chambers' narrative, of course, Lawrence recognizes himself as a fool, constructs himself as passive victim, foolish, shamed; despite all this, he asserts his newfound will: it *will* be poetry. That it is Chambers who records this moment, however, ironically lends credence to this worry about being, and becoming, only what others make of him, and it endows her with power both in the past of their relationship and the future of her memoir to make him a writer: to give his writing an origin and him a beginning. What we have of Lawrence's beginnings are all texts of this ambiguous kind, including his own numerous early poems—texts seeking to re-member elusive beginnings and equivocal transgressions.

I will focus in this essay on another important beginning, one which was also an occasion to recall the past: a culminating moment in the first phase of Lawrence's development as a poet when, in 1913, he published his first volume of verse, *Love Poems and Others*. I am interested here, not so much in the poet whose "experiences were hammered out in poetry almost as they came to him" (as John Worthen describes the juvenilia in the Cambridge biography, 262), as in the writer remembering the text of his life and revising those remembrances. Other people did most of the selecting and arranging of poems for this first book; and most of its readers did not find it foolish—the book was well received as the fresh, "intense" verse of a "modern" writer from the working class (Draper 52, 57). The poems included in, and revisions Lawrence made for this volume, however, are motivated less directly by class interests than by a dual sexual and literary self-consciousness; what on the surface of it might seem opposed concerns—sexual activity and literary artistry —were closely linked and freighted with ambivalence for Lawrence from the start.

Lawrence would later identify his sexual/literary renaissance with the period of his affair with Frieda Weekley and with the poetry produced during that affair, while hinting that most of his earliest poetry was merely that of a conventional young man suppressing his "real demon" (*Complete Poems* 27–28); so it is noteworthy that he revised the poems for *Love Poems and Others* while he was writing *Look! We Have Come Through!*. But a preoccupation with his sexuality pervades even the earliest drafts of poems in his first book, though these were written primarily with—as Lawrence put it—other "heroines" in mind (Boulton 462). What the revisions disclose is not a different level of sexual awareness in the drafts of 1908–11 and the 1913 published versions, but differing degrees of "impersonality" (a term Lawrence used in 1911 to discriminate among them, Boulton 340) and artistry and, more interestingly, different positions in relation to his sexuality. He struggles in these revisions—to return to the imagery of Chambers' memoir—between being the fool of others and becoming his own man and master. Moreover, he oscillates between taking up a female position and taking up that of the male, whether literally by shifting from dramatic monologues to dramatic lyrics or implicitly by shifting from evincing a conventionally female sexual receptivity to a conventionally male severity.

To describe Lawrence's emergence into authorship in psycholinguistic terms, the stories of his early adulthood echo a Lacanian story of infancy: the acquisition of language, of sexuality, and of subjecthood were bound up together for Lawrence, and these acquisitions brought with them the cost of a fissured consciousness. As Lawrence himself saw it, writing to Blanche Jennings in May 1908, he "began to write" when his "boyhood . . . [was] rudely shaken," as if "sick, having lost the health of my laddishness, all the humour that was the body of my mind's health dead" (Boulton 50). The popularized formulation of Lacanian theory closely resembles Lawrence's own accounts of the connections between writing and crisis in his early adulthood.[1] In suffering these fissures, this mirror-stage "loss" of his "laddishness," Lawrence sought a new mastery through his writing and over himself as well as others, seeking deliberately to trespass across the artificial boundaries of family, class, and sex. Thus he ultimately reconstituted new boundaries, a new "imaginary," newly divided between the wit and the fool, the high and the base, as well as between man and woman. Yet, as the Lacanian story also suggests, these different positions are entangled in each other: to be constructed by others and to produce one's own constructions are one and the same process, in the realm of the sexual as well as the artistic, and there are no wits without fools, no real masters, no essential men or women. Nor can there be any real winners in power struggles such as these, only competing memories, competing memorials.

In Worthen's remark that Lawrence's "experiences were hammered out in poetry almost as they came to him," the choice of the word "hammer" rather than, say, "express" was probably deliberate: the larger context of the biography makes it clear that Worthen sees Lawrence not as someone whose spontaneous utterances were unabashed or unmediated expressions of feeling, but someone who cast roles for himself and for whom writing was a vehicle for self-exposure *and* self-formulation. Moreover, in addition to recasting almost everything that happened to him, he did so from within the framework of an established literary world in which he and his women friends were immersed. Worthen thus stresses both how private the act of writing was initially for Lawrence (in contrast to his painting) and how insistently he sought a sympathetic audience (134). He hid his notebooks, recoiled from criticism, and shared his writing easily almost exclusively with Jessie Chambers. But he also shared it entirely with her: as her memoir makes clear, he had in her the new "public" that he sought. Lawrence was clearly anxious about the public response—of his family and community—yet he was not merely lucky to tumble into the hands of editors like Hueffer and Garnett, who embraced him nearly as unreservedly as Chambers. By keeping up with the latest journals and reading as widely as they could, Chambers and Lawrence groomed Lawrence-the-poet for recognition.

The publication history of Lawrence's poetry illuminates its role in his larger career. When Lawrence proved too anxious to do it for himself, Chambers personally selected a few poems from Lawrence's college notebooks and submitted them to the *English Review*. Its editor Ford Madox Hueffer promptly invited both Lawrence and Chambers to meet with him and then accepted the poems, thus giving Lawrence an entry into London literary society (Worthen 215–17). It was, of course, as a working-class writer that Hueffer thought Lawrence could rise into the upper reaches of the literary marketplace, so Hueffer introduced Lawrence to this world as a great new writer from a miner's family. Lawrence's preoccupation with all kinds of relationships that were—not necessarily sexual—but sensual and intimate (with babies, boy-students, and women) is palpable in these poems, but Hueffer's comments in this period reveal that what he wished to promote was a voice from the working class. He hoped Lawrence would produce a novel situated in his Eastwood background; nonetheless, he recommended that Lawrence send his first novel (then called "Nethermere"), which was middle-class in its settings, to William Heinemann (Worthen 221–22) where it would reach the large, lucrative middle-class market.

Hueffer only became unhappy with the direction of Lawrence's work when he read *The Trespasser*, a novel that closely followed the diary of another important female friend and supporter, Helen Corke. The book's eroticism, Hueffer feared, would damage Lawrence's reputation, and he disliked its "formless" lyricism, which was self-consciously literary and emotional (Boulton 339). Heinemann's reader Frederick Atkinson did not even finish reading the book, and Heinemann rejected it. Much as he had feared in that early conversation with Chambers, Lawrence seemed to hover uncertainly between winning a higher status and jeopardizing it.

It was Hueffer who first suggested to Lawrence in the fall of 1909 that he publish a book of verse, but this project did not move forward until the fall of 1911 when Edward Garnett encouraged Lawrence in the plan (Boulton 144, 309). Lawrence turned to Heinemann with this project in hopes of repairing their relations (Boulton 317); the poems sat beside *The Trespasser* in Heinemann's office without a response for four months and were then rejected. Meanwhile the poems had found two readers—Atkinson and Walter de la Mare, who replaced Atkinson in January 1912—and both had liked Lawrence's poetry. De la Mare had gone so far as to select and arrange some of the poems for publication. While waiting to hear from Heinemann, Lawrence imagined that Atkinson had decided against the poems out of dislike for their "rotten form" (Boulton 352), but after the poems' rejection and the disclosure of De la Mare and Atkinson's approval of them, Lawrence concluded that the poems' overt sexuality must have disturbed Heinemann. Lawrence wrote nastily that he supposed they had "shocked the modesty of his Jew-ship" (an early example of the way Lawrence countered assumptions of class superiority with racism; Boulton 442). After Heinemann's rejection, another six months passed before discussion of publication of the poems reopened with Garnett. Garnett not only liked Lawrence's "erotic" novel and poems, but encouraged Lawrence to develop still more explicit descriptions of love. So, as Garnett had done previously with *The Trespasser*, he now shepherded the poems toward publication with Duckworth. Garnett's son David changed De la Mare's arrangement slightly with the addition of five poems previously published in periodicals ("Violets," "Lightning," and three "Schoolmaster" poems). Proofs were ready by October, and the book appeared in February 1913.

Scholars have not considered the publication of *Love Poems and Others* as of much moment in Lawrence's career; it appeared after he had already published two novels and after the original experiences recorded in the poems (*after* the events reported in the opening volume of the Cambridge biography, the turbulent early years 1885–1912), and it has been overshadowed by interest in the lengthy revisions of his third novel *Sons and Lovers*, which was finally published in May 1913. In August 1913 Lawrence himself damned the book neatly when he mockingly renamed it "'Asphodels Among the Cabbages'—or 'Asphodels in the Kitchen Garden'" (Boulton 442). If the "asphodel" was simply a trope for the "conventionalised literary person," as Lawrence said in December of that year, then this was a good joke on Hueffer and his ilk, whose approval depended on there being something "nice" among the miner's son's cabbages (Boulton 491). Yet these jokes arose in the midst of hilarious teasing by Frieda and David Garnett, and Lawrence's repetition of their pokes was partly self-protective—he feared being anyone's fool, especially his own. He had struggled long and hard to see this first book of poems into print, and in a remark made later in September, he was also proud of it: "I thought the book awfully nice—I loved it." Then he added that it had failed to earn Frieda's "respect": "Frieda refuses to have sufficient respect for it—but there, she *would*. There are in it too many heroines other than herself. Queer, there is one poem to her. I wish it had been the last in the book" (Boulton 462). Lawrence's final comment about "Bei Hennef" is occasionally cited as signalling his sense of sexual and literary breakthrough with Frieda, a different kind of "heroine," and Lawrence later placed the poem to Frieda in *Look! We Have Come Through!* where it "starts the new cycle" (*Complete Poems* 28). But these comments also show us a Lawrence struggling with contradiction, with a sense of embattlement with others and of having at least two "masters," divided in this case between the literary establishment and Frieda, between himself and her.

These remarks are typical of the ambivalence with which he described his first book of poems, as if he were uncertain whether it was mediocre or not, whether he must consider it an important new threshold or merely a text groomed to please the critics—whether he could claim it as his own or not. Thus, earlier in September he had told Arthur McLeod that "It won't be a big book—rather a smallish one—a bit exquisite, the collection—à la De la Mare—to convince the critics I was well brought up" (Boulton 455). Obviously reluctant to betray his interest in the book, he reduces it to a "small" conventional work and someone else's selection, at that. But in 1911, he had told Atkinson that he preferred to publish "only . . . about 25 of the best, impersonal pieces," clearly indicating his own definite purpose to produce a short, punchy first book (Boulton 340). The history of this book's publication and Lawrence's anxieties about it indicate that in 1912–13 he would have seen *Love Poems and Others* as not merely a "pretty" miscellany (Boulton 445), but as a bold, "erotic" first book.

Lawrence's pride especially at a moment when he was freshly in love with Frieda and writing batches of new poems about her suggests that this book mostly satisfied his image of himself as a sexual-and-literary adventurer "making history" (Garnett's phrase, quoted by Lawrence, Boulton 390). The reviewers certainly thought so, proclaiming *Love Poems and Others* "the book of the moment," "the most important book of poems of the season," "unique . . . unexpected . . . new" (Draper 51, 53, 56).[2] Moreover, they considered the book the opposite of "conventional," not missing the "amorousness": "he does not write smoothly, sweetly and with dignity; nor does he choose subjects, such as blackbirds at sunset, which ask to be so treated"; "for its intensity of sensuous passion it may, at any rate, be called exciting" (Draper 51–52, 56). Still, this was also a volume groomed by others; though set aside by Heinemann, it had been prodded along and eventually prepared for public appearance, both by supportive friends like Chambers and Corke and by public literary men—by Hueffer, Atkinson, De la Mare, and the two Garnetts. For a self-consciously transgressive writer, literary success must itself carry a price: the price of uncertainty as to whether or not he had merely played the fool of others.

While scholars have paid relatively little attention to the production of *Love Poems and Others*, the record of its history is readily accessible through the biographies and letters of Lawrence, and the basic facts recounted above will only be surprising if you had assumed—as Lawrence might lead you to do in his 1928 note to the *Collected Poems* —that his first poems meant nothing more than a safe or easy start as a conventional young poet. That assumption is readily enough complicated by a careful review of the book's history. Less widely known are revisions to the poems that show Lawrence shifting position in relation to a sexual encounter or epiphany from one draft to the next, as he struggles with his sexuality, on the one hand, and with its literary articulation, on the other, alternately playing the passive recipient, the abruptly wakened lover, and the hostile opponent of another. His revisions result, moreover, in a greater "impersonality," through editing out a male speaker's foolishness or through distancing himself from the speaker by means of a dramatic monologue. At stake, nonetheless, in these revisions is Lawrence's own sexual and literary power.

One of the "Helen" poems, "Repulsed," for example, shows Lawrence shifting boldly from seeing himself as a fool of the cosmos to presenting himself as a major player in a cosmic battle. In the first full draft in MS E320.1 (the second of two college notebooks containing Lawrence's early poetry), he is shrunken like an empty dandelion stalk between the great clash of earth and sky, receiving the "doom" of the night and terrified of his "fate." Then in MS E213 (the holograph manuscript closest to *Love Poems and Others*), he identifies himself with the earth crouching in fierce, animal opposition to the sky, and he stands as firmly opposed to Helen as "the world of activity" is to "the dream that goes on high"—the two of them hating "each other tonight" (Ferrier 1 poem 62).

More complex in its successive permutations, another of the "Helen" poems, "Coldness in Love," is based on a poem originally written by Corke herself. Lawrence thus claimed another's memory for himself. The gender of the speaker becomes uncertain in Lawrence's first draft of this poem in MS E320.1 as he changes what had been a poem about the protagonist's sudden awakening in the middle of a dream into an antagonistic sexual struggle between the speaker and an unnamed, teasing other. Moving beyond the anecdote of "Repulsed," this conflict is also a struggle over "words": between a counterfeit as opposed to a boundary-breaking art. In the MS E213 version Lawrence drops this bold, explicit allegory of artistic creation and returns to the poem's original focus on the speaker's awakening. In returning, he reincorporates a specifically female point of view. But he also retains the anecdote of power struggle and replaces what had been a sisterly and heroic figure in Corke's poem with a sexually awakened virgin, ripely awaiting someone—presumably Lawrence.

Corke explained that she wrote "Fantasy" (her title for the poem) in response to an experience she had while spending the weekend in Sussex with Lawrence (Ferrier 2 100–01). In her poem, the speaker awakens in the cold dawn, "Very far indeed from my own ghost land . . . strayed into . . . a strange house in a land of loneliness." Disoriented and still half-asleep, she cannot decide whether she has returned to her troubled past (and, by implication, her dead former lover) or whether she is firmly in the present with her friend Lawrence: she goes looking for her "Little Brother," wondering if she can find him (and "Red warmth" in his sleep) or if in fact the dawn has "pointed the way / To my little land of ghosts." When she is reassured by hearing him moan in a dream, she maternally hushes him—and herself—pausing with her hand on his doorknob so as not to waken him: "rest quiet again / I have my hand on the latch— / Hush!" Then she offers herself as a kind of night-goddess (an Athena perhaps) to guard his threshold: "I guard against the Dawn the gate of your dream." Ambiguously, yet compassionately (in obvious response to her own recent anxiety), she guards "against" the dawn that would awaken him and the nightmarish "dream" that a too-sudden dawn might bring.

Lawrence transforms this sisterly anti-epiphany into a frustrating confrontation between the two of them, entitled "A Plaintive Confession" (Ferrier 1 and 2 poems 63 and 315). In his first version, it is not possible to tell whether the speaker is male or female; he/she asks the other to "remember" a cold afternoon when the speaker "recoiled" from the "raw cold," while the other "leapt about on the rocks, and threw / Me words that rang with a brassy counter's chime."[3] The "warm" past becomes (in figures borrowed directly from Corke's poem) a refuge from the "cold" present of his/her unsatisfying relationship: gradually the speaker "deadened" until nighttime "memories . . . crowded me warm with companionship, / Like ghosts." Instead of feeling, as in "Fantasy," an uncanny dislocation, as if the familiar and the unfamiliar had become entangled—"strayed into . . . a strange house" in the "deathly" dawn—the speaker of "A Plaintive Confession" feels upon awakening a simple, immediate need for the other: she/he "rose in fear, needing you fearfully." Moreover, the speaker imagines the other not merely "warm" but warm as a "jet of blood" to plunge into. When the speaker hears the other moan in sleep, she/he feels not protective, but newly fearful and "dare[s] not enter." This speaker is far more involved in the relationship with the sleeping person than in Corke's version and more timid (poem 63).

Gone, then, is the focus on a solitary, independent speaker. But still more dramatically different is the allegory to art that Lawrence next develops (poem 315). After a bath in the sea, Lawrence's speaker is "worn with cold" like a moon's shell, but the other still "mint[s] . . . that chinking counterfeit / Of gaiety." "Too often," says the speaker, "you . . . pay me thus / Barrenly . . . cheat[ing] / Me with . . . glinting jests." This version of the poem culminates by allegorizing their failed relation as a failure also of art: the speaker cries out, "Coin me words in your heart's full furnace heat!" and calls the other a "melting-pot" for the "old metal of meanings" where "the blossoms of shape are begot." Since in other poems, Lawrence generally associates himself both with the imagery of an alchemical furnace and with a fecund artistry, one could easily read the speaker of this poem as female, whose task it is to cry the man–poet awake. The title hints that the poem is one person's pleading "confession" to the other: 'she,' then, wants to "cast / My all in your molten flux." But whether the speaker is a she or a he, the poem plays out Lawrence's own yearning for sexual and poetic power. "A Plaintive Confession" firmly substitutes for the lone, exploratory Helen of "Fantasy" a dramatic encounter between two selves who are embattled with each other and face a simple choice between the gilded (middle–class) "counterfeit" of "barren" jests and empty words and the fiery, implictly authentic, fleshly powers of destruction and creation.

In "A Plaintive Confession," the speaker "came back clean" from the sea's cold bath, but yearning for a phoenix–like resurrection. While the next version dwells at still greater length on the details of the speaker's numbness and memories of "old days" in contrast to the other's "brassy" and "cold" shallowness, it develops the same essential anecdote until the end. But the ending is very different. This version, now called "Coldness in Love" (Ferrier 1 poem 63), ends with the sea bath and with the speaker renewed by the sea, not returning even glancingly to the "brassy" other and eliminating altogether the figure of the sexual/literary furnace. It closes instead by envisaging the speaker's "love" resurrected and by characterizing this as a virginal love: "and strange it seems / That my love has dawned in rose again, like the love of a maid." Possibly concerned about the ambiguity of the speaker's gender, Lawrence clarifies it with this last line and subdues her role: no hint remains of a fiery Sibyl or a Volumnia arousing the man to action. She waits gently at the end for whatever may happen, aware only of her pristine love. We are not likely to identify this "maid" with Lawrence; on the contrary, this woman is a potential mate for him. Yet even in this version, the speaker resembles Lawrence in resisting others' "teasing," their "brassy" love and language.

Though less revealing than are these revisions of Lawrence's multiple identifications with fool and fighter, with man and maid, the published forms of this verse and, as it happens, the organization itself of *Love Poems and Others* preserve some shifts of position through juxtaposition of dramatic monologues spoken by women with dramatic lyrics uttered by a Lawrencean persona. The book opens with the dramatic monologue "Wedding Morn" (*Love Poems* i–ii) in which a woman wonders what kind of "coin" she has gotten in her new husband. Here the woman is "master," and she "long[s] to see" her sleeping husband "In my power utterly," but the poem ends with second thoughts for the "limbs that I shall weep to know / Lie under my mastery." As if it had delivered a challenge to the male, this poem acts as the opening to a volume in which "love" is routinely enacted as power struggle. Subsequent monologues are spoken by women bewildered by or yearning for a masterful male figure, as in "Cruelty and Love" (poem 3, which later became the widely anthologized "Love on the Farm") and "Coldness in Love" (poem 6), and these are interspersed with dramatic lyrics whose male speaker quietly insists on his own centrality—on his "heart" as "pivot"—even as he is whirled into a sexual "dance of a dervish" with a woman in "Kisses in the Train" (poem 2 iii–iv); detachedly watches a woman to see if she has any "tears" in "Cherry Robbers" (poem 4 viii); or suffers sudden deflation when he sees his lover "hurt" by his burning love in "Lilies in the Fire" (poem 5 ix–x). A mild irony threads through many of these poems, undercutting the woman of "Wedding Morn," for example, so that "winners" become losers (and losers winners).

The book ends with two special sections, first of fictionalized dialect poems (which Pound later singled out for praise as "great art," Draper 54), and then of a few poems from the sequence "The Schoolmaster" about Lawrence's experiences in teaching boys. *Love Poems and Others* thus particularizes Lawrence's rural and educational background and foregrounds his skills as an "objective" writer of dramatic narratives (Corke's term, Ferrier 2 101). But even the poems in the last two sections typically involve efforts to represent or recall a personal crisis and power struggle of some kind, whether in his own voice or in that of a woman.

The revisions for "Repulsed" and "Coldness in Love" show how concerned Lawrence was with the roles he—or a fictionalized she—played in conflicts with sexual and literary (and even cosmic) dimensions. But while these poems disclose Lawrence experimenting with different parts in sharply focused dramatic conflicts, other revisions explore more subjective dimensions of sexual conflict. The intriguing revisions for the poem "Dream-Confused" show him unsure whether he is faced with himself rather than with an (opposed) other, and so it discloses a more precarious, intimate, and psychologically revealing struggle for sexual identity and power. (See appendix for complete texts of these variant versions.)

Probably due to its simplicity, the absence of reference to any identifiable occasion or person in Lawrence's life, and the didacticism of its final form in the 1928 *Collected Poems*, "Dream-Confused" has been almost universally ignored.[4] But although it has gone nearly unnoticed until now, this is a poem that rewards a second look—testimony not only to the fascinations of earlier versions of Lawrence's revised poetry, but to the different kinds of success one may find there.[5] Of thirteen poems that had previously appeared in the *English Review* (the innovative journal where Lawrence had his debut as a poet)[6] "Dream-Confused" is the only one republished in *Love Poems and Others*; so we may compare not only earlier drafts, but also a previously published form to those of 1913 and 1928. Lawrence included "Dream-Confused" among the first poems in his 1928 collection (poem 6), and since he asked us to see these as representing a chronological order (*Complete Poems* 27), he thereby designated "Dream-Confused" one of his earliest compositions. Worthen meanwhile assigns a tentative and (given the flood of poetry Lawrence had been writing since 1906) relatively late date of Autumn 1909 to the first manuscript version (483) on the basis of its belated position in the first college notebook (MS E317) where it is found at the end of the group of poems published together in spring 1910 in the *English Review*.

My object, however, is not to assign singular events or moments to individual poems; rather it is to show how the poems travelled with Lawrence through time, enunciating different positions for Lawrence and attaching themselves to changing occasions as they travelled. Retrospectively in 1928, Lawrence linked "Dream-Confused" to his earliest writing at home in Eastwood, but if it emanated from those days, it had changed dramatically by the time it reached its final form in *Collected Poems*. In the *English Review* in 1910, it appears among a series of poems published under the single title "Night Songs," which record dramatic night visions—amorous encounters or missed encounters—from his life in Croydon and London, including "Hyde Park at Night," "Piccadilly Circus at Night," "At the Window," and "Rebuked."[7] In its

1913 publication in *Love Poems and Others*, it is linked thematically and positionally to a series of poems inspired by Corke (whom he met in spring 1909), appearing at the end of a group comprised of "Red Moon-Rise," "Return," "The Appeal," and "Repulsed"—all "erotic" poems—and it is followed by less personal, but consciously arty poems about nature, working men, and the landscape, including "Corot," "Morning Work," and "Transformations." It thus marks a turning point in *Love Poems and Others* as the volume moves from "love poems" to "others."

Like Corke's poem "Fantasy," "Dream-Confused" focuses on the speaker's sudden awakening; in repeated revisions, Lawrence seems to hesitate between developing this epiphany into yet another power struggle with a lover or letting it remain instead one man's "dream." It develops from the first version in his college notebook in which it conjoins two kinds of poems—melodrama and self-confession; through a transitional second draft in the college notebook, where Lawrence tried to pull its two halves closer together; to a third version—its first published version in the *English Review*—in which dream consciousness is replaced almost entirely by a realistic narrative of a man and woman's erotic encounter at night; to its second published form in *Love Poems and Others* where narrative is again cloaked in the mist of dream, yet personality also is submerged in a carefully crafted, impersonal epiphanic lyric; finally to the mildly didactic last version of *Collected Poems* where "I" and "she" are both replaced with "we."

"Dream-Confused" records the speaker's response to a kiss. Kissing was a central, often final, erotic act in Lawrence's early poetry, featured in nine other poems in *Love Poems and Others*, but unlike what happens in most of these others, even the kiss becomes, in some versions of "Dream-Confused," the speaker's fantasy.

The first draft in MS E317[8] gets off to a false start, its first six lines cancelled. They describe a big red moon rising, "Is that the moon / At the window, so big and red," and the sound of a woman—or is it a bird—rushing down the stairs. Lawrence asks himself, is "No one in the room?—no one near the bed?" When he began the poem again, Lawrence set aside metaphors and vague scene setting and focused directly on an event that had just passed: "She kissed me a moment ago." His response to this event is what most changes in subsequent drafts: "She kissed me a moment ago / And waked my two fires on my breast." He first revised this second line to: "And waked my two kisses on my breast"; then he cancelled the entire line, to shift attention from his response to a somewhat clearer rendering of the scene of the kiss: "She kissed me a moment ago / Warm on the mouth, / And my breasts flare back two answering kisses." He was once again concerned about what his breasts did, however, and so he replaced "flare back" with "are lit up with." No matter what anxious change he made, however, his position remained that of passive respondent, and, of course, he inhabited a culture which associated both passivity and breasts more often with women than with men.

This draft of the poem next reintroduces the image of the moon, but now as a sympathetic reflector of the speaker: "The very moon is red in the south / With a bloody glow / And the {warm blood heat} wells up]from[in the night's abysses."[9] Lawrence completes the simile in the final lines by analogizing the hot blood of the moon more explicitly both to his sexual desire, his "kisses," and to his uncertainty and frustration: "{Is it And it's} only the moon / Going slowly out of the west / Like the kisses sinking unanswered in my breast." The moonrise becomes a cosmic mirror of Lawrence's own sexual uncertainty. In Lacanian terms, Lawrence shivers on the threshold of a realm of linguistic order, of language and the "symbolic"; of fundamental division between the childlike self and the (m)other; and of gendered division from the mother by the "Law" of the father. But he yearns to return to "imaginary" identification with the mother's breast, to see himself mirrored in her gaze, even (in this version) to identify her flesh with his own—blood with his blood, breast with his breasts: to be both mother and child.

Lawrence is only answering a wake-up call, yet it is he who in the end goes unanswered. But then again the call itself may be only a mirage, "only the moon" awakening him. This early draft of the poem is called "Dream," and the poem as a whole suggests that Lawrence has been startled into sexual feeling by practically nothing—by a dream from the abyss or by simple absence itself.

More could be said about the six cancelled lines at the beginning, which refer to an imagined woman rushing away and compare her to a bird beating against the window, as if trying to escape the "stare" of the moon. More stereotypical than the rest of this draft, this depiction of a woman fleeing the man she has aroused offers a faintly dramatic context for Lawrence's desire and frustration. Moreover, it suggests a different relation between male and female, in which the female is not identified with the male, but instead is subject to his gaze. One can see Lawrence in these lines crafting his remembered sexual epiphany into a more comfortable anecdote about male/female conflict. Even these lines, however, produce an impression of dreamlike enigma, not only through the persistent questioning about what is occurring in this moment, but also through syntactical parallelism that produces a curiously dual identification of the moon with her as well as with him: "Is that the moon / . . . / No one in the room? . . . / Is it the sound of her shoon." The uncertainly located moon creates an impression strengthened by the rest of this draft of a Lawrence poised not as a sharply defined persona in a clear melodrama, but as a resident in a house of mirrors.

Two concerns run alongside each other in this early version, and the rest of this essay will trace their evolution: this is a poem in which we see the poet struggling with being alone with his sexuality but at the same time trying to recast this struggle as a conflict between male and female. The uncancelled part of the first draft presents a persona in a feminized role in which he experiences himself as lacking.

In the next draft of the poem, still called "Dream," Lawrence restored most of the first six cancelled lines and then continued in much the way he had before; but instead of producing a disjointed effect, as if two different kinds of poems—or attitudes—had been conjoined, he manages to integrate them. He does this by reemphasizing the persistent questions, leaving his imagined alternatives of the first six lines entirely uncertain. Enigma submerges the melodrama: "Is that the moon / . . . ? / No one in the room?—no one {nearer near} the bed? / Listen!—her shoon / Palpitating down the stair! / —Or a beat of wings at the window there?" He also omits the "stare" of the moon, thus removing the hint of contest between the moon and the bird/woman.

The rest of the poem, however, is so uncertain as to seem unfinished rather than merely enigmatic. He delays his response to her kiss, and he seems more tentative than ever about when and how to articulate it:

The very moon is red in the south
With a bloody glow.
]fierce risen[
]Like my breasts' responsive kisses[
Welled up from the night's abysses
At her kiss, like my risen breasts' two kisses.
]To answer my breasts' two roused kisses[

His physical and emotional reactions—the "breasts' two kisses"—are not merely "responsive" but "fierce" in their rising. His responsive "kisses" remain located in his "breasts" as well as in "the night's abysses." The poem is left in a seemingly unresolved state in this draft (the middle section cited above seems particularly confused and repetitive). The poem is surrendered as if to its own feared oblivion. In the last line, once again the speaker is "unanswered": "]As the[Unanswered ˆthe risenˆ kisses sink in my breast."

But Lawrence resurrected the poem, and in some manuscript apparently now lost to us revised it yet again for publication; the next extant version is the one published in the *English Review* in April 1910 (7). This published version reveals that Lawrence subsequently found the second draft closer to a finished form than it seems. But some crucial changes have taken place. Through a few relatively simple alterations and choices, the poem has ceased to be an enigmatic dream and has become instead a crisply outlined narrative of a man's roused desire for a woman; the new version is called "Wakened" (also see Ferrier poem 6).

Lawrence has built a kind of redundancy into the middle section, which narrates the kiss: he frames his response with the reiterated act of *her* kiss. In doing this he manages to insist that his response has not come from nowhere; it comes from her kisses:

A moment ago
She kissed me warm on the mouth. . . .
The very moon is red in the south
With a bloody glow,
Welled up from the night's abysses
At her kiss, at her fervent two kisses!

He also assigns the new adjective "fervent" to her kisses, thus investing her with the fiery quality that before had characterized the moon and himself.

At the same time, the response of his breast has been moved as far away from the rousing kisses as possible, mentioned now only in the last line where "the kisses sink back" in his breast. It is the moon, not his breast, that "wells up" in response. Thus suppressing himself, he also shifts the focus, first, from the site of his response to her provocation and, second, from preoccupation with his reactions to abrupt let down. The moon and he are annoyed: "And now the moon / Goes slowly out of the west, / Sullenly—as the kisses sink back in my breast." And while the woman appears more aggressive in this version and Lawrence himself less central, he is also less feminine than before. "Breast" functions here as a standard metaphor for "heart" rather than as the primary site of his physical response, and his "sullenness" hints at a fiercer Lawrence of the future.

If it is not a great poem, it is not a bad poem either in its spare, objectified narrative. Lawrence naturalizes the curve of emotion in this version through the extended analogy to the circling moon. He continues to identify the moon closely with himself, but in the poem as a whole, there is greater exchange of response between the man/moon and the woman. Her greater fervor is matched by his greater disappointment, and she glows nearly as much as the moon, producing something more dynamically interactive than in the gender-typed melodrama or abysmal dream of the previous draft. Lawrence plays the fool: teased and abandoned by his lover, he is not allowed a masterful part.[10] But it *is* a part he plays; his role is clearer and he is at least another's fool, not his own. These changes, moreover, mark a greater "mastery" on the part of their author—they mark a deliberate move away from the introspection of the previous drafts toward control of himself as speaker and of the poem as craft. While not unappealing, this draft is also less intriguing, less ambiguous, less open to psychoanalytic exploration.

In the next version (MS E213), the manuscript closest to that of the printed poem in *Love Poems and Others*, Lawrence is still playing with the final lines of the last two verse paragraphs.[1] Changes in the section about the kiss regularize the metrical patterns. But there are also more substantive changes, which result in a still less personal poem. Neither moon nor man is depicted as responding directly to the woman's kisses. The moon's glow can be identified with him or her, but more precisely it symbolizes the event itself of kissing: "The moon from far abysses / Signalling those two kisses." Still more striking are changes in the last section, for Lawrence has suppressed not only the imagery of his breasts' physical responsiveness, but also the allusion to his subsequent frustration: his kisses "are sinking, soon / To leave me at rest."

This version of the poem bears the title "Dream-Confused," suggesting that it has all been a dream after all, and Lawrence will go back to sleep now that it is over. In this version, the poem insists on the transience of this sexual epiphany and explains this ephemerality as merely a dream phenomenon. One could become interested in the poem from a psychoanalytic vantage, but there is also less at stake in this version than in the first one:

> Is that the moon
> At the window so big and red?
> No one in the room,
> No one near the bed—? (xxxii)

This version is (in the style Lawrence sought) impersonal—its emotions implied by event and image, not stated. Only a comma was added (replacing an ellipsis at the end of line 9) for publication in *Love Poems and Others*.

This last version is significantly different from the one revised years later in 1927–28 for publication in *Collected Poems*. If forced to choose, I would not take the *Collected Poems* version (*Complete Poems* 37) over the earlier ones. Gone is the impersonality, but in its place is not the exposed self-consciousness of the earlier drafts; instead one finds (as one might expect of a revision for *Collected Poems*) a new morality in place expressed in an additional final "sentence," literally a terminal judgment, which operates like a fortune cookie message: "We misunderstood!" The moon of the third stanza is more cheerfully "ruddy" instead of "bloody," slightly diminishing the intensity of this line. Lawrence may have made this change because of yet another alteration; for he now has the kisses sink back not into the speaker's "breast" but into his "blood"—the doctrinal location which Lawrence later settled upon for his passions and one that resists any specifically feminine or sentimental associations. In the fourth stanza the moon bears the brunt of the new symbolism (and rhyme scheme), for it does not "[Go] slowly out of the west," but rather "Goes clouded, having misunderstood," while the kisses do not leave the speaker "at rest" but are "soon / To be under the flood." Like "Piano"—whose closing lines this one echoes—this version of "Dream-Confused" describes a young Lawrence lost in the ebb and flow of unexpected emotion, but with none of the crisp imagistic detail and irony of "Piano." There were, of course, more effective revisions than this of the early verse in *Collected Poems*, but "Dream-Confused" is not alone in possessing a history more interesting than could ever be guessed from its final state. Much as Lawrence relegated his early poems generally to second-class status as mere "Rhyming Poems" in his *Collected Poems*—as opposed to the breakthrough verse of "Unrhyming Poems"—he assigned the interesting epiphany of "Dream-Confused" to the "misunderstanding" of his "conventional" youth.

What "Dream-Confused" demonstrates about the first phase of Lawrence's development as a poet, culminating in the 1913 *Love Poems and Others*, is the poet's early preoccupation with an ambiguous and elusive sexuality and his repeated efforts not merely to rewrite a potent sexual memory, but to achieve control through language over a situation which was by its very nature beyond his control. In successive drafts of the poem he seems more rather than less restrained, increasingly aware of, but also guarded against, his fragile position—particularly in relation to the anonymous woman who haunts his bedroom. He becomes less rather than more willing to draw attention to himself. One sees Lawrence gradually developing the poem away from self-revelation toward gender-marked anecdotalism.

But at the same time he succeeds even in the 1913 version in a limited exhibition of sexual desire, and no matter how impersonal the poem becomes, it remains implicitly an exhibition of what is at once a sexualized and linguistic coming to consciousness: an awakening both of desire and of the impulse to encode the moon—to make it "signal" his desire. The poem betrays, moreover, a recognition that the cycle of awakening closes, not in a bliss of wholeness with others or in himself, but in a never-ending lack of answer. As in the more dramatic power plays of *Love Poems and Others*, there is no real winner and no real loser in this little drama; the poem, the desire, end only in brief "rest."

Notes

I wish to acknowledge with gratitude permission to reprint the published and unpublished versions of "Dream-Confused," granted by Lawrence Pollinger Ltd. and the Estate of Frieda Lawrence Ravagli; Viking Penguin; the University of Nottingham Library; and the Harry Ransom Humanities Research Center at The University of Texas at Austin.

1. I refer to the "popularized" version of Lacan's concepts because what have proved useful to many Lacanian critics are clarified reformulations of Lacan's deliberately obscure works. Abundant examples exist, but see the useful account both of Lacan's ideas and of his purposely difficult writing in Juliet Mitchell and Jacqueline Rose, Introductions I and II, *Feminine Sexuality*, 1–57. In Lacan's *Ecrits*, see especially "The mirror stage as formative of the function of the I" and "The function and field of speech and language in psychoanalysis" 1–7, 30–113.
2. Lawrence was unhappy, however, that the book did "miserably—sold 100," which he attributed to Duckworth's slowness in publishing them (Boulton 548, 545); and he thought the reviewers were too "faint" (548). But while Pound's two reviews began by criticizing "the disagreeable qualities" of some of Lawrence's poems, in particular their romantic "enthusiasm," he praised them too (Draper 53); all the reviews catalogued by Cowan heap encomiums on *Love Poems and Others* (see nos. 18, 26, 27, 32, 40, and 55). Lawrence's disappointment thus indicates how very highly he thought of these poems; as he said to Garnett, meditating on the poor showing also of *Sons and Lovers*, "I *know* I can write bigger stuff than any man in England." (His self-praise was somewhat more measured in a letter to David Garnett, "No, I don't think I'm the greatest poet that ever lived—I'm not very conceited. I should not like to say I thought myself as great a poet as Lord Tennyson—perhaps when I've finished, I shall, perhaps I shan't. But let me finish first. You are only twenty yet—I'm only 27," Boulton 536.)
3. In "A Plaintive Confession," Lawrence suggests that the speaker's complaint against the dancing, mocking other (man?) is legitimate; he suggests the opposite in another poem, "Tarantella" (whose earliest draft appears in the first college notebook, though it was not published until 1918). In addition, the speaker of "Tarantella" is female. In the poem "Tarantella," the speaker dances "a tarantella on the rocks, and the croon / Of my mockery mocks at him"; he is too "earnest," with "none / Of the night in his soul" (*Complete Poems* 130). The comparison of the two poems illustrates how much Lawrence liked to vary a repeated anecdote.
4. The only critical attention of which I am aware appears in an endnote in Mandell's extensive study of Lawrence's revisions where, in conjunction with "Love on the Farm," she argues that it produces a "metaphoric relationship

between physical and mythical realities. The metaphors suggest that the physical world thinly veils a metaphysical world. The question, then—a device Lawrence consistently uses to initiate metaphor—becomes central to the poem's development" (237 n11). In addition, I mention "Dream-Confused" briefly in discussion of its place in part one of *Collected Poems*, "Rhyming Poems" (*Self and Sequence* 186).

5. See also my more extended argument to this effect in "Excavating the Early Poetry."
6. Austin Harrison had succeeded Hueffer as editor of the *English Review* in December 1909 and wrote to encourage Lawrence to continue submitting his work (Boulton 152), so Hueffer was not influential in publication of "Wakened." Indeed, Lawrence claimed that Harrison had chosen "just the verses I don't want him to put in, I am rather mad" (Boulton 156). Lawrence clearly liked two of the poems better than the others, however, since he permitted publication of "Dream-Confused" in his first book and included "At the Window" in his second book, his elegiac sequence *Amores*. He never republished a third poem, "Rebuked," and he did not republish "Hyde Park at Night" or "Piccadilly Circus at Night" until he was more or less clearing out his college notebooks for his mistitled book, *New Poems*, in 1918.
7. "Hyde Park at Night" and "Piccadilly Circus at Night" were also paired together in the *English Review* and called "Workaday Evenings: I. Yesternight [and] II. To-morrow Night." I have used their final titles here for the reader's convenience in referring to their anthologized versions in *Collected Poems or Complete Poems*.
8. See appendix. The reader may refer also to Ferrier 1 poem 6 for the first two drafts of "Dream-Confused" in MS E317. My transcription includes slight corrections of Ferrier's versions. I wish to express my thanks to the Manuscripts Department of the University of Nottingham Library for permission to consult the original manuscript.
9. The brackets symbol {} indicates that the second letter, or word, or phrase has been written over the first. The inverted square brackets symbol][indicates deletion. The double caret symbol ^ ^ indicates an insertion into a line.
10. Interestingly, the poem preceding "Dream" in MS E317 is called "Fooled" (retitled "Rebuked" in the *English Review*) and recounts an episode in which the Lawrencean speaker feels he is being mocked by the (female) moon: "The moon is high—I am little— / She leans forward her smooth pale face / And smiles at my shamefast shadow / Dodging along in disgrace" (MS E317; Ferrier does not record these variant lines to "Rebuked," poem 220).
11. I wish to express my thanks to the Harry Ransom Humanities Research Center at the University of Texas at Austin for permission to consult the original manuscript, and to thank Cathy Henderson for her aid with information about the MS E213 draft.

APPENDIX:
"Dream-Confused"

1. Vasey MS E317; Ferrier MS1a; University of Nottingham Library La L 2/70 (dated Autumn 1909 by Worthen).

Dream

]Is that the moon[
]At the window, so big and red[
]No one in the room?—no one near the bed?[

]]Is it[{t T}he sound of her shoon[
]Quickly running]muffled stairs in haste down the stair?[[
]]Passing[the]stairs in haste?[[
]Or a beat of wings on the window against the moons red stare?[

She kissed me a moment ago
]kisses[
]]And waked my two /]fires[on my breast[[
Warm on the mouth,
are lit up with
And my breasts]flare back[two answering kisses.
The very moon is red in the south
With a bloody glow
in
And the {warm blood heat} wells up]from[the night's abysses.
{Is it And it's} only the moon
Going slowly]out[out of the west
Like the kisses sinking unanswered in my breast.

2. Vasey MSE317; Ferrier MS1b; University of Nottingham Library La L 2/71 (dated Autumn 1909 by Worthen).

Dream

Is that the moon
Against the window, so big and red?
No one in the room?—no one {nearer near} the bed?
{H L}isten!—her shoon
 Palpitating down the
]Rapidly passing the muffled[stair!
—Or a beat of wings at the window there?

A moment ago
She kissed me warm on the mouth—
The very moon is red in the south
With a bloody glow.
                    ]fierce risen[
]Like my breasts' responsive kisses[
Welled up from the night's abysses
  At her kiss, like my risen breasts' two kisses
]To answer my breasts' two roused kisses[

———

And now the moon
Goes slowly out of the west:
                              the risen
]As the[Unanswered / kisses sink in my breast.

3. *The English Review* (April 1910).

Wakened

Is that the moon
At the window, so big and red?
No one in the room—no one near the bed?
  Listen, her shoon
  Palpitating down the stair!
  —Or a beat of wings at the window there?

A moment ago
She kissed me warm on the mouth. . . .

The very moon is red in the south
With a bloody glow,
Welled up from the night's abysses
At her kiss, at her fervent two kisses!

And now the moon
Goes slowly out of the west,
Sullenly—as the kisses sink back in my breast.

4. Vasey MS E213; Ferrier MS14.

Dream-Confused

Is that the moon
At the window so big and red?
No one in the room,
No one near the bed—?

Listen, her shoon
Palpitating down the stair?
—Or a beat of wings at the window there?

A moment ago
She kissed me warm on the mouth. . .
The very moon in the south
Is warm with a bloody glow,
The moon from far
]Over the night's[abysses
Signalling th{e ose} two kisses.

And now the moon
Goes slowly out of the west,
And slowly back in my breast
My kisses are sinking, soon
To leave me at rest.

5. *Love Poems and Others* (1913).

Dream–Confused

Is that the moon
At the window so big and red?
No one in the room,
No one near the bed—?

Listen, her shoon
Palpitating down the stair?
—Or a beat of wings at the window there?

A moment ago
She kissed me warm on the mouth,
The very moon in the south
Is warm with a bloody glow,
The moon from far abysses
Signalling those two kisses.

And now the moon
Goes slowly out of the west,
And slowly back in my breast
My kisses are sinking, soon
To leave me at rest.

6. *Collected Poems* (1928).*

Dream–Confused

Is that the moon
At the window so big and red?
No–one in the room?
No–one near the bed?

Listen, her shoon
Palpitating down the stair!
—Or a beat of wings at the window there?

A moment ago
She kissed me warm on the mouth;
The very moon in the south

Is warm with a ruddy glow;
The moon, from far abysses
Signalling those two kisses.

And now the moon
Goes clouded, having misunderstood.
And slowly back in my blood
My kisses are sinking, soon
To be under the flood.

We misunderstood!

Works Cited

Boulton, James T., ed. *The Letters of D.H. Lawrence: Volume I: 1901–13.* Cambridge: Cambridge UP, 1979.

Chambers, Jessie. *D.H. Lawrence: A Personal Record.* 1935; Cambridge: Cambridge UP, 1981.

Cowan, James C. *D.H. Lawrence: An Annotated Bibliography of Writings About Him.* Vol. 1. De Kalb: Northern Illinois UP, 1982.

Draper, R.P. *D.H. Lawrence: The Critical Heritage.* New York: Barnes & Noble, 1970.

Ferrier, Carole. "The Earlier Poetry of D.H. Lawrence: A Variorum Text." Vols. 1 and 2. Diss., University of Auckland, 1971.

Lacan, Jacques. *Ecrits: A Selection.* Trans. Alan Sheridan. New York: W.W. Norton, 1977.

—-. *Feminine Sexuality: Jacques Lacan and the "école freudienne".* Ed. Juliet Mitchell and Jacqueline Rose. New York: Norton, 1985.

Laird, Holly. *Self and Sequence: The Poetry of D.H. Lawrence.* Charlottesville: University Press of Virginia, 1988.

—-. "Excavating the Early Poetry of D.H. Lawrence." *The D.H. Lawrence Review* 23.2–3 (1991): 111–28.

Lawrence, D.H. *Collected Poems.* Vol. 1. London: Martin Secker, 1928.

—-. *The Complete Poems.* Ed. Vivian de Sola Pinto and F. Warren Roberts. 1964, 1971; New York: Penguin, 1982.

—-. *Love Poems and Others.* London: Duckworth, 1913.

—–. "Night Songs." *The English Review* 5 (April 1910): 4–8.

Mandell, Gail Porter. *The Phoenix Paradox: A Study of Renewal Through Change in the "Collected Poems" and "Last Poems" of D.H. Lawrence*. Carbondale: Southern Illinois UP, 1984.

Vasey, Lindeth. "A Checklist of the Manuscripts of D.H. Lawrence." In Keith Sagar. *D.H. Lawrence: A Calendar of His Works*. Austin: U of Texas P, 1979. 191–266.

Worthen, John. *D.H. Lawrence: The Early Years 1885–1912*. Cambridge: Cambridge UP, 1991.

9

The Two Analyses of D.H. Lawrence*

JAMES C. COWAN

In a now famous case study, Heinz Kohut in 1979 gave an account of "The Two Analyses of Mr Z," as a means of showing the clinical relevance of the new psychoanalytic theories of self psychology that he had been developing for twelve years. Each analysis lasted about four years and the two were separated by an interval of five and a half years. During the first analysis, Kohut says, he "was viewing analytic material entirely from the point of view of classical analysis." The second analysis, which was in progress while Kohut was deeply involved in writing *The Analysis of the Self* (1971), coincided with his development and testing of a new frame of reference, his emerging theory of a separate line of development for the self, which allowed the analyst "to perceive meanings" he had not "consciously perceived" before and thus to give the patient "access to certain sectors of his personality that had not been reached in the first part of the treatment" ("Two Analyses of Mr. Z" 3). I intend to return to the contrasting psychoanalytic theories on which these two analyses were based, but I want to turn now to an analogous situation in the psychoanalytic reception and criticism of the work of D. H. Lawrence.

First Analysis: The Oedipus Complex

When *Sons and Lovers*[1] was published in 1913, it was almost immediately perceived by members of the London psychoanalytic community as a masterpiece illustrating such Freudian theories as the Oedipus com-

---

*This paper was originally presented at a scientific meeting of the North Carolina Psychoanalytic Society, November 20, 1992.

plex, psychosexual development, and unconscious motivation. Ivy Low, whose aunt, Barbara Low, and uncle by marriage, David Eder, M.D.,[2] were both London psychoanalysts, wrote enthusiastic postcards to friends: "Be sure to read *Sons and Lovers*!" "This is a book about the Oedipus complex!" (Litvinov, qtd. in Nehls 1:215). Further consideration of both the novel and Lawrence's early life suggests additionally, the influence of preoedipal issues, such as those articulated by Margaret Mahler and by Heinz Kohut.

Among those who initially saw the theme in oedipal terms was D. H. Lawrence himself, whose letter to his editor, Edward Garnett (19 November 1912) (*Letters* 1:476–77) presents a basically oedipal synopsis of the novel. Earlier (26 April 1911), Lawrence describes the *Oedipus Rex* of Sophocles as "the finest drama of *all* times" (*Letters* 1:261). In the unpublished "Foreword to *Sons and Lovers*," he writes: "The old son-lover was Oedipus. The name of the new one is legion. And if a son-lover take a wife, then she is not his wife, she is only his bed" (*Letters*, ed. Huxley 104). It is fair to say, however, that Lawrence saw himself as adapting the materials of his own childhood, adolescence, and young manhood to the fictional form of the realistic English Bildungsroman rather than as writing a case history to illustrate the theories of Sigmund Freud, whose work he had not read.

Frieda von Richthofen Weekley, whom Lawrence met (17? March 1912) and with whom he eloped six weeks later (3 May 1912), was acquainted with Freud's theories through Otto Gross, a brilliant but erratic young psychiatrist, who was briefly on the fringes of Freud's circle in Vienna and with whom she had a love affair and a passionate correspondence while she was married to Professor Ernest Weekley.[3] During Lawrence's final revision of *Sons and Lovers*, Frieda influenced the psychoanalytic emphasis on oedipal material and sexual symbolism that was already inherent in the manuscript. She may also have influenced the oedipal slant that Edward Garnett gave the manuscript by editing out some realistic material unrelated to that theme. She wrote to Garnett (September 1912), "I think L. quite missed the point in 'Paul Morel.' He really loved his mother more than anybody, even with his other women, real love, sort of Oedipus. . . . He is writing P.M. again, reads bits to me and we fight like blazes over it, he is so often beside the point." Later she reinforces her view of the delineating theme by telling Garnett: "The mother is really the thread, the domineering note"

(*Memoirs and Correspondence* 171). On their return to England in 1914, Lawrence became friends with Barbara Low and David Eder, and was acquainted with Ernest Jones, then President of the London Psycho-Analytical Society.[4]

The first psychoanalytic criticism of the novel came in a review by the American psychoanalyst Alfred Booth Kuttner (1915), which he expanded into an article for the *Psychoanalytic Review* (1916), which Barbara Low sent to Lawrence. *Sons and Lovers,* Kuttner says, has the "double quality" of ranking "very high as a piece of literature" while embodying a scientific theory and illustrating it with astonishing completeness. Kuttner clearly sets forth the classic psychoanalytic issues underlying the novel:

- The contrast between the parents, Walter Morel, warm, sensuous, and indulgent, whom Gertrude Morel, puritanical like her father, comes to loathe;
- Her determination to atone to her third baby, Paul, for having been unwanted (*SL* 73–74);
- The children's common hatred and contempt for their sometimes drunken and violent father (*SL* 101);
- The psychologically incestuous relationship that develops between mother and son, as presented in scenes that often resemble courtship, such as their visit to Lincoln (*SL* 297–303);
- Paul's praying for his father's death (*SL* 99), while bringing to his mother the tributes of flowers, his school prizes (*SL* 102), and his art work;
- The rivalry between Mrs. Morel and Paul's adolescent girl friend, Miriam Leivers, whose love he rejects in preference for his mother (*SL* 267);
- Paul's elaborate fantasy of not marrying but of sharing his life with his mother in a cosy little house, perhaps in middle age taking a staid wife who would be no rival for his mother (*SL* 130, 420)—which Kuttner calls a remarkably childish picture of the good life for a young man to have;
- His passionate involvement with Clara Dawes, married though separated from her working-class husband, and thus suitably debased to be available sexually while not competing with his mother for his spiritual side (*SL* 418);
- Paul's inability to love another woman while his mother lives (*SL*

418), yet his finding no freedom in her death but only increased allegiance to her internalized imago;

- His breaking his relationships with both Miriam and Clara out of fidelity to his mother;
- His finally drifting derelict without the mooring his mother had provided (*SL* chap. 15).

Kuttner's discussion briefly develops several related psychoanalytic issues: Because of the father's "unnatural position in the family," "where there should have been an attractive standard of masculinity to imitate," Paul "can only fear and despise" (95). Paul's inability to detach himself from dependency on the mother by means of the father's countervailing influence is further distorted in that his "early fixation" on his mother is actively encouraged by her "abnormally concentrated affection for her son" as a surrogate for her "unappeased love" in the marital situation (95). Paul's infatuation with his mother has a "paralyzing influence" on his love-making (95). Unable to "free himself from the incubus of his parents," Paul "remains enslaved by his parent complex" in "a kind of bottomless childishness." "Paul goes to pieces because he can never make the mature sexual decision away from his mother" nor "accomplish the physical and emotional transfer" (96).

There are several classically psychoanalytic elements that Kuttner does not notice, most of them clearly interpreted in a later applied Freudian analysis by Daniel A. Weiss or in psychoanalytically tinged discussions by others. Kuttner does not comment on the role of Clara's husband, Baxter Dawes, who, as Weiss points out, resembles Paul's father closely enough to serve as a father surrogate (26), to whom Paul responds with the same marked ambivalence (30–31), and with whom he can enact a reparation by proxy. First, in a fight over Clara, Paul allows himself to be beaten by Dawes as if in acceptance of deserved punishment (*SL* 433–35; Weiss 31–33); then he placates the man, staging a "rescue fantasy" and befriending him when he is in hospital (*SL* 448–51); and finally he returns Clara to him and reunites husband and wife as he could never do with his parents (*SL* 474, 478–80; Weiss 33–35).

Following Ernest Jones's psychoanalytic study of *Hamlet* (1949), Weiss develops several rich parallels between Hamlet and Paul:

- Their intense oedipal love for their mothers, both of whom are named Gertrude (Weiss 17–18);
- Their projection of incest guilt as hatred of the father, degraded as the

brutal step-father, whom they request the mother to refrain from sleeping with (*SL* 269; Weiss 18, 20, 24);
- Their attributing excessive purity to Ophelia and Miriam, whom they refer to as nuns (*SL* 309; Weiss 50);
- Finally, their use of parental surrogates to resolve issues relating to the "family romance," with Paul employing Baxter and Clara Dawes as Hamlet employs the player king and queen for this purpose (Weiss 67).

Certainly, for both Hamlet and Paul, these psychological issues come down to the question of whether "to be or not to be."

Kuttner does not acknowledge the ambiguity of the final paragraph, in which Paul, clenching his jaw and his fist and turning sharply, walks "towards the faintly humming, glowing town, quickly" (*SL* 492), as most readers see it, toward life. To which Mark Schorer appends the reservation: "as nothing in his previous history persuades us that he could unfalteringly do" (Schorer 12). Kuttner foresees for Paul only a compulsion to repeat in an endless round of temporary relationships with women, each of whom will be compared to his mother, found wanting, and then rejected as he moves on to the next woman.

Kuttner's article is quite favorable, but Lawrence reacted with dismay to find his creative work reduced, as he saw it, to a set of complexes. As he wrote to Barbara Low: "You know I think 'complexes' are vicious half-statements of the Freudians. . . . My poor book: it was, as art, a fairly complete truth: so they carve a half lie out of it and say 'Voila.' Swine!" (*Letters* 2:655). Lawrence's strong resistance to having his psychological issues uncovered and analyzed without the mask of art was activated by his reading of Kuttner's article.

Sons and Lovers *as Self Analysis*

The oedipal meanings of *Sons and Lovers* were obvious not only to Frieda Weekley but also to Jessie Chambers, the original of Miriam, who, aware that Lawrence had placed her in a hopeless position of rivalry with his mother, wrote to their mutual friend Helen Corke (23 March 1913): "The Miriam part of the novel is a slander, a fearful treachery. David has selected every point which sets off Miriam at a disadvantage, and he has interpreted her every word and action, and thought in the light of Mrs. Morel's hatred of her" (Chambers, *Collected*

Letters 27). "In *Sons and Lovers*," she says, "Lawrence handed his mother the laurels of victory" (Chambers, *D. H. Lawrence* 202).

Although such statements as these are colored by Jessie Chambers's emotional involvement in the situation, her perspective also provides insights that warrant being taken seriously. When she and Lawrence read Shakespeare's *Coriolanus*, Jessie felt the play had a special significance for him: "'You see, it's the mother who counts,' he said, 'the wife hardly at all. The mother is everything to him'" (Chambers, *D. H. Lawrence* 62). After his mother's death, Lawrence told Jessie: "I've loved her—like a lover—that's why I could never love you" (Chambers, *Collected Letters* 54). This insight is echoed in his subsequent statement to Frieda, "If my mother had lived I could never have loved you, she wouldn't have let me go" (Frieda Lawrence, *"Not I, But the Wind"* 56). Jessie believes that "the necessity he felt to justify his mother" in the novel resulted in his utter failure to face the issue (Chambers, *Collected Letters* 66).

Without recourse to Freudian theory, Jessie Chambers accurately observes: "It seems to me that one result of D.H.L.'s relationship with his mother was the complete divorce in his mind and attitude between love and sex" (Chambers, *Collected Letters* 78). Lawrence's critical biographer Emile Delavenay, who does know his Freud, comments: "With every woman he approached, Lawrence experienced the same split: he found himself incapable of loving those he respected and of respecting those he dared desire" (156). The implications of drive theory for the classically oedipal material are still apparent today.

These oedipal elements were, I believe, the issues Lawrence was referring to earlier when he wrote to his friend Arthur McLeod (26 October 1913) with reference to *Sons and Lovers:* "one sheds ones sicknesses in books—repeats and presents again ones emotions, to be master of them" (*Letters* 2:90). Kuttner expresses a similar idea: "Mr. Lawrence has escaped the destructive fate that dogs the hapless Paul by the grace of expression. . . . He cures himself by expression in his art" (100).

These are the first two statements of the widespread but questionable view of *Sons and Lovers* as a kind of self analysis, in which Lawrence, by *remembering* his experience in relation to his mother and representing it in fictionalized detail, employed the transformations of art in *working through* his Oedipus complex and so freed himself from it and healed his major psychological splits. Both Harry T. Moore (52) and Father Martin Jarrett-Kerr (25) subscribed to this view. In Freud's terms in "Remembering, Repeating, and Working Through" (1914; *SE* 12:145–56), Lawrence's statement is not about *remembering* but about *repeating* one's emotions in an effort to master them. Such personal growth can be achieved, however, only by means of a more distanced perspective than is possible in the midst of emotional repetition. Mark Schorer comments that Lawrence's theory is acceptable "only with the qualification that technique, which objectifies," affords this perspective: "For merely to repeat one's emotions . . . is also merely to repeat the round of emotional bondage." (Schorer 11–12). Frieda's account of Lawrence's rewriting *Sons and Lovers* in Italy confirms that he was not only remembering the original experiences but reliving the emotional situation with abreaction: "when he wrote his mother's death he was ill and his grief made me ill too" (Frieda Lawrence, *"Not I, But the Wind"* 56). But nothing Frieda says would support the conclusion that Lawrence's task of mourning was thereby completed, and he continued to struggle with the original emotional constellation in countless repetitions throughout his life.

Later psychoanalytic interpretations have found defensive maneuvers that suggest Lawrence may have wanted to avoid shedding too many sicknesses. Mark Schorer, linking the issues of artistic technique and therapeutic effectiveness, points out that "Morel and Lawrence are never separated. . . . Lawrence maintains for himself in this book the confused attitude of his character" (Schorer 13). Daniel A. Weiss, in a Freudian interpretation that runs counter to much previously received opinion, finds a psychoanalytic subtext of defenses and resistance: "In *Sons and Lovers* the artistic recognition of the material becomes itself a false recognition, a feint to catch the artist's eye while the real legerdemain of symbolic transformation does its work below the surface." Weiss approvingly summarizes Schorer's view that "Lawrence failed to resolve his ambivalent feelings toward his parents—his identity with and his alienation from his father, his wish to be free of and his dependence on his mother" (Weiss 14; Schorer 13). Schorer proposes: "If our books are to be exercises in self-analysis, then technique must—and alone can—take the place of the absent analyst" (12). Delavenay, who does not address the question of aesthetic distance, comments: "The attempt at self-analysis is a failure, not as a novel, but as a cure: it does not enable Lawrence to make a new start" (516).

Kuttner also must have recognized the limitations and incompleteness of *Sons and Lovers* as self analysis when, as a consultant to the publisher on another Lawrence manuscript, "The Wedding Ring," he was pained by signs of "deterioration . . . in a gifted writer, knowing as I do that it is of neurotic origin." In his opinion, "A rigorous Freudian analysis would make Mr. Lawrence both a happier man and a greater artist" ("Report and Letter on 'The Wedding Ring,'" in *WL* 483–85).

Lawrence, of course, was never psychoanalyzed, and the parallel I have drawn with Kohut's two analyses of Mr. Z is just that: an analogy with the applied psychoanalysis of literary interpretation at some distance from the deeply invested transference and uncovering process of a personal analysis. If we see the synthesis of Lawrence's literary art as a major factor enabling him to build up a compensatory structure, it is not to see it reductively but to recognize its importance in the maintenance of self-cohesion.

Second Analysis: Preoedipal Issues

What would it add to our understanding to re-analyze the Lawrence of *Sons and Lovers* along lines developed in more recent psychoanalytic theory? Although oedipal issues are consciously addressed, preoedipal issues are also implicit in the novel but are not worked through or understood on a conscious level. My observations on Lawrence's preoedipal issues must be considered as materials for a second analysis that is still in progress, for at this point I am unable to draw any final conclusions, and I do not want to foreclose what may yet emerge. Fred Pine, who has attempted an integrative approach to "the four psychologies of psychoanalysis" (i.e., the psychologies of drive, ego, object, and self), suggests that from the perspective of a "psychology of the self" (not specifically Kohutian self psychology), among the useful questions "are those having to do with boundaries, integration, and esteem."(Pine 582). Keeping these and related questions in mind "as potential modes of conceptualizing" the subject,[5] I will focus, in the remainder of this paper, on the two most important of Lawrence's preoedipal self issues: the difficulties of separation–individuation deriving from Lawrence's symbiotic relationship with his mother, and the internal deficit resulting from his inability as a child to make a positive identification with his devalued father.

Despite the obvious activation of oedipal feelings in the split between sexual and spiritual love in Paul Morel, Lawrence's emphasis throughout much of his work on the dangers of merger versus respect for otherness, as Judith Ruderman has pointed out, does not derive from triadic oedipal conflicts but from the dyadic relationship of mother and child (174–77). Jessie Chambers recognizes the psychic injury left by Lawrence's relationship with his mother: "What seems to me perhaps the most sinister feature is that intellectual awareness of the part his mother had played in his life was not sufficient to set him free. Some real inner injury had been done to him, and he could not heal himself" (*Collected Letters* 70). In self-psychological terms, the cognitive understanding of the oedipal issues, even with abreaction and some attempt at working through, could not heal the narcissistic injury.

In a letter to Rachel Annand Taylor[6] (3 December 1910) (*Letters* 1:190–91), Lawrence examines his family history, or mythology, to explain how that situation came about and what its effects are. Written one week before Lydia Lawrence's death, this letter expresses some remarkable perceptions that would enable Lawrence ultimately, with relative success, to negotiate the passage through separation–individuation. This task was made the more difficult in Lawrence's childhood by the familial rejection of the father and his unavailability as an idealizable object who could provide a way out of the dilemma. In the letter to Mrs. Taylor, Lawrence recognizes the attractive, desirable qualities of his father: "My father was dark, ruddy, with a fine laugh. He is a coal miner. He was one of the sanguine temperament, warm and hearty." The father's less attractive qualities, seen entirely from the mother's perspective, are magnified: "He lacked principle, as my mother would have said. He deceived her and lied to her. She despised him—he drank" (*Letters* 1:190). In the symbiotic merger with the mother, instituted from his birth, the boundaries of the self were seemingly dissolved and mother and son shared, as it were, a common boundary. The father, hated and rejected from birth, occupied a position outside that union; consequently, both the good paternal qualities of dark, ruddy life and fine laughter and the bad paternal qualities of instability and lack of principle, were consciously defined as outside the self, even while, on a deeper level, Lawrence also unconsciously identified his masculine self with the vitality as well as the irrationality and violence of the only masculine model he had.

The fusion with his mother that Lawrence describes in the letter to Rachel Annand Taylor was a world unto itself, seemingly containing everything necessary for life, a golden globe in which empathic immersion afforded almost total access to the mother so that sensitivity replaced the need for speech. There is, however, a further split. Lawrence's description of the experience sounds so idyllic at first that the gratification seems close to ecstasy. Yet the feeling of merger is also potentially destructive: "It has been rather terrible, and has made me, in some respects, abnormal" (*Letters* 1:190).

"This peculiar fusion of soul," Lawrence says, "never comes twice in a life-time." When it does come, it is in the form of total immersion in the flood of shared consciousness that affords mutual, intuitive "understanding." Lawrence's relation to his mother was his only model for love, and his sense of reality was grounded in this relationship. The impending loss, then, poses the threat of self dissolution, and he must find an anchor in reality elsewhere. As the experience of merger has left him with a feeling of abnormality, Louie Burrows, an old girl friend, suddenly emerges as the representative of healthy normality, and he impulsively asks her to marry him. The two feelings are simultaneous: "There is no hostility between the warm happiness and the crush of misery: but one is concentrated in my chest, and one is diffuse—a suffusion, vague." "Muriel," Lawrence's poetic name for Jessie Chambers, cannot provide a mooring in reality against such identity diffusion, since his mother has hated the girl and he believes that she, like his mother, wants to devour his soul (see *SL* 211). Louie, with her "healthy, natural love," "will never plunge her hands through my blood and feel for my soul," he says. "Nobody can have the soul of me. My mother has had it, and nobody can have it again. Nobody can come into my very self again, and breathe me like an atmosphere" (*Letters* 1:190–91).

The threatened loss of self cohesion—in Kohut's term, the *disintegration anxiety* (*How Does Analysis Cure?* 16–19)—that Lawrence describes in the last chapter of *Sons and Lovers* was real. Eighteen years later he recalled: "I was twenty-five, and from the death of my mother the world began to dissolve around me, beautiful, iridescent, but passing away substanceless, till I almost dissolved away myself, and was very ill: when I was twenty-six" ("Foreword to *Collected Poems*" 851). Lawrence's lung diseases, his pneumonia in that year and later the pulmonary tuberculosis that ultimately caused his death, with their common symptom of breathing difficulties, served psychologically, by his own account, to convey the effects of a smothering love. In *Fantasia of the Unconscious*, Lawrence attributes the etiology of such diseases to exploitation of the child's love: "any excess in the sympathetic mode . . . tends to burn the lungs with oxygen, weaken them with stress, and cause consumption. . . . No child should be induced to love too much. It means derangement and death at last" (*Fantasia* 97) This statement, as unscientific as it may be, speaks to the need to dispel the destructive mother.

According to Margaret S. Mahler and her associates, "the child with a predominantly symbiotic organization seems to treat the mother as if she were part of the self, that is, as not separate from the self but rather fused with it" (Mahler, Pine, and Bergman 7). In Mahler's conception, the "process of separation-individuation has two intertwined . . . developmental tracks": "the track of individuation, the evolution of intrapsychic autonomy, perception, memory, cognition, reality testing"; and "the track of separation that runs along differentiation, distancing, boundary formation, and disengagement from mother. All these structuralization processes will eventually culminate in internalized self-representations, as distinct from internal object representations" (Mahler, Pine, and Bergman 63). In these terms, at twenty-five, Lawrence's separation-individuation was ambivalent and less than complete. Judith Ruderman, employing Mahler's concept of separation-individuation and its subphases (176–77), thinks that Lawrence's difficulty in separating from the mother is "evidenced by the tension between the desire for merger and the need for independence that informs all his work" (175–76).

What evidence do we find in *Sons and Lovers* of the symbiotic relationship I am discussing? In an early childhood scene, Lawrence describes Mrs. Morel's feelings toward the infant Paul:

> In her arms lay the delicate baby. Its deep blue eyes, always looking up at her unblinking, seemed to draw her innermost thoughts out of her. She no longer loved her husband; she had not wanted this child to come, and there it lay in her arms and pulled at her heart. She felt as if the navel string that had connected its frail little body with hers had not been broken. A wave of hot love went over her to the infant. She held it close to her face and breast. With all her force, with all her soul she would make up to it for having brought it into the world unloved. She would love it all the more now it was here; carry it in her love. Its clear, knowing eyes gave her pain and fear. Did it know all about her? When it lay under her heart, had it been listening then? Was there a reproach in the look? She felt the marrow melt in her bones, with fear, and pain. [*SL* 74.]

Psychoanalytically, what is striking about this passage is not only the young adult male author's intuitive grasp of his mother's most intimate feelings but also his fantasies about his infantile relationship with her. As Lawrence presents the situation imaginatively, since the mother no longer loves her husband, the infant son, early in the oral incorporative stage, has already effectively won the oedipal rivalry with his father. Thus, although originally unwanted, he has been chosen as her favorite. They are bound together as if by an uncut umbilical cord. Although in time this tie will become a tether from which even his mother's death will not entirely free him, it is, at this point, a source of strength. Through Paul, Lawrence presents himself, not only in infancy but throughout childhood and even beyond, as a delicate, physically frail youngster whose strength lies in his ability to gain intuitive knowledge of the other, an ability this passage suggests he may have acquired prenatally and further developed in the strong empathic relationship he shared with his mother.

That Paul Morel as a child shares everything with his mother is a given; beyond that, he feels that nothing has really happened until it has been shared with her (*SL* 102). More significantly, I want to reconsider two passages that are sometimes cited as evidence of Paul's oedipal fixation. The first is from his childhood:

> Paul loved to sleep with his mother. Sleep is still most perfect, in spite of hygienists, when it is shared with a beloved. The warmth, the security and peace of soul, the utter comfort from the touch of the other, knits the sleep, so that it takes the body and soul completely in its healing. Paul lay against her and slept, and got better. Whilst she, always a bad sleeper, fell later on into a profound sleep that seemed to give her faith. [*SL* 107]

To my mind, what the passage illustrates is not only the triumph of Paul's oedipal wishes but, more profoundly, the gratification of his merger needs in the global union with his mother. In the fantasy he returns in sleep to a pre-separation state in which mother and child share, in effect, a single consciousness.

As Paul develops into adolescence, his mother exploits both his oedipal wishes and his dependency needs to preserve the symbiosis for the gratification of her own needs. When Mrs. Morel bitterly objects to Paul's growing interest in Miriam, "Instinctively he realized that he was life to her. And, after all, she was the chief thing to him, the only supreme thing." Paul immediately declares, "I talk to her, but I want to come home to you." When his mother pleads, "And I've never—you know, Paul—I've never had a husband—not really—," he accedes to the obvious manipulation of his oedipal feelings and accepts the role of surrogate (*SL* 267).

This is something more than the usual Oedipus complex that is passed through in the normal stages of development. I believe that the strength and persistence of Lawrence's oedipal pathology is to be understood in terms of the preoedipal issues it served, in Jessie Chambers's words, the "inner injury," or as he put it, the "wounds to the soul, to the deep emotional self" (*Complete Poems* 620). Lawrence says of his autobiographical character: "There was one place in the world that stood solid and did not melt into unreality: the place where his mother was. Everybody else could grow shadowy, almost non-existent to him, but she could not. It was as if the pivot and pole of his life, from which he could not escape, was his mother" (*SL* 278). As the letter to Rachel Annand Taylor makes clear, Lawrence's relationship with his mother was the ground of his reality.

* * *

The psychoanalyst Jessica Benjamin traces the roots of idealizing love to the rapprochement subphase of separation-individuation, the period from about sixteen to twenty-four months during which the child must resolve the conflict between the wish to remain in symbiotic union with the mother and the wish for autonomy as a separate individual (Moore and Fine 181). As "the father begins to assume the crucial role of standing for freedom, separation, and desire," Benjamin says, "Here begins the child's relationship to the father that has been adduced to explain the power of the phallus." It is through identification with the father "that boys escape the depressive mood of rapprochement and deny the feeling of helplessness that comes with the realization of separateness." "The father of rapprochement is internalized as the ego ideal of separation and, like the oedipal superego, can be seen as a psychic agency that embodies a specific resolution of the rapprochement conflict." "The upshot of this analysis is that for boys . . . the issues of recognition and independence become organized within the frame of gender" (Benjamin 121–24).

What happens, however, if the father is not available for identification and idealization? In Lawrence's family of origin, and in *Sons and Lovers*, the position of the depreciated father, living in internal exile in his own home, precluded his providing a stable model for safe passage through separation–individuation to individual identity and autonomy. For Lawrence, the rapprochement conflict of dependency versus independence could not be resolved at a phase–appropriate age, and his childhood gender identity was at best unstable.

Sons and Lovers provides evidence that despite his protestations, Paul Morel needed the idealizing relationship he had never had with his father. He takes delight in Walter Morel's stories about Taffy, the pit pony, who likes a bit of tobacco, though the stories seem to go nowhere (*SL* 103–104). Seeing his father at his bath, Paul gazes admiringly at his still "wonderfully young body, muscular, without any fat," and smooth, clear skin: "It seemed strange they were the same flesh" (*SL* 250). Jessie Chambers mentions Lawrence's pleasure in the dancing skills of the father he generally despised (*D. H. Lawrence* 30).

The potential relationship with his father, however, derailed from birth, could not be restored. The letter to Rachel Annand Taylor shows clearly how that situation came about. "I was born hating my father: as early as ever I can remember, I shivered with horror when he touched me. He was very bad before I was born," Lawrence writes. Then in a juxtaposition that implies a causal connection, he adds: "This has been a kind of bond between me and my mother" (*Letters* 1:190). It is not his personal recoil but his mother's active interference that prevented Lawrence from developing any positive relationship with his father.

Heinz Kohut says that, in this kind of situation, behind the mother's "depreciating attitude" toward the father, and her "manifest preference for the (thus overstimulated) child (the son)," there is "regularly a covert attitude of admiration and awe toward her own oedipal love object," her father. "The son participates in the mother's defensive belittling of his father, and elaborates this emotional situation by spinning out grandiose fantasies; he senses, however, the mother's fear of the strong male figure with the adult penis and realizes (unconsciously) that her exaltation of him, the son, is maintained only so long as he does not develop into an independent male" (*Analysis of the Self* 146–47). Kohut's interpretation describes the emotional situation between Lawrence and his mother with uncanny accuracy.

Despite his need for paternal connection, Lawrence rejected his father's overtures. Lawrence's boyhood friend George Neville recalls

Arthur Lawrence's coming to the sickroom with awkward, unspoken concern for his son when Lawrence was ill (Neville 63). In the parallel scene in *Sons and Lovers*, instead of responding to his father's solicitous inquiry, Paul says, "No; is my mother comin'?" "How long will she be?" (*SL* 106). But in the return of the repressed in later novels—notably in Lilly's therapeutic massage of the flu stricken Aaron in *Aaron's Rod* (96) and Birkin's fantasy of being taken care of in his delicate health by stronger, working-class men in the "Prologue" to *Women in Love* (502) —Lawrence enacts the fantasy of being the recipient of masculine tenderness during illness.

I postulate an additional psychic element as a constituent of Lawrence's difficult separation-individuation: the function his phallic-stage discovery of his penis must have had in his gradually developing sense of separateness from his mother and as a part object that he came to regard with the idealization he could not invest in the whole object, his father. In his novel *Aaron's Rod*, Aaron's phallic flute, metaphorically recalling Moses' brother Aaron's miraculous rod, is associated with Aaron Sisson's individual, creative self (*AR* 108, 129). In *Lady Chatterley's Lover*, the penis is represented as the phallus with quasi-sacral properties and personified with a separate identity, culminating in Mellors's memorable address to his phallus as an autonomous being with a will of its own (*LCL* 210). In Lawrence's novella *The Escaped Cock*, the risen Christ-figure's erect phallus becomes the source of his resurrection and the sacramental sign of his transcendence (*EC* 57). If one may take a great leap back to the childhood psychological situation depicted in *Sons and Lovers*, Lawrence's later pervasive use of the phallus as an image of autonomous selfhood suggests that the penis early came to represent an area of the self that was independent of the relationship with the mother. If this hypothesis is correct, then idealizing the penis was a way of avoiding the danger that he might fall into and be engulfed by the mother or her female surrogates. The first part of his life that Paul Morel does not share with his mother is his sexuality in what Peter Blos has called "the second individuation process of adolescence." "There was now a good deal of his life of which necessarily he could not speak to his mother. He had a life apart from her—his sexual life. The rest she still kept" (*SL* 411-12). Despite his split between spiritual and sexual love, Paul's allowing himself in late adolescence this single area of relative independence from his mother is a positive sign that foreshadows his ultimate success, however attenuated or incomplete, in establishing his own separate identity.[7]

Whatever John Arthur Lawrence's limitations, the family constellation already in place when D. H. Lawrence was born required the son's rejection of the father as the price of the simultaneously sustaining and devouring relationship with the mother. The father's abdication meant that he could meet few if any of his son's early psychic needs. In Benjamin's theory, what "boys get from their fathers in the normal course of rapprochement" is "a vehicle of solving that conflict between separation and dependency that preserves grandiosity and omnipotence, salvaging self-esteem and independent will and desire" (Benjamin 132). Lacking such a vehicle, Lawrence must fight that battle as best he can without it.

In his young manhood, Lawrence's individuation, like Paul Morel's, was conditioned not only by the strength of his overidentification with his mother but also by the perceived deficits in his relation to his father. In face of the father's unavailability, such a son must look elsewhere for masculine identification, as Lawrence sought to do in his idealization of male bonding; in the homoerotic impulses that tended to return in the anxiety of crisis situations such as he experienced in the Cornwall period; in the attempted sublimation of his longing in rituals of Blutbrüderschaft or leadership; and in his mythic idealization of the phallus. However overdetermined these masculine elements may be and whatever literary themes they may embody, I believe that all of them derive in large part from Lawrence's unmet need in relation to his father.

Lawrence's continuing issues in this regard, his repeated attempts to find a nurturant man, an idealizable man, or viable male bonding, are related "to the reactivation of the needs of the unconscious nuclear self," with regard to the pole of its masculine ideals. In Heinz Kohut's terms, Lawrence, unable to idealize his father but massively disappointed in his unavailability, had no opportunity to de-idealize him gradually as he inevitably discovered the father's realistic flaws, and hence Lawrence had no means of making transmuting internalization of the paternal self-object in the integration of the ideals with other parts of his personality (*Restoration of the Self* 217). In the figure of Walter Morel, Lawrence depicts his father as exiled from family life and raging alone in his own home (*SL* 101–102). But his absence left an injury that Lawrence tried to heal in the compulsion to repeat the ambivalent pattern of overidealization, inevitable disappointment, disruption, and undervaluation in relation to other men.

The wide emotional swings of this pattern derived, I believe, from

Lawrence's wishful fantasies regarding the earliest objects of his internal representational world. For all his insistence on otherness and the repeated strictures against merging throughout his work, Lawrence's only early model for closeness was his relationship with his mother. Whereas the repetition compulsion in relation to men derived from his sense of deprivation and longing for the relationship he felt he had never had, its emotional intensity came from his overgratification in the relationship he had had and lost. Although Lawrence was able to work through the disintegration anxiety of his "sick year" following his mother's death, his mourning for the lost feeling of merger with her was lifelong, and he could not entirely suppress the wish to reinstate this model in other close relationships. This wish may have returned whenever the possibility of closeness presented itself, but it returned with particular strength in his repeated fantasies of being tenderly nurtured by another, usually stronger, man. So did his disappointment at the inevitable failure of the attempt and his underlying despair about the impossibility of such a relationship.

In Kohut's second analysis of Mr. Z, idealization of the analyst was "replaced by a mirror transference of the merger-type": "the patient became self-centered, demanding, insisting on perfect empathy, and inclined to react with rage at the slightest out-of-tuneness with his psychological states, with the slightest misunderstanding of his communications." Although in the first analysis Kohut had seen such behavior as defensive, he now looked on it as an "analytically valuable replica" of a time in early childhood, when Mr. Z "had been alone with his mother, who was ready to provide him with the bliss of narcissistic fulfillment at all times," "when a condition of overgratification had prevailed which, in turn, led to the fixation that hampered further development" ("Two Analyses of Mr. Z" 11–12).

In his Introduction to Kohut's correspondence, Geoffrey Cocks sets forth the hypothesis that "The Two Analyses of Mr. Z" contains "[t]he most revealing account of Kohut's early years": "It is likely that this essay describes Kohut's training analysis with Ruth Eissler in the 1940s . . . and a subsequent self-analysis in the 1960s." Cocks, who says that Kohut's wife and son as well as colleagues and friends had intuited that he was Mr. Z, supports his argument with a series of striking parallels between Kohut and the pseudonymous patient: "An examination of the case study in fact reveals only lightly camouflaged events in Kohut's life" (Introduction to Kohut, *Curve of Life* 4–5). If Cocks is correct in his view of the autobiographical origin and "personal status of what [Kohut] regarded as the seminal case for self psychology," then Kohut stands in relation to "The Two Analyses of Mr. Z" in a position comparable to Lawrence's in relation to *Sons and Lovers*. Possibly both men were employing their respective literary forms in the process of working through major issues of their early lives.

Kohut's comments, both in this essay and elsewhere, open a fascinating area for further exploration in regard to Lawrence. In a typical Lawrencean split, if women potentially threatened to repeat the danger of engulfment by the devouring mother, men could be seen in wish-fulfillment fantasy not only as the available and idealizable father but also as the potentially nurturing father, who could provide the kind of gratification Lawrence had experienced in the merger with his mother but not in relation to his father. In several late autobiographical pieces, Lawrence revised the view of his parents as presented in his letter to Rachel Annand Taylor of 3 December 1910. This change implies an attempt to revise the internal representation of his earliest objects. In one unpublished manuscript, he writes:

> My mother fought with deadly hostility against my father, all her life. He was not hostile, till provoked, then he too was a devil. But my mother began it. She seemed to begrudge his very existence. She begrudged and hated her own love for him, she fought against his natural charm, vindictively. And by the time she died, at the age of fifty-five, she neither loved him nor hated him any more. She had got over her feeling for him, and was "free." So she died of cancer. ["Getting On" (1926), qtd. in Worthen 501]

In the revised version of Lawrence's family myth, his mother's fatal cancer has a psychosomatic etiology in her vindictive hatred of his father, and the father has become the model of natural charm and instinctuality. In later years Lawrence said to Frieda: "I would write a different 'Sons and Lovers' now; my mother was wrong, and I thought she was absolutely right" (Frieda Lawrence, *"Not I, But the Wind"* 56). Where the father was concerned, Lawrence did write a correction to *Sons and Lovers*. It is in *Lady Chatterley's Lover*, in the idealized portrait of the gamekeeper, Oliver Mellors, a working class man who speaks in the Midlands dialect, delivers a strong polemic for life and against a corrupt society based on mechanism and money, and expresses genuine tenderness in a heroic masculine sexuality.

Notes

1. References to *Sons and Lovers* will be cited in the text in the version edited by Edward Garnett for the first edition (1913), reprinted with only minor corrections of a few misprints, as edited by Keith Sagar (1981), rather than in the expanded text, reinstating Garnett's editorial excisions, as edited by Helen Baron and Carl Baron for the Cambridge University Press edition (1992). It was, of course, the first edition text that Kuttner reviewed and that Schorer, Weiss, and other critics discussed here assessed. The extracts I cite, however, are substantially the same in both texts, and the psychoanalytic meaning of this material, as in actual life, is not essentially altered by the elaboration of its traditionally "realistic" context. It should also be noted that, despite his reservations, Lawrence reviewed and approved Garnett's "pruning" of the manuscript (*Letters*, 1:517) and dedicated the novel to Garnett (*Letters* 1:477).
2. See Edward Glover, "Eder as Psychoanalyst."
3. See Otto Gross and Frieda Weekley, *The Otto Gross–Frieda Weekley Correspondence*, transcribed, translated, and annotated, by John Turner, with Cornelia Rumpf–Worthen and Ruth Jenkins. Published as a special issue of *The D. H. Lawrence Review* 22, no. 2 (Summer 1990): 137–227, the letters are printed both in English translation and in the original German. Turner's introduction, pp. 137–63, is indispensable. See also Sigmund Freud and C. G. Jung, *The Freud/Jung Letters: The Correspondence between Sigmund Freud and C. G. Jung*, ed. William McGuire, trans. Ralph. Manheim and R. F. C. Hull (Princeton, N.J.: Princeton University Press, 1974), pp. 141, 151, 152, 155–57. Freud, who recognized Gross's pathology, referred him for analytic treatment to Jung, who ultimately diagnosed his illness as dementia praecox, i.e., schizophrenia. Ernest Jones, for whom Gross was his first instructor in the technique of psychoanalysis, concurs with that diagnosis. See Jones, *Sigmund Freud: Life and Work*, .2:33.
4. According to Phyllis Grosskurth (158), Ernest Jones founded the London Psycho-Analytical Society on October 30, 1913, with himself as president and David Eder as secretary. Although Freud recognized Eder as the first, and for a time the only, practitioner of psychoanalysis in England, differences developed between Eder and Jones over Eder's expression of Jungian views. As a result, Jones dissolved the Society and on February 20, 1919, inaugurated a new group.
5. Pine's proposed questions concern the relative stability of "a sense of undifferentiated self-boundaries," the presence of "fantasies of merger, enactments of merger, or panics regarding loss of boundaries," the extent of "derealization or depersonalization" or of "discontinuity of the self-experience," the extent to which the individual experiences "himself or herself as the center of action in his or her own life," and "the ongoing sense of self-value, of esteem." Finally, he asks, "What pathological efforts to right imbalances in that subjective state of self are present—grandiosity, denial, flights into

activity, disdain of others?" (562)

6. Lawrence met Rachel Annand Taylor, a Scottish poet nine years older than himself, at a poets' supper party at Ernest Rhys's home in Hampstead in the spring of 1910, while Lawrence was teaching in Croydon. According to Majl Ewing, "Her cultural sophistication, her Pre-Raphaelite beauty, and her romantic poetry so strongly impressed Lawrence that when, in the autumn, he was asked to give a paper on a living poet before a Croydon literary group, he chose her as his subject." See Majl Ewing, "Foreword" to D. H. Lawrence, *Eight Letters by D. H. Lawrence to Rachel Annand Taylor,* [p. 1]. See also Lawrence's lecture "Rachel Annand Taylor." For further information on Rachel Annand Taylor, see Nehls, 1:525.
7. How much early developmental issues may be understood in terms of classical psychoanalytic drive theory is illustrated in Blos's comment on an adolescent male patient: "only after the castration anxiety in relation to the archaic mother was recognized, could the phallic modality assert itself and counteract the passive submissive trend" (165).

Works Cited

Benjamin, Jessica. "The Alienation of Desire: Women's Masochism and Ideal Love." *Psychoanalysis and Women*, ed. Judith L. Alpert, 113–37. Hillsdale, N.J.: Analytic Press, 1986.

Blos, Peter. "The Second Individuation Process of Adolescence," *The Psychoanalytic Study of the Child* 22 (1967): 162–86.

Chambers, Jessie [pseud. E. T.]. (1935), *D. H. Lawrence: A Personal Record*. New York: Knight Publications, 1936.

———. *The Collected Letters of Jessie Chambers*. Edited and with an Introduction by George J. Zytaruk, with Illustrations by Jack Bronson. Pub. as *The D. H. Lawrence Review* 12, nos. 1–2 (Spring–Summer 1979): iii–xxxiii, 1–238.

Delavenay, Emile. *D. H. Lawrence: The Man and His Work, The Formative Years, 1885–1919*, trans. Katharine M. Delavenay. Carbondale and Edwardsville: Southern Illinois University Press, 1972.

Freud, Sigmund. *The Standard Edition of the Complete Psychological Works of Sigmund Freud*. Translated under the General Editorship of James Strachey, in collaboration with Anna Freud, Assisted by Alix Strachey and Alan Tyson. London: Hogarth Press and the Institute of Psycho-Analysis, 1958. [Cited as *SE* followed by volume and page numbers.]

Freud, Sigmund, and C. G. Jung. *The Freud/Jung Letters: The Correspondence between Sigmund Freud and C. G. Jung*, ed. William McGuire, trans. Ralph Manheim and R. F. C. Hull. Princeton, N.J.: Princeton University Press, 1974.

Glover, Edward. "Eder as Psychoanalyst." *David Eder: Memoirs of a Modern Pioneer*, ed. J. B. Hobman, 89–116. Foreword by Sigmund Freud. London: Victor Gollancz Ltd., 1945.

Gross, Otto, and Frieda Weekley. *The Otto Gross–Frieda Weekley Correspondence.* Transcribed, translated, and annotated, by John Turner, with Cornelia Rumpf-Worthen and Ruth Jenkins. Pub. as *The D. H. Lawrence Review* 22, no. 2 (Summer 1990): 137–227.
Grosskurth, Phyllis. *Melanie Klein: Her World and Her Work.* New York: Alfred A. Knopf, 1986.
Jarrett-Kerr, Father Martin [pseud. Father William Tiverton]. *D. H. Lawrence and Human Existence.* London: Rockliff, 1951.
Jones, Ernest. *Hamlet and Oedipus.* New York: W. W. Norton, 1949; rpt. Garden City, N. Y.: Doubleday Anchor Books, 1955.
———. *Sigmund Freud: Life and Work,* 3 vols, rev. ed. London: Hogarth Press, 1974.
Kohut, Heinz. *The Analysis of the Self.* New York: International Universities Press, 1971, rpt. 1987.
———. *The Curve of Life: Correspondence of Heinz Kohut, 1923–1981*, ed. Geoffrey Cocks. Chicago and London: University of Chicago Press, 1992.
———. *How Does Analysis Cure?,* ed. Arnold Goldberg with Paul Stepansky. Chicago: University of Chicago Press, 1984.
———. *The Restoration of the Self.* Madison, Conn: International Universities Press, 1977, rpt. 1988.
———. "The Two Analyses of Mr Z." *International Journal of Psychoanalysis* 60 (1979): 3–27.
Kuttner, Alfred Booth "Report and Letter on 'The Wedding Ring'" (November 10, 1914). In Appendix III in *The Rainbow*, by D. H. Lawrence, ed. Mark Kinkead-Weekes, 483–85. Cambridge, U.K.: Cambridge University Press, 1989.
———. "*Sons and Lovers.*" *The New Republic* 10 (April, 1915): 255–57.
———. "*Sons and Lovers*: A Freudian Appreciation." *Psychoanalytic Review* 3, no. 3 (July 1916): 295–317. Rpt. in *D. H. Lawrence and "Sons and Lovers": Sources and Criticism*, ed. E. W. Tedlock, Jr., 76–100. New York: New York University Press, 1965. [Cited in the Tedlock collection.]
Lawrence, D. H. *Aaron's Rod.* Edited by Mara Kalnins. Cambridge, U.K.: Cambridge University Press, 1988. [Cited as *AR.*]
———. *The Complete Poems of D. H. Lawrence.* New York: Viking Press, Compass Book, 1971.
———. *Eight Letters by D. H. Lawrence to Rachel Annand Taylor.* Foreword by Majl Ewing. Pasadena, Calif.: Grant Dahlstrom at the Castle Press, 1956.
———. *The Escaped Cock.* Edited by Gerald M. Lacy. Los Angeles: Black Sparrow Press, 1973. [Cited as *EC.*]
———. "Foreword to *Collected Poems*" (1928); rpt. in *The Complete Poems of D. H. Lawrence*, ed. Vivian de Sola Pinto and F. Warren Roberts, 849–52. New York: Viking Press, 1971.
———. *Lady Chatterley's Lover, A propos of "Lady Chatterley's Lover."* Edited by Michael Squires. Cambridge, U.K.: Cambridge University Press, 1993. [Cited as *LCL.*]
———. *The Letters of D. H. Lawrence.* Edited and with an Introduction by Aldous

Huxley. 3rd printing. New York: Viking Press, 1932, rpt. 1936. [Cited as *Letters*, ed. Huxley]

———. *The Letters of D. H. Lawrence*, Vol. 1: *September 1901–May 1913*. Edited by James T. Boulton. Cambridge, U.K.: Cambridge University Press, 1979. [Cited as *Letters* 1, followed by page numbers.]

———. *The Letters of D. H. Lawrence*, Vol. 2: *June 1913–October 1916*. Edited by George J. Zytaruk and James T. Boulton. Cambridge, U.K.: Cambridge University Press, 1981. [Cited as *Letters* 2, followed by page numbers.]

———. "Rachel Annand Taylor." In *Young Lorenzo: Early Life of D. H. Lawrence Containing Hitherto Unpublished Letters, Articles and Reproductions of Pictures*, by Ada Lawrence and G. Stuart Gelder, 249–68. Florence: G. Orioli, 1931. Rpt. in *Phoenix II: Uncollected, Unpublished, and Other Prose Works by D. H. Lawrence*, ed. Warren Roberts and Harry T. Moore, 217–20. New York: Viking Press, 1968.

———. *Sons and Lovers* (1913). Edited and with Introduction and Notes by Keith Sagar. Harmondsworth, Middlesex, England: Penguin Books; New York: Viking Penguin, 1981, rpt. 1986. [Cited as *SL*.]

———. *Sons and Lovers* (1992). Edited by Helen Baron and Carl Baron. Cambridge, U.K.: Cambridge University Press, 1992.

———. *Women in Love*. Edited by David Farmer, Lindeth Vasey, and John Worthen. Cambridge, U.K.: Cambridge University Press, 1987. [Cited as *WL*.]

Lawrence, Frieda. *Frieda Lawrence: The Memoirs and Correspondence*, ed. E. W. Tedlock, Jr. New York: Alfred A. Knopf, 1964.

———. (1934), *"Not I, But the Wind . . ."* Afterword by Harry T. Moore. Carbondale and Edwardsville: Southern Illinois University Press, 1974.

Litvinoff, Ivy Low. "A Visit to D. H. Lawrence." *Harper's Bazaar* (October 1946): 411–18; rpt. in *D. H. Lawrence: A Composite Biography*, Vol. 1: *1885–1919*, ed. Edward Nehls, 215-22. Madison: University of Wisconsin Press, 1957. [Cited as Litvinov, in Nehls 1.]

Mahler, Margaret S., Fred Pine, and Anni Bergman. *The Psychological Birth of the Human Infant: Symbiosis and Individuation*. New York: Basic Books, 1975.

Moore, Burness E., and Bernard D. Fine, eds. *Psychoanalytic Terms and Concepts*. New Haven, Conn., and London: The American Psychoanalytic Association and Yale University Press, 1990.

Moore, Harry T. (1954), *The Priest of Love: A Life of D. H. Lawrence*. Rev. Ed. New York: Farrar, Straus, and Giroux, 1974.

Nehls, Edward, ed. *D. H. Lawrence: A Composite Biography*, Vol. 1: *1895–1919*. Madison: University of Wisconsin Press, 1957.

Neville, G. H. *A Memoir of D. H. Lawrence (The Betrayal)*, ed. Carl Baron. Cambridge, U.K.: Cambridge University Press, 1981.

Pine, Fred. "The Four Psychologies of Psychoanalysis and Their Place in Clinical Work." *Journal of the American Psychoanalytic Association* 36, no. 3 (1988): 571–96.

Ruderman, Judith. *D. H. Lawrence and the Devouring Mother*. Durham, N.C.: Duke

University Press, 1984.
Schorer, Mark. "Technique as Discovery" (1948), *Hudson Review* 1 (Spring 1948): 67–87. Rpt. in Mark Schorer, *The World We Imagine: Selected Essays*, 3–23. New York: Farrar, Straus, Giroux, 1968. [Cited in the Schorer collection.]
Weiss, Daniel A. *Oedipus in Notthingham: D. H. Lawrence*. Seattle: University of Washington Press, 1962.
Worthen, John. *D. H. Lawrence: The Early Years, 1885–1912*. Cambridge, U.K.: Cambridge University Press, 1991.

10

Lawrence and Crowd Psychology

GINETTE KATZ-ROY

Lawrence became increasingly concerned with individual fulfilment and saviour-figures as he felt that man was being threatened by the rise of mass civilization. Many critics have analysed the theme of leadership in his work,[1] yet his attitude to crowds has been somewhat neglected—and not totally without reason—since in Lawrence's fiction, leader figures are not necessarily followed by crowds (one follower or disciple is enough for Birkin or Rawdon Lilly). The other Lawrencian heroes are not very often confronted with large groups of people either. Graphic descriptions of the First World War are conspicuously absent from his fiction. Crowds play an active role only in *Touch and Go, Kangaroo*, *The Plumed Serpent* and *Movements in European History*. Elsewhere, they are more or less part of the background. But even if they rarely come to the forefront, they are Lawrence's constant preoccupation from 1915 on, as his letters, poems and essays show clearly enough. Whether visible or invisible, they determine Lawrence's outlook on history and politics, his philosophy and his choice of specific forms of art.

Many of Lawrence's reflections on the subject are representative of the Zeitgeist and are marked by social Darwinism.[2] At the turn of the century, some thinkers had attempted a methodical study of the attitude of crowds. The "psychology of crowds" was a science founded by two Frenchmen who were near contemporaries of Lawrence: Gustave Le Bon (1841–1931) and Gabriel Tarde (1843–1904).[3] I will refer mostly to what we could call their best-sellers: Le Bon's *Psychologie des foules* (1895) and Tarde's *L'opinion et la foule* (1901). These works had an incredible influence on political and scientific thinking in Lawrence's time and after. There were forty-five editions of Le Bon's book between 1895 and 1963. It was translated into sixteen languages and read by people as different as Clémenceau, Mussolini, Hitler and Franklin D. Roosevelt as well as

Jung, Freud, Bergson and Adorno. It gave inspiration to the British psychologist William McDougall and the American sociologist Edward A. Ross for the first works of social psychology written in English-speaking countries.[4]

I cannot argue that Lawrence had read Le Bon and Tarde but his outlook on crowds often coincides with theirs, for a number of reasons—besides the fact that the Frenchmen's ideas were in the air. First, they had a common interest in Charles Darwin, Herbert Spencer and the latest discoveries in anthropology and biology (Lawrence had read the works of other naturalists who upheld evolutionism, such as Thomas Huxley, Ernst Haeckel and Wilfred Trotter[5]), second they had the same type of nineteenth century cultural heritage marked by post-French Revolution social or racial theories (Carlyle and Nietzsche on the one hand, Taine and Gobineau on the other), thirdly, Le Bon's and Tarde's vision permeated the works of authors that Lawrence had an opportunity to read or hear of (e.g. Renan, Jung, Bergson, Freud[6]). Thus, these two scientists' theories may help us to define Lawrence's position in the ideological or scientific context of the period and the specificity of his outlook.

In 1895, Le Bon was predicting the beginning of the "era of crowds," and deploring the growing power of the masses, evidence of which he found in trade-unionism and parliamentary representation. This was the last stage before the disintegration of the West, a phase of chaos[7] preceding the birth of a new civilization. The most traumatic experience Lawrence had of this chaos was the First World War and its aftermath. The social difficulties and the political problems of the period led him to this very pessimistic conclusion to *Movements in European History*: "So Europe moves from oneness to oneness, from the imperial unity to the unity of the labouring classes, from the beginning to the end" (252). We find many echoes of the unrest of the labouring classes in his writings; "The bull of the proletariat has got his head down," as he says in his poem "St Luke" (*CP* 137). His history manual teems with menacing throngs: "the vulgar populace of Rome" (35), "floods of fierce unknown people" (43) "black clouds of human beings" (65), or the "delirious" mobs of the French revolution (200).[8] He shows the same anxiety in his letters: "the mob shall not crush us nor starve us nor cry us to death" (*L II* 273). At the end of his life, in *Apocalypse*, he still holds a very Nietzschean stance and denounces the rule of the weak, of that frustrated mass who, for lack of real power, can only resort to bullying. Le Bon and Tarde as well as Lawrence describe natural crowds as violent, irrational, instinctive, suggestible, close to primitive man, the savage or the child, even feminine in their desire for submission to a strong power. They are fickle and unpredictable like women.

In "Education of the People," written in 1918, Lawrence hints that crowds are like children manipulated by idealists. The images he uses in relation to crowds in this text are telling. First, the new generations are identified with Briareus, one of the hundred-armed and fifty-headed sons of Uranus and Ge (Heaven and Earth) who tried to overthrow Zeus. Thanks to the triumphant modern woman, this "baby-in-arms" has become the new god in our society; he has defeated "the man who is supposed to be the responsible party" (*Ph* 661)—a situation which recalls Darwin's thesis of the rivalry between the father and sons in the primitive horde.[9] This mythical monster traditionally represents the gigantic forces of Nature, and here, for Lawrence, obviously the wild power of the rising masses. Further on in the essay, the baby monster turns into Demogorgon,[10] the people avid for democracy, an androgynous being, since a Gorgon or Medusa (who is one of the three Gorgons) is female. It is a rather greedy, immature, gullible and stupid creature by whom one must refuse to be impressed or paralyzed. In the same essay, he proclaims:

> We want quality of life, not quantity. We don't want swarms and swarms of people in backstreets. We want distinct individuals, and these are incompatible with swarms and masses. (*Ph* 606)

"Bare Fig-Trees," a poem written about 1920 in Sicily, associates Demos and the Gorgon again and denounces the ideal of equality.[11] Here the comparison of the fig-tree to a seven-branch candelabrum conflates Biblical imagery and the scientific notion of a common origin of humanity, which Lawrence had already developed at the end of *Movements in European History*:

> Oh many-branching candelabrum, oh strange up-starting fig-tree,
> Oh weird Demos, where every twig is the arch twig,
> Each imperiously over-equal to each, equality overreaching itself
> Like the snakes on Medusa's head,
> Oh naked fig-tree! (*CP* 300)

Later, in "More Pansies," Lawrence claims that "demos" should serve the happy few who look "beyond humanity," and several other poems of the same period are built on this opposition between the few and the many:

> Democracy is service, but not service of demos.
> Democracy is demos serving life
> And demos serves life as it gleams on the face of the few,
> and the few look into the eyes of the gods, and serve the sheer gods.
> (*CP* 650)

The mob sometimes chooses to follow the wrong masters. Even though Gerald in *Women in Love* is not Lawrence's ideal of an enlightened leader, the miners submit passively to his iron will and manly authority, whereas they had reacted like rebellious children to Thomas Crich's paternalistic rule. As Lawrence puts it in "Reflections on the Death of a Porcupine" (1925), "Every lower order seeks in some measure to serve a higher order: and rebels against being conquered" (*Ph II* 473). Le Bon shows that the crowd rebels more easily against a lenient master than against a strong one and Gerald corresponds quite well to his idea of the strong leader as an alienated and neurotic hero.

For Le Bon and Tarde, the crowd is always intellectually inferior to the isolated individual.[12] It acts under the influence of its spine rather than of its brain. Lawrence says that communication between leader and followers does not require more than "brainless intelligence." It is based on a sort of telepathy, a "reversion to the premental form of consciousness" (*K* 329). In "Touch and Go" (1920), Willie Houghton, addressing a group of colliers, complains: "I've lived in this blessed place for fifty years, and I've never seen the spark of an idea, nor of any response to an idea, come out of a single one of you" (*CPl* 325). In a crowd, the individual becomes an automaton deprived of any will-power like the miners in *Women in Love* who, in the last stage of industrial decadence, become "strange machines, heavy, oiled" (115), robots made of inanimate matter; Lawrence asserts bluntly: "Most men *don't* think" (*Ph II* 623)[13] and still more abruptly, "Very few men have being at all" (*Ph II* 384).[14] He often sees crowds as amorphous organisms, composed of creatures of a lower order, either sheep, rats, insects, bugs, beetles, wood-lice or ants: "Half-made creatures, rarely more than half-responsible and half-accountable, acting in terrible swarms like locusts" (*PS*,

106). These comparisons, both apocalyptic and biological, were not uncommon in that age of scientific research on animal societies. The French philosopher Taine had already described the crowd as "an animal of a lower order, an invertebrate, a monstrous worm which has a diffuse sensitivity and still wriggles with disorderly movements after its head has been more or less severed from its body."[15]

What are we to make of this rather depressing picture of a mass civilisation doomed to regression (or what Lawrence, using a scientific term, calls "devolution")? The age of crowds is presented as a movement backwards towards barbarism and dissolution. Yet Le Bon shows that since "a crowd is a herd which cannot do without a master" (68), its domination cannot last long. He believes in the education of an élite who will exercise a military and political power over the masses, not in the teaching of useless knowledge to the many (and Lawrence shares his opinion on this last point).

For Le Bon as for Lawrence, history is a succession of cycles: "The cycle of a people's life consists in passing from barbarism to civilisation trying to fulfill a dream, then in declining and dying when this dream has lost its power" (*LB* 124). Hence the importance of leaders which, curiously enough, in the case of Le Bon, goes with the conviction that a parliamentary regime is the best system for avoiding personal tyrannies. He dreams of a democracy with a leader elected by plebiscite. The whole is not terribly coherent but it sounds like a remote cousin of Lawrence's philosophy. It reveals the same tension between pessimistic observation and faith in a possible change, the same hesitation between different forms of ambiguous political solutions. Tarde also believes in the necessity of having strong leaders, but their power must be balanced by public opinion. The end of *Movements in European History* may appear as even more confusing since Lawrence advocates at the same time "a good form of socialism" and natural aristocracy.

* * *

Le Bon's and Lawrence's conception of history as cyclical does not strike us as literally Darwinian; it is rather Spencerian in the sense that a biological pattern serves to describe the life and death of a society conceived as an organism. This recalls as well Blake's mythical construction or the theory of the French eighteenth century scientist Cuvier who imagined successive creations after natural catastrophes. Does not Lawrence repeatedly prophesy the end of the world in apocalyptic terms? "The French revolution was only a bit of a brief inundation. The real deluge lies just ahead of us. [. . .] all that remains is to be a Noah, and build an ark," he writes in 1926 (*Ph* 754). The same biblical overtone can be found in the title of *The Rainbow* which traces the history of a family through three generations without any notion of evolution in the sense of progress (Ursula will prove to be one of the happy few in *Women in Love* only). The rainbow which appears in the sky at the end offers a faint gleam of hope for the future but above all it marks the end of the cycle of disintegration that goes with the pseudo-progress of an industrial society. At the end of *Women in Love*, Birkin thinks of the future of mankind in terms of a sudden mutation of the species: "The eternal creative mystery could dispose of man, and replace him by a finer created being: just as the horse has taken the place of the mastodon" (479).

Even though Darwinism[16] haunts his writings, Lawrence rejects it emphatically several times. Some of his most attractive characters seem to be a challenge to the notion of evolution: Count Dionys in "The Ladybird" is "a bit like a monkey" (164), Hepburn in "The Captain's Doll" is perceived by Hannele, who is torn between fascination and irritation, as "a sort of psychic phenomenon like a grasshopper or a tadpole or an ammonite" (94). Let us note that the function of Lawrence's animal imagery can only be understood in its context and in the wider context of Lawrence's ontology. Here the comparison with a creature of a lower order is not totally pejorative; it is ironical in Hannele's mind; it has negative connotations for an orthodox evolutionist, but it may have positive ones for Lawrence who often thinks that primitive creatures are better adjusted to their environment than man. In the Foreword to *Fantasia of the Unconscious*, he asserts: "Floods and fire and convulsions and ice-arrest[17] intervene between the glamorous civilizations of mankind [. . . .] I do not believe in evolution, but in the strangeness and rainbow-change of ever-renewed creative civilizations" (8). There is no other evolution than this progressive change followed by a sudden break-up. The epilogue of *Movements in European History* shows that he even denies the validity of transformism and calls into question the idea of a common descent. For him, "Man has descended from man" (255). In "The Crown," he condemns all scientific certainties as idealistic heresies: "our will–to–live contains a germ of suicide, and our survival of the fittest the germ of degeneracy" (*Ph II* 397). Yet the following passage from "Study of Thomas Hardy," sounds thoroughly Spencerian as it stresses the continuity between inanimate matter and living organisms and insists on the principle of change from homogeneity to heterogeneity:

> Life starts crude and unspecified, a great Mass. And it proceeds to evolve out of that mass ever more distinct and definite particular forms, an ever–multiplying number of separate species and orders, as if it were working always to the production of the infinite number of perfect individuals, the individual so thorough that he should have nothing in common with any individual. (42)

In spite of his repeated and misleading attacks on evolutionism, Lawrence always thought that the sole purpose of life was differentiation, and this conditioned his attitude to crowds.

We cannot avoid addressing this problem of Darwinism or social Darwinism, however briefly, when dealing with the psychology of crowds, since crowds organized in masses[18] are a party to the struggle for life in modern society, even more than in the past. We have seen that most of the time, Lawrence rejects all evolutionary theories and notions of progress wholesale without telling us which brand of evolutionism he is calling into question. Like many people, he has an oversimplified view of Darwin's theory. Nevertheless, he is a little closer to Darwin than to Spencer on the subject of natural selection[19] since he makes it clear that he refuses to consider the struggle for life and free competition as natural phenomena in society (or in the world between races and nations). In the epilogue of *Movements in European History*, commenting on the notions of "progress" and "free competition," he writes: "Since the war these words make us feel sick, they have proved such a swindle" (257). Yet, we know that he refuses "Liberty, equality, fraternity" as well, though at times he defends a sort of material equality to solve the problem of poverty. The struggle for life is just as inacceptable as its contrary. There must be a struggle for something other than existence, production or power.

The labouring classes reveal the same greed for power and money as their exploiters. When asked by Gerald what he thinks of the British working man in *Touch and Go*, Oliver answers: "I think he's in nearly as bad a way as the British employer: he's nearly as much beside the point" (*CPl* 363).[20] In the industrial system, workers and bosses are equally doomed to regression. Clifford Chatterley is also described as a crab or a lobster, which is unambiguously pejorative here. In fact, our life should be a struggle for consciousness, and as is suggested in *Lady Chatterley's Lover*, a struggle for *being* as opposed to *having*. In trying to find a solution to the conflict between the workers and their capitalist boss in *Touch and Go*, Oliver cries: "Why can't we try really to leave off struggling against one another, and set up a new state of things?" (384). As he dreamed of this new state of things himself, Lawrence had replaced the concept of evolution by that of "unfolding": "the truth of evolution is not true. There is no evolving, only unfolding" (*L III* 39). This theme is also developed in the first pages of "Study of Thomas Hardy": "The final aim is the flower [. . .]. The final aim of every living thing, creature or being is the full achievement of itself" (12). In his concern for individual fulfilment and harmonious social life, he had no real quarrel with Darwinism[21] or post-Darwinism even if he was not aware of it.

* * *

Le Bon has been called the Machiavelli of mass societies. Lawrence, Le Bon and Tarde all try to exorcise their fear of crowds by imagining ways of counteracting the destructive drives of the masses. One of these ways is to insist on the role of the individual in the shaping of history, which brings the temptation of relying on great leaders. The other consists in using one's understanding of the psychology of crowds to cause a substantial change in mentalities. Tarde's original contribution is to highlight the importance of communication and propaganda before MacLuhan. He even considers conversation as an embryonic social relationship that may have a considerable impact on public opinion: "The evolution of Power can be explained by the evolution of Public Opinion which itself can be explained by the evolution of conversation" (*T* 121).

Le Bon and Tarde seem to offer recipes for the manipulation of crowds. According to Le Bon, crowds are easily hypnotized and do not think rationally but in images (he even says "image-thoughts," using the same term that Lawrence uses in *Apocalypse* to define a form of primitive thought); crowds are sensitive to exaggeration, violent assertions and repetition, they love myths and the supernatural, they are attached to the traditions and spirit of their race: "Myths and legends are indeed the true bases of a civilization" (*LB* 35). We find a perfect illustration of all this in *The Plumed Serpent* with the revival of an ancient religion and its rites, the incantatory rhythm of its hymns, its haunting drum-beating sessions, its propaganda more akin to art than rational discourse and its insistence on hypnotism. Even Kate is "mesmerised" by Ramón (The Lawrencian hero is always fascinating). In a recent study,[22] Tony Pinkney stresses the importance of the theme of communication through writing and public reading in *The Plumed Serpent*. One of the striking aspects of the new leaders' propaganda is that it relies so much on art forms: poetry, music, dance and costume design. Nevertheless, Ramón's main weapon remains language: "With his words, Ramón was able to put the power of his heavy strong will over the people" (337).

* * *

There is no denying that, in spite of his avowed contempt and even repulsion for crowds, Lawrence was concerned with the problem of mass-communication and that his art is an art of persuasion. But his dismissal of "the ordinary newspaper cant" through Birkin in *Women in Love*, his critical use of newspaper clippings in *Kangaroo* and his defence of "*a* people's" theatre as opposed to "*the* people's theatre" in the preface to *Touch and Go*, reveal his yearning for a more meaningful type of relationship with the public which goes together with a desire to find a satisfactory solution to the life of the individual in a mass society. The role of newspapers is not always negative in his fiction. They often have a premonitory function,[23] or at least they provide the first hints of a topic which will become central in the book. In "The Captain's Doll," Hannele hears about Mrs Hepburn's death through a newspaper before she can talk about this accident with Hepburn. What must be noted is that public information becomes meaningful only when it is discussed between two individuals. In Lawrence, we often find a dialectic movement from the impersonal to the personal and back to another type of impersonal connection which he calls the "non-human."

This miner's son, who had come out of the mass himself, was never content with ignoring the masses. We find innumerable examples of his hatred of contact with the crowd and his disgust for collective man, whether in small or large groups. His heroes or heroines often share his feeling: Gudrun stifles when she is in the streets of Beldover and she feels she is "sinking into one mass with the rest" (118); Kate hates "the degenerate mob of Mexico City"; and Mellors, like Birkin, even contemplates the extermination of the human species. Nevertheless, if we examine carefully the Brangwen sisters,' Kate's or Connie's reactions, we discover obvious traces of sympathy which are also the author's. The Coal Dust chapter in which Gudrun is fascinated by the "strange glamour" (116) of a group of miners is a case in point. Lawrence could almost say with Ramón, "I detest and despise masses of people. But these are my own people" (250). In his essay "Nottingham and the Mining Country," he depicts the miners' community he knew in his youth as "deeply alive" and deplores the fact that the sense of organic life which existed then has been lost. He complains about this in the poems too:

> Oh I have loved the working class
> where I was born,
> and lived to see them spawn into machine-robots
> in the hot-beds of the board-schools and the films.
> (*CP* 644)

Several poems in "More Pansies" show that he was becoming increasingly conscious of the fact that the masses were the victims of our civilization: "What have they done to you, men of the masses creeping back and forth to work?" (*CP* 630). At times, he even seems to hope that the great change he is looking forward to will come from them. At the end of the poem "St Luke," the author exhorts the bull of the proletariat to become conscious of its destructive and creative powers: "let him roar out challenge on the world and throwing himself upon it, throw off the madness of his blood" (*CP* 327). After the General Strike of 1926, he wrote to a friend: "This strike will have done more to preparing for industrial revolution, than fifty years of ordinary life would have done" (*L V* 533). We find the same revolutionary mood in a letter of December 1928: "We want a revolution not in the name of money or work or any of that, but of life [. . . .] I get more revolutionary every minute, but for *life's sake*" (*L VII* 99). In short, Lawrence is distrustful of the masses as they have become; he imagines they were rather more "alive" in the past, and, in his most optimistic and prophetic moments, hopes they will recover their consciousness, vitality and instinct of community if the world hears the right gospel. This would be a universal gospel which has nothing in common with Christian indoctrination or purely political propaganda—perhaps an art capable of suggesting the right questions, "since the business of art is never to solve but only to declare" (*STH* 72).

He often describes men in a crowd as "uncreated" or "half-created" as if something or someone could one day bring them to the fullness of their humanity. In his essay "Democracy," Lawrence claims that "The highest Collectivity has for its true goal the purest individualism" (702). Hence his apparent hesitation between private and more or less public forms of communication in his fiction. Eventually, we are bound to acknowledge that for him, the most persuasive forms of communication are private: conversations, letters or the contact between two people. In this, he joins Tarde. For instance, Mellors' letter at the end of *Lady Chatterley's Lover* contains a long speech on the evils of mass civilization. Incidentally, we may note that the tone of many of Lawrence's essays is conversational and we may also think of his activity as a compulsive letter-writer. From *Women in Love* on, all his novels are based on individual exchanges—even his leadership novels. Who must be convinced of the validity of Ramón's venture if not Kate? What is the central theme of *Aaron's Rod* if not the relationship of Aaron and Lilly? Who does Ben Cooley try to win over if not Somers? No wonder we return to the intimacy of the couple in *Lady Chatterley's Lover*. No wonder Parkin, in becoming Mellors in the third version of the book, has lost his political commitment as a communist. Persuasion begins at home.

The beginning of Chapter XVI in *Kangaroo* is a sharp criticism of any attempt to study collective psychology—a somewhat paradoxical criticism, given Lawrence's interest in the subject:

> The study of collective psychology to-day is absurd in its inadequacy. Man is supposed to be an automaton working in certain automatic ways when you touch certain springs. These springs are all labelled, they form a keyboard to the human psyche, according to modern psychology. And the chief labels are herd instinct, collective interest, hunger fear, collective prestige, and so on. (324)

This might almost be construed as an attack on Le Bon and Tarde. Although his observations, his fears and his belief in the individual were the same as those of the French scientists, his approach to the psychology of crowds was definitely more religious or visionary, a matter of philosophical belief rather than rational analysis and pragmatic speculation.

His lifelong dream was to reach separateness in union, to challenge the division between "you" and "me" without losing the sense of otherness:

> How one craves [. . .] that I and you and my neighbour should each be distinct in clarity from each other, perfectly distinct from the general mass. Then it would be a melody if I walked down the road, if I stood with my neighbour it would be pure harmony. (*STH* 43)

In his fiction, his longing for a successful integration of the individual into the mass is best expressed in lyrical and utopian terms at the end of the unfinished "The Flying Fish" when Gethin Day admires the harmonious and silent underwater ballet of a school of porpoises. The same wordless and happy communion can be found in the description of the collective dance[24] in another unfinished text entitled "Autobiographical Fragment" in *Phoenix*. Why were these texts left unfinished? Were these visions too ideal or too remote from what Lawrence, with his usual sense of relativity, considered the true business of art, namely the "changing rainbow of our living relationships"? (*STH* 175).[25] As we have penetrated further into the era of crowds, many thinkers since Lawrence have taken the same path as he did and expressed in terms sometimes very close to his their desire to save the man in the crowd or to defend otherness. Among them, we may cite: Theodor W. Adorno, Elias Canetti, Georges Bataille, Gilles Deleuze, Emmanuel Lévinas[26] etc. Lawrence even proved to be a philosopher of "difference" or "differ*a*nce" long before Derrida defined it as: "the historical and epochal *unfolding* of being or of ontological difference."[27]

In spite of his repeated attacks on mass civilization, Lawrence never spoke of crowds as a total outsider. Like Darwin and many nineteenth century thinkers, he believed that social life gives meaning to individual life. Even if this did not inspire him with undue optimism, he considered that *there* were his roots, *there* was the soil that would permit the creation of the self which was his lifelong concern.

> Just as a tree is only perfect in blossom because it has groping roots, so is man only perfected in his individual being by his groping, pulsing unison with mankind. The unknown God is within, at the quick. But this quick must send down its roots into the great flesh of mankind. (*K*, 332)

His story "The Man who Loved Islands" reads like a tragic satire of a man who did not love crowds. Divided between his faithfulness to the working-class and the solipsism of the artist, between his scientific curiosity and his spiritual aspirations, he spent most of his life groping for a solution in terms of the smallest possible social unit, the couple or—better still—the author and his privileged reader. It is only in this encounter between two individuals that he finally tried to find the best conditions for real communication.

Cue-Titles

CP de Sola Pinto, Vivian and E. Warren Roberts, ed. *The Complete Poems of D.H. Lawrence*, London: Heinemann, 1964.

CPl Lawrence, D.H. *The Complete Plays*. London: Heinemann, 1970; 1st publ. 1965.

K Lawrence, D.H. *Kangaroo*. Harmondsworth: Penguin Books, 1960; 1st publ. 1923.

L Boulton, James T., ed. *The Letters of D.H. Lawrence*. Cambridge UP, Vol. 1 to 7, 1979–91.

LB Le Bon, Gustave. *Psychologie des foules*. Paris: Presses Universitaires de France, 1963; 1st publ. 1895.

Ph McDonald, Edward D. ed. *Phoenix, The Posthumous Papers of D.H. Lawrence*. London: Heinemann, 1967, first published 1936.

Ph II Roberts, Warren and Harry T.Moore. ed. *Phoenix II, Uncollected, Unpublished and Other Prose Works by D.H. Lawrence*. London: Heinemann, 1968.

PS Lawrence, D.H. *The Plumed Serpent*. Cambridge University Press, 1987.

STH Lawrence, D.H. *Study of Thomas Hardy*. Cambridge University Press, 1985.

T Tarde, Gabriel. *L'Opinion et la foule*. Paris: Presses Universitaires de France, 1989; 1st publ. 1901.

Notes

1. One of the recent studies in this area is Barbara Mensch's *D.H. Lawrence and the Authoritarian Personality* (Macmillan, 1991) which, like a number of other works, sets out to clear Lawrence of any charges of fascism and depicts him, rather oddly, as a defender of equality and a liberal. The author abstains from mentioning the controversial essay "Education of the People."
2. Herbert Spencer, the founder of social Darwinism, applied the laws of selection to social and moral structures and coined the notions of "survival of the fittest" and "the struggle for life."

in 1894, accused Le Bon of plagiarism.

4. Though Le Bon and Tarde are now considered as outdated and reactionary, their ideas are still referred to in many recent studies on the origins of fascism or on crowd psychology; for instance, Zeev Sternhell's *La droite révolutionnaire, Les origines françaises du fascisme* (Paris: Editions du Seuil, 1978) or Serge Moscovici's *L'Age des foules* [*The Age of Crowds*] subtitled *A Historical Treatise on Mass Psychology* (Paris: Fayard, 1981).
5. His reaction to Trotter's *Instinct of the Herd in Peace and War* (1916) was absolutely negative. He returned the book to Dollie Ratford who had lent it to him with this note: "I send you back Trotter also. I didn't like him very much. Oh, I *cannot* stand this scientific talk of instincts and bee communities and wolf packs and such like, as if everything worked from a mechanical basis [. . .] I think all science, but particularly the sciences of psychology and sociology, are loud-mouthed impertinence: impertinent, that is what they are" (20 Dec. 1916), *L III* 59). With Lawrence, a critical attitude of this type never means that the work in question had no impact on him.
6. Freud's essay "Group Psychology and the Analysis of the Ego" is entirely devoted to an analysis of Le Bon's *Psychologie des foules*. He finds that Le Bon shares with him an interest in "the life of the unconscious soul."
7. Oswald Spengler's *Decline of the West* was first published in 1917 (translated into English in 1926–28). Lawrence mentions it in *The First Lady Chatterley* (Harmondsworth: Penguin Books, 1973, p. 18): "by the time *Untergang des Abendlands* appeared, Clifford was a smashed man [. . .]." For Spengler, "cultures are organisms" and our "Faustian" Western civilization is nearing its end. He denounces the power of money, the machine and the masses in modern society.
8. Spengler uses even more pejorative terms to evoke the French revolutionary masses: "dregs of society, rabble, the populace."
9. A theme taken up by Freud in his study of Le Bon.
10. The name "Demogorgon" appears in the works of several authors Lawrence had read: Spenser's *Fairie Queene*, Milton's *Paradise Lost* and Shelley's *Prometheus Unbound*. Lawrence's Demogorgon has much in common with Aristophanes' Demos, a stupid character who personifies the Athenian people in the satirical play entitled "*The Knights*."
11. He had already denounced it in "Education of the People" and does so repeatedly: "It is obvious that the old ideal of Equality won't do" (*Ph* 600).
12. Tarde writes: "in fact, any fruitful initiative is born from individual thought" (*T* 70). Lawrence shares this opinion: "Vitally, intensively, one human being is always more than six collective human beings" ("Education of the People," *Ph* 637).
13. "On Human Destiny."
14. "The Crown"
15. Hippolyte Taine, *Essais et Mélanges Sociologiques*, p. 67–68, quoted by Gabriel Tarde in *L'Opinion et la foule* (Paris: Presses Universitaires de

France, 1989; 1st publ. 1901)

16. In his *One Long Argument. Charles Darwin and the Genesis of Modern Evolutionary Thought* (Harvard University Press, 1991), Ernst Mayr shows that no two authors interpret Darwin in the same way. Among the five main themes of Darwin's theory (evolution, common descent, multiplication of species, gradualism, natural selection), Lawrence seems to retain only the first two in some of his writings, but his position may vary.
17. Hence the logic of making Gerald die in the snow at the end of *Women in Love*.
18. Le Bon, Tarde and many of their followers try to classify the different types of crowds according to various principles. In his essays, Lawrence only takes up Spencer's distinction between masses organized for military domination and masses organized for production. In *Kangaroo*, Chapter XVI, he differentiates between organized mass and mob: "The spirit of vengeance belongs to a mass which is higher than a mob" (323).
19. Patrick Tort insists on what he calls the "reversive effect" of Darwinian selection, referring to a passage from *The Descent of Man* in which Darwin asserts that "natural selection" selects the civilisation which opposes natural selection. ("L'effet réversif de l'évolution" in *Darwinisme et Société*, ed. Patrick Tort. Paris: Presses Universitaires de France, 1992). This was a reassuring and moral complement to the law of natural selection in society.
20. In the introduction to this play, Lawrence represents the war between the proletariat and capitalism as the grotesque fight of two dogs for a bone, one dog being Plebs and the other Bully.
21. The conclusion of *The Origin of Species* shows that Darwin cared about the fate of the individual: "Natural selection acts only for the benefit of each individual [. . .]."
22. *D.H. Lawrence* (London: Harvester Wheatsheaf, 1990)
23. See *Women in Love* p. 54, *The Plumed Serpent* p. 56, *Kangaroo* p. 185.
24. Once again the fish is the ideal model. The dancers are compared to "a shoal of fish or a flock of birds dipping and spreading in the sky." (*Ph* 832).
25. "Morality and the Novel."
26. See T. W. Adorno, *Minima Moralia*, 1951; Elias Canetti, *Masse und Macht*, 1960; George Bataille, *La Part Maudite*, 1967; Gilles Deleuze and Félix Guattari, "Micropolitique et segmentarité" which pays a tribute to Gabriel Tarde, in *Mille Plateaux*, 1980; Emmanuel Lévinas, *Entre Nous, Essais sur le penser-à-l'autre*, 1991.
27. "La différance" in Jacques Derrida, *Marges de la philosohpie* (Paris, Les Editions de Minuit, 1972) p. 23.

11

D. H. Lawrence: Illness, Identity, and Writing

WAYNE TEMPLETON

Susan Sontag once wrote: "One cannot use the life to interpret the work. But one can use the work to interpret the life" (*Saturn* 111). Perhaps, if one can "make selective use of the life" (111), one can do both. Certainly that is my intention in this essay, which began as a quest to ascertain the reasons why Lawrence's fiction changed so dramatically in manner (particularly of characterization), theme, and even methodology, and why, specifically, it changed during the war years. Of course the war itself was one reason, as was his deteriorating relationship with his wife Frieda and with close friends such as John Middleton Murry and Katherine Mansfield. Yet another was the intense despair that began to affect both his life and his writing, especially the work at hand during that time: *Women in Love*, which Lawrence once had seen as a simple sequel to *The Rainbow*. By about 1916, however, it had become a new novel, with a new style of writing and new themes, informed in part by the effects of a world war and, more importantly, of personal anxiety upon individuals. In this respect *Women in Love* (and subsequent novels in other ways) reflects both the psychological and the social components of cultural experience in ways that fundamentally differentiate it from previous novels.

Biography, then, does inform Lawrence's works, which often became significantly different and more complex as they were developed, for they were affected by Lawrence's own ongoing confusion, alienation, and conflicts: his desire to be loved and respected, for example, while simultaneously, for a variety of interrelated reasons, despising the very people and social institutions from which he would command that love and respect. And central to this ambiguity lies an ailment, pulmonary tuberculosis, Lawrence himself rarely referred to, and then (although, as I hope to establish, for sound reasons) only in a decidedly abstruse way;

and yet this ailment not only "strongly influenced . . . [his] life and character" (Meyers 325) but actually reformed his personality and indirectly restructured his art. The ailment's symptoms had devastating effects on Lawrence's sense of self.

From birth Lawrence was chronically ill, and this sickliness, indirectly at least, first began to affect his identity in that attempts to cope caused him to develop certain characteristics, perceptions, and opinions which set him apart from healthier, more conformist peers. Even when he wanted to be accepted (a desire he seldom felt, or at least seldom articulated), he seems to have been continually unsuccessful in any efforts he made. He was a sickly infant. William Edward Hopkin described him at a few weeks old as a "puny, fragile little specimen," while the author himself recalled being "a snuffly-nosed little beggar, seldom without a cold" (Nehls 1: 21). He suffered a variety of respiratory diseases that kept him from school until age seven. This age difference, of little consequence in itself, can perhaps be seen as portentous of the harrowing experiences which were to follow, partly resulting from the fact that to his peers—the sons of Nottinghamshire miners—he was different and therefore an appropriate target of their derision. A boyhood friend, George Neville, later recalled that in contrast to the rowdy, soccer-playing other boys of his age Lawrence was "a thin, pale, weakly lad . . . with no energy for our oft-times over-robust games, and no apparent inclination to attempt to join us." Neville recalled as well "that little, troublesome, hacking cough that used to bring his left hand so sharply to his mouth—a cough and an action that he never lost" (Neville 38, 40).

That cough, which was to plague Lawrence the rest of his life, was a symptom of chronic pulmonary problems, including the tuberculosis from which he eventually died. However, although he suffered that and a number of other symptoms, Lawrence rarely admitted he was ill. Even after he knew the nature of his illness, he would still dismiss his incapacitation as temporary: at worst a comparatively minor irritant that kept him from his work. Even when he was told to his face what he had and that he could only expect to live one year more, he wrote to Dorothy Brett from Mexico (5 February 1925) that his "flu" had "got tangled up with *malaria*: these houses have malaria mosquitoes from that little river, so I am still in bed—having quinine injections shoved into me." And to Curtis Brown ten days later: "Been having the devil of a time with malaria—think it's got under." Only days before his death, in fact, Frieda remembered that when "the doctors examined him and asked him questions about himself, he told them: 'I have had *bronchitis* since I was a fortnight old'" (*Not I But the Wind* . . . 292; emphasis mine).

It may seem odd that Lawrence never mentioned tuberculosis by name. Indeed, he spent most of his adult life flatly denying any chronic ailment and where necessary stating quite boldly that doctors who suggested otherwise were a bunch of quacks. But from earliest childhood, too ill to be a part of normal routine and pastimes, kept out of school for two years because of respiratory problems, Lawrence undoubtedly suffered from what psychologists call an identity crisis. All children, Erik Erikson has noted, as they forge from themselves a sense of self, attempt to detect some meaningful resemblance between what they see in themselves and what observation tells them others judge and expect them to be. This sounds like common sense, Erikson adds: "like all health, however, it is a matter of course only to those who possess it. . . . Only in ill health does one realize the intricacy of the body; and only in crisis . . . does it become obvious what a sensitive combination of interrelated factors the human personality is" (14). When we add to this the philosopher Charles Taylor's definition of self as that which seeks dignity, or "the characteristics by which we think of ourselves as commanding (or failing to command) the respect of those around us" (15), then we can perhaps appreciate that in the face of what he would understandably see as an increasing dissipation of dignity, Lawrence would not openly name or admit to having a chronic, and certainly not a terminal illness. Rather, he would be moved to develop a coping mechanism and even to reinvent himself, as it were: presenting to the world, at least through his essays and novels, a healthy, vibrant, virile D.H. Lawrence (as indeed most people before Moore's biography thought he was).

Besides health and dignity, identity depends upon a sense of oneself as a "being who is growing and becoming" (Taylor 50), a being, therefore, with some sense of both past and future. Indeed, Taylor believes that we can never exhaust the question of who we are, because we are "always . . . changing and *becoming*" (47). A sense of identity, therefore, would be profoundly affected by the realization of a terminal illness, and for a writer this would be compounded by the impending end not just of life but of creation. If for Proust identity depended upon the recovery of the meaningful past, for Lawrence it depended upon the likelihood of a meaningful future, a future he granted himself not only in refuting tuberculosis but also in creating an ideology which was a prescription for survival achievable not instantaneously but over time. We can see in his projected narrative yet another link between identity and writing.

That prescription would comprise a combination of will, determination, and the development of an inner strength; for disease, Lawrence believed, was a symptom of weakness. It was also symptomatic of excess. One of the few times he ever broached the subject of tuberculosis, in an essay on Poe, he elaborated upon this assertion. Tuberculosis, he wrote, is related specifically to an excess of love (by which he meant sexual passion). Such excess becomes disintegrative because it breaks down that which is and must remain "intrinsically isolate and single" in an individual, causing "the neuroticism of the day." And excess is the "prime cause of tuberculosis" because the excitement involved weakens the "sympathetic tensions of the chest—the lungs—or the throat, or of the lower brain, and the tubercles are given a ripe field" (*Studies* 75–77). Given the number of Lawrence's affairs, often concurrent, before 1911 (the year I believe his tuberculosis became active), the juxtaposition of those two phenomena—the "excess" and then the tuberculosis—may have seemed to him more than coincidence. Of greater relevance here is that after 1911 those affairs stopped abruptly, and he also severed his relationship with Louie Burrows, the woman to whom he was engaged to be married.[1]

This assumption of excess is not so eccentric as it may seem. In *Illness as Metaphor* Susan Sontag notes that the Victorians were convinced illness was a punishment for moral dereliction and since tuberculosis, or consumption as it was then termed, invariably led to impotence while at the same time heightening sexual desire (modern researchers speculate that this is a result of the slight but constant fever the ailment produces), it was a particularly vengeful and therefore appropriate punishment (*Metaphor* 4–7). The belief, in other words, is that the individual causes the disease; by the early twentieth century this was thought to be a consequence of repression and especially with tuberculosis, of repressed passion. This, again, is of particular relevance in a consideration of Lawrence, who also accepted the common belief that sexual intercourse is potentially the most debilitating of activities, for it involves an expense of energy not easily regained. What Lawrence had to do, obviously, was to release sexuality from repression while at the same time harnessing it. This would be achieved, he suggested (in *Women in*

Love, for example), by releasing the body transcendentally from the oppressiveness of both reason and illness, or weakness, and by expanding the notion of non-intellectual experience generally. This would entail a kind of epistemological re-engagement: being aware of primary sensations before they are objectified by mental processes. He called this "blood-consciousness."

Before continuing an investigation of Lawrence's responses to terminal illness, I think it advisable first to attempt a more definite date of contraction and then to consider the tuberculosis itself. There is reason to believe that Lawrence may have initially acquired the disease even earlier, during childhood, after which it characteristically remained dormant for several years; however, the illness he experienced while teaching at Croydon in 1911, shortly after his mother's death, definitely was tuberculosis. This fact, of course, is not mentioned in his "Autobiographical Sketch" wherein he admitted to pneumonia from which he nearly did not recover during the winter of 1901–02, but added, casually, that after his mother died he "went on teaching for another year, and then again a bad pneumonia illness intervened. When I got better I did not go back to school" (594). At the time of his illness in 1911, however, there is evidence that even he believed it was more serious than that. Certainly his sister Ada did; in a letter to Edward Garnett, 2 December, she wrote that although her brother was recovering, there was still the possibility of a relapse. Fifteen days later, apparently after Lawrence had assured her that it was only pneumonia, she wrote again to Garnett that he had "really made wonderful progress the last week. The report concerning the expectoration was very satisfactory. No [tubercular] germs were discovered, and since then both lungs have almost completely cleared up. Of course my brother will be very liable to consumption and as the doctors say will always need great care. He has to give up school too" (Jefferson 146).

On the same day, to the same man, Lawrence was even more optimistic, and typically disdainful of the medical profession. "The doctor says I mustn't go to school again," he wrote, "or I shall be consumptive. But he doesn't know." Was Lawrence not telling the truth? Or did he in fact *not* have tuberculosis? Or had he been misdiagnosed? On the one hand the latter was possible in 1911, when little was known of the disease. On the other hand, a substantial body of evidence exists which clearly indicates that Lawrence did have the disease as early as 1911 and that what he wrote and what he told family and friends was an understatement of the kind he was to use to describe his health for the rest of his life. Richard Aldington has written that in November of 1911 "Lawrence was smitten with tubercular pneumonia affecting both lungs," leaving him "weak and with shattered health, always thereafter under the threat of tuberculosis, which suspended its attack but never left him." This has been corroborated in Jeffrey Meyers' biography by the observation of Dr. William Ober that the illness of 1911 may very well have been a reactivation of "an arrested juvenile tubercular infection" (73). Aldington adds that the doctor warned Lawrence that "he must give up school-teaching and 'live out of doors.'" That, Aldington believed, was a "polite way of telling him that with tuberculosis he would not be allowed again in schoolrooms" (97–98).

Helen Corke has also corroborated this in her memoirs, where she recalled that Lawrence had contracted pneumonia after being caught in a rainstorm en route to the Garnetts "one November evening" in 1911. During his convalescence "it was discovered . . . that he had tuberculosis, though he would never admit it and, indeed, was never heard to pronounce the word. He realized, however, that it meant the end of his career as a teacher, for nobody with a history of TB was permitted to work in school" (Hahn 55). Echoing Corke's recollections, Ford Madox Ford,[2] by than a close associate, wrote in his memoirs that during the previous year Lawrence had already suffered not only from the loss of his mother but also from the daily toil of teaching: of being "subject to the drag of the minds of the schoolchildren for hours of every day in a fetid atmosphere," after which, even though of "tired mind," he would write "in the odd moments of silence" during the evenings. "And then came the scourge! He was pronounced tubercular . . . I don't think he ever mentioned it to me; perhaps he did not to anyone. It was a subject that he was always shy of mentioning" (319). Nevertheless, his friends and relatives knew what the problem was, as did the Kent County Council who refused to renew his teaching contract. Consumption was even the reason given for his exemption from active military duty during the war.[3]

Even more indisputable evidence of tuberculosis can be discovered once we are aware of its symptoms, many of which were evident to those who knew Lawrence, especially those with experience of tuberculosis: Katherine Mansfield, for example, and the friends who watched her succumb to the disease. Some are evident even to us as we read about the man. He was often sick, or sickly, pale, gaunt, increasingly so as he lost weight in later years, flat or hollow-chested, lacking in physical stamina, although this was often overlooked because he had a nervous energy, and with that an irritability and aggressiveness which seemed to imply great stamina. He often suffered from loss of appetite, fever, rapid pulse, night sweating and nightmares, chronic coughing and expectoration, hemoptysis—hemorrhaging of the blood vessels and the coughing up of blood—and a raspy, asthmatic breathing. Although some of these symptoms can be attributed to other, related, diseases, such as bronchopneumonia, acute lobar pneumonia, or bronchitis, taken together, especially as chronic symptoms, they point clearly to tuberculosis.

This brings us to a consideration of the disease itself. Tuberculosis is a contagious malady, although not highly so, contracted from another's heavy coughing or sputum, or in infants from contaminated milk. Before the development of penicillin it was a common disease, particularly in the first quarter of the twentieth century when, exacerbated by poor working conditions, poor diets, and no cure, it reached epidemic proportions. In 1930 the mortality rate in Britain per 100,000, although declining, was estimated to be near 100; the rate was highest for men in the 45–54 year range (158 per 100,000). People of the working class had the highest overall rate—unskilled labourers: 267 per 100,000 compared to 94 for the upper class and 76 for farmers (see Clarke; Long; Mooney). This rate was because the contaminated air of the work environment and crowded working conditions caused an increase in irritated lung tissue, thus making the individual more susceptible and increasing the likelihood of contagion. Tuberculosis was particularly endemic in coal-mining towns where coal dust, silica, and asbestos—fine enough to be spread throughout a town by normal airflow—eventually cause the formation of scar tissue in the lungs. This in turn destroys large areas of lung tissue as well as lymph nodes, which are responsible for the creation of lymphocytes, the basis of bacilli destruction and immunization. After sufficient exposure to these contaminating industrial dusts, the lungs are no longer immune to pulmonary diseases, of which tuberculosis is the most common.

Medical research has determined that there are two states of pulmonary tuberculosis: the primary, or initial, and the secondary, or chronic. The first is usually contracted at an early age, but the children who experience it are usually strong enough and have healthy enough lungs to develop an indigenous immunization. However, where a large dose of tubercle bacilli is ingested, or when the child's resistance is low as the result of having suffered other pulmonary diseases, the bacilli can spread before resistance can be accomplished, resulting in secondary infection. This infection can often lie dormant for some time, although usually by the age of 40 or so even the strongest individual succumbs as aging itself lowers resistance. In a person suffering other pulmonary problems, however, the disease usually begins to be active by late adolescence or early adulthood, especially if the individual suffers a traumatic experience or chronic anxiety. This certainly describes Lawrence in Croydon in 1911, as he struggled to continue teaching while trying simultaneously to become a writer, plagued by doubts concerning both pursuits, troubled by several of his relationships with women, and grieving the recent death of his mother.

During the chronic stage, heavy coughing of blood occurs as the bacilli erode blood vessels in the lungs. As the disease then spreads, it travels through the bloodstream either to the brain, causing tubercular meningitis, or—partly as the result of ingestion of coughed-up particles of bacilli-contaminated blood—to other organs, mostly those of the reproductory system. In men these include the testes and the prostate, where they in turn form lesions in the prostate and seminal vesicles. This spread does not necessarily result in outward symptoms but does invariably lead to the destruction of these vesicles, and therefore to sterility and impotency.

The increased likelihood of tubercular reactivation following trauma, the refusal to accept the fact of a terminal illness (a refusal likely contributing to trauma), the nervous energy, a probable consequence of the slight but continuous fever associated with the disease, and with that an increase in work: all these characterize a considerable number of other, particularly artistic, tubercular victims (Kafka, Chopin, Beardsley come to mind). They are certainly also true of Lawrence, who worked ceaselessly, obsessively, often on several projects at once, and who was sickly, temperamental, and restless for most of his adult life. But while these symptoms definitely affected his personality, his relationships, the extent and even the style of his work, none would have been more significant than sterility and impotence, which relate directly to the sexual ideology that informs some of his best and most famous works.

That he was in fact suffering these symptoms is highly probable, given the medical evidence and the supportive biographical evidence, including most recently that of Jeffrey Meyers, who rather casually lists "sexual impotence" as one of the various symptoms of tuberculosis from which Lawrence suffered (325), and who states later that "though sterile," he enjoyed "healthy physical relations with Frieda" (331).[4] As early as 1911 the doctors were advising Lawrence either to abstain from sexual intercourse or to accept the probability of sterility. This can be confirmed by the fact that he had at one time considered marriage and children—"'You know,'" he used to tell Helen Corke, "'when I'm middle-aged, I shall probably be . . . settled, and take my family to church every Sunday—Best so'" (Corke 62)—but then, rather abruptly, he wrote to Louie Burrows after his illness that he had been "thinking what the doctor at Croydon and the doctor at Bournemouth both urged on me: that I ought not to marry, at least for a long time, if ever. And I feel myself my health is so precarious, I wouldn't undertake the responsibility" (4 February 1912). Although the former, to Helen Corke, is partly a romanticization, and the latter a way of ending his engagement with Louie, nevertheless he was not fabricating advice but, rather, choosing in his subsequent relationship with Frieda to ignore it.

In a letter to Catherine Carswell, cited by Paul Delany, John Middleton Murry wrote that "'Lawrence was incapable of begetting children and that at one time he was deeply distressed by it.' The time referred to would most likely be late 1914, since before then the two couples [the Lawrences and the Murrys] had not been in close and continuous contact." This failure, Delany speculates, "would inevitably arouse jealousy of Weekley [Ernest, Frieda's first husband, who at the time] . . . still regularly offered to take Frieda back, and who had fathered her three children. Lawrence admitted this rivalry in 'Meeting Among the Mountains,' where the poet, encountering a brown-eyed peasant driving a bullock wagon, is reminded of Weekley." As in real life, there is no overt action in the poem; instead the poet "is 'frozen' and his lungs 'turned to stone' as if Lawrence himself were subconsciously accepting impotency and tuberculosis as condign punishments for ousting Weekley from Frieda's affections" (Delany 22–23).[5]

It is apparent elsewhere as well that the early prowess, manifested in a number of affairs before the autumn of 1911, had become by the war years somewhat "cerebral. . . . It might not be true," wrote Cecil Gray, "to say that Lawrence was literally and absolutely impotent—this, I am assured on medical authority, is a very rare physical condition—but I am certain that he was not very far removed from it" (Nehls 1: 436–37). Although according to *Mr Noon* he may have been only sterile during the first years of their marriage, according to Frieda by 1926 Lawrence was completely impotent. Long before then, however, he had begun discussing sexuality as an abstraction, as an artistic theme, as a means of satisfying "bodily and spiritual want . . . in one and the same draught," for it "seems to me," he wrote Henry Savage (31 October 1913)—interestingly, after having spent more than a year with Frieda in Europe—

> that the chief thing about a woman—who is much of a woman—is that in the long run she is not to be had . . . by any of the catch words, love, beauty, honor, duty, worth, work, salvation—none of them—not in the long run. In the long run she only says 'Am I satisfied, or is there some beastly unsatisfaction gnawing and gnawing inside of me.' . . . So she goes for man, or men, after her own fashion, and so is called a Sphinx, and her riddle is that the man wasn't able to satisfy her—riddle enough for him: And an artist—a poet—is like a woman in that he too must have this satisfaction.

In that letter we see the beginning of Lawrence's coping mechanism: his program for recovery. How *does* he contend with a woman he cannot satisfy and with an artistic vision of (among other things) virility, sexuality, that growing awareness of the need to be both sexually and intellectually mature that we see Paul Morel experiencing? How can even artistic vision offer an alternative to the plight of Siegmund MacNair if the artist is being betrayed by his own body? The solution would have to focus on a quest for strength and sources of strength other than the usual or the obvious. It would have to deal with ways to end conflicts between the mind and the body, for certainly his mind was strong and willing. It would have to embrace the notion of will and determination, of mind over matter, and it would also find in the body itself another spring, another source of energy, for mind over matter by itself is simply another way of describing post-Enlightenment Europe, that industrial world which Birkin hates so much: a "vast abstraction of ice and snow" which fulfills only the "mystery of ice-destructive knowledge, snow-abstract annihilation" (*Women in Love* 254).

This ideology, which would have a profound effect upon Lawrence and his writing, particularly *The Rainbow* and *Women in Love*, Lawrence first began to develop seriously in his "Foreword" to *Sons and Lovers* in

January, 1913, and then in his long essay, "Study of Thomas Hardy" (1914), in which he describes the need for individuals to acknowledge and develop the other side—which for men he called the "feminine side" —of the self.[6] This ideology, which required an equilibrium to be established between what he termed Will-to-Motion (the intellectual, rational side) and Will-to-Inertia (the instinctual, sensuous side), Lawrence derived primarily from Henri Bergson's notion of the *élan vital* and from Schopenhauer, a philosopher famous for his celebration of the will.[7] "In the healthy state," the latter once wrote, "the will lies at the foundation of all organic functions; but with the appearance of disorders that threaten its whole work, it is vested with dictatorial power, in order to subdue the rebellious forces . . . [that is, the disease], and to lead everything back on to the right track" (Schopenhauer 2: 260).

By willing himself to be strong, Lawrence would throw off the disease, and while this may seem rather rashly optimistic, in fact he extended by about ten years the average life expectancy of a tuberculous victim before the advent of antibiotics. He did so by making death subordinate to life, ill-health subordinate to recovery. And he had reason to believe he would succeed, partly from having by this time become acquainted as well with the works of William James, a man who argued from personal experience that the will could achieve a harmony between mind and body whereby the vitality of the former would be channeled to the ailing latter. Lawrence had read several of James' works by this time, including *The Varieties of Religious Experience*, where James states that if the divided self is to be unified, the two forces humans possess, "one carnal, the other spiritual," must be "harmonious and well balanced" (144, 147). Lawrence had also read *The Principles of Psychology*, in which James included a long chapter titled "Will," where he argues that just as the will can repeatedly produce a sense of pleasure, so too can it be trained to dissipate pain. James believed that through sheer determination he could cure himself and as he was pleased to testify, in the years following his decision to act upon his theory of free will, his health improved quite remarkably.

What is noteworthy here is not just that James or Lawrence believed in the will but that they committed themselves to these convictions: James in the testimonials and case studies that form an important part of his work, and Lawrence in his essays and especially in his fiction, where strong characters without purpose invariably disintegrate and die while physically weaker characters, often suffering from ill-health as well but possessing determination, survive and even prosper or are on the verge of doing so as the narrative ends. For the writer, Charles Altieri has observed, art is particularly effective in this, for art entails a process of objectification necessary for self-reflection. Self-awareness, in other words, is achieved through expression (Altieri 236), which as a means of directing the will works well by providing a model or blueprint expressed publicly, thus urging its author to commitment and responsibility. Further to this, Taylor points out, there is invariably a valuable additional need to forge a new language in order to bring to expression "the meaningful forms and relationships which undergird . . . ordinary perception, as they emerge and take shape from the materiality of things" (468).

In attempting to make use of the will and in his terms to work towards a balance between Will-to-Motion and Will-to-Inertia, thus achieving a revitalization of self, Lawrence begins with the belief that we do not *have* a self as we have, say, a head or an arm. Identity is neither stable nor finite but more like a soul, greater than the sum of its parts and constantly in a state of flux. For that reason he was not interested in self-interpretation (he hated Freud), but self-discovery: not being but becoming. He also was not interested in unity and certainly not in the post-Enlightenment version of unity in which sensibility or the instinct is subordinated, even vanquished, by reason.[8] Following from Bergson, what Lawrence wanted is what has been called unmediated unity, or in Blakean terms a polarized or dualistic identity. Here Lawrence was particularly influenced by Bergson's doctrine of the *irreducibility* of experience to external explanation: the *élan vital*. "An *individual*," Lawrence once wrote, "is that which is not divided or not dividable" ("Democracy" 74).

To talk about a state of flux does not mean of course that there is no such thing as a substantial self; indeed Kant, in refuting Hume's argument that this is precisely the case, asserted in his "Third Paralogism" (*Critique of Pure Reason*) that the "dictum of certain ancient schools, that everything in the world is *in a flux* and nothing is *permanent* and abiding . . . is not refuted by [a belief in] the unity of self-consciousness," for although "we must necessarily judge that we are one and the same throughout the whole time of which we are conscious . . . we are unable from our own consciousness to determine whether, as souls, we are permanent or not" (342–43). In other words, while a person changes throughout a lifetime, that person does not consider those changes substantial enough to see himself or herself as a different person. In fact Rey believes that identity should not even be our primary concern, for it is *survival* that matters most, and survival depends not upon identity but "our continuing identity" (43), which Lewis defines as the relationship between "the I who exists now and the surviving I who will, I hope, still exist then"—in the future (18). And while of course survival presupposes identity, Rey argues for an identity not only in flux but consisting equally of what he calls "*bodily* and psychological criteria" (58; emphasis mine).

Lawrence, although defining identity as constantly changing, at the same time also clearly perceived self wholistically.[9] For him an individual ceases to exist *in divido*; separated into parts, as the Latin expression implies, it is ultimately destroyed. As a result there also can be no superior part such as the mind. To Lawrence the mind was only one part of a functioning self, and while it along with the nervous system is often perceived as being more important for being cognitive, he argues that this need not be—that we possess a physical cognitive ability as well, which he variously termed intuition, blood consciousness, sensuality, or, as Birkin describes it, "the great dark knowledge you can't have in your head—the dark involuntary being" which is "death to one's self—but it is the coming into being of another" (*Women in Love* 43).

James Cowan has pointed out that at one point in *Lady Chatterley's Lover* Connie states that "I believe in the resurrection of the body" (87). Cowan writes that Lawrence intended Connie to mean this literally, as he did. "For Lawrence, 'a resurrection of the body' meant, in part, 'resurrection of the flesh'" (56). He believed in a "resurgence of the flesh and the deep, intuitive knowledge available to [a] man through sensual awareness [blood consciousness] as equal in value to the mind and the mental–spiritual knowledge elevated by the Protestant–capitalist–materialist ethos of modern industrial society. If the emphasis in Western culture upon rational, objective knowledge validated in the laboratory may be seen as the masculine thrust of spirit, the externalization of Idea . . . then Lawrence's reaffirmation of intuitive, subjective knowledge validated experientially in the body is an attempt to redeem the feminine, the inward, the mutable as a significant mode of knowing lost to whole generations immured in the scientific method" (57).[10]

This is the Will–to–Inertia, which must develop alongside Will–to–Motion. This is also a rejection of the spiritual, external, abstract, intellectual, scientific worlds of the Church, which held that the problem was moral, the solution in God's determinist hands, and of medicine, which pompously claimed that Lawrence had an incurable disease. (Rhys Davies, whose offers on more than one occasion to find a doctor for Lawrence as he coughed up blood and struggled to breathe were rejected, wrote: "It seemed to me that he believed a submission to medical art was an act of treachery to the power within him, his gods" [Nehls 3: 315].) Lawrence was engaged in an exploration, in the feminine, of an alternative source of vitality, and in blood consciousness, of a differently focussed will even than James's. I would point out, by the way, that although he sought in Will-to-Inertia physical renewal—progress, in other words—he was not being contradictory. As Daleski notes, Will-to-Inertia has to do with roots, eternality, feeling, "full life in the body," nature, while Will-to-Motion, although having to do with knowledge, mind, spirit, "multiplicity and diversity," also includes community, "self-subordination," "service of an idea" (30). In other words, in *personal* (as opposed to social) terms the mental life is one of stasis and abstraction (note that Lawrence uses the term motion and not movement), while the physical life is one of regeneration, vitality, and concrete relation to nature. This is the ideal, of course. For the victim of tuberculosis the opposite tends in fact to be true: the fevered mind is highly active while the body is lethargic, often incapacitated, even impotent.

As Cowan points out, from the ideal introduced in "Study of Thomas Hardy," Lawrence developed a "vitalist philosophy . . . rooted in a nonanthropomorphic religion whose gods 'were not *beings*, but symbols of elemental powers'" (60). This he elaborated in *Psychoanalysis and the Unconscious* and *Fantasia of the Unconscious*, where he reveals his belief in the existence of not two but "four great primary centres of consciousness" (*Fantasia* 97): two objective, on the upper plane of being, and two subjective, on the lower plane. The latter, Lawrence points out, is where the evolution to *homo sapiens* began, because in the beginning was *not* the word. Language comes later, on the upper plane, where it describes and intellectualizes (and kills) the life that came before it. The lower plane is also where the source of individual vitality resides, for there we find our central reality: the "spontaneous, living, individual soul" (*Fantasia* 183). While this is an "intuitive" system, based not on "objective fact but on metaphor," the value for Lawrence "lies in formulating a personal myth to affirm what the body knows as opposed to what the mind knows" (Cowan 62). And what the body knows is that it can overcome TB.

Oscar Wilde states in *The Critic as Artist* that part of the value of a work of art lies in its independence from the intellect that engendered it. This is what we want, he believed: "'we desire the concrete, and nothing but the concrete can satisfy us.' . . . In Art, as in the dance, 'the body is the soul'" (Kermode 46). In *Mr Noon* Lawrence makes the same distinction—the soul, different from the spirit, is the repository of or lies at the centre of an individual's vitality (on the lower, the concrete or physical, plane of being). Here we find the *élan vital*, the imaginative or creative as opposed to the simply mimetic, and, related to that, what Taylor calls the potential for epiphany: that additional revelation of something previously inaccessible, or some greater significance. And here we see how Lawrence might believe he could achieve an epiphany—in this case (re)create himself (as a man with a curable pulmonary problem)—because he was no longer held in check by Western rationalism or by the notion of humanity reflecting or embodying something of the perfection of God. Interestingly, to do this he *has* to refute modern psychology and especially Freudian psychology because it too suggests that we are, by the age of six or so, firmly established psychologically. Not coincidentally, the psychologist Lawrence showed most interest in—Trigant Burrow—believed that the modern sense of self is an image the individual holds to be true, although it is often an idealistic image and thus more of a goal than a reflection. It is, however, an image that can be changed. And as the image changes, so too does the identity. This is of course related to James's concept of will and his belief that one can be what one wants to be if one possesses sufficient determination. To will is first to desire; it is in modern psychological terms a matter of both conation (desire or inclination) and volition (free choice) leading to resolve. For Lawrence it was also, as I have said, a matter of vitality and of finding a second source of vitality, for the original one was being depleted. Here the soul, or body as soul, becomes relevant.

In *Mr Noon* the narrator tells us that the soul is "that deep core of individual unity where life itself, the very God, throbs incalculably, whose throbbing unfolds the leaves and stem of the body, and brings forth the flower of the mind and the spirit. But the spirit is not the soul. Ah no. The soul has deep fibrilled foliage in the damp earth, has its dark leaves in the air" (189). The soul is the primal, sensual tree of life through which flows "the dark sap of life, stream of eternal blood" and in it resides as well the "gorgeous mystery of sensual individuality" (190). So the soul, the body, contains the sap of life *and* individuality: vitality *and* identity. This means that a body, though racked with tuberculosis, is capable of healing itself so long as the sufferer is in touch with —can tap—this source of vitality. We are speaking here of the feminine side: the intuitive, non-scientific, physical plane of being. The soul, which is concrete, is opposed to the abstract spirit, the body to the mind, sickness (including psychological sickness: neurosis, repressed desire) to health, social being to individual or personal being.

I think it possible to see Lawrence's philosophy at this point as one that also calls for a move from passivity and stasis (which he believed endemic in Western civilization) to personal choice and regeneration. The spirit, products of the mind, etc., are abstract trifles, blown about by the winds of time; life—and not just human life—realizes its continuum (its permanence or immortality) and its universal significance in the physical. In Romantic terms the body thus becomes the symbol of life and especially of life everlasting. I am not sure Lawrence would have been comfortable with this use of "symbol"; nevertheless he does seem to come close to suggesting that there is a communalism here—that we are not so much autonomous trees as branches tapping into a common source of vitality.[11]

The remaining question here is: Did Lawrence succeed? And the obvious answer is that ultimately of course he did not; he died at the age of forty-four. However, it also seems clear that he did not succumb passively to the tuberculosis that killed him at such an early age—he did not "stew in his consumption" as he accused Katherine Mansfield of doing—but fought to overcome the illness, to repudiate its "evil force" (Nehls 3: 315), and to live his life as fully as he could. If he failed it was not in personal but theoretical, ideological terms, and it was also not the failure of the individual but of relationships, a failure most clearly dramatized in *The Rainbow* and especially in *Women in Love* where, as I have argued elsewhere,[12] the Birkin marriage ends as a result of a further relational problem: that of the individual to society. Part of the reason for these failures is that relationships served within his coping mechanism as scapegoats. Rather than becoming depressed or disillusioned with his own incapacity, Lawrence would instead criticize society and the institution of marriage, for reasons similar to those articulated by Rupert Birkin, who at one point sees connubial satisfaction and bondage as synonymous. (See, for example, *Women in Love* 199–200.)

Theoretically, in his essays, he solved this problem by assuming that two like-minded people could live in harmony because each would automatically accept the other's need for autonomy while simultaneously and intuitively knowing when that other would conversely require assistance or support. But because he was a talented novelist who could create characters with independent lives, when he came to applying the theory those characters—whom he always (for the first few novels at least) allowed the freedom to resist didactic authority—could not conform. As Ursula and Rupert discover in their attempt to reify his idea of freedom in love, it is impossible to retain complete independence and still be part of a relationship. A compromise must be agreed to, on both sides, and yet while that seems commonsensical and fairly straightforward, Lawrence appears to have resisted (i.e., his characters do not do this), possibly because the devastating effects of tuberculosis mediated against such action in his life. He could not, and his characters often would not, relent. For Lawrence that meant never admitting to his illness and never weakening in his conviction that each person must be as strong, as self-assured, as convinced of the essential value of his or her own uniqueness as possible in order that individuals could then form meaningful relationships within a new society whose values and goals reflected human needs and desires.

This was the dilemma with which Lawrence and some of his most significant, most complex characters continually wrestled. And yet in some respects that in itself—the lack of resolution—accounts for much of Lawrence's greatness as a novelist. And, too, the specific nature of his illness, and especially the psychological consequences of it, help establish the link between the artist and the man, between the social and the personal, by revealing enigma, contradiction, and suffering as evidence supporting the belief that literature cannot be written in a vacuum, but must derive from the artist's experience. For Lawrence, perhaps the most profound component of that experience was tuberculosis, a disease, as he struggled to vanquish it, which led him to the discovery of insightful observations concerning human behavior and potential. The most significant and yet deceptively simple of these he recorded on the last page of his final work, *Apocalypse*. "For man," he wrote, "the vast marvel is to be alive. For man, as for flower and beast and bird, the supreme triumph is to be most vividly, most perfectly alive" (149). It was an ideal which he had upheld, personally and artistically, all his life.

Notes

1. This raises the question, of course: why, and especially so soon after ending his engagement with Louie, did Lawrence turn to Frieda? Daniel Schneider speculates that it had something to do with her foreignness, that like Tom Brangwen with Lydia Lensky, he embued her with the magical ability to solve his problems, to grant him a new life, a rebirth. "I feel as if I can't breathe while we're in England," he wrote her on the eve of their departure for Germany (*Letters*, 1: 389, 30 April 1912). In Germany he would breathe again, he would absorb some of the vitality of this woman Catherine Carswell once described as a "force of nature" (Nehls 1: 394). Frieda von Richthofen Weekley was also remarkably different from Louie Burrows: she was strong, independent-minded, experienced in love and life, a mother and perhaps in certain respects a mother figure.
2. I realize that Ford is not always reliable, but in this instance his statements are not out of line with those of other witnesses, or with medical literature on the subject, which notes that stress and trauma are invariably at least partially responsible for the activation of TB.
3. "I got my complete exemption," he wrote Barbara Low, 8 July 1916, "because I was able, spiritually, to manage the doctors. . . . I said [to the military doctor] the doctors said I had had consumption." According to Zytaruk and Boulton, he apparently had a certificate from Dr. Ernest Jones attesting to the fact that he did have chronic tuberculosis (*Letters* 2: 623n3).
4. Even more recently, John Worthen has observed: "It has been claimed that DHL's [sic] illness 'made him sterile'; the claim rests on the assumption that DHL's pneumonia [the bout of 1901] was followed by 'a serious illness, rather like mumps.'" He concludes that the "case for his sterility is unproven" (527n82).

   It is certainly unproven if pneumonia in 1901 followed by a mump-like illness is said to be the cause. But this story comes from Barbara Weekley, hardly a reasonable source in a discussion of events that occurred a decade before she had ever heard of the man.
5. In a conversation I had with Paul Delany in June, 1993, he said that he wished to retract the suggestion that Lawrence was responsible for the lack of children. This was because Frieda, who had had several unprotected sexual liaisons since the birth of her last child, had not become pregnant, indicating that it was more likely she who was sterile. But medical research prevents us from eliminating Lawrence, leading to the ironic conclusion that perhaps both were sterile. Whatever the case, Delany's analysis of Lawrence's recorded problems with Weekley, especially as dramatized in "Meeting Among the Mountains," is insightful, and Murry's sense of Lawrence's distress also, I believe, sheds light on this complex state of affairs.
6. See Daleski, Ch. 1 for further discussion of this ideology.
7. For a time he considered Nietzsche as well, but by the time of *Women in Love*

he refuted his idea of *Wille zur Macht*. Lawrence was interested in becoming, not being, and certainly not in power. For a lengthier discussion of this, see Foster, Ch. 4.

8. See Horkheimer and Adorno for an elaboration of this subject. Their discussion coincides with Lawrence's views on Western civilization as being ruled by an hegemony of reason.
9. I tend to use the terms "self" and "identity" interchangeably, defining the former as basically the Old English version of the Latin *idem*—that which is unique about a person, or more or less consistently the same (*idem*=same). Sometimes the distinction is made between identity as uniqueness and self as that which maintains uniqueness. Some psychologists see identity in terms of roles; de Levita, for example, defines self as "the sum total of one's reflections upon oneself" and identity as "the cluster of roles one is enacting, i.e., the psychological representatives of these roles" (110). Using these definitions we could say that Lawrence as self is a chronically ill man, but as identity is a determined, willful man who *identifies* with health, harmony, vitality, will. Schachtel, who similarly associates identity with role, persona, personality (73, 75), also points out further distinctions other psychologists have made between, for example, the "real self" and the "idealized self-image" (74).
10. In "The Man Who Died," written the year before *Lady Chatterley's Lover*, Lawrence makes a similar point. The man who died does not die in the flesh and ascend in the flesh to Heaven, as he was expected to do. Rather, he transcends the petty life of the flesh—of excess, and greed—to achieve the greater life of the body, a life full of vitality and virtue, similar to the cock's. He achieves "his immortality of being alive without fret" (180), a goal his author had sought for some years.
11. See his review of Trigant Burrow's *The Social Basis of Consciousness*, and a letter to Aldous Huxley (14 November 1927) in which he describes Beethoven's inability to have meaningful relations as his "crucifixion into isolate individuality."
12. See *States of Estrangement*, especially Chs. 4 and 5.

Works Cited

Aldington, Richard. *Portrait of a Genius But. . . .* 1950. New York: Collier Books, 1961.

Allen, Gay Wilson. *William James: A Biography*. New York: Viking, 1967.

Altieri, Charles. *Canons and Consequences: Reflections on the Ethical Force of Imaginative Ideals*. Evanston, IL: Northwestern UP, 1990.

Clarke, Brice R. *Causes and Prevention of Tuberculosis*. Baltimore: Williams and Wilkins, 1952.

Corke, Helen. *D.H. Lawrence: The Croydon Years*. Austin: U of Texas P, 1965.

Cowan, James C. "D.H. Lawrence and the Resurrection of the Body." In *Healing*

Arts in Dialogue: Medicine and Literature. Ed. Joanne Trautmann. Carbondale: Southern Illinois UP, 1981.

Daleski, H.M. *The Forked Flame: A Study of D.H. Lawrence*. Evanston, IL: Northwestern UP, 1965.

Erikson, Erik. *Young Man Luther*. New York: Norton, 1958.

Ford, Ford Madox. *Your Mirror to My Times*. New York: Holt, Rinehart and Winston, 1971.

Foster, John Burt, Jr. *Heirs to Dionysus: A Nietzschean Current in Literary Modernism*. Princeton, NJ: Princeton UP, 1981.

Goodheart, Eugene. *The Utopian Vision of D.H. Lawrence*. Chicago: The U of Chicago P, 1963.

Green, Martin. *The von Richthofen Sisters: The Triumphant and the Tragic Modes of Love*. New York: Basic Books, 1974.

Hahn, Emily. *Lorenzo: D.H. Lawrence and the Women Who Loved Him*. New York: J.B. Lippincott, 1975.

Horkheimer, Max, and Theodor W. Adorno. *Dialectic of Enlightenment*. Trans. John Cumming. 1944. New York: The Seabury Press, 1972.

James, William. *The Principles of Psychology*. 1890. Cambridge: Harvard UP, 1981.

———. *The Varieties of Religious Experience*. 1902. New York: Macmillan, 1961.

Jefferson, George. *Edward Garnett: A Life in Literature*. London: Jonathan Cape, 1982.

Kant, Immanuel. *Critique of Pure Reason*. Trans. Norman Kemp Smith. 1787. New York: St. Martin's Press, 1965.

Kermode, Frank. *Romantic Image*. London: Routledge and Kegan Paul, 1957.

Lawrence, D.H. *Apocalypse and the Writings on Revelation*. Cambridge: Cambridge UP, 1980.

———. "Autobiographical Sketch." *Phoenix II: Uncollected, Unpublished, And Other Prose Works by D.H. Lawrence*. Ed. Warren Roberts and Harry T. Moore. Harmondsworth: Penguin, 1978. 300–302.

———. *The Complete Poems*. Ed. Vivian de Sola Pinto and F. Warren Roberts. Harmondsworth: Penguin, 1977.

———. "Democracy." *Reflections on the Death of a Porcupine and Other Essays*. Ed. Michael Herbert. Cambridge: Cambridge UP, 1988. 61–83.

———. Foreword to *Sons and Lovers*. *The Letters of D.H. Lawrence*. Ed. Aldous Huxley. London: Heinemann, 1932. 95–102.

———. *The Letters of D.H. Lawrence*. Eds. James Boulton et al. 6 vols. to date. Cambridge: Cambridge UP, 1979– .

———. *Lady Chatterley's Lover*. Harmondsworth: Penguin, 1961.

———. *Mr Noon*. Ed. Lindeth Vasey. Cambridge: Cambridge UP, 1984.

———. *Psychoanalysis and the Unconscious* and *Fantasia of the Unconscious*. New York: Viking, 1960.

———. *The Rainbow*. Ed. Mark Kinkead-Weekes. Cambridge: Cambridge UP, 1989.

———. Rev. of *The Social Basis of Consciousness*, by Trigant Burrow. *Phoenix: The Posthumous Papers of D.H. Lawrence*. Ed. Edward D. McDonald. Harmonds-

worth: Penguin, 1978. 377–82.
———. *St. Mawr and the Man Who Died*. New York: Vintage, 1953.
———. *Studies in Classic American Literature*. New York: Doubleday, 1951.
———. "Study of Thomas Hardy." *Study of Thomas Hardy and Other Essays*. Ed. Bruce Steele. Cambridge: Cambridge UP, 1985. 3–132.
———. *Twilight in Italy. D.H. Lawrence and Italy*. New York: Viking, 1972.
———. *Women in Love*. Ed. David Farmer, Lindeth Vasey, and John Worthen. Cambridge: Cambridge UP, 1987.
Lawrence, Frieda. *Not I, But the Wind . . . .* London: Macmillan, 1934.
Levita, David J. de. *The Concept of Identity*. Paris: Mouton, 1965.
Lewis, David. "Survival and Identity." Rorty 17–40.
Long, Esmond R. *A History of the Therapy of Tuberculosis*. Lawrence: U of Kansas P, 1956.
Lucas, Robert. *Frieda Lawrence*. London: Secker & Warburg, 1973.
Meyers, Jay Arthur. *Fighters of Fate*. Freeport, NY: Books for Libraries Press, 1927.
Meyers, Jeffrey. *D.H. Lawrence: A Biography*. New York: Knopf, 1990.
Mooney, Elizabeth. *In the Shadow of the White Plague*. New York: Thomas Y. Crowell, 1979.
Moore, Harry T. *The Priest of Love: A Life of D.H. Lawrence*. Rev. ed. London: Heinemann, 1974.
Nehls, Edward, ed. *D.H. Lawrence: A Composite Biography*. 3 vols. Madison: U of Wisconsin P, 1959.
Neville, George. *A Memoir of D.H. Lawrence*. Ed. Carl Baron. London: Cambridge UP, 1981.
Rey, George. "Survival." Rorty 41–66.
Rorty, Amelie Oksenberg, ed. *The Identities of Persons*. Los Angeles: U of California P, 1976.
Schachtel, Ernest G. "On Alienated Concepts of Identity." In *Man Alone: Alienation in Modern Society*. Ed. Eric and Mary Josephson. New York: Dell, 1962.
Schneider, Daniel J. *The Consciousness of D.H. Lawrence: An Intellectual Biography*. Lawrence: Kansas UP, 1986.
Schopenhauer, Arthur. *The World as Will and Representation*. Trans. E.F.J. Payne. 2 vols. New York: Dover, 1969.
Sontag, Susan. *Illness as Metaphor*. New York: Farrar, Straus and Giroux, 1978.
———. *Under the Sign of Saturn*. New York: Farrar, Straus and Giroux, 1980.
Taylor, Charles. *Sources of the Self: The Making of the Modern Identity*. Cambridge: Harvard UP, 1989.
Templeton, Wayne. *States of Estrangement: The Novels of D.H. Lawrence, 1912–17*. Troy, NY: Whitston, 1989.
Worthen, John. *D.H. Lawrence, The Early Years: 1885–1912*. Cambridge: Cambridge UP, 1991.

12

Modernist Dialogics of Form in *The Rainbow*

JOAN DOUGLAS PETERS

One inherent issue confronting scholars of D.H. Lawrence is the general lack of respect currently given his work in the larger field of modernist criticism. While Lawrence is in the forefront of the modern British novelists, he is rarely treated as an important "modernist" in the tradition of Woolf, Joyce, and Beckett. The consequence is a diminishing of reputation, not only for Lawrence but also for those who work in the field of Lawrence scholarship. The fault, it seems to me, lies primarily, if not completely, with Lawrence's celebrity as "dark priest" philosopher. This categorization, established in the 1950s and 60s, unfortunately still flourishes and largely determines the trajectory of even the most sophisticated Lawrencian scholarship today.

The underlying critical assumption is that Lawrence is a single–voiced metaphysician, who uses plots, characters, themes, language, and imagery to act out or speak directly to some single philosophical system of thought, thus making his novels monological allegories of his own personal sexual and social beliefs. This premise, of course, places Lawrence in an antagonistic relationship to the larger tradition of the modernist novel, where the emphasis on strategies of narrative works both philosophically and rhetorically to exclude such didactic readings. Moreover, instead of applying disinterested critical terminology to the novels, Lawrencian criticism tends to trap itself in Lawrence's own unique metaphysical vocabulary, thereby isolating him from other modernists whose work has withstood, and been enriched by, larger, independent theoretical methodologies.

Most of the major modernist novelists, from Conrad to Graham Greene, shared the belief that a novel's philosophical designs should be expressed structurally and narratologically, rather than directly and didactically as critics read Lawrence. *Ulysses* and *To the Lighthouse*, for example, are obviously divided formally into chapters or sections, but what distinguishes their structures as modernist is the way that each part is dominated narratologically by the point of view of a single focalized and focalizing character (Stephen Dedalaus, Bloom, and Molly Bloom in their sections of *Ulysses*; Mrs. Ramsey, Mr. Ramsay, the unseen narrator, and Lily Briscoe in *To the Lighthouse*), all of whom indirectly address each other philosophically, linguistically, and, in the process, dialogically. Through the differences in character, linguistic style, and ideological viewpoint, worked directly into the texture of narratives of the different parts of the novels, the metaphysical structures in the books are created.

As Bakhtin describes structural metaphysics in his definition of the polyphonic novel, the narrative patterns that make up structure thereby create, by interacting with each other, open-ended, unfinalized, if coherent, philosophical "discussion," without authorial intrusion or philosophical didacticism. Linda Hutcheon points out, moreover, that one (if not *the*) major metaphysic characterizing the modernist novel is a meta*fictional* one; in other words, it is how the modern novel speaks about and defines itself as modernist through its own structure and narrative technique.

My larger thesis is that Lawrence himself is actually squarely within this same modernist tradition. Rather than representing philosophy in his novels through the direct words and actions of fictionalized characters or omniscient narrators with authorial sanction, Lawrence creates his greater metaphysic out of dialogical oppositions evolving out of narrative patterns that form philosophical arguments making up the structures of his major works. In the *Study of Thomas Hardy*, one of the more direct mines of Lawrencian critical theory, Lawrence in fact points to structure as *the* place for developing metaphysic in a novel: "Because the novel is a microcosm, and because man in viewing the universe must view it in light of a theory," he says, "therefore every novel must have the background or the structural skeleton of some theory of being, some metaphysic. But the metaphysic must always subserve the artistic purpose beyond the artist's conscious aim. Otherwise the novel becomes a treatise" (*Phoenix* 479). When metaphysic is developed as structure, rather than as a direct acting out or talking out of the author's own personal ideologies, it envelops the tale without interfering with or determining it, creating a tension between story and metaphysic that works to prevent the kind of allegory that critics have traditionally, with varying degrees of sophistication, read into Lawrence's works. The larger metaphysic structuring all Lawrence's major novels—as, I would say, it structures the novels of most of Lawrence's modernist counterparts—is a dialogical discussion of the novel as form, how it represents itself as genre, specifically in modern times.

What is particularly interesting about *The Rainbow* in this light is that Lawrence wrote it in conjunction with his *Study of Thomas Hardy*, a clearly doctrinal thesis aimed at investigating the place of the novel as genre in relation to a larger system of metaphysics—social, religious, artistic, sexual. Robert Langbaum points out, unfortunately without explanation, that the *Study of Thomas Hardy* "provides the skeletal structure" of the final version of *The Rainbow*, paraphrasing Lawrence's description of metaphysic as "structural skeleton" in the *Study* itself. He maintains that the *Study of Thomas Hardy* was written so that Lawrence could "better understand himself as a novelist, to understand where he comes from and where he is going" (70). This same exploratory impulse to place the novel as genre then, I would say, *does* become the structural metaphysic of *The Rainbow*, the specific novel emerging immediately out of that larger theoretical investigation. *The Rainbow* can be read metaphysically and metafictionally as Lawrence's effort to explore through his own novel the evolution of the novel as genre into its modernist form.

The Rainbow, in fact, metafictionalizes itself formally in a number of significant and complex ways. First, the familial structures that make up plot and theme in this work—where one generation emerges out of, negates, and then in many ways repeats the patterns of the previous generation, until the realities of modern times make such patterns infeasible—also serve as its metafictional, metaphysical narrative structure. Second, Lawrence actually uses the last half of *The Rainbow* as metafiction to reject and sometimes even to parody the idealism of his own personal metaphysic enacted in the first half of the book, making a didactic reading of the whole novel virtually impossible. Third, and most important I think, is that in *The Rainbow* Lawrence uses a woman's narrative point of view to present metafictionally the realities of the modern novel in dialogical opposition to its other forms. Indeed, the gender determined categories established at the opening of the novel make this narrative role for women not arbitrary but obligatory. Through his own metafictional strategy, then, Lawrence vitally empowers women in such a way as to challenge feminist critical complaints that he uses women only in roles of sexual submission. Here Lawrence gives "woman" control of fully half of the narrative and, as a result, metaphysical control of half the structural argument of the book.

Even the most useful and intelligent critical discussions of Lawrence's language (I am thinking primarily of Michael Bell's *D.H. Lawrence: language and being*) ultimately finalize and make static his narrational use of language, as other critics do his philosophical systems, because they do not recognize the distinctions in narrative voice created by the particular character focalizing through the words. Like many of his contemporaries, particularly Woolf and Joyce, Lawrence wrote mostly in the form of third-person free indirect discourse. That is, the narration for the most part reflects not an omniscient point of view but the personal viewpoint of specific characters represented in third-person, not first-person, form. That way, while there *is* a single narrative line running throughout the novel, it is comprised of different narrative voices interacting dialogically within the texture of the overall narration. All of Lawrence's major novels, like a surprising number of many other modernist works, are formally divided into sections dominated by one or sometimes two narrative points of view. These dominant narrative viewpoints come to characterize the narrational language and the metaphysics of their particular sections, each functioning as part of a larger metaphysical discussion, in direct dialogical confrontation with the narrative voices and consciousnesses dominating the other sections, thereby diversifying the dynamics of the novel's discourse while exploring stylistically as argument the nature of the novel as form.

As he does with other novels, Lawrence establishes a structural blueprint for *The Rainbow* in its opening pages—this time along gender lines. The kinds of essentialist categories of gender that begin *The Rainbow* are just the sort that many readers legitimately find disturbing and didactic when these are viewed, erroneously I think, as allegorical statements of Lawrencian philosophy played out in the fiction of his books. As structural paradigms, the same generalizations, devoid of gender allegory and largely independent of the fiction, become not only palatable but also functionally critical because they determine the dynamics of the style of narration that create the formal dialogics of the novel. Men are described from the onset as living life as pure experience:

> It was enough for the men, that the earth heaved and opened its furrows to them, that the wind blew to dry the wet wheat, and set the young ears of corn wheeling freshly round about. . . . So much warmth and generating and pain and death did they know in their blood, earth and sky and beast and green plants, so much exchange and interchange they had with these, that they lived full and surcharged, their senses full fed, their faces always turned to the heat of the blood, staring into the sun, dazed with looking towards the source of generation, unable to turn around . . . (10–11)

Therefore the first section, dominated by Tom Brangwen, might be seen metaphysically through the quality of the narration, as representing this experiential "male" way. Women, on the other hand, are in these opening pages generalized and thus represented as experience consciously conceived and uttered. The second half of the novel, dominated in fiction and narrative by Ursula, can be seen metaphysically and metafictionally to embody that idea: "The women were different. . . . [They] looked out from the heated blind intercourse of farm–life, to the spoken world beyond. They were aware of the lips and the mind of the world speaking and giving utterance, they heard the sound in the distance, and they strained to listen" (18). Between this early Tom section and the final Ursula section is the portion devoted to the marriage and narrative perspective of Will and Anna, who together, and in opposition to each other, focus the narration on intellectualized issues of sex and abstract religious dogma.

These three major narrational agencies create various bi–structural metafictional combinations operating either in conjunction with, or in opposition to, one another. By this dualistic interaction, the progress of the narrative transforms the governing structural metaphysic back and forth from a model of finalized dialectics to open–ended dialogical argument, the mode in which the novel ends. In the first half of the book, for example, the Will and Anna narrative works in opposition to the preceding Tom section—one arguing for pure experience, the other for dogma. This duality is, in a way, resolved in the Ursula section comprising the second half, where concrete, particularized experience is itself intellectually evaluated, consciously and artistically.

At the same time, with both Tom and Lydia *and* Will and Anna, man and woman live in direct opposition to each other, creating within each couple a metaphysical duality, which eventually resolves itself in a "third state" of sexual union and procreation. This kind of resolution, in turn, is unavailable to Ursula because the conditions of modern industrialism and the new opportunities and roles for women make such a resolution incongruous. Thus the first half of the novel, consisting of a kind of Blakean dialectic enacted separately and differently by both couples, is set off against the Ursula section, where such resolution cannot exist. The dialectic enacted by the men and women of the previous generations is thereby transformed into an unresolved dialogic for Ursula and, in turn, for the structure of the novel as a whole. The metafictional argument implicit in this final structural movement into the dialogical is that this is the same course the novel must take as genre if it is to be vital artistically and metaphysically in modern times, an argument that is implicitly performed and illustrated by the modernist dialogical structure of *The Rainbow* itself.

The first structural movement of *The Rainbow* is determined narratologically by Tom Brangwen. Tom is from the beginning depicted as a man who feels life deeply but is absolutely incapable of articulating that feeling or conceptualizing what he thinks or believes. Unlike Ursula, who with full adolescent vigor investigates and then interrogates every complexity of every life experience she encounters, Tom is described as having a "complete inability to attend to a question put without suggestion" (11). The narrative texture characterizing the Tom section of the novel, when he is focalized and/or the focalizing agent, is, by reflection, generally obtuse—dominated stylistically by short declarative sentences, statements of facts without analysis, simplistically broad metaphysical questions, and little or no dialogue or concrete physical description. In the following passage, for example, the narration rendering the simplicity of Tom's analysis of his marriage to Lydia, including a very basic understanding of his own deep fears, creates a metaphysic within the narrative style of the novel that is primal and uncomplicated as well:

> He realized with a sharp pang that she belonged to him, and he to her. He realized that he lived by her. Did he own her? Was she here for ever? Or might she go away? She was not really his, it was not a real marriage, this marriage between them. She might go away. He did not feel like a master, husband, father of her children. She belonged elsewhere. Any moment, she might be gone. And he was ever drawn to her, drawn after her, with

> ever-raging, ever-unsatisfied desire. He must turn home, wherever his steps were taking him, always to her, and he could never quite reach her, he could never quite be satisfied, never be at peace, because she might go away. (58)

From the beginning Tom distinguishes himself from the other male Brangwens by his desire to intuit a larger metaphysical explanation of his own life experience; but his efforts are thwarted and his narrational perspective prevented from fully realizing that metaphysic because he is unable to articulate even the possibilities of what his experience might mean. As a result, the relationships, events, and feelings portrayed by the narrative in his section of the novel are made more obliquely unfathomable than they might otherwise be, for the most part because the focalizing agent is constitutionally unable to interpret them speculatively with any kind of sophistication or clarity. A duality built into the texture of this section suggests that this limitation may be a deliberate narrative function of gender.

With the introduction of Lydia, Lawrence offers the first instance of direct dialogue (a meaningless exchange between Tom and Tilly, notable for calling attention to itself simply as "dialogue," with no other recognizable purpose), includes more concrete description, and, when the narrative perspective shifts momentarily to Lydia's consciousness, allows the reinstitution (from the opening of the novel) of poetry into the prose. The paragraphs reflecting Lydia's thinking are generally longer, and her feelings are revealed metaphorically rather than bluntly and obtusely. Under Lydia's gaze, the narrative focus is momentarily on the real, recognizable, detailed natural world rather than on simple thoughts and events:

> Summer came, the moors were tangled with harebells like water in the ruts of the roads, the heather came rosy under the skies, setting the whole world awake. And she was uneasy. She went past the gorse bushes shrinking from their presence, she stepped into the heather as into a quickening bath that almost hurt. Her fingers moved over the clasped fingers of the child, she heard the anxious voice of the baby, as it tried to make her talk, distraught. (51–52)

Even within the narrative texture of this first section, then, Lawrence builds a metafictional opposition between men and women that will come to determine the larger stylistic structure of the book. As with Anna in the next section of the novel, however, Lydia loses all control over narrative language and perspective in this section once she gets married and starts bearing children—as if for the women in these earlier generations the act of procreation naturally replaces, or displaces, the conceptually creative impulse that expresses itself in words. So her stylistic contribution to the narration here is short-lived. Throughout the Tom section, Lawrence primarily endeavors through his narrational style to emphasize that pure, inarticulate experience cannot and perhaps should not be artistically conceptualized or consciously articulated and analyzed. He does this, with some notable exceptions, by keeping the focus as enigmatic and general as possible.

The introduction of Will Brangwen into the novel shifts the narrative focus from Tom and Lydia first to Anna, then to Anna and Will. In "Girlhood of Anna Brangwen," the chapter serving as narrational transition, Lawrence builds opposition into the narrational style by paralleling young Anna's experience, actual and subjective, with Tom's. For example, as adolescents both Tom and Anna feel similar kinds of frustration and alienation at school, feelings that both evaluate internally in the same self-defensive way. Anna's response, however, infiltrates into the narrative with a kind of abstract, formalized, metaphysical mode of thinking and articulating—albeit a childish one—that strongly contrasts with the kind of narrational discourse describing young Tom, as in the following passage on his problems with others at school:

> But when it came to mental things then he was at a disadvantage. He was at their mercy. He was a fool. He had not the power to controvert even the most stupid argument, so that he was forced to admit things he did not in the least believe. And having admitted them, he did not know whether he believed them or not; he rather thought he did. (10)

Metaphysical complexity is built into the narrational discourse of Tom's narrative largely through his inability to analyze metaphysically. He simply represents the situation as it is, allowing contradictions implicit in his own feelings to stand unresolved. In young Anna's narrative, however, these natural complexities are replaced by larger, formally metaphysical, abstract questions (all implicitly answered) and fierce, definitive judgments against those on the other side:

> She never felt quite sure of herself whether she were wrong, or whether the others were wrong. She had not done her lessons: well, she did not see any reason why she should do her lessons, if she did not want to. Was

> there some occult reason why she should? Were these people, schoolmistresses, representatives of some mystic Right, some Higher Good? They seemed to think so themselves. But she could not for her life see why a woman should bully and insult her because she did not know thirty lines of *As You Like It*. After all, *what* did it matter if she knew them or not? Nothing could persuade her that it was of the slightest importance. (95)

Through these parallel responses, the basic differences between Tom and Anna reveal themselves metaphysically as a "dialogue" built into the narrative style of the novel, not rendered as direct "authorial" commentary or represented as allegory in the fiction.

Tom is explicitly contrasted with Anna, as character and as narrative focalizor, not only by his inability but also by his absolute *unwillingness* to conceive and articulate formally what his experience might mean, a determination that creates a distinct duality between them: "Sometimes Anna talked to her father. She tried to discuss people, she wanted to know what was meant. But her father became uneasy. He did not want to have things dragged into consciousness. Only out of consideration for her he listened" (101). Yet at Anna's wedding, the point at which he turns Anna over to Will and, in effect, the narrative perspective over to the new couple, Tom is very insistent about publicly articulating the meaning of his abstract doctrine of marriage, the metaphysic that has evolved out of his own experience and, consequently, the experience of the novel to this point. "For the first time in his life," the narrative points out explicitly, "he must spread himself wordily" (133).

Although the actual discourse of Tom's philosophy of marriage is simplistically phrased and made awkward by constant audience interruptions, it is also conceived and articulated, in the form of an interactive dialogue with the other guests, as a system of greater metaphysics—"'*If* we've got to be Angels,' went on Tom Brangwen, haranguing the company at large, 'and if there is no such thing as a man nor a woman amongst them, then it seems to me as a married couple makes one Angel'" (134)—and reflects a strong determination to articulate consciously his own experience in metaphysical form before surrendering point of view to the next generation. It is as if Tom, and the novel itself, must *speak* personal experience as doctrine in order to *depersonalize* it and thereby make the metaphysic of pure experience, in the form of dialogue, a dialogical part of the greater whole.

In immediate contrast to the metaphysic of inarticulate experience governing the first section of the novel, the metaphysical preoccupation of the second section, once Anna Brangwen marries Will, is represented largely in terms of abstract opposition on deeper issues that are for these two characters already mental abstractions, each side deliberating constantly, inwardly and aloud, about the way things *should* be. He wants her to be possessed by him; she wants to possess herself. He wants religion to be mystical and inarticulate; she wants it to be what she can see. The quality of the narration of this section, because it repeats and reflects the abstract metaphysical thinking of these characters, is also predominantly abstract in style, and this style is illustrated and in some sense *performed* within the fiction of the novel by the direct discourse that goes on between the characters on the subject of abstract ideas. In this sample exchange over a book of religious prints, for example, Anna and Will articulate their basic, intuitive beliefs about life as oppositional dialogue on the abstract subject of religion, thus displacing their private, unconscious metaphysics in a way that could never have occurred between Tom and Lydia in the fiction of the first section of the novel:

> "I do think they're loathsome," she cried.
> "What?" he said, surprised, abstracted.
> "Those bodies with slits in them, posing to be worshipped."
> "You see, it means the Sacraments, the Bread," he said slowly.
> "Does it," she cried. "Then it's worse. *I* don't want to see your chest slit, nor to eat your dead body, even if you offer it to me. Can't you see it's horrible?"
> "It isn't me, it's Christ."
> "What if it is, it's you! And it's horrible, you wallowing in your own dead body, and thinking of eating it in the Sacrament."
> "You've to take it for what it means."
> "It means your human body put up to be slit and killed and then worshipped—what else?"
> They lapsed into silence. His soul grew angry and aloof. (149–50)

What is fascinating about this passage in terms of its role in the larger structural opposition of the book is that it fictionally performs a direct dialogue between the metaphysics of the first two sections of the novel, at the same time that it structurally represents only one side of that duality. Although Anna articulates her point of view in the form of abstract debate, in pointed contrast to the experiential style of indirect discourse in the Tom section of the novel, she actually speaks directly *for* that experiential way of perceiving and interpreting in this particular argument, *in opposition to* the abstracting and symbolizing of experience directly promulgated by Will. Thus Will and Anna, as characters in the fiction, make personal, dialogical, and unresolved the metafictional issues that are static, dialectical, and absolute in the larger structure of the novel —creating a dynamic tension between fiction and structure in the total metaphysics of the book. This formal interaction of fiction and structure, in turn, itself dramatizes metafictionally the more precise terms of Lawrence's own critical theory of form for the novel as genre. In the *Study of Thomas Hardy* he writes:

> The adherence to a metaphysic does not necessarily give artistic form. Indeed the over-strong adherence to a metaphysic usually destroys any possibility of artistic form. Artistic form is a revelation of the two principles of Love and Law in a state of conflict and yet reconciled: pure motion struggling against and yet reconciled with the Spirit: active force meeting and overcoming and yet not overcoming inertia. It is the conjunction of the two which makes form. And since the two must always meet under fresh conditions, form must always be different. Each work of art has its own form, which has no relation to any other form. (*Phoenix* 477)

In this way Lawrence establishes that metaphysic in the novel genre is realized not only through dialogical oppositions in narrative structure but also in a concurrent oppositional relationship between the statics of that structure and the dynamics of the fiction it envelops.

The first half of *The Rainbow*, encompassing the first two sections of the novel, ends with the death of Tom in the flood—death by drowning being a familiar modernist symbol indicating the overcoming of the old by new life. The second half begins with Lydia talking to Ursula, discoursing on the metaphysical relations between men and women, so that in effect woman is turning the narrative over to woman in the transitional phase of the structural metaphysics of this book. In light of this transition, the metaphysical debates between Will and Anna in the second section (as well as the narrational differences between Tom and Lydia in the first) enforce the idea that the greater *metafictional* dichotomy of this novel is a metaphysic based on and articulated by an opposition of gender.

Earlier in the novel, Lydia explicitly perceives that her life experience with Tom will be one that will require her to create for herself, and implicitly for him, a new *form*: "She would have to begin again, to find a new being, a new form, to respond to that blind, insistent figure standing over her" (39). In *The Rainbow* the thematic evolution of life out of old patterns into modernity is represented fictionally and narrationally in terms of the evolution of a particular woman, Ursula, into new form, both for herself, and, consequently, for the novel as genre. Ursula's narrative consciousness takes over almost exactly, to the page, half-way through the novel, setting her woman's narration in direct dialogical opposition to the first two sections already discussed. Metafictionally, then, it would seem that Lawrence is deliberately using woman's narrative point of view to suggest that the new form for the novel is one set in implicit contrast to existing patriarchal conventions of genre—including, by implication, his own.

Although both the first two sections of *The Rainbow* are obviously exploring within the form of a novel larger dualistic metaphysical concerns, the narrational styles of both sections together contribute to a lack of the novelistic in the texture of the first half of the book that the Ursula narrative of the second half, in contrast, provides. Although Anna as a child, in keeping with her metaphysical role as woman, has a wonderfully original sense of language and a talent for inventing words—"We don't live with *you*, she bellows at Tom, "You—you're—you're a bomakle," (67)—young Ursula is described as having a fascination with the larger relations between words and things. Her intuitively metaphorical way of conceiving language inherently formalizes words as literature in this half of the novel, an impulse that becomes more and more conscious as she matures. By her adolescent infatuation with the wording of her own statement, "If I were the moon I know where I would fall down," we see how, for example, Ursula's internal prose inherently stresses the formal connection between feeling, trope, and grammar: "It meant so much to her that sentence. She put into it all the anguish of her youth and young passion and yearning" (308–309). This self-consciously metaphorical manner of conceiving language incorporates into the narration a firm grounding of metaphysics in the language of the concrete world, producing a new linguistic realism for the novel that contrasts markedly with the narrative texture of the first half.

In opposition to both the obtuse vocabulary of intuition dominating the Tom section and the language of intellectual abstraction characterizing the Will and Anna section, for Ursula and concurrently for her narrative, "words must have a weekday meaning, since words were weekday stuff. Let them speak now: let them bespeak themselves in weekday terms. The vision should translate itself into weekday terms" (264). As character, Ursula also has an intuitive sense of the vital connection between life and literature, the relationship obviously most crucial to Lawrence's critical theory of genre, despite her inherited familial antipathy towards the authoritarianism of formal reading: "Only in odd streaks did she get a poignant sense of acquisition and enrichment and enlarging from her studies; one afternoon, reading *As You Like It*; once when, with her blood, she heard a passage of Latin, and she knew how the blood beat in a Roman's body; so that ever after she felt she knew the Romans by contact" (310). It is noteworthy that Ursula's critical response to reading *As You Like It* contrasts with Anna's cited earlier.

As narrative consciousness, Ursula transforms the structural metaphysic in the second half of the novel from a dialectical opposition between two static belief systems into a self-generating dialogical metaphysic continually in flux. As a person, Ursula has an intuitive self-honesty that causes her to be constantly evaluating her own character, specifically in relation to life as she experiences it. This self-evaluation carries over into the narration, in contrast to the earlier sections, as narration constantly questioning itself. She is also habitually interrogating her own moral experience and the lessons she has inherited or been taught. This inquisition, perhaps because of her better education and world experience, is conducted on a level of complexity heretofore absent from the narration, allowing for full, complex exploration of those experiences and beliefs for the whole book. We are aware throughout her section of the novel that Ursula herself is always in process, always developing. While the earlier narrative focalizors do come to "realizations" about their marriages and themselves, these discoveries are rendered in the form of final epiphanies, stratified in the novel through the symbol of the rainbow. There is no sense of ongoing development in the minds of these characters throughout their sections, nor, in consequence, of their narrational points of view. As metafiction, Ursula's constant questioning and challenging of her own metaphysics in the light of her real life experience, reflects and enacts narratologically Lawrence's own conviction that the fiction (or life) of a novel should always relate to its own governing philosophy in that interrogatory way.

Ursula, moreover, is described from the beginning, specifically in contrast to Gudrun, as being "the one for realities"; and the narrative of her half of the novel reflects this keen appreciation and awareness of life's realism. With Ursula's narrative consciousness, specific social ideological concerns are introduced into the novel—including the modern educational system, industrialism, women's rights, and the evils of war—all explored directly in the fiction in terms of Ursula's real experience, not simply expounded upon in her focalized mind and consciousness. At the same time, the narrative notes, "it pleased her also to know that in the East one must use hyperbole or else remain unheard; because the eastern man must see a thing swelling to fill all heaven, or dwindled to a mere nothing before he is suitably impressed. She immediately sympathized with this eastern mind" (258). In this spirit, while much of the metaphysic in this section is conveyed in a rather conventionally realistic way (consider Ursula's experience as a teacher in Ilkeston, for example), Ursula is also given free rein to rant and rave inwardly, with typical adolescent intensity and self-contradiction, about her own developing unrooted, metaphysical beliefs.

Certainly Ursula's personal metaphysics, as well as her political ideas about the social world at large, very nearly mirror Lawrence's own. Because her presentation of her metaphysical beliefs is so melodramatic, so changeable, so self-contradictory, however, her narration manages to resist the didacticism that might destroy this novel metafictionally as a "novel" in the generic sense as Lawrence critically defines the form. Whenever political ideology is overtly addressed by Ursula in characteristically Lawrencian terms, in turn, it is always expressed Socratically in the form of dialogue with another character, as for example Ursula's argument with Skrebensky on the evils of democracy and monied aristocracy (426–28) where she clearly adopts both Lawrence's personal political beliefs and his rhetorical style. In this section of the novel, then, formal Lawrencian philosophy is always presented as developmental and changeable, or else it is rendered literally as a dialogic in the form of a fictional dialogue between Ursula and someone with a contrary point of view; it is never articulated didactically as authorial discourse within the fabric of the book.

In fact, the melodrama and self-contradiction implicit in the doctrinal absolutes built into Ursula's own developing metaphysical consciousness in this half of the novel actually allow the narrative to laugh at the intensity of those metaphysics and thereby further to undermine their validity as Lawrencian doctrine. Take, for example, Ursula's dramatic moment of clarity as she looks at life under the microscope in Dr. Frankenstone's laboratory (a setting that emphasizes the joke), sparking this exclamatory epiphany: "Suddenly she had passed away into an intensely-gleaming light of knowledge. . . Self was a oneness with the infinite. To be oneself was a supreme, gleaming triumph of the infinite" (409). Moments later, after she is suddenly reunited with Skrebensky, Ursula realizes with equal force and hyperbole a new epiphany, one that explicitly but unconsciously and absolutely contradicts the first: "She was no mere Ursula Brangwen. She was Women, she was the whole of Woman in the human order. All-containing, universal, how should she be limited to individuality?" (412). Ursula's flagrant, nonapologetic contradicting of her own absolutes in this novel is very reminiscent of Lawrence's rhetorical strategy in his critical prose, a strategy that I would maintain is used in both places deliberately to argue *against* the metaphysical validity of "absolutes" in life and literature at all.

Not only does Lawrence undermine Ursula's metaphysics by mocking their intensity in this narrational way, he actually uses the Ursula section in order to *parody* retrospectively the intensity of the metaphysics expressed internally and externally as doctrine in the earlier sections of this novel. Through this parody, Lawrence calls into question the legitimacy of any novel that represents metaphysic directly through character, narration, dialogue and plot—even his own. His larger metafictional conviction that this kind of representation is not viable for the modern novel, as suggested by Ursula's necessary break with familial patterns of the past generations, is particularly poignant in light of the fact that most Lawrencian scholars are still reading Lawrence's own modern works in that way.

Indeed in the Ursula half of the novel, Lawrence dramatizes as parody the possibility that his own metaphysics, enacted mostly in the Tom section of the novel, are themselves completely incongruous to modern life, and by association the modern novel that must reflect such life. When Tom decides to marry Lydia, he knows intuitively and absolutely by instinct, blood-consciousness if you will, that even though she barely knows him she will accept him as her husband; and not surprisingly she does. "He was a long time resolving definitely to ask her to marry him. And he knew, if he asked her, she must really acquiesce. She must, it could not be otherwise. . . . 'Yes I want to,' she said impersonally, looking at him with candid, newly-opened eyes, opened now with supreme truth" (40, 44). The reliability of the metaphysic built into the language of this implicit exchange is seriously undermined as metaphysical doctrine when it is compared to a similar situation in the second half of the novel. When Anthony asks Ursula, without any previous romantic or sexual contact, to marry him and come live on the farm, the absurdity of such a marriage ever actually coming to pass for the modern generation is made patently clear in Ursula's response, a response which, as rendered, almost directly mocks the earlier scene:

> She realized with something like terror that she was going to accept this. She was inevitably going to accept him. His hand was reaching out to the gate before them. She stood still. His hand was hard and brown and final. She seemed to be in the grip of some insult.
>
> 'I couldn't,' she answered involuntarily. (386)

What this comparison suggests both metaphysically and metafictionally is not that the interaction between Tom and Lydia was unrealistic, but that because "life" has changed, the novel itself may not be able to convey life experience and the relations between people, particularly between men and women, as intuitive and inarticulate any longer in any realistic way. In fact, to attempt to represent life in this manner may risk making the novel form itself obsolete, even ridiculous. What Lawrence believes in and loves philosophically, then—his faith in the essential, vital inarticulateness of living experience—paradoxically may no longer work for the novel as Lawrence loved and believed in the form, as the "book of life" as life is lived.

The sexual union through marriage that resolved, and in the process opened up, the relationships in the first half of *The Rainbow* is portrayed in the second half as a form of absolute closure that would be impossible for Ursula, and metafictionally for the kind of novel she implicitly narrates. (In fact in this section when Lawrence is "finished" metaphysically with characters like Winifred Ingers and Skrebensky, he deliberately marries them off.) As Ursula sees Skrebensky in the final stages of their affair, "He seemed added up, finished. She knew him all around, not on any side did he lead into the unknown. Poignant, almost passionate appreciation she felt for him, but none of the dreadful wonder, none of the rich fear, the connection with the unknown, or the reverence of love" (438–39). This sentiment could as well express the metaphysical relationship of the second half of *The Rainbow* to the first, and it points to the end of the novel, which, rather than finalizing the story line, actually works to prevent fictional and structural closure.

The final paragraph reinstitutes the symbol of the rainbow; this time, however, the governing trope encompasses the whole large industrial world, instead of simply a man and a woman and child, opening up the symbol, and the novel, to a newer, physically more expansive reality of life—in direct contrast to its structural function of closing off the relationships of the earlier couples.

The quality of language describing this new symbol is so transparently ugly as well ("the sordid people who crept hard-scaled and separate on the face of the world's corruption were living still"), especially in contrast to its earlier manifestations, that it actually functions linguistically to undermine the legitimacy of any kind of symbolic resolution in the novel at all. By representing dualistically both the decay and the "new germination" of the evolving industrial world, the final paragraph contrasts dramatically and directly with the lovely, coherent pastoral representation of Marsh farm that opens the book, establishing a dialectical relationship between the beginning and the end of the novel that itself prevents closure. Because this dialectic frames, and can therefore never be resolved within, the structure of this novel, the duality between the two represented worlds is thereby transformed into an on-going state of dialogue, creating for the fiction an overall structural metaphysic in dialogical form that could only be described as modernist.

Works Cited

Bakhtin, Mikhail. *Problems of Dostoevsky's Poetics*. Ed. and Trans. Caryl Emerson. Minneapolis: U of Minnesota P, 1984.

Bell, Michael. *D.H. Lawrence: language and being*. Cambridge: Cambridge UP, 1991.

Hutcheon, Linda. *Narcissistic Narrative: The Metafictional Paradox*. Waterloo: Wilfred Laurier UP, 1980.

Langbaum, Robert. "Lawrence and Hardy." In *D.H. Lawrence and Tradition*. Ed. Jeffrey Meyers. London: The Athlone P, 1985.

Lawrence, D.H. *Phoenix: The Posthumous Papers of D.H. Lawrence*. Ed. Edward D. McDonald. N.Y.: Viking P, 1936.

———. *The Rainbow*. Ed. Mark Kinkead-Weekes. Cambridge: Cambridge UP, 1989.

13

The Lawrencean Flame-Water Antithesis in *Lady Chatterley's Lover*

GEORGE J. ZYTARUK

Commentaries on Lawrence almost invariably cite that famous letter written to Ernest Collings on 17 January 1913 asserting: "My great religion is a belief in the blood, the flesh, as being wiser than the intellect" (1: 503). I do not question the importance of this antithesis in attempts to understand Lawrence's fundamental ideas, nor do I wish at this time to quarrel with the many ways in which this particular formulation of Lawrence's creed has been used and abused by critics over the years. What I find remarkable, however, is that surprisingly little attention has been paid to that part of the letter immediately following Lawrence's one-sentence definition of his "great religion":

> I conceive a man's body as a kind of flame, like a candle flame forever upright and yet flowing: and the intellect is just the light that is shed unto the things around. And I am not so much concerned with the things around;—which is really mind:—but with the mystery of the flame forever flowing, coming God knows how from out of practically nowhere, and being *itself*, whatever there is around it, that it lights up. (503)

Taken as a whole, the passage becomes significant in two ways: first, it encapsulates the basic Lawrencean doctrine of duality; second, it features Lawrence's deliberate formulation of the flame image (some would say trope), which recurs in an infinite variety of forms as he struggles to present his artistic vision.

This is not to say that I date all of Lawrence's uses of flame imagery from this time in his career, although given its predominance in the work which was shortly to absorb all his energies (I am referring to the "Sisters"), the occasion is certainly noteworthy. Some of the very early poems, however, reveal that the flame image already constitutes a unique mode of metaphoric expression. In "The Wild Common," for example, "The quick sparks on the gorse-bushes are leaping/Little jets of sunlight texture imitating flame" (*The Complete Poems* 33); in "Dog Tired," the "vetch-clump still burns red!" (35); in "Lightning," "Her breath flew warm against my neck,/Warm as a flame in the close night air" (61); and, in "At a Loose End," Lawrence writes, "Many years have I still to burn, detained/Like a candle-flame on this body" (115). Finally, allow me to quote in its entirety that remarkable poem entitled "The Enkindled Spring":

> This spring as it comes bursts up in bonfires green,
> Wild puffing of green-fire trees, and flame-green bushes,
> Thorn-blossom lifting in wreaths of smoke between
> Where the wood fumes up, and the flickering, watery rushes.
>
> I am amazed at this spring, this conflagration
> Of green fires lit on the soil of earth, this blaze
> Of growing, these smoke-puffs that puff in wild gyration,
> Faces of people blowing across my gaze!
>
> And I, what sort of fire am I among
> This conflagration of spring? the gap in it all—!
> Not even palish smoke like the rest of the throng.
> Less than the wind that runs to the flamy call! (116)

These are only a few examples from among hundreds of such variations of flame images in Lawrence's poetry. Having read all of his works with the flame-water antithesis in mind, I am now convinced that what we are witnessing in Lawrence's writing is what Northrop Frye sees as a common feature of all great creative artists: "the fact that every poet has his private mythology, his own spectroscopic band or peculiar formation of symbols, of much of which he is quite unconscious" (505). Of course, Lawrence's choice of the phoenix as his own particular emblem should have long ago alerted us to pay special attention to his unique poetic signature.

My examples have thus far focused on the "flame" dimension of the antithesis, although from the sources quoted it would be easy enough to illustrate the "water" dimension as well. Let me, however, turn to some other works to indicate the degree to which the flame-water antithesis really forms a unified whole. My first example comes, oddly enough, from *Etruscan Places*, which, I believe, functions as a kind of intertext for *Lady Chatterley's Lover* and which, for this reason alone, is doubly relevant here. This is what Lawrence says:

> The universe, which was a single aliveness with a single soul, instantly changed, the moment you thought of it, and became a dual creature with two souls, fiery and watery, for ever mingling and rushing apart, and held by the great aliveness of the universe in an ultimate equilibrium. . . . And everything was dual, or contained its own duality, for ever mingling and rushing apart. (84)

In one of his very late works, *Apocalypse*, we find this passage:

> Fire and water, the two great living elements and opposites, gave rise to all substance in their slippery unstable, 'marriage.' But when one triumphed over the other, there was "injustice".—So, when the sun-fire got too strong for the sweet waters, it *burnt* them, and when the water was burnt by fire, it produced salt, child of injustice. (112–13)

Finally, an example from that fascinating work, *Mr Noon* which will show how the flame–water antithesis is applied by Lawrence to human relations:

> Ultimately, a woman wants a man who, by entering into complete relationship with her, will keep her in her own polarity and equipoise, true to herself. *The man wants the same of woman* [my italics]. It is the eternal oscillating balance of the universe. It is the timeless inter-related duality of fire and water. (212)

Rather than explicate these passages (which, of course, would have to be considered in their particular contexts) and become mired in theoretical pronouncements, let me proceed directly to illustrate how the flame–water antithesis works in *Lady Chatterley's Lover*. Throughout this discussion, when I speak about the flame–water antithesis I will include all sorts of variations of the two elements; thus, "flame" will encompass "sparks," "glow," "gleam," "sun," "warmth," and a variety of colours that suggest a "flame" connection. Similarly, water images will include such variations as "rain," "flood," "cold," "ice," "snow," and a host of other permutations and combinations. Owing to space constraints, it will not be possible to explain each variation, but I think once attention has been drawn to the recurring pattern of these images, the individual instances will be clearly relevant to the overall flame–water antithesis. Let me also stress that this novel is not the only work in which I find Lawrence employing his unique "spectroscopic band" of imagery. An equally persuasive case can be made for the novels *The Rainbow* and *Women in Love*, as well as for the novellas *The Virgin and the Gypsy*, *St. Mawr*, and *The Escaped Cock*.[1] And I have already referred to the poems.

Turning to *Lady Chatterley's Lover*, let me begin with Wragby Hall itself, which is a house where there is "no touch, no actual contact"; and we are told: "No warmth of feeling united it organically" (16). It is Connie's "second winter at Wragby" (17), when she realizes that she is "going to pieces in some way. Vaguely she knew she was out of connection: she had lost touch with the substantial and vital world" (19). Even the wood where she would sometimes "lie prone in the bracken" (like Birkin), "her one refuge, her sanctuary" is "not really a refuge, a sanctuary, because she had no connection with it . . . She never touched the spirit of the wood itself" (19); of the men at Wragby, she says, "Instead of [them] kissing you, and touching you with their bodies, they revealed their minds to you. It was great fun! [not really] But what cold minds!" (34). Tommy Dukes, who knows what a "mental lifer" he is, characterizes them all: "We're all as cold as crétins, we're all as passionless as idiots . . . God! when one can only talk!" (37–38).

The image of this "cold" world is underlined in Chapter 5 where Clifford and Connie go for a walk across the park to the wood. It is "a frosty morning," the "frost [lies] bluish in the sockets of the tufts" (39) of the grass, the gravelled path itself is covered with "hoar frost," and the old leaves on the ground still have "frost on their underside." There is an allusion to the "snows of yesteryear." Into this world of frost and snow strides the gamekeeper "like the sudden rush of a threat out of nowhere" (43). I want to stress, however, that even in this first introduction, Mellors is already being marked out through special flame images: first, attention is drawn to his "red face and red moustache and distant eyes" (43), certainly appropriate colours for one who will eventually be delineated as the bearer of the life flame; second, he is singled out as "a curious, quick, separate fellow, alone, but sure of himself" (44). While Clifford looks at Mellors with "curious, cool wonder," Connie's perception is quite different: "She saw in his blue impersonal eyes a look of suffering and detachment, yet a certain *warmth* [my italics]" (44–45). We must pay attention to these qualities; they will steadily be expanded as the novel proceeds. For the moment, there is still "a raw coldness. It was going to snow" (45).

Mellors's vitality is, for the moment, "quenched," but "quenched" does not mean that his inner fire cannot again flame into being, which is exactly what happens. Connie can no longer endure trying to relate to the men in Clifford's circle; to her "these men seemed so old and cold. Everything seemed old and cold" (54), which becomes a sort of refrain on her current state of affairs. Sometimes, she weeps bitterly, saying to herself: "Silly fool, wetting hankies!" (59); "Wragby, the Lady Chatterley business, money and fame. . . . Love, sex, all that sort of stuff, just water ices" (60). One day, "after it had rained as usual, and the paths were too sodden for Clifford's chair" (61), Connie sets out alone for the wood. It seems like "the end of all things!" (61), but this will in fact be the beginning of new life for her.

What does she see as she comes out of the wood on the north side? It is "the keeper's cottage, a rather dark, brown stone cottage, with gables and a handsome chimney . . . [and] a thread of smoke [rising] from the chimney" (61). We might very well overlook this detail, except that the well-worn proverb teaches us—"Where there's smoke, there's fire." Rounding the side of the house, Connie comes upon the keeper unawares. That Mellors is for the moment immersed in water, in the element that usually opposes the life flame, underlines how "utterly alone" he is. Yet the effect on Connie is "a visionary experience" that hits her in the middle of the body. The entire passage is worth noting:

> She saw the clumsy breeches slipping down over the pure, delicate, white loins, the bones showing a little, and the sense of aloneness, of a creature purely alone, overwhelmed her. Perfect, white, solitary nudity of a creature that lives alone, and inwardly alone. And beyond that, a certain beauty of a pure creature. Not the stuff of beauty, nor even the body of beauty, but a lambency, *the warm, white flame of a single life, revealing itself in the contours that one might touch: a body*! [my italics]. (62)

Coming face to face with him a little while later, Connie notices how "his eyes looked warm and kind, particularly to a woman, wonderfully warm, and kind" (63). His eyes are "warm and blue," and "when the eyes ceased to laugh they looked as if they had suffered a great deal, still without losing their warmth" (63).

Connie goes up to her bedroom and looks "at herself naked in the huge mirror" (65). Her body looks "as if it had not had enough sun and warmth" (65). She sees herself old at twenty-seven "with no gleam and sparkle in the flesh" (65). "Her belly had lost the fresh, round gleam it had" (65). Her "haunches and buttocks had lost [their] gleam" (66), which was there when the German boy had loved her; but in the past ten years, she has had "no healthy human sensuality, that warms the blood and freshens the whole being" (66). What follows is a metaphorical battle between images of "warmth" and images of "cold" focussed, for the most part, on the relationship between Clifford and Connie. A deep sense of injustice against Clifford is registered, not because he is sexually impotent, but because, "he was never really warm," at best only considerate in a "cold sort of way!" (67). Even Connie's father still possesses "the warmth of man . . . who could still comfort a woman with a bit of his masculine glow" (67); but to Clifford and his lot "warmth to them was just bad taste . . . keep yourself cold" (67), and what Connie has been serving in her self-sacrifice to Clifford has been "a cold spirit of vanity, that had no warm human contacts" (67).

The arrival of Mrs. Bolton at Wragby enables Connie to spend more time by herself, and it is the older woman who suggests that Connie ought to see the daffodils behind the keeper's cottage. The yellow colour of the flowers ought to alert us to their significance; these are flowers of the sun, even if their source is the darkness of Hades. Connie is about to "pass the porches and the portals," to enter a new world, but in the imagery of the flame-water antithesis it is "a cold morning" and "cold breaths of wind came," and from overhead "only cold currents came down" (79). In contrast, the stone of the cottage is being "warmed in a burst of sun"; there is "a sparkle of yellow jasmine," and the "daffodils turn golden, in a burst of sun that was warm on her hands and lap" (80).

The next afternoon when she returns to the wood, she comes upon the "secret little clearing, and a secret little hut" (81), where, as Mellors explains in his own special language, he is "gettin' th' coops ready for th' young bods" (81). Mellors asks Connie to come inside the hut and very simply asks: "Am Ah t' light yer a little fire?" In "a moment the yellow flame was running up the chimney" [as predicted by the earlier smoke imagery] (82). Connie has entered "a sort of little sanctuary" where she "sat and warmed her hands at the blaze" and "grew warm by the fire" (82). This is the flame world of Mellors presented in stark contrast to Clifford's cold world of Wragby; but while the presence of Mellors "touched Connie's womb," the effect of her presence on him is profoundly disturbing. Nevertheless, "a little thin tongue of fire suddenly flickered in his loins, at the root of his back, and he groaned in spirit" (83). Mellors is, after all, "only a hired man" who has, in any case, been avoiding "any further close human contact" (83). His anger "against the self-willed female" is of long standing, and when he looks at Connie, his eyes "had a cold, ugly look of dislike and contempt" (84). So this meeting ends in stalemate.

In the meantime, the relationship between Connie and Clifford continues to deteriorate; Connie has only "her own warmth," and during her visits to the hut in the wood it is still raining, and cold; her own warmth is not enough to sustain her spirits. Ironically, Clifford seems "verily to be re-born" (101), since Mrs. Bolton replaces Connie as the woman behind him. His talk fills Connie with "dismay and repulsion" (104); Connie asks herself: "What man in his senses would say such things to a woman! . . . What man with a spark of honour would put this ghastly burden of life-responsibility" (104) on a woman? "She never even touched him nowadays, and he never touched her . . . they were so utterly out of touch" (104).

We now come to what is surely the turning point in the relationship between Connie and Mellors. One afternoon, just after she has been watching "the water bubbling coldly in John's well" (104), the keeper gives Connie her own key to the hut in the wood. This gesture in itself is certainly important, but what is even more interesting is the scene that Connie encounters when she enters the hut by herself. Mellors, she sees, has "left a little pile of kindling and small logs" (105) near the fireplace; in Lawrence's special imagery, the necessary life-materials are ready in the hut. While everything at Wragby makes "her go cold," everyday when Connie comes to see the hens, they are "the only things in the world that warmed her heart" (105). She reflects on "how terrible it was that it should be spring, and everything cold-hearted"; only the hens are "warm with their hot, brooding female bodies" (106). In Lawrence's most moving instance of flame imagery in this novel, Connie is pictured on a "lovely sunny day" looking at a newly hatched little chick; "it was the most alive little spark of a creature in the seven kingdoms at that moment. . . . Life, life! Pure, sparky, fearless new life! New life! So tiny and so utterly without fear!" (106).

Connie has not yet touched this "atom" of life, but during a subsequent visit, she tells Mellors that she would "love to touch" one of the chicks. When she holds the chick, she is so moved by this "atom of balancing life trembling" in her hands that "a tear fall[s] on her wrist" (107). The effect on Mellors is rendered in the appropriate language: "[S]uddenly he was aware of the old flame shooting and leaping up in his loins, that he had hoped was quiescent for ever" (107). He is moved by something "mute and forlorn" in Connie, and "compassion flamed in his bowels for her" (107). "At the back of his loins the fire suddenly darted stronger" (108). Lawrence adds, "His heart melted suddenly, like a drop of fire" (108).

In the first sexual encounter that follows, Connie participates with a sort of "queer obedience," although Mellors touches her "soft warm body" with "exquisite pleasure." The flame-water antithesis is crucial here. Mellors touches her with "his wet body," but there is also an "afterglow" from the moonlight over the oaks. His are "kisses of warmth" (110), and when Mellors returns to the cottage, he "started the fire" and "the fire was bright." He sits "by the fire" thinking about what he has begun with Connie, and in spite of the complications that the affair is certain to bring, he experiences "the stirring restlessness of his penis, the stirring fire in his loins!" (112). He has, in a word, begun "Life" again.

Connie goes to the wood next day "with a sort of warm naive kindness" that "opened her womb" towards Mellors. Although it is a grey afternoon, Connie is conscious of the "heave of the sap" that pushes its way "into the flamey oak-leaves, bronze as blood" (113–14). The keeper "does not come this afternoon"; it is "raining again," the "drizzle of rain" is like a veil; but Connie cannot stay away; she goes into the wood after dinner. I think "the fine rain" foreshadows the sexual failure that occurs in this second encounter; but perhaps we ought not to expect too much, too soon! Connie has anticipated the encounter, for "under her frail petticoat she was naked" (117). Mellors caresses "the delicate, warm, secret skin of her waist and hips," and Lawrence evokes the "warm, live beauty of contact, [which] is so much deeper than the beauty of vision," but Connie feels "herself a little left out"; to her "the man was intensely ridiculous in this posture and this act!" (118). Mellors attempts to keep her legs "warm"; his is an "undoubting warmth."

Mellors asks, "Are yer cold?" Upon her return to Wragby, we are told that Connie "would take her bath . . . she must take her bath" (119), which underlines the failure in the cottage.

Connie does not go into the wood for the next three days, so long as she feels or imagines that "the man is waiting for her, wanting her" (120). On the fourth day, when it is "almost warm," she sets out towards Marehay Farm, ostensibly to see Mrs. Flint's baby. Again, Lawrence symbolically endorses the value of this incident. We are told, "Mrs. Flint's eyes glowed again . . . the kettle was boiling by the fire," and, naturally, "the baby [is] a perky little thing . . . with red hair" (121). "How warm and lovely it was to hold a child in one's lap," thinks Connie, and she "got a deep voluptuous pleasure out of its soft young warmth" (122). And like the pheasant chick in the wood, the baby embodies "Young life! And so fearless!" (122). Lawrence also notes: "Mrs. Flint flushed and glowed and bridled with excitement" (122). Connie muses, "How warm and fulfilling somehow to have a baby" (123).

The incident with the baby also serves as dramatic preparation for the next encounter with Mellors, an encounter that has not been deliberately anticipated or planned. This will be the third time that the lovers come together, this time outdoors, in a "place where there was a little space and a pile of dead boughs" (124). It is here that Connie first experiences "new strange thrills rippling inside her," a feeling which Lawrence describes as "a flapping overlapping of soft flames . . . exquisite, exquisite and melting her all molten inside" (124). This is, of course, the first really satisfying love-making that Connie has; "his life sprang out into her. . . . And they lay and knew nothing" (125).

The passage has been extensively discussed and analysed, but I want to add the observation that there is a remarkable similarity between this passage and Lawrence's comment on one of the paintings in the Tombs of Tarquinia. In the novel, Connie is "like a sea-anemone under the tide," and Mellors carries his flame into her. In *Estruscan Places*, we find this passage describing the dolphin's plunge into the sea: "He is so much alive, he is like the phallus carrying the firey spark of procreation down into the wet darkness of the womb. The diver [in the painting] does the same, carrying like a phallus his small hot spark into the deeps" (89). Now the flame has penetrated Connie's womb; "another self was alive in her, burning molten and soft in her womb and bowels . . . . In her womb and bowels she was flowing and alive now" (126). Significantly,

Lawrence says: "Connie would not take her bath this evening" (128). The "warm flame of life was stronger" than Clifford, from whom the "real things were hidden" (129).

Let me now turn to Chapter 12 in which Connie again goes to the wood. The opening paragraph is remarkable for its evocation of sexual vitality. The color "yellow" is there in "the dandelions making suns"; there are "yellow celandines." "It was the yellow, the powerful yellow of early summer"; in the cottage the "fire was red"; everything is alive. But when Connie tells him about her desire to have a child, Mellors speaks "cold, good English" (156); he thinks he is merely being used; there is "a cold silence." Connie has again anticipated having sex, for she has left her "underthings off," yet when they come together the whole act again seems "ridiculous" to Connie. "Cold and derisive" her female soul stands apart. She is left "like a stone on a shore"; it "was no good that time." The complete absence of flame imagery here is telling, but when Mellors takes Connie "in his arms again," and once she has given up her "inward anger and resistance," she begins to "melt in marvellous peace"; now "she felt him like a flame of desire, yet tender, and she felt herself melting in the flame" (162). In what is surely her most profound sexual experience, she feels "she was like the sea, nothing but dark waves rising and heaving . . . she was ocean rolling its dark, dumb mass" (163). Like the diver in the Etruscan painting, Mellors's phallus has carried "his small hot spark into [her] deeps"; "a sudden little flame of new awareness went through her" (164). When Mellors returns (he leaves briefly to shut up the hens), Connie is "still lying there, glowing like a gypsy" (166).

"Tha mun come one naight ter th' cottage," (166) says Mellors, and after that emblematic scene in which Clifford attempts to take his bath–chair into the sacred wood, and where he fails so miserably, where he is suggestively described as "on the last wild waters, sailing in the last voyage of our civilization" (173), where the only evidence of fire is in a momentary touch of Connie's hand by Mellors, when "the flame of strength went down his back and his loins, reviving him" (179), Connie makes her plans for the first all–night encounter in the cottage. Clifford sends "out a skeleton's cold grizzly *will* against her" (182), but despite "a certain rebellion burning in her heart," with not really "the right sort of heart to take to a love–meeting," she sets out for the cottage. Although her shoes are "wet," there is a "red fire," burning inside; she sits "by the fire"; "it was warm after the chill outside" (184). Later she goes out "alone into the darkness" and feels "her shoes getting wetter again" (192). Mellors is "sitting in front of the low fire" when she returns. "He put sticks on the fire, and fetched more, till they had a good crackling chimneyfull of blaze. The rippling running yellow flame made them both happy, warmed their faces and their souls" (192). Connie slips into Mellors arms "before the fire" (192). "He held her close, in the running warmth of the fire. The flame itself was like a forgetting. And her soft, warm, ripe weight!" (192).

That night, Mellors recounts his sexual history, from which Connie concludes that they "*are* a couple of battered warriors" (192). Using very plain terms now, Mellors tells Connie what he believes in:

> Yes, I do believe in something. I believe in being warm-hearted. I believe especially in being warm-hearted in love, in fucking with a warm heart. I believe if men could fuck with warm hearts, and the women take it warm-heartedly, everything would come all right. It's all this cold-hearted fucking that is death and idiocy. (193)

And he adds: "Anything for a bit of warm-heartedness . . . I tell you it takes two even to be tender and warm-hearted" (193). "I'd rather die," Mellors insists, "than do any more cold-hearted fucking" (194). This frankness almost causes a rupture between them, and Mellors is about to leave, when Connie pleads for understanding. Note that in the reconciliation, as Mellors feels Connie under her clothing, we are told "she was smooth and warm." After making love very briefly, they gain "a measure of equanimity," as Lawrence phrases it; in the morning, let us note, "the sun rose over the wood." Connie sees how "warm and smoothed out" Mellors looks, lying there beside her, his eyes "look so warm," and Connie's breasts are "faintly golden." Lawrence says

> To Connie he was suddenly piercingly beautiful again, as when she had seen him that afternoon washing himself. Gold of sunshine touched the closed white curtain. . . . The sun . . . sent in a beam that lit up his thighs and slim belly and the erect phallus rising darkish and hot-looking from the little cloud of vivid gold-red hair. (195–96)

As in the previous two vital encounters, Connie's feelings are associated with "sharp soft waves of unspeakable pleasure [washing] over her,

[and] as he entered her," she again experiences "the curious molten thrilling that spread and spread till she was carried away with the last, blind flush of extremity" (197–98). Mellors's eyes now darken "with another flame of consciousness"; he sits naked on the bed "in the invisible flame of another consciousness" (198). Connie herself "lay naked and faintly golden like a Gloire de Dijon rose" (199). The lovers are "together in a world of their own" (199). On another occasion in the cottage, as "the rain was rushing down" and "thunder crashed outside" Connie sees the cottage as "a little ark in the Flood" (202–203).

After having taken such pains to show how the variations of flame or fire are consistently used by Lawrence to evoke the life-giving qualities in Connie's and Mellors's relations, and indicating how images of water are invariably antithetical to the life flame, what are we to make of the lovers' encounter in the pouring rain? It is by no means unusual to see this scene interpreted as representing a sort of cosmic union between the lovers and the natural elements. Such readings are partially sanctioned by the text, especially if we take into account what Lawrence says elsewhere about the necessity for vital relationships with the "circumambient universe." When I consider, however, how consistent Lawrence is in his use of water images to indicate those forces which are hostile to life and those mental attitudes which constantly threaten the possibility of a vital life, I would insist that in this part of the novel the significance of water imagery is still antithetical to flame. Let me attempt to explain.

To begin with, when Connie opens the door and looks outside, she sees "the straight heavy rain, like a steel curtain" (206); she dances "in the rain with the eurhythmic dance-movements she had learned so long ago in Dresden" (207). Neither the "steel curtain" nor the "movements . . . learned so long ago" points toward her new-found awareness. Mellors joins her in what I would only call a spirit of bravado, being caught up as it were in Connie's impulsive actions. Yet even here, we should note that (in the midst of the heavy rain) Connie's "blue eyes blazed with excitement" (207), and when he takes her in his arms, her "chilled female flesh . . . became quickly warm as flame, in contact" (207). Once again, flame triumphs over water. It is the presence of the flame that redeems this union—not some beneficent quality of the rain. Mellors, in fact, does not "like the rain," and by the time Connie follows him indoors, he "had already started a fire" (207). Note, too, that they both proceed to rub themselves dry, and that the "fire [which is] blazing up" is the means of restoring their mutual warmth. Both their bodies are "open to the fire"; Connie even holds "her head to the fire" (208). When Mellors touches Connie's "rounded tail," the vital flame asserts its dominance; "it seemed as if a slippery sort of fire came from it into his hands. And his two finger-tips touched the two secret openings to her body, time after time, with a soft little brush of fire" (208). What is being endorsed here is the flame component of the flame-water antithesis, not the reverse; but I am sure that this explanation will not settle the matter so neatly.

If trying to sort out the flame-water antithesis in the scene we have just been discussing seems problematical, "the night of sensual passion," which I want to look at now may prove to be even more difficult. By the time Connie goes to spend her last night with Mellors, she has already declared openly her belief in "the life of the body . . . [as] a greater reality than the life of the mind" (219). She tells Clifford that "the human body is only just coming to real life. With the Greeks it gave a lovely flicker, then Plato and Aristotle killed it, and Jesus finished it off" (220). She has arranged with Mellors that "if everything promised well for their night together, she would hang a green shawl out of the window. If there were frustrations, a red one" (220-21). I would certainly have preferred to see these colours reversed here, since "red" would fit in much better with my theory—nonetheless, it is an "emerald-green" shawl that signals to Mellors that all's well.

A good deal has already been written about this memorable night in Mellors's cottage, but not much has been said about the flame images that so thoroughly permeate the scene. Connie obediently takes the "burning" candle upstairs, which in itself signals endorsement of what is to follow. "It was," we are told, "sensuality sharp and searing as fire, burning the soul to tinder" (231). This is reductive fire imagery, and what it conveys is essentially a "burning out of the shames," something we are told, that is "forever necessary, to burn out false shames and smelt out the heaviest ore of the body into purity. With the fire of sheer sensuality" (231). Still, it is the "sensual flame" through which the purification is accomplished; it is the "sensual fire" that reveals the true phallic vision to the lovers. Lawrence's comment is unequivocal: "It needs sheer sensuality even to purify and quicken the mind. Sheer fiery sensuality, not messiness" (232). Connie later tells her sister Hilda that one needs both: "real tenderness [and] real sensuality . . . with the same person" (236).

Connie leaves Wragby and Mellors and travels to Venice, where, not surprisingly, she realizes that she is pregnant. When she hears from Clifford about the "beastly things" that Mellors is supposed to have done to Bertha Coutts, she falls "into a state of funk"; she remembers "the last night she had spent with him, and shivered," wondering whether Mellors "had known all that sensuality, even with Bertha Coutts" (247). But she does not repudiate her latter–day "Apollo" of Wragby Wood (I borrow Clifford's epithet here). He had given her "an exquisite pleasure and a sense of freedom and life . . . . He had released her warm, natural sexual flow" (248). Her refusal to go back on her life with Mellors is reasserted in a number of flame images. She recalls "the odd grin flickering on his face," "his hand warmly and softly closing over her tail," the "warmth . . . [running] through her womb, and the little flames flicker[ing] in her knees" (248). Finally, she says: "Oh, no! I mustn't go back on it! I must not go back on him. I must stick to him and to what I had of him, through everything. I had no warm, flamy life till he gave it me. And I won't go back on it" (248).

And that is exactly what Connie does; she stands by Mellors. She returns to London, where for the first time she sees the gamekeeper "in a formal suit of thin dark cloth." They meet (where else?) "outside the Golden Cock in Adam Street" (256). It is a tender and moving reunion, and Lawrence very subtly indicates to us that the commitment of the lovers towards each other is unwavering. A variety of flame images reinforces their steadfastness. Not only is the pub aptly named but also Connie's recollection of her stay in Venice is in sharp contrast to what now exists between her and Mellors: "Not all the sunshine of Venice had given her this inward expansion and warmth" (257). When she tells Mellors, "I'm going to have a child" (257), he looks at her "like some dark–flamed spirit" (257). When she tells him, firmly, "I want to live with you," we note: "In spite of himself, little flames ran over his belly as he heard her say it" (258). Several times during this meeting attention is drawn to the "flickering" in Mellors's face. To Mellors, Connie looks "so lovely and warm and wistful" (260). The love–making, characterized as it is by "tenderness," also incorporates the flame image: "And he went into her softly, feeling the stream of tenderness flowing in release from his bowels to hers, the bowels of compassion kindled between them" (261).

This is the last time in the novel that Mellors and Connie will appear together, but their absence from each other will not extinguish the flame that has come to burn between them. It is true that at times during the period of uncertainty, Mellors feels his "inside turn to water," yet he remains confident that "all the bad times that ever have been, haven't been able to blow the crocus out: not even the love of women" (281). "So they [the hostile world]," he asserts, "won't be able to blow out my wanting you, nor the little glow there is between you and me" (282). "I believe in the little flame between us," Mellors continues, "now the little flame is all I care about in my life" (282). Two books about Lawrence have featured titles from Mellors's letter to Connie. The first is an early book (1965) called *The Forked Flame* by H.M. Daleski; the second is titled *Flame into Being* (1985) by Anthony Burgess. Despite such tantalizing titles neither volume considers the centrality of the flame–water antithesis that I have been documenting. Mellors's belief is a repudiation of the "old Pentecost" and is here presented in the image of "the little forked flame between [him and Connie]" (282): "I'll stick to my little pentecost flame . . . . And I won't let the breath of people blow it out" (282). Here, as throughout the novel, the flame symbolizes the "higher mystery, that doesn't let even the crocus be blown out" (282).

Formerly, the antithetical water images have constantly threatened the survival of the flame, but here they are accepted as Mellors writes about chastity, which he now loves "as snowdrops love the snow"; chastity is "like a snow drop of forked white fire" (282); it is good to be chaste, he says, "like a river of cool water in my soul" (282). In a linguistically daring assertion, Mellors sums up the achieved relationship: "We fucked a flame into being," and he is confident that when they come together again, they "can [again] fuck the little flame brilliant and yellow, brilliant" (282). Mellors's message to Connie and, by extension, Lawrence's message to us, hearkens back to his pronouncement in the letter with which I began this paper: "We really trust in the little flame, and in the unnamed god that shields it from being blown out" (283). It is the same injunction that Lawrence urges in his short poem entitled, "Be It So":

> O, if a flame is in you, be it so!
> When your flame flickers up, and you flicker forth
> in sheer purity
> for a moment free from all conceit of yourself,
> and all afterthought
> you are for that moment one of the gods. . . . (674)

Note

1. For a very perceptive analysis of the "fire and water" imagery in *The Escaped Cock*, see Robert H. MacDonald, "The Union of Fire and Water: An Examination of the Imagery of The Man Who Died." MacDonald argues that Lawrence's "imagery makes plain the equal and reciprocal power of the opposites" (41); my own view is that "fire and water" are antithetical elements, and Lawrence's images consistently invoke the hostility between the two.

Works Cited

Burgess, Anthony. *Flame into Being: The Life and Work of D.H. Lawrence*. London: Heinemann, 1985.

Daleski, H.M. *The Forked Flame: A Study of D.H. Lawrence*. London: Faber and Faber, 1965.

Frye, Northrop. "The Archetypes of Literature." In *Criticism: The Major Statements*. Selected by Charles Kaplan. New York: St. Martin's Press, 1991: 500-14.

Lawrence, D.H. *Etruscan Places*. New York: Viking, 1932. Compass Books Edition, 1957.

———. *Apocalypse and the Writings on Revelation*. Ed. Mara Kalnins. Cambridge: Cambridge UP, 1980.

———. *The Letters of D.H. Lawrence*. Vol. 1. Ed. James T. Bolton. Cambridge: Cambridge UP, 1979.

———. *Lady Chatterley's Lover*. Afterword by Harry T. Moore. Signet Modern Classic. New York: New American Library, 1959.

———. *Mr Noon*. Ed. Lindeth Vasey. Cambridge: Cambridge UP, 1984.

———. *The Complete Poems*. Vol. 1. Ed. Vivian de Sola Pinto and Warren Roberts. New York: Viking, 1964.

MacDonald, Robert H. "The Union of Fire and Water: An Examination of the Imagery of *The Man Who Died*." *The D.H. Lawrence Review* 10.1 (Spring 1977): 34–51.

14

A Question of "Dual Forces": D.H. Lawrence and Buddhism—A Comparative Approach

KAIEN KITAZAKI

Lawrence's idea of "Dual Forces," conspicuous in his "Study of Thomas Hardy," has been interpreted by scholars before and since the Cambridge edition of his essay published in 1985.[1] My purpose is to examine a Japanese, especially a Japanese-Buddhist, understanding of "Dual Forces" and to show how such an understanding could be of help to scholars outside of Japan. In introducing the interpretation of Amida-Buddha by Saint Shinran, Master and Founder of the Shin Sect of Buddhism[2] in thirteenth-century Japan, I intend to make the "Dual Forces" of Lawrence more understandable to Christians; conversely, I can achieve a significantly new view of the traditional interpretation of "Amida-Buddha"[3] through a comparative study of Lawrence and Buddhism.

Both Lawrence and Shinran think that there is an "Original Power" or "impersonal forces" (Worthen 56) forever working in this universe: Lawrence uses expressions such as "Holy Spirit," "Dark Sun," "Father Sun" or "Creative Power" (e.g., *The Plumed Serpent* 123–25). Saint Shinran refers to "Amida-Buddha," which originated from India as one of the Buddhisms taught, especially by Hinayana Buddhism, in China, Korea and Japan. Lawrence saw "Holy Spirit" working as "Dual Forces" or "Male and Female" in his "Study of Thomas Hardy."[4] Shinran saw "Amida-Buddha" working as "Dual Forces," "Kannon and Seishi," in his *Wasan* or Japanese hymns.

To make the Amida-Buddhist "Dual Forces" or "Two Laws" more concrete, let me first quote the beginning part of *Shōshin Nembutsu Ge, The Gāthā of True Faith in the Nembutsu* by Saint Shinran:

> I rely upon the Tathāgata of Immeasurable Life;
> I take refuge in the Inconceivable Light. (17)

"Tathāgata" in Sanskrit means "thus-come," used as an epithet for the Buddha, the enlightened One. The expressions "Immeasurable Life" and "Inconceivable Light" are translations of the Sanskrit "Amitāyus" and "Amitābha" respectively: they are called "Amida" in one phonetic rendering. Here Shinran understands "Amida" working as "Dual Forces": "Immeasurable Life" and "Inconceivable Light." Then he interprets this Amida as Dual Forces revealed to the human being; he tries to interpret "Dharmākara" who appears as a monk seeking his real or "alter ego" in *The Greater Sutra*:

> Dharmākara, the Bodhisattva, during His causal state,
> Being in the presence of the Buddha Lokeśvararāja,
> And having examined the causes of Buddhas' Pure Lands
> And the good and evil of those Buddha Lands and of the heavenly and
> human realms,
> Established the highest, most excellent Vow
> And brought forth the rare Great Universal Vow.
> After contemplating for five kalpas,[5]
> He chose the best of them.
> Again, He vowed that His Name would be heard in the ten quarters. (18–19)

The Monk or Dharmākara, Incarnation of Amida–Buddha, is a kind of "alter ego" or archetypal human being. Shinran finds in him his own image and feels familiar with the Monk. Finally he found in this Monk the significance of his life–long travel seeking his "true self." This means that Amida–Buddha or Dual Forces is forever coming down into the human soul of a man and bringing the illumination of Amida–Buddha himself.

This anecdote is reminiscent of Aaron Sisson seeking his true self, "the man in a man," in *Aaron's Rod* (25) or Kate Leslie's "alter ego" or Owen's "real self" in *The Plumed Serpent* (10). While Aaron at the Royal Oak talks with the "landlady," "the little doctor," and others, he feels unhappy and uncomfortable, realizing that there was a "hard, opposing core in him, that neither the whisky nor the woman could dissolve or soothe, tonight" (*Aaron's Rod* 22). He sees in the doctor as well as in the landlady the same danger, the same menace: "wise speech and good intentions—they were invariably maggoty with these secret inclinations to destroy the man in a man" (25). This "opposing core in him" or "the man in a man" takes us to the "alter ego" Kate finds in herself. At the "Beginnings of a Bull-fight," before the game, the "fun" begins among the audience:

> "Look at that!" said Owen. "Isn't that fun!"
> "No," said Kate, her little *alter ego* speaking out for once, in spite of her will-to-happiness. "No, I don't like it. I really hate common people." (*The Plumed Serpent* 9)
> As a socialist, Owen disapproved, and as a happy man, he was disconcerted. Because his own real self, as far as he had any left, hated common rowdiness just as much as Kate did. (*The Plumed Serpent* 10)

Shinran, Kate and Aaron share the common "archetype" which seeks a balanced way of living, the reconciliation of the "Dual Forces." Let me quote again from Saint Shinran:

> Kannon and Seishi
> Together illumine the world with the light of compassion,
> Never resting even for a moment
> From bringing to Nirvana those with mature conditions. (*Jodo Wasan* 47)

Also:

> If one says "Namu Amida Butsu,"
> Kannon and Seishi,
> Together with Bodhisattvas numerous as the
> Ganges' sands or dust-particles,
> Follow him like the shadow that follows one's body. (142)

The term "Kannon" in Japanese, means the Buddha Avalokiteśvara who hears the voices of worldly people full of sufferings, and "Seishi" means "the Buddha with Wisdom and Light"; these are the two virtues of Amida-Buddha. There are always dual forces working that make us complete as human or sentient beings. The "Kannon Power" or "Love Urge" reveals itself in the world with such things as sunshine, air, food, water, clothing, and forms of recreation that make us enjoy this life. Whereas the "Seishi Power" or "Power Urge" is revealed in strong summer heat, severe cold in winter, flood or typhoon, famine, earthquake, lightning, fire, senility, illness, and death. These things we cannot welcome; we try to evade them. But this "Seishi Power" is a factor that checks our laziness when we come to depend too much on "Kannon Power" and awakens us to a more balanced way of living. It is a "balance of Natural Powers" that Lawrence discusses at various times and places.[6]

As we have seen, Aaron recognizes the imbalance in nature, listening to the voiceless voice of "the man in a man" from his "invisible or second self" (286–87). Kate realizes her "alter ego" speaking out, and Owen too has his own "real self." What is this call or speaking out but the working-out of the two forces within him and her? And this calling of the "true self" is being born at any moment at any place. We cannot see where the "Holy Spirit" or "Amida" is. But it is at work in "the man in a man," in Aaron's two selves. Aaron's "two selves" remind us of Kate Leslie's "two selves," one belonging to Cipriano and Ramon and the other belonging to her past. Finally, by saying "I must have both," she seems to be taking the way to Cipriano and Ramon, her sensitive, desirous self" (*The Plumed Serpent* 439).

Seen through Buddhist eyes, Aaron is undergoing a struggle towards finding his true self, like Shinran's reliance upon and taking refuge in the Tathāgata, "Immeasurable Life and Inconceivable Light" upon whose balance his true self rests. Here we are able to see the workings of "Holy Spirit" or "Amida-Buddha," and it conveys a truth to inward experience that has its relevance today.

When Lawrence says, "Now the aim of man remains to recognize and seek out the Holy Spirit" (*Phoenix* 514), he thinks of the "Originator" who drives the twin principles of Law and Love across the ages. His "Study of Thomas Hardy" is written from this point of view: he considers whether or not Love and Law ruled by the Holy Spirit have enough contact or relation in Hardy's novels and other artistic expressions.

Lawrence, discussing Hardy's novels, gives an example of the incompleteness of the characters; he gives us an example of the denial of "one major force" in the unbalanced way of life led by Clym Yeobright. Why does Clym come back to Egdon when he discovers the vanity of life in Paris and the *beau monde*? Is it to reunite himself with the flow of life that rose out of Egdon as from a source? Naturally not. Clym comes,

> to preach to the Egdon eremites that they might rise to a serene comprehensiveness without going through the process of enriching themselves." As if the Egdon eremites had not already far more serene comprehensiveness than ever he had himself, rooted as they were in the soil of all things, and living from the root! (*Phoenix* 417)

"Could the sound of his own words affect the working of the body of Egdon?" "The will and words," which militate against "the great reality of Egdon," are the only vanity. Lawrence concludes that Clym, whom he satirically describes as "preaching out of sheer emptiness," must "learn what it is to be at one, in his mind and will, with the primal impulses that rise in him."

Comparing Alec and Jude, Lawrence further points out that Jude wanted to arrest all his activity in his senses, while Jude wanted to arrest all his activity in his mind. In this way both wanted to escape from the trouble of living as a "complete person, a full individual." To live as "complete," "full" individual is to live by a "balance of Natural Forces," meaning we should be careful not to stick too much to the "one force" only.

Born in the world of Protestantism, Lawrence knew quite well that it put too much reliance upon the Bible and on an individual revelation through the Bible. He thought this world as balanced on the side of "Power Urge" or "Infinite Light," in the appeal it makes to the spirit of conflict and dissent, or to the "Male Impulse." He saw a kind of abstracting in the work of J.M.W. Turner in his "Study of Thomas Hardy." Lawrence tells us that "I cannot look at a later Turner picture without abstracting myself, without denying that I have limbs, knees and thighs and breast" (475).

He says Turner sought a consummation of the Spirit, rather than a mating of body with Spirit. Turner's quest for Light, the quest to "make light transfuse the body," is a denial of one major force. He identified the dissident of Protestantism with this denial or imbalance.

At the same time, Catholicism is not immune from denial or imbalance. If we take a look at Doña Carlota in *The Plumed Serpent*, her love-centered or egoistic self-will was not broken until her death. She could not have a chance to see a "balance of Natural Forces" to the end of her life. Her insistence on her love of her husband and children shows that she denies "Dual Forces." She sacrificed herself to one major force, the "Love Urge" or female or sexual impulse (*Plumed Serpent* 206–207).

Another example of imbalance in *The Plumed Serpent* occurs in "The Bishop of the West" chapter when Ramón and Cipriano meet in order to ask permission to introduce Quetzalcoatl as a religion for the Mexicans. But to their regret, the Bishop shows little interest in their request:

> "Your Church is the Catholic Church, Father?"
> "Surely!," said the Bishop.
> "And Catholic Church means the Church of All, the Universal Church?"
> "Surely, son of mine."
> "Then why not let it be really catholic? Why call it catholic when it is not only just one among many churches, but is even hostile to all the rest of the churches? Father, why not let the Catholic Church become really the Universal Church?"

> "It is the Universal Church of Christ, my son."
> "Why not let it be the Universal Church of Mohammed as well: since ultimately, God is One God, but the peoples speak varying languages, and each needs its own prophet to speak with its own tongue. The Universal Church of Christ, and Mohammed, and Buddha, and Quetzalcoatl, and all the others—*that* would be a Catholic Church, Father." (264)

Thus, neither the Bishop's version of Catholicism nor dissident Protestantism can guarantee a "natural or complete" self balanced by "Dual Forces." Lawrence's departure from his Midlands and journey to the south of Europe and his return to his home country from America tell us that he was always dealing with the deep working out of the imbalance of the "Dual Forces." Lawrence's "savage pilgrimage" around the world tells us that he was well aware of this imbalance in his soul.

Now we come back to Saint Shinran to trace briefly his life-long pursuit of Amida-Buddha, Incarnation of "Kannon and Seishi Power." Shinran was born in A.D. 1173, in the Kamakura Area as the son of the noble Fujiwara family. In consequence of his distinguished birth, his earthly prospects were full of promise. But his mother died when he was very young, followed by his father's death before Shinran was nine years old. These unhappy events led him to the monastery of the venerable Jiyen, where he had his head shaved by this noble priest and was given the Buddhist name, Hanyen (Suzuki *Collected* 169-90). Here we can notice that in Shinran was born "the man in a man" or Dharmākara who is Amida Buddha being incarnated Himself as a Bodhisattva. He went up to Mount Hiei, a Mecca of the Tendai schools, one of the main streams of Mahayana teachings introduced to Japan from China by Saicho, the Founder of this sect on this mountain.

Shinran wanted to study and practice religious disciplines but found this life unsatisfying. During the first year of Kennin (1201 CE) when he was twenty-nine years old, he went down from Mt. Hiei to call on the Genkū Shōnin at his Yoshimizu monastery; he wished to walk in the right way of Easy Practice;[7] he found it very uncertain to plod along the narrow path of Difficult Practice in these later days when humanity had become so degraded. As soon as he met the venerable Genku, Shinran instantly came to realize the inmost meaning of the doctrine of salvation through Amida Buddha: Amida's all-embracing love for sentient beings. He found that in his soul lived Amida Buddha, incarnated as a Bodhisattva Dharmākara, letting him seek the balance of "Dual Force," "Kannon and Seishi Powers" to make him complete as a human being. Or rather he found out that he was always surrounded by the workings of the "Dual Force"; he came to realize that humanity was so degraded because it was so lazy or impudent and ignorant about itself. Once we are well aware of "Dual Forces" forever working for us, that awakening saves us from a lopsided way of life, saves us from "the imbalance of Natural Powers."

In order to keep our awakening alive and to live fully as sentient beings, we are taught to say "Namu-Amida-Butsu," the recitation of the Buddha's name and to live as humbly and modestly as possible. The authority for this faith is found in *The Sutra of Meditation* and *The Greater Sutra*, two of the three Buddhist sutras Shinran selected out of many:

> If a man, bowing in reverence to Amida Buddha and pronouncing his Name, is desirous of being born in Amida's Country, the Buddha would send out an immeasurable number of Buddhas and bodhisattvas such as Kannon and Seishi, all in their transformation-bodies, in order to keep the devotees well guarded. (Suzuki *Kyōgyōshinsō* 39–40)

Or in the *The Greater Sutra*, Shinran again confirms his faith: "When I attain Buddhahood, if all beings in the ten quarters pronouncing my Name up to ten times were not reborn in my Country, I would not attain the Supreme Enlightenment" (40).

These two quotations tell us that Amida-Buddha is now seen as having attained Buddhahood; Amida's dual forces, "Kannon and Seishi" or "Male and Female" Forces have always been working to let "sentient beings" live in the ideal Country or "Pure Land." This "Pure Land" should not be taken literally. As J. Campbell points out in *The Power of Myth*, "Every religion is true one way or another. It is true when understood metaphorically. But when it gets stuck to its own metaphors, interpreting them as facts, then you are in trouble" (56). Buddhists too should be careful not to interpret "Pure Land" as some concrete land somewhere (see Note 3). Taking the ascendance of Jesus to heaven, Campbell advises us to see this in terms of its metaphoric connotation: "he has gone inward—not into outer space but into inward space, to the place from which all being comes, into the consciousness that is the source of all things, the kingdom of heaven within" (56). "Pure Land" too is the place from which all being comes; it is a "metaphor of returning to the source, alpha and omega, of leaving the fixation on the body behind and going to the body's dynamic source" (57). This is a kind of "Becoming" world, not a "Being" world as F.L. Baumer says in his *Modern European Thought* (3 and 45–49).

In the "Becoming" world, "the body's dynamic source," "Birth-and-Death" is identical with Nirvana just as Shinran sings in his *The Shōshin Ge: The Gāthā of True Faith in the Nembutsu*:

> When Faith is raised in a deluded and defiled ordinary man,
> He is made aware that Birth-and-Death is identical with Nirvana. (36)

"Birth-and-Death identical with Nirvana" is seen from the viewpoint of an enlightened being, or one born in the Pure Land. The idea "identical" ("soku" in Japanese, "identity of differences" in English) is seemingly peculiar to Mahayana Buddhism. But when we remember, for example, W. Blake's famous poem *Auguries of Innocence*, this "identity" can be commonly or universally applied to the Westerners as well as to the Buddhists of Japan.

> To see a World in a grain of sand,
> And Heaven in a wild flower,
> Hold Infinity in the palm of your hand,
> And Eternity in an hour. (Keynes 431)

We can see in this poem that there is a clear contrast and a close affinity between "Infinity" and the "finite," "Eternity" and "moment," "Worldly world" and "Heavenly world," and "Extremely small world" and "Extremely large world." We can understand, as Blake does, that these two worlds of extremes are identical. This interpretation of the world we have already seen in Lawrence's criticism of Clym Yeobright, of Jude, and of the painter Turner. Lawrence concludes that the "Dual Forces" of Thomas Hardy lead us 'to recognize and seek out the Holy Spirit, the Reconciler, the Originator, He who drives the twin principles of Law and Love across the ages" (514). And on the development of true art, he says "there shall be the art which knows the struggle between the two conflicting laws, and knows the final reconciliation, where both are equal, two in one, complete. This is the supreme art, which yet remains to be done" (515–16).

Lawrence's attitude to art also can be applied to his understanding of Buddhism (though it is the southern, Hinayana Buddhism) through a letter to his American friend Achsah Brewster:

> True Nirvana is a flowering tree whose roots are passion and desire and hate and love. *(Letters,* 3: 712*)*

This reminds me of Saint Shinran's statement that "Birth-and-Death is identical with Nirvana." Shinran was sent into exile to the northern part of Japan because his revolutionary fame in Kyoto angered orthodox schools of Buddhist teachers, and there he met many illiterate farmers and fishermen. But he found in them the clue to the "True Nirvana." He embraced those who were unable to free themselves from the chain of birth-and-death; he realized again and again that "passion and desire," "hate and love," delight and sorrow are the "roots" only from which a beautiful tree or flowers grow.

In the same letter to Brewster, Lawrence further comments on Nirvana: "Nirvana is all right if you get at it right. It is a sort of all-inclusive state, and therefore includes sorrow, does *not* supersede sorrow: no such impertinence" (712). The "all-inclusive state" means that if the ideal of Nirvana is likened to the "Male Force" then the other "Female Force" suggests an analogy of the "roots" that send up new shoots. Lawrence insists in his letter that the final "reconciliation" of the "Dual Forces" should accord with his understanding of the ideal of Buddhists. Lawrence tries to avoid "Nirvana" being "a cut blossom." Brewster's Nirvana, being "too much a one-man show," inevitably leads to "navel contemplation" (712); he not only admonishes Brewster but also checks himself from falling into "navel contemplation," excluding either "Force of Male or of Female."

Why did Lawrence make fun of Brewster's "Nirvana"? Because with either Buddhists or Christians, "the shift from a nature religion to a sociological religion" (Campbell 56) makes it difficult for them to remember their likeness to nature. Lawrence sought the "Dual religion" from his earliest days as a writer, just as Shinran sought the balance of "Dual Forces" early in his childhood when he lost both of his parents. Shinran, too, supports a "nature religion" rather than "sociological religion." He says in his letter to his followers in the Kanto Area during his late life in Kyoto, "Amida-Buddha is the medium through which we are made to realize *jinen*, or nature" (Ueda 30).

To conclude, I should point out that both Lawrence and Shinran advocate a type of "nature religion," and they share in common an understanding of Nature; the "Original Power" of Nature always takes on two forms: "Male Force" and "Female Force," or "Kannon Power" and "Seishi Power," trying to make all living things on earth complete, perfect in themselves. Another similarity between them, suggesting their common "nature religion," is that both touched the "Original Power" directly, not through indirect media such as "sociological religion." Shinran met

"Amida" directly as he says, "When I carefully consider the Vow which Amida brought forth after five kalpas' contemplation, I find that it was solely for me, Shinran, alone!" (*The Tanni Sho* 79). Lawrence writes, "I believe that Jesus is one of the Sons of God: not, however, the only Son of God." He cannot believe in a Church of Christ that declares there is only one way to God (*Reflections* 385).

In this way both of them try to identify themselves directly with the "Original Power." In fact, to say that "I and the Father are one," as Jesus said, is blasphemy for us (Campbell 57). But as Campbell further points out, "in the Thomas gospel that was dug up in Egypt some forty years ago, Jesus says, 'He who drinks from my mouth will become as I am, and I shall be he'" (57). Thus we are all manifestations of Buddha consciousness or Christ consciousness. Although this may seem a heresy to some, to wake up to the Christ or Buddha consciousness within us is to be awakened, after all, to the workings of "Dual Forces," of "God" being "one God," or of "Creative Power," of "Amida-Buddha."

Notes

1. Before the Cambridge Edition, J. Worthen, for example, aptly summarizes in his *D.H. Lawrence and the Idea of the Novel*: "The ideas which dominate the 'study' are those of impersonal forces existing in and through and behind human beings, in terms of which we can understand ourselves and our history. Lawrence sometimes calls them Law and Love, sometimes the Male and Female principles" (56).

   In their 1988 study, *D.H. Lawrence's Non-Fiction: Art, Thought and Genre*, Howard Mills and David Ellis successfully place "Study of Thomas Hardy" in an appropriate or historical context (10–39) and point out "the polarity of male and female principles" (35 and 38).
2. One of the traditional thirteen schools of Japanese Buddhism and a major form of PURE LAND BUDDHISM. Its founder, SHINRAN (1173–1263), used the term Jodo Shinshu to denote the "true essence" *(shinshu)* of Pure Land teaching as expounded by his teacher Honen. The basic goal of Shin Buddhism coincides with that of Mahayana Buddhism: realizing the wisdom to see things, including the self, as they truly are. In this tradition, however, such wisdom is brought forth from within each person by the transforming powers of Amida's Primal Vow and not through calculative thinking or self-generated effort.
3. There were many suicides who dived into the Sea of "Naniwa" (old name of present-day Osaka) supposing that there existed a Paradise far in the distance of the ocean. This kind of suicide came from the belief that at the very Western direction from the West-Gate of Shitennoji Temple in Naniwa opened the

East–Gate or the doorway to Paradise, of Pure Land. Travelling to Paradise in this way was very popular among the people between the end of Heian Period and the beginning of Kamakura Area (from the 9th century C.E. to 12th century C.E.).

In modern times, we often hear it said that "if the existence of 'Amida–Buddha' or of 'Pure Land' is scientifically proved, then I believe it." This type of question is quite similar to the one in the former example, because both share in common the view that they accept Pure Land or Amida–Buddha as existing objectively in this universe. But, in fact, we have to accept it as metaphor as J. Campbell points out, or Lawrence himself says: "Great religious images are only images of our own experience or of our own state of mind or soul" in his "The Risen Lord."

4. See E.D. McDonald (ed.), *Phoenix 1936* (New York: The Viking Press, 1968), "Study of Thomas Hardy," for examples of such expressions.
5. *Kalpas* means aeons of time.
6. Apart from "Study of Thomas Hardy" we have referred to, we could quote Lawrence writing in *The Symbolic Meaning* (the early version of *Studies in Classic American Literature*), discussing Hector St. John de Crèvecoeur: "He opened the dark eyes of his blood to the presence of bees, birds and serpents. He saw them in their magnificent struggling division, and their wonderful coexistence in luminous strangeness."
7. *The Tanni Sho: Notes Lamenting Differences*, p. 13, refers to the Path of Easy Practice in which one has only to utter the Nembtsu in accordance with Amida's Vow in order to be born in the Pure Land and realize Enlightenment. The term is contrasted to *Nangyo*, difficult practice, or the Path of Difficult Practice in which one performs various practices for a long period of time.

Works Cited

Campbell, Joseph, and William Moyers. *The Power of Myth*. New York: Doubleday, 1988.

Chung, Chong–Wha. "In Search of the Dark God: Lawrence's Dualism." In P. Preston, editor, *D.H. Lawrence in the Modern World*. Macmillan, 1989.

Fugen, Daien, translator and annotator. *The Shoshin Ge: The Gatha of True Faith in Nembtsu*. Kyoto: Ryukoku UP, 1962.

Fujimoto, Ryukyo, et al., translators and annotators. *The Jodo Wasan: The Hymns on the Pure Land*. Kyoto: Ryukoku UP, 1965.

Japan: An Illustrated Encyclopedia. Tokyo: Kodan Sha, 1993.

Keynes, G., editor. *Blake: Complete Writings to the Variant Readings*. Oxford: Oxford UP, 1972.

Lawrence, D.H. *Aaron's Rod*. Cambridge: Cambridge UP, 1988.

———. *Letters*. Vol. 3 edited by Boulton and Robertson. Cambridge: Cambridge UP, 1984.

———. *Phoenix*. Edited by E. MacDonald. New York: The Viking Press, 1968.

———. *Reflections on the Death of a Porcupine and Other Essays*. Cambridge: Cambridge UP, 1988.

———. *The Symbolic Meaning*. London: Centaur Press, 1975.

Mills, Howard, and David Ellis. *D.H. Lawrence's Non-Fiction: Art, Thought and Genre*. Cambridge: Cambridge UP, 1988.

Shozomatsu Wasan: Shinrans' Hymns on the Last Age. Kyoto: The Ryukoku University Translation Center, 1980.

Suzuki, D.T. *Collected Writings on Shin Buddhism*. Kyoto: Shinshū Otaniha, 1973.

(Suzuki), translator. *The Kyogyoshinsho: The Collection of Passages, Expounding the True Teaching, Living, Faith, and Realizing of the Pure Land*. Kyoto: Shinshu Otaniha, 1973.

Teruaki, T., translator. *Kin Gendai Yoroppa No Shiszo*. Tokyo: Daishukan Shoten, 1992. (Originally *Modern European Thought* by F.L. Baumer, London: Macmillan, 1977).

The Tanni Sho: Notes Lamenting Differences. Kyoto, The Ryukoku University Translation Center, 1990.

Worthen, John. *D.H. Lawrence and the Idea of the Novel*. London: Macmillan, 1979.

15

The Edward Garnett Editing of the *Sons and Lovers* Ms.

JOHN HENRY RALEIGH

The famous Edward Garnett edition of the MS. of *Sons and Lovers* has often been mentioned or discussed but has hardly ever been examined systematically or in detail, the aim of the present study. (It should be said that the new Cambridge edition, edited by Helen and Carl Baron, of *Sons and Lovers* (1992) restores all Garnett cuts).[1] The Garnett edition has been celebrated by several literary critics beginning with Mark Schorer in his introduction to the publication of the facsimile of the MS. in 1977,[2] regretted by a smaller number, with some others in between the pro and the con. Garnett's major purposes in making his multiple excisions, about 1/10 of the original MS., are obvious and well-known: to sharpen and heighten and concentrate the mother-son story of Mrs. Morel and Paul by eliminating in great part the presence of sibling William Morel. This was Garnett's most substantial diminution. But also he diminished Walter Morel, both by cutting out some of the expositions of his mining background and by eliminating two or three of the few occasions when Morel was seen in favorable light. Garnett also diminished the general social context of England in the early twentieth century by cutting out some matters relating to the suffragette movement and some other instances of social context. Such then were the major excisions or diminutions, and I shall not discuss them since their purpose is clear.

What I was interested in was whether there could be found some kind of pattern in Garnett's cuts, that is, not so much the subject matter of the cuts, as all-important as that is, but was there some technical aspect of the novel that perhaps set off Garnett's diagonal slashes? And I think there are several, as I shall attempt to show. First, for some figures. Schorer and the Barons say that Garnett made about 79–80 deletions, from quite tiny ones—a word, a line or two—to quite substantial ones, sometimes involving two or three pages. My own interest was not in Garnett's tiny deletions but in those diagonal slashes whereby he cut out anything from a short paragraph or a brief dialogue to one or two or more pages. My estimate is that there are about 64 of these kinds of cuts, and the majority of these are dialogues or parts of dialogues. That is to say, of Garnett's 64 excisions about 42 are pure dialogue and approximately another 5 are made up mostly of dialogue, with some description. This makes a total of around 47 dialogic excisions, or approximately 73% of my total of 64. For example, in Chapter VI, (Death in the Family), all seven cuts are of dialogue. So whatever Garnett was doing, diminishing William or Walter Morel or down-playing the suffragette movement, he was doing it in large measure by eliminating dialogue. (He was also of course eliminating non-dialogue which I shall discuss later.) I next set myself the question: what kinds of dialogue were being excised either in whole or in part and could one guess why Garnett was eliminating them? the answer to this, I believe, is "Yes" for many of them but not for all.

The greatest number of whole or partial removal of the same type or kind of dialogue are some eleven arguments or disputes or tiffs, either eliminated or truncated: four between Mr. and Mrs. Morel; one between Mrs. Morel and Mrs. Anthony; two between Mrs. Morel and William; and four between Paul and Clara. As for the reasons, arguments between married couples, like the Morels, tend to be quite repetitious and are thus easily reduced. Of the four here cut down, two are arguments about his drinking and one is about whether William should be punished for roughing up Mrs. Anthony's son. The fourth is a more limited disagreement carried out in front of Mr. Heaton, the minister. The argument between Mrs. Morel and Mrs. Anthony is about the dispute between their sons and is, needless to say, quite repetitious. Mrs. Morel's two brief interchanges with William concern his girl-friend Gypsy, and are cut out completely, along with all the other excised material about William. One of Paul's arguments with Clara is about the equality or rather the disequality of the sexes, one of the themes of the novel that Garnett had diminished. Two of the other three tiffs between Paul and Clara are concerned with his quizzing her about her relations with Dawes, which at times seem to touch on the same matter of the equality of the sexes. The third features Paul being rather ill-natured and will be mentioned in my next category, a discussion of another kind of dialogue-cut by Garnett: his removal of what he regarded as inappropriate utterances by the central characters.

This second type of dialogue cuts, slight but important, involves characterization with Garnett removing statements made by central characters when, evidently, these statements in his opinion are out of keeping with his sense of that character. There are some seven of these, three of them for Mrs. Morel. Two of them involve her being furiously angry. The first is a cut from the first, and rather lengthy, argument with Morel in Chapter I (The early life of the Morels) about his drinking. One of Garnett's cuts here—there are others—has Mrs. Morel saying, "I'd smite you down, you cowardly beast, if only I could." Garnett, I am guessing, thought this somewhat out of character for the ladylike Gertrude Morel (although I would add it sounds rather like a seventeenth century Puritan, from whom, after all, Mrs. Morel is descended). In C. VII (Lad-and-Girl Love) the Morels and others are driving to their sea-side cottage, and the trip is taking longer than it was said to be by the woman who sold them the ticket. Mrs. Morel exclaims "That stinking hussey," so loudly that her daughter Annie says, "Don't shout so mother." I think I agree with Garnett on these two Mrs. Morel excisions; they are somewhat out of character. The third Mrs. Morel cut is from her conversation with Mr. Heaton in C. II (The Birth of Paul and another Battle). Heaton has been giving her a symbolical interpretation of Christ changing the water to wine at Cana. But Mrs. Morel rejects this with a much more earthy, naturalistic version, making, as Lawrence comments, "the bible real to the people." It appears to me that Mrs. Morel here is a pure mouth-piece for her creator, D.H. Lawrence, and is, once more, somewhat out of character.

Paul Morel also has some of his dialogue censored on at least four occasions. There are two instances in C. VIII (Strife in Love) in conversations with Miriam. In the first one he is sounding off to Miriam on the powers of the unconscious—"But you are what your unconscious self makes you—"and she is both fascinated and repelled. In the second one he is explaining to her the conventionalizing of art into stylized, geometric designs and how the force of gravity is the great shaper of things. These monologues are Paul at his most "profound" and perhaps confusing (the Barons had to supply scholarly footnotes for each sequence.) Garnett, I guess, thought all this a bit much for two young lovers.

Another excision for Paul was in C. III (The young life of Paul). Here Garnett has cut out a very brief section of dialogue between Paul and his mother when the boy is explaining his embarrassment at how he was treated by the paymasters when he went to collect his father's pay. Why was this cut? I am not sure. Perhaps because the situation itself has already been dramatized at the pay-station. I mentioned above the excision of an argument between Paul and Clara. This occurs in C.X. (Clara) where the two are exchanging barbed taunts. Of Paul's behavior here Lawrence remarks, "He began to lose his head" and, "Now he had lost his head, and gone too far." Garnett simply removed the entire interchange.

A third class or kind of dialogue often cut down or out by Garnett is playful banter, especially when it is rather arch, between two or more people. There are at least six instances of this kind of exclusion. One is a little interchange in C.V (Paul Launches into Life) between Paul and Louie, "handsome and brazen," at Jordan's place of business. Another one in this same sequence is an interchange between Fanny, the little humpback woman, who has a nice singing voice, and Paul, with him urging her to sing, which she finally does. Since the conversation with Fanny had been preceded by the cancelled interchange with Louie, which itself was quickly followed by the excision of a brief dialogue between Paul and Pappleworth, before the cancelled Fanny-Paul duet, the conclusions seems to be that Garnett wished to play down Paul's relations with his fellow-workers, thus further reducing the social context of the novel. Still another fairly large excision is some playful joking between Paul and Mrs. Morel at dinner before they go to the Leivers in C. VI (Death in the Family). In the group outing to Wingfield Manor that the young people take in C. VII (Lad-and-Girl Love) Garnett cut out one brief piece of dialogue and another more substantial one, both of them meant to be jocular. In the brief one there is a joking interchange between Leonard, Dick, Paul, and Annie about the fact that Leonard and Dick had a drink in a public house. The lengthy one—a whole page in the Baron edition—involves Leonard, Dick, Paul, Geoffrey, Miriam, and Annie. They are inside the decayed manor and are pretending to be ancient lords and ladies, all in a very arch and coy manner. Still another little episode in this same chapter involves Miriam, Paul, Mrs. Morel, and Mr. Morel, bantering about the significance of the name "Elizabeth." It is rather labored humor, and even Morel gets in a joke that makes the others laugh, constituting perhaps still another reason for Garnett to cut it since it would make Morel more attractive. In C. VIII (Strife in Love) a small piece of banter, involving Beatrice getting a cigarette from Paul, with Miriam looking on, was removed. Finally in C. XIII (Passion) a page long dialogue between Mrs. Morel and Paul joking about whom he will marry was taken out. As commentary on all these kinds of cuts, I would offer the judgment that jocular or high-spirited dialogue was not one of Lawrence's strong points.

But all excisions by Garnett were not of dialogue, as I have already mentioned. And in eight of the prose descriptions that have been removed I found, I think, another esthetic principle of Garnett's editorializing. These are all Lawrence's descriptions of the state of mind and/or emotions of one of his central characters at some stage of their lives and often involving their relationships and feelings about another character. For example, in C. II (The Birth of Paul) Mrs. Morel has a fairly lengthy mental summation on her relationship to her husband, how she is destroying his authority, how poor they were, how mean he was, how he drank too much, how the children were on her side, and so on. Garnett cut this because it did not have to be said; it had already been dramatized previously by dialogue and action. In this type of cut I think one can discern the fine hand of Henry James, whose novelistic principles would by the time of the completion of *Sons and Lovers* be generally known: the necessity for *dramatizing* everything and not just summarizing things in what James liked to call "a seated lump of information." (This was also one of Flaubert's exclusions). Thus Garnett cut out seven other such summaries because the reader would have already known their gist from previous characterization, dialogue, and action. The other "seated lumps of information" are: still in C. II after a quarrel with the drunken Morel, Mrs. Morel thinks how she loathes him; in C. III (The Casting off of Morel) a description of how baby Paul does not like his father and how his father is afraid of him (some dialogue here); again in C. III Mrs. Morel's sadness at the prospect of William's departure; in C.V (Paul Launches into Life) Paul's thoughts at his mother's question "What do you want to be?" Not surprisingly, he thinks he did not want to do or be anything; still in C.V, Lawrence's description of Paul telling his mother about his first day at Jordan's; in C. IX (Defeat of Miriam) Lawrence's description of Paul's complex and contradictory feelings about Miriam and his mother's role in this; in C. XI (The Test on Miriam) Paul's thinking about how all his feelings about Miriam always turn into abstractions.

A different kind of "seated lump of information" is found in the letters by Paul to Miriam at the end of C. IX (The Defeat of Miriam) beginning with one on her twenty-first birthday. Both Lawrence himself and Garnett cut several passages of these lengthy effusions. Another Garnett principle appears to have been that if something does not advance the action then that something should be cut out or cut down. Certainly these letters do not advance matters.

So far I have been talking about the Garnett cuts that seem to be susceptible of an explanation by guessing at what was his assumption or principle. But I did find some of his excisions that, for me anyway, made little sense and I confess to not seeing why he made the cuts, although at times I think I can offer some speculations on these matters. The largest single inexplicability occurs in C. VII (Lad-and-Girl Love), the visit on a rainy night by Paul and Miriam to the Bestwood Library. In the Baron edition this occupies a good 3 1/2 pages, the single largest excision in the Paul-Miriam story and the largest cut in the entire MS., being even larger than the huge one of William, C. III (The Casting off of Morel). Paul arrives at the Library first and converses with Mr. Sleath, the librarian, and also with a Mr. Smedley. Then Miriam arrives, they talk, and soon leave to walk home in the rain, talking the while; at last Paul arrives home and converses with his disapproving mother who neither likes him walking in the rain nor talking with Miriam.

I can guess at some of the reasons for Garnett cutting this. First, it is eminently detachable, having no roots in the past nor intuitions to the future, and is a once-only experience in the book as a whole. Second, it introduces two once-only secondary characters, the librarians, and since Garnett often reduces social context in the novel as a whole, he decided to jettison these men along with their library. Third, it is a quite happy experience for both Paul and Miriam. His conversation is "quick and vigorous" and her soul "expanded" in listening to it. She then goes on home with "her heart glowing" and he goes home "glowing" as well. Did Garnett think that this was too unalloyed a happiness for this usually complicated, entangled, and ultimately doomed relationship? I don't know—just guessing. But I do think that it was a real loss to the original *Sons and Lovers*. And, according to John Worthen's *D.H. Lawrence*, Jessie Chambers especially regretted the excision of this passage, thinking it showed most emphatically the real relationship between her and Lawrence.

This is the largest instance of a difficult to explain excision. There are, of course, many lesser ones, even more difficult to explain since they do not reduce the size of the novel by much and one of Garnett's concerns was a commercial one, to reduce the size of the novel for the economy of publishing it. For example, in C.V (Paul Launches into Life) Paul and his mother are travelling by train to Nottingham to try for the job at Jordan's. She suddenly exclaims that she thinks he will get the job and he is embarrassed that she talked loud enough for other people to hear, all in a total of five lines. In this same chapter after the interview they are outside in the street, deciding where to eat. Paul decides they should do it in style and damn the expense. This one is all dialogue, six lines, and is cancelled for what reason I cannot guess. There are other removals I find equally difficult to understand or explain.

I now wish to make some observations on Garnett's general editing of the MS. as a whole with some concluding remarks on D.H. Lawrence's prose style and method of composition.

The Garnett cuts are mostly in the first ten chapters. In C. XI, XII, XIII they dwindle quite markedly (Garnett or someone censored lightly here some matters relating to sex), and in C. XIV and XV, they disappear. So the bulk of Garnett's editing was performed on the first two–thirds of the MS. Since the last third was written by the same writer with the same stylistic and compositional techniques and offered the same opportunity for cuts as did the first two–thirds, one wonders why Garnett virtually ceased and desisted after C.X. Did he think he had diminished the MS. sufficiently in the first ten chapters. Had he become bored with the process? There are no answers to these questions. But there is an interesting parallel in Garnett's career as a publisher's reader. In 1916 Joyce's *A Portrait of the Artist As a Young Man* was submitted to Duckworth's and, as with *Sons and Lovers*, Garnett was the reader. Ellmann in his biography of Joyce publishes Garnett's report. Among other things, Garnett says: "James Joyce's 'Portrait of the Artist as a Young Man' wants going through carefully from start to finish," and "In the earlier portion of the MS. as submitted to us, a good deal of pruning can be done."[3] This is surely a most interesting editorial "might–have–been:" Joyce's *A Portrait* with its first part pruned and its entirety "gone over" by Edward Garnett.

The larger consideration of whether Garnett's editing was good or bad for the first publication of *Sons and Lovers* has been endlessly debated. In Lawrence's own correspondence can be found statements both praising and regretting that editing. Critics have agreed and disagreed. As remarked earlier, Mark Schorer, my dear departed friend and respected colleague, was unqualifiedly enthusiastic in his introduction to the facsimile of the MS. he edited. H.S. Saxena thinks it all a mistake.[4] Or Hugh Kenner argued that since in part a novel is a matter of small balances, when you remove something you alter those balances.[5] Other critics, like Mark Spilka, are "Yes" and "No."[6] (I count myself one of these.) The Barons in their introduction to their edition argue that Lawrence more regretted than approved of Garnett's excisions and therefore reprint in its entirety the pre-Garnett MS. In addition the Barons establish that Lawrence's original punctuation was substantially changed —some 4,000 to 5,000 times—by the printers and they restore the originals. In one such restoration they show that the printers' change in punctuation altered Lawrence's meaning. Because of all their restorations the Barons claim their edition is a new book and establish copyright beginning in 1992, a claim contested by David Trotter in his review in the *TLS* in September, 1992. On balance I am in favor of what the Barons have done, even though I think some of Garnett's cuts quite justified. Restoring William Morel's full presence helps to underline the use of plurals in the title *Sons and Lovers*. Humanizing Morel and establishing him in his profession of mining was not only truer to the original person, Arthur Lawrence, but makes him less of a pure lout than he tends to be in the novel. Those who knew the father disagreed with this conception and Lawrence himself later came to regret it. Only he, of all the Lawrence children, felt so strongly about this matter. The suffragette movement was of great importance in those days—Mrs. Lawrence herself was prominent in a local branch of the women's movement and so were several of the young women Lawrence knew.

Beyond these alterations, a survey of all of Garnett's cuts and truncations show that he is attempting to alter the novel in some important ways. In the large sense Garnett appeared to be trying to make "Sons and Lovers" more like a Henry James novel and less like one by, say, H.G. Wells or Arnold Bennett, by concentrating on one central, complex relationship, Paul and his Mother, and diminishing the social context generally. He was even, so it appears, trying to make it less of a working–class novel, the very quality that was so prized by many readers when the novel first appeared ("At last, the authentic voice of the working class"). Hence the down–playing of Morel and his miner–context, the fashioning of Mrs. Morel into a somewhat more genteel personage, the diminution of Paul's relationship to his fellow workers in Jordan's, and the diminishing of contentiousness and argumentativeness in the novel as a whole—in the folklore of these matters it is the lower class folk who are supposed to be the most assertive and loud in verbal contention. The most striking single incidence of this down–playing of working–class life was Garnett's removal of much of the "Barm–O" episode in C. III (The Casting off of Morel, the Taking on of William). "Barm–O" was a yeast dispensed by an old man with a cart who came through the streets singing hymns and crying out "Barm–O." Like all the other working–class women in the neighborhood, when Mrs. Morel heard the cry of "Barm–O," she went down into the alley with her mug to get some yeast. Garnett not only removed a good deal of this episode, but also, as mentioned above, a considerable amount of the angry interchange which happens in connection with "Barm–O" between Mrs. Morel and Mrs. Anthony about their sons' dispute. There is a distance at first between the two women and they must shout at one another, and then they come together when the "Barm–O" man fills each cup with yeast and dispenses a little badinage to each woman (all this removed by Garnett). After the "Barm–O" man passes on Garnett lets the text resume with the conclusion of the dispute between the two women. The large cuts in this classic little vignette of domestic working–class life tends once more to elevate the social "tone" of the novel, besides preventing, once more, Mrs. Morel from raising her voice.

That a middle–class editor should have tried to make a working–class novel by a writer from a working–class background a bit less of a working–class affair should come as no surprise given the overwhelming importance of class in English society. In fact, it would be a plausible question to ask whether Garnett himself was fully aware of what he was doing; perhaps he only thought he was making the novel more tidy and esthetically more coherent. If in French literature (and life?) the watchword should be, "*Cherchez la femme*," in English literature and life it has to be, "Look to the class."

In short, Garnett had somewhat narrowed the sociological spread or scale of the novel. Lawrence himself, on the other hand, seemed to have thought of his novel as having a very wide social compass among the working classes. And in a description he wrote for the dust-jacket of *Sons and Lovers* he placed social scope and variety first and "sons and lovers" last.

> Mr. D.H. Lawrence's new novel covers a wide field: life in a colliery, on a farm, in a manufacturing centre. It is concerned with the contrasted outlook on life of two generations. The title, *Sons and Lovers*, indicates the conflicting claims of a young man's mother and sweetheart for predominance.[7]

This, of course, may have been a purposeful blurb to promote sales, but I think it also reveals some pride by the author on his own sociological range among the lower orders. The Baron edition more fully certifies to this fact.

One of the most interesting aspects of the Garnett editing considered from the perspective of Lawrence as a writer was, for me anyway, the ease with which Garnett removed passages, some of them extensive. By "ease" I mean he had to do little patch-work by way of adding transitions. The Barons point out how slight this had to be: once a name "Mrs. Morel" substituted for a pronoun "She" or adding an occasional short sentence, e.g. "She was relieved." But most of the time one just removes the lines or paragraphs or pages and the seamless web of the prose forms a new entity without a ghost of a regret or a shade of ambiguity. In their Preface discussing the fact that most of Lawrence's texts are corrupt, the Barons remark on a distinct instance of this characteristic of Lawrence's prose:

> Then there were extraordinary lapses like the occasion when a typist turned over two pages of MS. at once, and the result happened to make sense. (VII)

That is to say, a whole page was left out and it did not matter in the continuity of the narrative. But there was nothing "extraordinary" about it—Garnett was doing the same thing throughout his editing of *Sons and Lovers*.

Now this same characteristic may be true for other writers. But we have few, if any, other cases like that of *Sons and Lovers*: a MS. that is extraordinarily neat and clear with excisions that are also neat and clear made all the more so by the fact that hardly any transitions are needed when cuts are made. So what does it tell us of Lawrence's compositional methods? I am not sure I know, and can only offer some speculations.

Lawrence's story appears to be less a narrative than it is a string of episodes. Although the episodes are strung together in a temporal sequence, they do not always have a logical sequence—*post hoc ergo propter hoc*—i.e., a mutual dependency. It is rather as if Lawrence were emitting spurts of prose energy. The past is always being left behind, cut off from the present and the future. I think this same trait is found in the large sense in all of Lawrence's work. Just as his great contemporary Joyce was always oriented toward the past, Lawrence was always oriented to the future and the casting off of the past, as in the conclusion of *The Rainbow*. This same impulse or tendency underlies virtually all of Lawrence's work. To illustrate at random: there is always the insistence on break–out or rebirth, with the past destroyed and a transformed future emergent, the favorite metaphors being the phoenix and the chrysalis and the butterfly. That the past should be obliterated and no memory of it preserved is an insistent theme. In *Women in Love* the venerable country home of Hermione, Breadalby, is admittedly lovely and stately, but it represents the past:

> And then, what a snare and delusion, this beauty of static things—what a horrible, dead prison Breadalby really was, what an intolerable confinement, the peace! (C. VIII)

In history itself, according to Lawrence, the past is always disappearing. In *Lady Chatterley's Lover* he said, "This is history. One England blots out another," and, never one for bothering about a foolish consistency, he locates in *Lady Chatterley* (1928) the cataclysm at various junctions in the more recent past: 100 years ago, 1828; 40 years ago, 1888; 20 years ago, 1908; 12 years ago, 1916. It was common, of course, for many Western writers, especially English writers, to locate the great break with the past in the 1914–1918 catastrophe. None asserted this divide between B.W. (before the Great War) and A.W. (after) as a major turning point in history more passionately or completely than did Lawrence. In *Kangaroo* he said that the old world ended in 1915 and that in the winter of 1915—1916 the spirit of old London collapsed; thus the soul of England went under in the Great War. Nothing of the human enterprise was permanent anyway, even ideas: "every idea is perishable."

A great Lawrencian dichotomy is between the universe and the humanity that inhabits a part of it; the universe is perpetual and endlessly creative; humanity, and all its history, is frail, perishable and in the last analysis unnecessary (Birkin in *Women in Love*).

The fragility of the past and the tenuousness of the connection between the present and the past is illustrated by some other properties of *Sons and Lovers*. Thus when Lawrence is describing the inner lives of his characters they have rather few memories of their own pasts, especially if compared to the central characters of *Ulysses*, Stephen Dedalus and Leopold and Molly Bloom. In addition, time in a Lawrence novel does not move by the clock—as, once more, it does in Joyce—but expands and contracts; moments can be expansive and years can slide by. For instance, take the process of Paul's aging, in C. VII (Lad-and-Girl Love) he is said to be 19; in C. XII (Passion) he is 25. Between these two age sign-posts Lawrence sprinkled some other ones—21, 23, almost 24—but still it might come as somewhat of a surprise to the casual reader that between the events of C. VII and those of C. XII six years have been consumed. I think that such an elastic time-sense also lessens the interdependency of the present and the past.

The only certain generalization that can be made about sequentiality in Lawrence's narratives is: *post hoc-fortasse* [perhaps] *aliquando* [sometimes] *temere* [haphazardly]—*propter hoc*.

Appendix: The Handwriting of the "Sons and Lovers" MS.

D.H. Lawrence's handwriting was remarkably clear and steady, underlining how effective had been his instruction in penmanship in school, which must have been enhanced by his three months as a commercial clerk. There are some crossings-out, with interlineated additions, but little of those massive deletions and/or additions that mark the MSS. of Joyce and Tolstoy and Proust. The *Sons and Lovers* MS. is thus an editor's delight, as Mark Schorer said. The steady clarity of the writing also tells us, of course, something about the character of the writer although I am not sure what it is. Lawrence himself concocted a nice irony on this matter by making Paul Morel have a "vile" and "execrable" handwriting.

But the handwriting of *Sons and Lovers* is not all of a piece, for it varies in size quite remarkably, as can be verified visually by looking at the printed facsimile of the MS. (cited in footnote #2). Thus p. 136 (Mr. Morel in the hospital) has 425 words; p. 498 (the fight between Morel and Dawes) has 840 words; p. 540 (the last page) has 532 words. The bulk of the book, Chapters I through XII, is written in approximately the same size hand as p. 136. It is in C. XIII (Baxter Dawes), that the handwriting becomes so tiny, beginning, as I see it, when Paul and Clara are at the sea-shore and continuing on after that. In C. XIV (The Release), a larger-size hand begins to appear although by no means entirely. The last parts of the book are written in a hand smaller than that of the first twelve chapters, but not as minuscule as parts of C. XIII. It is then the descriptions of the Dawes, wife and husband, that trigger the minuscule style. One can think of all kinds of easy psychological generalizations that could be made about this, but I shall forbear. I even consulted some works of graphology, a pseudo-science if ever there were one, and found some remarkably silly psychological observations on the character traits supposedly exhibited by small handwriting. The best that I can offer is to say that writing about both the Dawes together aroused some kinds of emotions in DHL's complex psyche that led to a condensation of his handwriting. Then in C. XIV (The Release), about his mother's death, pages of a larger hand appear at times when he is describing some of the symptoms of his mother's dying. So, what do we say to this? Again I do not know. The only generalization that I can derive from all this is that Lawrence's remembrance of things past included certain memories that revived in him emotions of such power as to alter his handwriting when describing them. He was quite aware of a tendency that the size of his handwriting was subject to diminution under the pressure of certain circumstances. Thus in a letter to Edward Garnett in May, 1913, he remarked: "Frieda sprawls so large I must squeeze myself smaller. I am very contractable." (*Letters*, I, 547)

Notes

1. *Sons and Lovers*, ed. Helen Baron and Carl Baron (Cambridge: Cambridge University Press, 1992).
2. *Sons and Lovers*, A Facsimile of the MS., edited with an Introduction by Mark Schorer (Berkeley and Los Angeles: University of California Press, 1977).
3. Richard Ellmann, *James Joyce* (New York: Oxford University Press, 1982), pp. 403–404.
4. H.S. Saxena, "A Study of the Facsimile of the Manuscript of *Sons and Lovers*," *D.H. Lawrence: An Anthology of Recent Criticism*, ed. Aruna Sitesh, (New Delhi: Ace Publications, 1990), pp. 106–15. Saxena's argument can be summarized in his/her own words: "The deletions have resulted in pushing into the background some of the major concerns of the novel. It is time that a new version of *Sons and Lovers* is published as Lawrence must have wished it to be" (107). The Barons 1992 edition does precisely that.
5. Hugh Kenner, "Restoring the Steamy Bits and More," *New York Times Book Review* (November 29, 1992), pp. 9–10.
6. Mark Spilka, "For Mark Schorer with Combative Love: The *Sons and Lovers* Manuscript," *DHL: A Centenary Consideration*, ed. Peter Balbert and Philip L. Marcus (Ithaca: Cornell University Press, 1985), pp. 29–44.
7. *The Letters of D.H. Lawrence*, Vol. 1, ed. James T. Boulton (Cambridge: Cambridge University Press, 1979), footnote #4, pp. 529–30.

16

D. H. Lawrence's Narrators, Sources of Knowledge, and the Problem of Coherence

MICHAEL SQUIRES

Readers of D. H. Lawrence have long been intrigued by the quality and texture of his prose. Its complex fragmentation has elicited widespread comment; its linguistic challenges are critical commonplaces. As part of what remains to be done, I want to examine Lawrence's use of fictional narrators and to focus on two related problems that it creates: the problem of coherence and, below that, the problem of the text's sources of knowledge. Analysis of Lawrence's narrators reveals that problems of coherence can be traced to his use of various narrative voices, and that these various voices depend on assumptions about his sources of knowledge which require careful scrutiny. My aim is to look across the wide span of Lawrence's fiction; to identify a line of technical development; to situate that line within the context of published criticism, both theoretical and practical, occasionally challenging received critical views; and, finally, as I reconsider some central passages in the Lawrence canon, to reach fresh conclusions about narrative coherence, sources of knowledge, and Lawrence's narrators.

This cluster of concepts has attracted extensive commentary, most of it designed to help readers understand Lawrence's characters and themes. Such understanding is not my purpose. Whereas Keith Sagar, Mark Spilka, and Stephen Miko regard Lawrence's narrators as vehicles of information or interpretation rather than as difficult constructs in the text, contemporary critics have located the sources of Lawrence's imaginative power in his highly developed intuitive and sensory equipment (Wallace 103–19), in his adaptation of the carnivalesque (Fleishman 17), or in his ability to "transcode" experience (Hyde, *D. H. Lawrence* 3); and they have derived his conception of knowledge from biblical typology (Hyde, *Risen Adam*), from Romantic poetry (Ragussis), or from Aestheticism

(Holderness 98–129, Fernihough). Diane Bonds understands this cluster of concepts as a narratological problem: but her deconstructive insights, though penetrating, are confined to the subversive features of Lawrence's texts. The philosophical and narratological connections between narrators, knowledge, and coherence remain therefore to be defined. I anticipate that some of my distinctions may help to refine a critical method—rhetorical in origin, comparative in application—for negotiating the vexingly difficult bond between narrator and character.

Two related issues require at least preliminary comment. First, the notion of coherence as an aesthetic aim was beginning to be challenged by many early-Modernist writers. Marcel Proust, for example, analyzing Ruskin's criticism, wrote:

> Apparently he moves at random from one idea to the next. But in truth the imagination which guides him follows his deepest inclinations, which impose on him a superior logic in spite of himself—so much so that, at the end, he finds he has obeyed a hidden plan which, when it is finally unveiled, imposes in retrospect a kind of order on the whole. (my translation, qtd. in Hayman 218)

Such deeper patterns of coherence, lying below the level of conscious planning or structuring, reveal the structural components of intuition as they manifest themselves in narrative choices.

And second, the concept of knowledge needs to be defined in a philosophical context. Whereas Conrad despairs at the loss of an underlying unity that would illuminate daily life, and whereas Woolf relies heavily on immediate sensory experience, Lawrence glimpses something beyond the mind that knowledge cannot reveal but that intuition—residing in the blood, "where we have our strongest self-knowledge" (Moynahan 30)—can. Whereas Kant views experience as already created "by the 'intuitions' of time and space . . . and known by no other means than those it names" (Brodsky 50), Patrick Whiteley writes:

> Lawrence rejoices that the lens [of unity] is shattered; he embraces the chaos that Western civilization wants to bring under its idea of order. For Lawrence, to be one with this darkness that grounds human existence is to turn the mind away from itself and back toward the body from which the mind arose before it became conscious of itself. (21)

For Lawrence mind and body ought ideally to form a monistic whole.

"But why do you persist in separating soul and body?" he demanded of Rachel Annand Taylor (26 October 1910). "I can't tell . . . one from the other" (i. 185). Yet that condition of wholeness can occur only when the mind can no longer inspect itself, and can no longer distinguish between imagination and knowledge. That this condition is rarely achieved generates a kind of narrative shock. Lawrence's narrators, inveighing more and more against their society, "voice the conscience of the individual trapped in a morally corrupt society" (Whiteley 21–22), thereby defining the implied relationship between a narrator and the characters about whom he writes. But the notion of giving conscience a "voice" begs the question of how a particular narrator discovers this moral–political content within each character—and how the mode of discovery changes in successive literary works.

In Lawrence's early fiction the lack of coherence among sources of knowledge within the text fosters narrative instability. *The White Peacock*, published in 1911 when Lawrence was only twenty five, and *Sons and Lovers*, published two years later, illustrate his early difficulties with narrative control. In *The White Peacock* the narrator wavers between involvement and distance, between sensuousness and physical restraint. Notice the final sentence of the following passage from chapter 5, where I have clarified the narrator's focalization[1] by employing italics to indicate what Lawrence *might* have written:

> We moved across to the standing corn. The sun being mild, [*I noticed that*] George had thrown off his hat, and [*that*] his black hair was moist and twisted into confused half–curls. Firmly planted, he swung with a beautiful rhythm from the waist. On the hip of his belted breeches hung the scythe-stone; his shirt, faded almost white, was torn just above the belt, and showed the muscles of his back playing like lights upon the white sand of a brook. There was something exceedingly attractive in the rhythmic body [*To me his rhythmic body seemed exceedingly attractive*]. (47)

Delight in the rhythmic sensuousness of work jostles against the narrator's attempt to efface his own pleasure. Like the tear in George's faded shirt, the passage opens inward toward discovery and visual stimulation. In the text knowledge enters through the eyes until the last sentence. There, the narrator's indirection muffles the lure of male musculature, which is displaced from observation to meditation. A comparison of Connie Chatterley's visual apprehension of Mellors, half naked at his wash–basin, nicely distinguishes her visual and emotional "shock" (*Lady Chatterley's Lover* 66) from Cyril's shift in perspective.

Later, when George and Lettie sit down in the forest, the narrator records the hum of bees and concludes: "The sight of their clinging, clambering riot gave satisfaction to the soul" (214). *Whose* soul? Two perspectives—that of the characters and that of the narrator—appeal for attention. The narrator does not yet know where to position himself so that he can plumb and then record depths of emotional experience. That skill will come as Lawrence develops a more expressive authorial voice.

In the meantime Lawrence's loss of his mother, who was "strong and steadfast" (i. 195) but also "rather scornful" (i. 174), affected him profoundly. Seeking to recover her presence vicariously, he introduced into his prose a fresh voice of judgment which had not been present in *The Trespasser*, the novel he drafted shortly before she died in 1910. The effect is curious. Lawrence introduced into *Sons and Lovers* the fresh technical problem of unifying judgment with narrative flow. To clarify the change, I compare two passages, one that I have recast in order to eliminate disruption, the other Lawrence's original, which reveals several fractures worth observing: first, the tenses *would be feeling* and *would reach out* shift incoherently to *felt* and *was*; second, the incoherent time signal *soon*, which reflects a continuing action, requires a modal verb; and third, in the words "Both felt," the focalization of the final sentences shifts to Walter and Gertrude Morel as a couple. Here are the two versions, their differences italicized:

Recast

> And Morel sitting there, quite alone, having nothing to think about, *felt* vaguely uncomfortable. *At such times* his soul reached out in its blind way to her and found her gone. *Then* he felt a sort of emptiness, almost like a vacuum in his soul. He *appeared* unsettled and restless, and, *feeling oppressed* in that atmosphere, he affected *her*. Both felt an oppression on their breathing, when they were left together for some time. *But once he had gone* to bed, *she could settle down* to enjoy herself alone, working, thinking, living.

D. H. Lawrence

> And Morel sitting there, quite alone, and having nothing to think about, *would be feeling* vaguely uncomfortable. His soul *would reach* out in its blind way to her, and *find* her gone. He *felt* a sort of emptiness,

> almost like a vacuum in his soul. He *was* unsettled and restless. *Soon* he could *not* live in that atmosphere, and he affected his wife. Both felt an oppression on their breathing, when they were left together for some time. *Then he went* to bed, *and she settled* down to enjoy herself alone, working, thinking, living. (63)

Apart from the way Lawrence perfectly frames the passage within the word "alone," the instability of perception (tenses, focalization) suggests that in 1913 Lawrence's sources of knowledge were diffuse or unreliable. Struggling to represent the soul's knowledge, Lawrence encounters a series of disruptions. The most interesting is the subtle way in which the narrator slants the words "having *nothing* to think about" and "His soul would reach out in its *blind* way" (my emphasis); the narrator's words reflect not his own voice but embody Mrs. Morel's criticism of her husband. This confirms Carol Sklenicka's point that "the perspective of Gertrude Morel governs much of the novel" (40).

Later, when Paul and Miriam are alone, reeling in the moonlight, Lawrence writes a passage in which two forms of disruption appear:

> He turned and looked at her. She stood beside him, for ever in shadow. Her face, covered with the darkness of her hat, was watching him unseen. But she was brooding. She was slightly afraid—deeply moved and religious. That was her best state. He was impotent against it. His blood was concentrated like a flame in his chest. But he could not get across to her. There were flashes in his blood. But somehow she ignored them. She was expecting some religious state in him. Still yearning, she was half aware of his passion, and gazed at him, troubled. (215–16)

This is characteristic Lawrentian writing, the flow of emotional responses initiated by a verbal stimulus; but its fractured focalization is notable. First, the choice of linking verbs—*was* or *were* occurs nine times—shows that the passage's perspective is disrupted from inner revelation to outer observation, as in the choice of "There were flashes in his blood" over the more interior "Flashes stirred his blood": so that the passage, sometimes angled unexpectedly toward objective rather than subjective forms of experience and knowledge, wavers. Second, the exterior judgment at the center—"That was her best state"—derives from an omniscient external voice that disrupts the passage's flow, so that the passage seems to stutter. The unit of blood-and-blockage created by "*His blood was concentrated like a flame in his chest. But he could not get across to her*" has to be immediately repeated (in paraphrase) as "*There were flashes in his blood. But somehow she ignored them*" (my italics). Such disruptions can be interestingly linked to similar disruptions of narrative presentation in E. M. Forster's *A Passage to India* (see Ragussis 133–71); but in 1913 Lawrence was still experimenting with narrative perspectives, not yet having found a voice that, when mastered, was uniquely his.

Early in *The Rainbow* (1915), when Tom and Lydia Brangwen attempt to reestablish their emotional connection, the narrator confronts the problem of depicting Tom metamorphosed into a new self while showing how awareness of change is thrust upon him, beyond his own power. I want to illustrate Lawrence's new control of language and coherence by examining a brief passage—first in my recast form—in order to separate my "active" from Lawrence's necessarily "passive" appraisal of Tom's change. (Italics distinguish the two forms.)

Recast

> *He felt as if* a daze had come over his mind, *as if* he had another centre of consciousness. *Another activity had started somewhere in his body—in his breast or in his bowels. He felt as if* a strong light were burning there, *as if* he was blind within it, unable to know anything, except that this transfiguration burned between him and her, connecting them, like a secret power.
>
> Since she had come to the house he *had gone about* in a daze. . . .

D. H. Lawrence

> A daze had come over his mind, he had another centre of consciousness. In his breast, or in his bowels, somewhere in his body, there had started another activity. It was as if a strong light were burning there, and he was blind within it, unable to know anything, except that this transfiguration burned between him and her, connecting them, like a secret power.
>
> Since she had come to the house he went about in a daze, scarcely seeing even the things he handled, drifting, quiescent, in a state of metamorphosis. He submitted to that which was happening to him, letting go of his will, suffering the loss of himself, dormant always on the brink of ecstasy, like a creature evolving to a new birth. (38)

About this pair of passages, two points are worth making. First, the kind of disruption evident in Lawrence's earlier work has largely disappeared. His technical grasp is more exact and mature: narrative knowledge (i.e., what is knowable for the reader) is restricted to Tom's emotions as understood by the narrator and as expressed in the narrator's lyrical phrases. Second, the implicit moral system of the novel has been transferred from omniscient statements in *Sons and Lovers* like "That was her best state" to images and analogies that encode the implied author's views. For instance, in the sentence that begins, "It was as if a strong light were burning there," the strong light represents less clearly Tom's analogy than the narrator's: and beyond it a reader can infer that feelings converted into analogies are implicitly admired and, for the narrator, are also a kind of "letting go of *his* will" and a waiting "on the brink"—not of emotional "ecstasy" (as for Tom) but of artistic ecstasy. That ecstasy leads the narrator to discover an interpretive system that only *appears* to be within Tom's focalization. It is of course outside, used often to explore the psyches of other characters. And as these analogies and images gradually acquire an evaluative function in each text, they also require us, in consequence, to distinguish the central ways in which critics like myself can talk about the bond between narrator and character.[2] Here, Tom and the narrator share what I call a "second degree" bond, in which both character and narrator draw from similar sources of knowledge but use different linguistic idioms. The "as if" structure is a doorway to a *complementary* idiom: what Paul Hernadi calls "substitutionary narration"—by which he means "the narrator's sympathetic substitution of his own words for [his character's] thoughts and feelings" (35–37)—and what Roy Pascal calls "dual voice."[3]

A more pointed example of this kind of narratorial bonding occurs in the novel's second generation, when Will and Anna resist each other, she crying, he accusing:

> "What are you crying for?" came the question again, in just the same tone. And still there was silence, with only the sniff of her tears.
>
> His eyes glittered, and as if with malignant desire. She shrank and became blind. She was like a bird being beaten down. A sort of swoon of helplessness came over her. She was of another order than he, she had no defence against him. Against such an influence, she was only vulnerable, she was given up. (143)

The sentence about Will's eyes holds special critical interest. Recast within Anna's focalization (as Lawrence might readily have done), the sentence would read: "To her his eyes glittered with malignant desire." The result? The rewritten sentence improves the passage's coherence since, as originally written, the words are the narrator's: it is he, not Anna, who interprets the glitter of Will's eyes,[4] which is viewed from outside Will's consciousness (hence *as if* with malignant desire). Since at this juncture the narrator does not offer certainty, he only records his own intuitive impression. Yet that impression, because it is followed by "She shrank and became blind," becomes implicitly part of Anna's focalization. Hence the incoherence. Gerald Prince says that "incoherent commentaries expressed by the narrating voice . . . cast doubt on the interpretive powers of the narrator" (548). A more useful way to view what Lawrence achieves is to see incoherence as *part of* the interpretation of the text—to see incoherence as a reflection of the idea that a character's conscience is trapped within a morally corrupt society. Ideologically, incoherence becomes the technical counterpart of entrapment.

Moreover, it is worth saying that the "as if" structure, by now a Lawrentian heuristic, becomes a central functioning unit of his imagination. It is a rhetorical device for regauging and reformulating what a character like Will expresses or what a character like Anna feels—not just more vividly, but in ways that offer clarification and illumination *for the novel's readers*. In passages of Free Indirect Style, each "as if" structure, simile, or metaphor generates a fresh layer of interpretive understanding—always at an *angle* to the character's focalization, forming usually a second-degree bond. For example, after Paul Morel looks into Miriam's eyes, these words follow: "He turned aside, as if pained" (210), where the "as if" changes the focalization from Paul to the narrator. And the sentence above, "She was like a bird being beaten down," which uses the narrator's simile, helps to form an interpretive layer that eventually opens a window onto the implied author's value system, which in Lawrence's fiction has often been difficult to assess. It is therefore too reductive to say about Lawrence's fiction that "the character and narrator together struggle for a language in which to express their realisations" (Worthen 41). Rarely do they struggle for, or in, the same language. A more precise and discriminating critical vocabulary is needed.

To move in that direction invites a pointed question about Lawrence's work: what happens when he approaches the borders of language function? What happens when he transcends the old language that, as Virginia Woolf put it, reveals "gig-lamps symmetrically arranged" and, instead, discovers the "luminous halo" of subjective experience (106)? Scott Sanders is surely right to say that Lawrence "forced his characters through the medium of words to the boundaries of language, beyond which they could sense powers and orders of being which neither he nor they could name" (82). In *The Rainbow* Lawrence, apart from experimenting with the angle of bonding between narrator and character, has—like Woolf or Proust—determined to reveal fresh layers of the dark unknown of intuition and instinct. That much is widely agreed. What is not, is Lawrence's peculiar use of heuristics—conceptual heuristics—to explore a *topos* of darkness that exists beyond and beneath the light of nineteenth-century rationalism.

In the splendid passage that follows, Lawrence responds to the problem of coherence by using binary form as the heuristic to explore dialectical forces. As he experiments with angles of bonding, he accumulates increments caught in a widening narrative net. Ursula's knowledge and idiom yield gradually to the narrator's without, however, reaching full separation. The two opening paragraphs reveal the narrator's presence (angle 2) in what Stefan Oltean calls a "highly articulated rendering of the [girl's] internal states" (709). The third paragraph modulates to the narrator's record—so assured as to be quoted—of the alien group's defensive certainty, not as Ursula might imagine it but as the narrator does: yet that record still falls, because of the narrator's extreme empathy, within the *range* of Ursula's intuitive awareness. The final paragraph, in which opposed forces join, is articulated entirely in the narrator's distinct idiom and barely sustains Ursula's awareness.

> [1] That which she was, positively, was dark and unrevealed, it could not come forth. It was like a seed buried in dry ash [of disillusion and falsity]. This world in which she [Ursula Brangwen] lived was like a circle lighted by a lamp. This lighted area, lit up by man's completest consciousness, she thought was all the world: that here all was disclosed for ever. Yet all the time, within the darkness, she had been aware of points of light, like the eyes of wild beasts, gleaming, penetrating, vanishing. And her soul had acknowledged in a great heave of terror only the outer darkness. This inner circle of light in which she lived and moved, wherein the trains rushed and the factories ground out their machine-produce and the plants and the animals worked by the light of science and knowledge, suddenly it seemed like the area under an arc-lamp, wherein the moths and children played in the security of blinding light, not even knowing there was any darkness, because they stayed in the light.
>
> [2] But she could see the glimmer of dark movement just out of range, she saw the eyes of the wild beast gleaming from the darkness,

> watching the vanity of the camp fire and the sleepers; she felt the strange, foolish vanity of the camp, which said "Beyond our light and our order there is nothing," turning their faces always inward towards the sinking fire of illuminating consciousness, which comprised sun and stars, and the Creator, and the System of Righteousness, ignoring always the vast darkness that wheeled round about, with half-revealed shapes lurking on the edge.

The dialectic between character and narrator, darkness and light, angel and beast culminates in a synthesis where opposed forces finally impinge on each other. The opening "Yea" signals an ironic register beyond Ursula's idiom:

> [3] Yea, and no man dared even throw a firebrand into the darkness. For if he did, he was jeered to death by the others, who cried "Fool, anti-social knave, why would you disturb us with bogeys? There *is* no darkness. We move and live and have our being within the light, and unto us is given the eternal light of knowledge, we comprise and comprehend the innermost core and issue of knowledge. Fool and knave, how dare you belittle us with the darkness?"
>
> [4] Nevertheless the darkness wheeled round about, with grey shadow-shapes of wild beasts, and also with dark shadow-shapes of the angels, whom the light fenced out, as it fenced out the more familiar beasts of darkness. And some [in the camp], having for a moment seen the darkness, saw it bristling with the tufts of the hyena and the wolf; and some, having given up their vanity of the light, having died in their own conceit, saw the gleam in the eyes of the wolf and the hyena, that it was the flash of the sword of angels, flashing at the door to come in, that the angels in the darkness were lordly and terrible and not to be denied, like the flash of fangs. (405–406)

About this passage—a favorite of critics—two matters require comment. First, the focalization is again curious, modulating outward in circles. It progresses from the narrator's description of Ursula acknowledging "the outer darkness" in paragraph 1; to Ursula's consciousness as it is increasingly revealed in the narrator's idiom (e.g., "System of Righteousness"); to the narrator's commentary, in biblical style, quoting the smug creatures who assume that "the eternal light of knowledge" shines on them alone; and finally to a focalization in which the narrator continues to limit himself to the symbols of the unconscious that populate Ursula's consciousness but emphatically uses his own language.

In a motion circling outward, the narrator strives to extend Ursula's perception, privileging his extension rhetorically, empowering it with the weight of authority, and, most important, participating vitally in her discovery of the depths of darkness. The narrator goes well beyond his normal function, in earlier works, of supplying metaphors; he is now a fresh source of knowledge about the *sub*conscious and its mysterious connections, through the gleaming eyes of light, to the conscious sphere. It is insufficient to say that "Ursula must get to know the familiar beasts of darkness better" (Miko 171). Ursula intuits, but the narrator contextualizes. She responds to sensory and para-sensory data; he penetrates it critically. She ascends, but he illuminates. This distance between internal and external focalization is wider than usually assumed—closer to Conrad than to Joyce.

It seems very likely that in composing *The Trespasser* (1912) and *Sons and Lovers* (1913) Lawrence found a niche of new perception when he discovered first that Siegmund and Helena, lying on the beach, comprise "two grains of life in the vast movement" of oceans, clouds, and circling spheres (78) and then, with rapidly developing insight, that Paul and Clara, after making love, had pierced the *known* in order to discover "life wild at the source" where, dwarfed by a "magnificent power," they comprise "only grains in the tremendous heave" (398). The *known* prefigures the light of the campfire, the darkness plumbing an order below language, below perception, below even consciousness. This order is articulated with great difficulty, may invite disruption, and may require the narrator's direct intervention. The "vastness" and "tremendousness" are overwhelming—to the characters, whose instinctual response is awe, and to the narrator, who must struggle both to open categories of perception and to negotiate rhetorical modes of expression.

Second—apart from the passage's focalization—its impressive coherence is, after all, disturbed in paragraphs 3 and 4 by the biblical voice, with its lordly repetitions and its "unto us is given." That voice, although it arguably extends Ursula's critique of the "Sunday" system of thought in chapter 10, nevertheless substitutes a *rhetorical* mode for the discovery of new knowledge which the passage centrally explores. The difficulty is real. Instead of discovering the function of the vital animal eyes as they connect light/consciousness and dark/unconsciousness, the narrator's heuristic of a three-part spatial model (i.e. light and dark, with eyes between) is skewed: it "discovers" a rhetoric of revelation and apocalypse in "the flash of fangs" and "the flash of the sword of angels." One cannot deny the grandeur of such language, nor the differences between it and the categorical absolutes of the Sunday system; but one can say that Lawrence, by drawing on a known rather than a partially unknown language system, compromises the deeper search for conduits of exchange between conscious and unconscious regions.

That deeper search, however, is only delayed. Near the end of *The Rainbow*—while the horses thunder near Ursula, impinging on her psyche—the gleaming points of animal eyes emerge, activated now, given clearer shape and sharper function, successfully mediating between Ursula's conscious and unconscious minds. In such writing Lawrence brilliantly captures the *space* between the two minds: it is a space full of dynamic activity, like atoms leaping in a chemical transaction. In the horses scene Ursula's new knowledge of herself derives not from the chafing of one rhetorical code against another but from the interplay of her conscious and her unconscious selves. Here, Lawrence fully controls his sources of knowledge, making them function both technically and thematically.

* * *

There is another approach to the conjunction of sources of knowledge and narrative coherence in Lawrence's work. In a later passage from *The Rainbow*, which follows Ursula and her lover Anton Skrebensky to the ocean's edge, I differentiate between the passage I have recast and the passage Lawrence wrote in order to show both the divided focalization and the problem it entails within this mixed perspective:

Recast

> Then there, in the great flare of light, she clinched hold of him, hard, as if suddenly she had the strength of destruction, she fastened her arms round him and tightened him in her grip, whilst her mouth sought his in a hard, rending, ever-increasing kiss, till *she felt that* his body was powerless in her grip; his heart *seemed to melt* in fear from *her* fierce, beaked, harpy's kiss. She *pressed in her mouth as if it were a beak*, till *she seemed to have* the heart of him. *She took no notice as the water washed again over their feet*; she seemed unaware.

D. H. Lawrence

> Then there, in the great flare of light, she clinched hold of him, hard, as if suddenly she had the strength of destruction, she fastened her arms round him and tightened him in her grip, whilst her mouth sought his in a hard, rending, ever-increasing kiss, till his body was powerless in her grip, his heart melted in fear from the fierce, beaked, harpy's kiss. The water washed again over their feet, but she took no notice. She seemed unaware, she seemed to be pressing in her beaked mouth, till she had the heart of him. (444)

Accounting critically for the differences between these two passages will illuminate Lawrence's narrative method, whose complexity can be daunting. A comparison yields several things. By positioning last the sentence beginning "She took no notice," the recast passage improves coherence because Ursula's distant awareness now *follows* her instinctual destruction of Skrebensky's spirit: but what one loses is Lawrence's odd rhythm that places a *pause* before the thrust of Ursula's beaked mouth. It is not an issue of "stylistic failure," as Graham Hough asserts (69). That pause, really a shift in perspective, is a useful reminder of the disruptive force that helps to map Lawrence's earlier work. In Lawrence's text the perspective modulates from the certainty of "his body was powerless" and "his heart melted," to the focally uncommitted "The water washed again over their feet," then to the narrator's *impression* of a gouging beak which is recorded by a narrator who watches Ursula but also understands the significance of her act. The area between the diegetic and mimetic poles of discourse, between "narrator" and "reflector," is especially striking.

Of broader concern, a comparison of passages shows Lawrence's narrator employing (as before) both his own language and Ursula's as conduits for impressions sent from her subconscious realm. That sort of discovery, typical of Modernism, is an immense narrative resource. Already the narrator *knows* that Skrebensky's "heart melted," that the water "washed again over their feet," that Ursula's mouth was "beaked": whereas these perceptions, recast wholly within Ursula's focalization, become subjective, known only to Ursula—as in "his heart seemed to melt," "She took no notice as the water washed again over their feet," her mouth seemed *like* a beak. As rewritten, Ursula's psychic rape of Skrebensky is imagined rather than witnessed; it is communicated to the reader unmediated rather than documented by the narrator.[5] When

Lawrence's narrator, like Forster's, assumes multiple locations within a single paragraph, the reader learns to accept the oscillation as part of the technical liquidity that Modernist writing invents.

Most of the critical commentary on this well-known passage (e.g., Albright 87, Ben-Ephraim 157-62, Bonds 60, Ross 41, Cowan 130-31) grapples with Ursula's aggression and Skrebensky's victimization as if the lovers, inverted, were Tess and Alec d'Urberville, his aggressive coarseness violating her "feminine tissue, sensitive as gossamer" (chap. xi). But what an interesting difference between the couples. Hardy's judging, moralizing voice ("the coarse appropriates the finer") is muted. Lawrence's narrator never asks, What is the moral scheme toward which a reader can be led? but rather, What does this character experience, deep inside, in a region of darkness or chaos, that can be communicated to a reader? And at what angle of bonding? Knowledge depends on narrative position.[6] If the narrator shifts his location—steps outside the region of darkness to *look* at the characters and their physical surroundings, tries to watch *and* to feel with them—then incoherence may result, as in "The water washed again over their feet, but she took no notice." For Lawrence the problem of focalization is always the problem of *when* to shift from inside to outside. It is as if the narrator's sources of knowledge recurrently dry up—or are shut off, or blocked—so that a *visual default* quickly fills in the space. Intuition is unstable, like the flash of fangs. Without inspiration or strict control, intuition—lapsing—allows a small narrative fissure to open. This is not a criticism of Lawrence's genius but an attempt to define the distinction of his technical resources and the uniqueness of his imagination.

As Lawrence's imagination operates more capaciously and begins more subtly to integrate forms of disruption, a major realignment takes place. The angle of bonding between narrator and character gradually shifts from a similarity of perspective (angles 1 and 2) to a dissimilarity of perspective (angles 3 and 4). This central shift characterizes Lawrence's work of the Twenties, but has its source in the later parts of *Women in Love* (1920), where the realignment of the narrator's sympathy is especially marked. I want to conclude my discussion of knowledge and coherence—and Lawrence's increasingly complex uses of them—by examining passages, from his final decade, that probe the minds of Gudrun Brangwen and then Oliver Mellors. Both passages illustrate how the sense of profound disruption remains but is now increasingly mastered, so that disruption is *masked* by the poise and authority of an assured narrative voice.

Readers of *Women in Love* always notice the subtle evolution of Gudrun's character from the narrator's cautious appreciation to his cold skepticism. But critical junctures along this path have been harder to isolate. A passage about Gudrun, which is both artistically accomplished and puzzlingly focalized, holds particular interest because of its subtle "rupture." Charles Ross (57) seconds F. R. Leavis's notion that the organization of *Women in Love* "is so rich and close" that there is "not a scene, episode, image or touch but forwards the organized development of the themes" (151). In a sweeping sense, surely that is true. But in individual passages one is often surprised to find—not lapses or flaws, nor even contradictions, but curious shifts (even dissonances) that reveal a counterforce through which some deeper structure can emerge. It is as if what Lawrence wrote about Etruscan art were also true of his own prose, with "one thing springing from another, things mentally contradictory fusing together emotionally" (*Etruscan Places* 121). These shifts need analysis.

In the passage below, the differences are instructive between what Lawrence wrote and what he might have written if he had focalized the passage to separate more fully Gudrun's mind from the narrator's. As Gudrun, awake and "destroyed into perfect consciousness," lay motionless, her "wide eyes staring . . . into the darkness," Gerald lay asleep with his arms encircling her. The recast passage transfers the brooding depths of revelation to Gudrun but cannot accommodate the narrator's central question:

Recast

> *As she lay, she seemed to hear waves breaking* on a hidden shore, long, slow, gloomy waves breaking with the rhythm of fate, so monotonously that *to her* it seemed eternal. This endless breaking of slow, sullen waves of fate held her like a possession, whilst she lay with dark, wide eyes looking into the darkness. *It seemed* she could see so far, as far as eternity—*yet it was as if she saw nothing*. She was suspended in perfect consciousness.

D. H. Lawrence

> She seemed to lie hearing waves break on a hidden shore, long, slow, gloomy waves breaking with the rhythm of fate, so monotonously that it

> seemed eternal. This endless breaking of slow, sullen waves of fate held her like a possession, whilst she lay with dark, wide eyes looking into the darkness. She could see so far, as far as eternity—yet she saw nothing. She was suspended in perfect consciousness—and of what was she conscious? (345)

In Lawrence's final clause the narrator queries the reader but delays his answer (she was at last "conscious of everything") until the sentence that follows: "This mood of extremity, when she lay staring into eternity, utterly suspended, and conscious of everything, to the last limits, passed, and left her uneasy" (345).

This is an immensely interesting passage. Its repetitions of wide eyes penetrating darkness—each repetition building on the previous one, extending it and enlarging it toward the extreme of "eternity"—illustrate Lawrence's rhetorical mastery. The passage is also interesting for the way the sequential motion across Gudrun's consciousness is interrupted. The reader, entering the dark recesses of Gudrun's subconscious mind, is given an impression ("She seemed to lie hearing waves") which is then glossed by the narrator (the waves break "with the rhythm of fate"). Then the sequential motion itself is broken—not by words like "yet it was as if she saw nothing" (which would sustain her *seeming* to hear waves breaking) but by the more forceful clause "yet she saw nothing." This clause offers a categorical judgment that the narrator infers from his own separate sources of knowledge. As if to increase the accumulating distance between character and reader, this clause is followed by a question aimed not at the character but at the reader: "and of what was she conscious?" This is not a matter of self-interrogation. The question forces the reader out of Gudrun's focalization and into the narrator's, inviting an intimacy between reader and narrator that supplants the bond between character and narrator. The final summary sentence invites us to think critically about a character who earns our grudging interest and our uneasy respect. It is the kind of narrative stance that Thomas Mann adopts in *Death in Venice*.

This shift from character to reader constitutes a core feature of Lawrence's imagination. What he learned early—to transfer experience from mother to son in *Sons and Lovers*, from female to male in *The Trespasser*, and from male to female in *The Rainbow*'s third generation—he continued to refine: valences shift according to his unstable focalization. The narrator's knowledge often depends on the distance between narrator and character, disruption signifying that the narrator's access to the character's psyche has been blocked, as the next passage demonstrates.

Once Oliver Mellors finds himself involuntarily mated to Connie Chatterley, he ponders in chapter 10 the implications of their union, searching for ways to connect their personal and social spheres. To clarify the point I will make, I have repositioned three contiguous paragraphs from *Lady Chatterley's Lover* (1928), taking them up individually.

The opening paragraph offers a series of recognitions, all of them focalized within Mellors's mind and in his idiom, opening outward, lily-like, from understanding to wisdom. Notice that the middle sentences could all be prefaced by the words "He knew."

> [1] He went down again, into the darkness and seclusion of the wood. But he knew that the seclusion of the wood was illusory. The industrial noises broke the solitude, the sharp lights, though unseen, mocked it. A man could no longer be private and withdrawn. The world allows no hermits. And now he had taken the woman, and brought on himself a new cycle of pain and doom. For he knew by experience what it meant.

What Mellors *knows* is extracted in his own sober idiom: Dorrit Cohn calls this *narrated monologue*—"a character's mental discourse in the guise of the narrator's discourse" (*Transparent* 14). The burden of Mellors's experience cuts a "vertical" incision into the narrator's wider experience and superior ability to generalize, as in "The world allows no hermits," with its gnomic present tense and its assurance. This kind of narrated monologue Lawrence has practised since about 1920, when his conception of audience began to change, and is refined in transitional works like *Mr. Noon* (completed 1921) and *St. Mawr* (1925), where the narrator's presence is pointedly visible.

Sustaining the outward progression of paragraph 1, the next paragraph is shaped into a *dialogue* between Mellors's voice and the narrator's—but so subtly that a reader almost misses Lawrence's fused perspectives. Here, with annotations in capitals, is the paragraph:

> [3] He thought with infinite tenderness of the woman. Poor forlorn thing, she was nicer than she knew, and [NOW THE NARRATOR ADOPTS BRIEFLY HIS OWN IDIOM] oh, so much too nice for the tough lot she was in contact with! Poor thing, she too had some of the vulnerability of the wild hyacinths, she wasn't all tough rubber-goods-and-platinum, like the modern girl. And they would do her in! As sure as life,

> they would do her in, as they do in all naturally tender life. Tender! Somewhere [THE NARRATOR REMINDS MELLORS] she was tender, tender with a tenderness of the growing hyacinths, something that has gone out of the celluloid women of today. But [AGAIN THE NARRATOR'S IDIOM] he would protect her with his heart for a little while. For a little while, before the insentient iron world and the Mammon of mechanised greed did them both in, her as well as him.

This is richer than it appears. Dickensian in its rhetorical motion, the paragraph oscillates between soft and hard, heart and greed, flowers and iron—oppositions that nonetheless mirror the much more subtle dialogue between character and narrator. Take phrasing. Throughout the novel, Mellors's laconic speech, like March's in *The Fox* (1923), masks his sensitivity and warmth: but the phrases "oh, so much too nice" and "he would protect her with his heart" are part of the narrator's idiom, typically more colloquial and sentimental than Mellors's. In their dialogue of sensibilities, Mellors's reaches inward, the narrator's reaches outward, enriching the keyboard registers of the character "inside" with darker and deeper tones. This is the essence of Lawrence's later style—not a juxtaposition, not a counterpoint, but a fusion of lighter and darker voices: horizontal and vertical textures at last merged coherently—"the upright through the horizontal," in the narrator's happy phrase (*Lady Chatterley's Lover*, textual note on 174:9). It is worth saying, with Graham Holderness, that Lawrence "has kept the rhetoric of his people" (135), though certainly Lawrence transforms it by embracing banality as a dominant ironic tone.

The final paragraph (it is Lawrence's second) demands a special kind of attention, even tolerance, as the narrator first summarizes—then extracts a conclusion from—the two paragraphs that (in my rearrangement) preceded:

> [2] It was not woman's fault, nor even love's fault, nor the fault of sex. The fault lay there, out there, in those evil electric lights and diabolical rattlings of engines. There, in the world of the mechanical greedy, greedy mechanism and mechanised greed, sparkling with lights and gushing hot metal and roaring with traffic, there lay the vast evil thing, ready to destroy whatever did not conform. Soon it would destroy the wood, and the bluebells would spring no more. All vulnerable things must perish under the rolling and running of iron. (119)

This paragraph, a climax to the sequence, edges outward from Mellors's voice into the narrator's. Repetition is more evident, and the language is more poetic than Mellors's, the diction crisper, the repugnance sharper, the moral fervor more urgent. To call the passage's effect "horrifying" (Fjågesund 148) only exaggerates. The rhetoric of authority reflects a narrowing of moral purpose while the novel's depth of understanding widens. Critics who argue that Lawrence has lost control of his narrative, who for instance chastise his "uncritical identification with Mellors" (Cavitch 200), misunderstand the role that the narrator assumes. The narrator chooses *not* to include what the narrator of version 2 (called *John Thomas and Lady Jane*) had included—namely, the direct series of Mellors's impressions introduced by the verb "seemed," as in:

> The lights at Stacks Gate and at Tevershall seemed wickedly sparkling, and the blush of the furnaces, faint and rosy since the night was cloudless, seemed somehow aware. A curious dread possessed him, a sense of defencelessness. Out there, beyond, there were all those white lights and the indefinable quick malevolence that lay in them. (*John Thomas* 115)

This is language that seeks what Lawrence, writing to Dorothy Brett, called "bottomless pools" (19 December 1926)—that which mines his character's psyche, penetrating vertically, "go[ing] way down into yourself, down till you really *feel* [what] would be right" (23 January 1927, letter to Gertrude Cooper). The narrator takes the phrase "Out there"—common to both versions—and reconfigures the double exchange of sights "out there" and their effect on Mellors, to a quite different exchange of sights within the narrator's horizontally encompassing sweep ("vast evil thing," "All vulnerable things"), which suppresses Mellors's feelings in order to display the narrator's. As Cohn remarks, "the more conspicuous and idiosyncratic the narrator, the less apt he is to reveal the depth of his characters' psyches" (25). This edging outward of narratorial discourse extends the larger ethic of masculine control that hides the voices of dissonance; yet this dissonance inheres in all of the structural irregularities of the late work.

Earlier, in the case of Ursula, the narrator allows a visual default to help him shape a scene; in the case of Gudrun, two perspectives join to form an assessment; in the case of Mellors, the narrator's poetry of anger draws on neither Mellors's idiom nor his sources of knowledge but in narrated monologue deliberately returns to the apocalyptic mode of *The*

Rainbow, divested now of biblical rhetoric. When one stops to consider in what other "interior" forms Lawrence might have expressed this final paragraph—psycho-narration (the narrator's discourse about a character's consciousness) or quoted interior monologue—these alternative forms prohibit the *drive toward certainty* that the narrator's own voice must project in order for the balance of voices coherently to reflect—and to reinscribe—the novel's confident architectural oppositions of Wragby and wood, Clifford and Mellors, insentience and sentience.

The search for knowledge in *Lady Chatterley's Lover* is not so much inward, into the psyche (as it was in Lawrence's middle works), but outward, into the culture that defines and constrains a character. What is especially worth saying is that the narrator participates in that constraint. In *Lady Chatterley's Lover* he does so by pushing the characters toward forms of knowledge that find closure, that chafe against the open forms toward which the characters, thinking about themselves, are regularly drawn—as, for instance, in Connie's awakening to her pregnancy (chapter 10), in the night of sensual passion (chapter 15), and in Mellors's final, embracing letter (chapter 19). At the end of Lawrence's career the lack of connection that exists between a character and his culture (as that culture is defined by the narrator) shows up *masked* in passages like the one that begins, "It was not woman's fault." The disharmony passes almost unnoticed, yet it signals a conflict between a mode of discovery and a mode of certainty.

The problem is real at another level, too. Lawrence did not place the final paragraph last, but second. Such disruptions of coherence can be illustrated frequently in his later work (see Squires 127–32: but also, however, Jackson). They subtly manifest Lawrence's well-known resistance to any form of social entrapment. But at the end, coherence and knowledge are unexpectedly linked in Lawrence's work: the narrator's early judging voice runs like a vein through the rest of the prose; but at the heart of his later fiction, judgment impedes patient development; and rhetorical modes, although yielding brilliant explorations, suffer some incompatibility in purpose and effect. Psychic disruption remains an enduring feature of Lawrence's imagination; its implications for his art, which help to explain the change in quality after *Women in Love*, are only now being analyzed.

If one may now generalize: recasting passages of a text to reveal their masked assumptions yields a sort of X-ray of an author's artistic motives. Recasting clarifies his choices; facilitates a fuller understanding of the narrator's complex stance; and allows readers more keenly to observe perceptual, conceptual, and artistic changes across the span of an author's work. By locating the intersection of psychic disruption, sources of knowledge, and aesthetic coherence in the work of D. H. Lawrence, this critical method does two things more: it demonstrates the need for a conceptual terminology that will differentiate degrees of bonding between character and narrator, and it points to the study of Lawrence's contemporaries, where similar interpretive problems emerge as cultural values change. Lawrence is poised to reveal this cultural moment, when assumptions about art and knowledge were undergoing ferment and revision, because his art, more clearly than that of his contemporaries, exhibits features that are both familiar from the Victorian novel and yet innovatively fresh. To study the properties of Lawrence's imagination is to index the cultural crisis of Modernism. I conclude, finally, that as these varied ruptures in focalization and coherence reflect the way the narrator's sources of knowledge "dry up" or shift or become striated with rhetorical excess, so also do they reflect the fragmentation endemic to Modernist culture. Indeed, this fragmentation is reinscribed into Lawrence's technical choices so seamlessly that readers have often missed seeing it.

Notes

1. As for the term *narrator's focalization* (the angle of vision through which a stroy is filtered), it is fair to say that narratological distinctions are still in flux. Gérard Genette distinguishes "Who sees?" from "Who speaks?": a distinction that Shlomith Rimmon-Kenan considers "a theoretical necessity" (72). Offering a slight variant, Seymour Chatman distinguishes *who narrates*, which he calls "slant," from *who sees*, which he calls "filter" (4). As interpreted by Dorrit Cohn, Franz Stanzel distinguishes *perspective*, which he applies to space (the visible outer world), from *view*, which he applies to the psyche (the invisible inner world): so that in his shcema perspectives range from external to internal, views range from outside to inside. Cohn, however, questions the accuracy and utility of Stanzel's distinction ("Encirclement" 176–78).
2. My conceptualization has four angles within a "square" of relationships. In *first-degree* angle of bonding, both narrator and character draw from similar sources of knowledge and use similar linguistic idioms; in *second-degree* angle of bonding, narrator and character draw from similar sources of knowledge but use

different linguistic idioms; in *third-degree* angle of bonding, narrator and character draw on different sources of knowledge but use similar linguistic idioms; and in *fourth-degree* angle of bonding, narrator and character draw on different sources of knowledge and use different linguistic idioms, yielding a shapr separation. Recasting a passage is the surest method of identifying the angle of angle of bonding.

3. But it has also led Graham Holderness to complain that in *The Rainbow* Lawrence replaces the "communal narrator" of *Sons and Lovers* with "a subjectivist narrator who constantly collapses into the immediate experience of individual character" (186).
4. Significantly, Lawrence added the words "and as if with malignant desire" to the typescript of the novel (Cambridge edition, textual note on 143:34).
5. Oltean argues that Free Indirect Discourse, broadly defined, "becomes a means of representing *acts of discourse* (external and internal) and *preverbal or nonverbal acts of mentation*" (712).
6. Marcel Proust wrote about 1908: "At the bottom of our consciousness, what is so dark and obscure cannot be brought into daylight without first making it traverse an intermediate region between our hidden inner self and our exterior intelligence: yet how to get it that far?" (my translation, qtd. in Hayman 329).

Works Cited

Albright, Daniel. *Personality and Impersonality: Lawrence, Woolf, and Mann.* Chicago, U of Chicago P, 1978.

Ben-Ephraim, Gavriel. *The Moon's Dominion: Narrative Dichotomy and Female Dominance in Lawrence's Earlier Novels.* Rutherford, NJ: Fairleigh Dickinson UP, 1981.

Bonds, Diane S. *Language and the Self in D. H. Lawrence.* Ann Arbor, MI: UMI Research P, 1987.

Brodsky, Claudia J. *The Imposition of Form: Studies in Narrative Representation and Knowledge.* Princeton: Princeton UP, 1987.

Cavitch, David. *D. H. Lawrence and the New World.* New York: Oxford UP, 1969.

Chatman, Seymour. *Coming to Terms: The Rhetoric of Narrative in Fiction and Film.* Ithaca: Cornell UP, 1990.

Cohn, Dorrit. "The Encirclement of Narrative: On Franz Stanzel's *Theorie des Erzählens.*" *Poetics Today* 2 (1981): 157–82.

Cohn, Dorrit. *Transparent Minds: Narrative Modes for Presenting Consciousness in Fiction.* Princeton: Princeton UP, 1978.

Cowan, James C. "D. H. Lawrence's Sexual Fallacies." *Journal of the History of Sexuality* 5 (1994): 115–41.

Fernihough, Anne. *D. H. Lawrence: Aesthetics and Ideology.* Oxford: Clarendon P, 1993.

Fjågesund, Peter. *The Apocalyptic World of D. H. Lawrence*. Oslo: Norwegian UP, 1991.
Fleishman, Avrom. "Lawrence and Bakhtin: Where Pluralism Ends and Dialogism Begins." *Rethinking Lawrence*. Ed. Keith Brown. Philadelphia: Open UP, 1990. 109–19.
Genette, Gérard. *Narrative Discourse*. Ithaca: Cornell UP, 1980.
Hayman, Ronald. *Proust: A Biography*. New York: HarperCollins, 1990.
Hernadi, Paul. "Dual Perspective: Free Indirect Discourse and Related Techniques." *Comparative Literature* 24 (1972): 32–43.
Holderness, Graham. *D. H. Lawrence: History, Ideology, and Fiction*. Dublin: Gill & Macmillan, 1982.
Hough, Graham. *The Dark Sun: A Study of D. H. Lawrence*. 1956. Reprinted London: Duckworth, 1968.
Hyde, G. M. *D. H. Lawrence*. New York: St. Martin's Press, 1990.
Hyde, Virginia. *The Risen Adam: D. H. Lawrence's Revisionist Typology*. University Park: Pennsylvania State UP, 1992.
Jackson, Dennis. "Chapter-Making in *Lady Chatterley's Lover*." *Texas Studies in Literature and Language* 35 (1993): 363–83.
Lawrence, D.H. *Etruscan Places*. London: Secker, 1932.
———. *John Thomas and Lady Jane*. New York: Viking, 1972.
———. *Lady Chatterley's Lover*. Ed. Michael Squires. Cambridge: Cambridge UP, 1993.
———. *The Rainbow*. Ed. Mark Kinkead-Weekes. Cambridge: Cambridge UP, 1989.
———. *Sons and Lovers*. Ed. Carl and Helen Baron. Cambridge: Cambridge UP, 1992.
———. *The Trespasser*. Ed. Elizabeth Mansfield. Cambridge: Cambridge UP, 1981.
———. *The White Peacock*. Ed. Andrew Robertson. Cambridge: Cambridge UP, 1983.
———. *Women in Love*. Ed. David Farmer, Lindeth Vasey, and John Worthen. Cambridge: Cambridge UP, 1987.
Leavis, F. R. *D. H. Lawrence: Novelist*. 1955. Reprinted New York: Simon & Schuster, 1969.
Miko, Stephen J. *Toward "Women in Love": The Emergence of a Lawrentian Aesthetic*. New Haven: Yale UP, 1971.
Moynahan, Julian. "Lawrence and the Modern Crisis of Character and Conscience." *The Challenge of D. H. Lawrence*. Ed. Michael Squires and Keith Cushman. Madison: U of Wisconsin P, 1990. 28–41.
Oltean, Stefan. "A Survey of the Pragmatic and Referential Functions of Free Indirect Discourse." *Poetics Today* 14 (1993): 691–728.
Pascal, Roy. *The Dual Voice: Free Indirect Speech and its Functioning in the Nineteenth-Century European Novel*. Manchester: Manchester UP, 1977.
Prince, Gerald. "Narratology, Narrative, and Meaning." *Poetics Today* 12 (1991): 543–52.

Ragussis, Michael. *The Subterfuge of Art: Language and the Romantic Tradition*. Baltimore: Johns Hopkins UP, 1978.

Rimmon-Kenan, Shlomith. *Narrative Fiction: Contemporary Poetics*. London: Methuen, 1983.

Ross, Charles L. *"Women in Love": A Novel of Mythic Realism*. Boston: Twayne, 1991.

Sanders, Scott. *D. H. Lawrence: The World of the Five Major Novels*. New York: Viking, 1974.

Sklenicka, Carol. *D. H. Lawrence and the Child*. Columbia: U of Missouri P, 1991.

Squires, Michael. *The Creation of "Lady Chatterley's Lover."* Baltimore: Johns Hopkins UP, 1983.

Wallace, M. Elizabeth. "The Circling Hawk: Philosophy of Knowledge in Polanyi and Lawrence." *The Challenge of D. H. Lawrence*. Ed. Michael Squires and Keith Cushman. Madison: U of Wisconsin P, 1990. 103–120.

Whiteley, Patrick J. *Knowledge and Experimental Realism in Conrad, Lawrence, and Woolf*. Baton Rouge: Louisiana State UP, 1987.

Woolf, Virginia. "Mr. Bennett and Mrs. Brown." *Collected Essays*. Vol. 2. London: Hogarth, 1966.

Worthen, John. *D. H. Lawrence*. London: Edward Arnold, 1991.

List of Contributors

JAMES C. COWAN, founder and former editor of The D. H. Lawrence Review, teaches at the University of North Carolina, Chapel Hill. His books include *D.H. lawrence's American Journey, D. H. Lawrence: An Annotated Bibliography of Writings about Him* (2 vols.), and *D. H. Lawrence and the Trembling Balance*.

H. M. DALESKI, Professor (Emeritus) of English, The Hebrew University, Jerusalem. Has published five books of criticism, including studies of Lawrence, Dickens, and Conrad. Has currently completed a book on Thomas Hardy.

PAUL DELANY is Professor of English at Simon Fraser University. His books include *D. H. Lawrence's Nightmare* (1978) and *The Neo-pagans* (1987). He is completing a book about English literature and money.

JANE EBLEN KELLER is Writer in Residence in the School of Communications Design at the University of Baltimore. She is also Director of the School's undergraduate program in Professional Writing and teaches in the master's program in Publications Design.

GINETTE KATZ-ROY, Professor of English Literature at the University of Paris X, has published many articles on D.H. Lawrence and various other authors or artists. She is the editor of the French journal *Études lawrenciennes*. She is also the co-editor and co-author of *D.H. Lawrence* (Paris, L'Herne 1988).

KAIEN KITAZAKI is a Professor in the Department of Humanities at Soai University in Osaka, Japan. His publications include Japanese translations of *Phoenix* and *Phoenix II*, co-productions of the Study Circle of D. H. Lawrence, Kyoto and of *Aaron's Rod*.

HOLLY LAIRD, Associate Professor of English at the University of Tulsa, is author of *Self and Sequence: The Poetry of D. H. Lawrence* and is Editor of *Tulsa Studies in Women's Literature*.

JOAN DOUGLAS PETERS is an Associate Professor of English at the University of Hawaii at Manoa. She has published articles on issues of narrative and genre theory in the work of D. H. Lawrence and other novelists and is executive committee member and past Program Chair of the D. H. Lawrence Society of North America.

CAROL PIERCE, Professor of English at The University of Baltimore. She is also President of the International Lawrence Durrell Society and Co-editor of *Deus Loci: The Lawrence Durrell Journal*. She has taught a seminar involving D. H. Lawrence for many years.

JOHN HENRY RALEIGH, Professor of English, University of California, Berkeley, author of *Mathew Arnold and American Culture*, *The Plays of Eugene O'Neill*, *Time, Places and Idea: Essays on the Novel*, *The Chronicle of Leopold and Molly Bloom*.

M. ELIZABETH SARGENT, Associate Professor of English and Director of the Honors Program at Western Oregon State College, regularly publishes essays on D. H. Lawrence and others. With Garry Watson (University of Alberta, Edmonton) she is currently co-editing a volume on Lawrence for MLA's series in Approaches to Teaching World Literature.

MARK SPILKA is currently working on a book to be called *Domestic Violence in Short Modern Fiction: A Critical Sample* in which his contribution to this volume will also appear. He has retired from teaching at Brown University but still serves as Editor for *Novels, A Form of Fiction*.

MICHAEL SQUIRES, Clifford A. Cutchins III Professor of English at Virginia Tech, is the author or editor of seven books on D. H. Lawrence. In 1995 he was given the Harry T. Moore Distinguished Scholar Award for Lifetime Achievement in Lawrence Studies.

NORA FOSTER STOVEL, Associate Professor of English at the University of Alberta, has published articles on twentieth-century writers, including D. H. Lawrence. She published *Margaret Drabble: Symbolic Moralist*, *Rachel's Children: Margaret Laurence's A Jest of God*, and *Stacey's Choice: Margaret Laurence's The Fire-Dwellers*.

WAYNE TEMPLETON, Professor of English at Kwantlen University College, has published a book, *States of Estrangement: The Novels of D. H. Lawrence, 1912-1917*, and several papers on the life and works of D. H. Lawrence.

GEORGE J. ZYTARUK is a Professor of English and the founding president of Nipissing University in North Bay, Ontario. He is the author or editor of three books on Lawrence and a number of essays. In 1992 he was awarded an Honorary Doctor of Letters degree by Laurentian University.

• Cap-Saint-Ignace
• Sainte-Marie (Beauce)
Québec, Canada
1996